CMDB Systems
Making Change Work in the Age of Cloud and Agile

CMDB Systems
Making Change Work in the Age of Cloud and Agile

Dennis Nils Drogseth

Rick Sturm

Dan Twing

AMSTERDAM • BOSTON • HEIDELBERG • LONDON
NEW YORK • OXFORD • PARIS • SAN DIEGO
SAN FRANCISCO • SINGAPORE • SYDNEY • TOKYO
Morgan Kaufmann is an imprint of Elsevier

Executive Editor: Steven Elliot
Editorial Project Manager: Benjamin Rearick
Project Manager: Punithavathy Govindaradjane
Designer: Mark Rogers

Morgan Kaufmann is an imprint of Elsevier
225 Wyman Street, Waltham, MA 02451, USA

ISBN: 978-0-12-801265-9

British Library Cataloguing in Publication Data
A catalogue record for this book is available from the British Library

Library of Congress Cataloging-in-Publication Data
A catalog record for this book is available from the Library of Congress

For information on all MK publications,
visit our website at www.mkp.com

Working together
to grow libraries in
developing countries

www.elsevier.com • www.bookaid.org

Contents

Preface...xv
Introduction: How to Use This Book..xvii
About the Authors...xxiii
Acknowledgments...xxv

SECTION 1   FAILURE IS NOT AN OPTION

CHAPTER 1   The Odds Are Against You **3**
    CMDB Opinions...4
    Who Should Care About a CMDB System?...5
    CMDB System DNA 6
        A CMDB Is Not...6
    OK, So Are the Odds Really Against You?..6
    Voices from the Industry, Voices from the Trenches 7
        No Vision or Strategy 8
        Not Understood and Not Communicated 9
        Lack of Confidence..9
        No Resources and High Costs 9
        Resistance to ITIL Can Also Be a Factor 9
        Shaky Senior Management..9
        Vendor Failure..10
    Back to the Drawing Board?...10
    Framing the CMDB System Conversation 11
        On the Other Hand, Can You Really Do Without a CMDB System?....11
    Summary Takeaways 12

CHAPTER 2   Why Bother? The Case for a CMDB System **13**
    A Few Initial Data Points..14
    CMDB Success Rates Revisited 14
    Some Short Answers..15
    Return on Investment..17
    Reasons for Going Forward: More Voices from the Trenches 18
        Drowning in (Siloed) Data?...18
        Optimizing IT OpEx Efficiencies in the Face of Rising Complexities....18
        Change Management and Change Impact Analysis....................19
        Asset Management and IT Financial Optimization 19
        Service Impact, Root Cause Analysis, and Troubleshooting.......20
        The Move to Cloud and Virtualization 20
    Bringing the Organization Together 23
    Summary Takeaways 23

SECTION 2   THE BASICS

CHAPTER 3   CMDB System Foundations **27**

CMDB Foundations Part One: Process 27
Why It's Good to Get to Know ITIL First...27
A (Very) Short History..29
A Human Face to Service Management 29
ITIL's Libraries..29
ITIL's Configuration Management Database (CMDB) 31
The Configuration Management System (CMS) 32
The Service Knowledge Management System (SKMS)...........................33
CMDB Deployments Underscore ITIL's Relevance.................................34
A Few Critical ITIL Processes...36
CMDB Data and Configuration Items: A Second Look 38
A Few Final Points 41
CMDB Foundations, Part One: Process—Summary Takeaways 42
CMDB Foundations Part Two: Technology...42
CMDB System Technologies: A Closer Look..43
A Reminder: "Big Vision, Baby Steps"...45
A Look at the Broader CMDB System and the Service Management
Ecosystem It Supports 46
CMDB System Foundations Part Two: Technology—Summary Takeaways........51

**CHAPTER 4   CMDB System Deployment Stages: An Eight-Step Ladder
to Success** **53**

Standing in the Middle of the Storm..54
What About "People?" 56
A Closer Look at the Third Vector 56
Climbing the Eight-Step Ladder to CMDB System Success....................57
Step One: Define Your Objectives and Consider Your Resources.............58
How Do You Know if You're Ready?...60
Step Two: Technology, Process, and Organizational Audit.....................61
Step Three: Evolutionary or Maturity-Level Assessment 64
Reactive Infrastructure Management..64
Active Operational Management 65
Proactive Service-Oriented Management 65
Dynamic Business-Driven Management 65
Step Four: Define Your Requirements, Architecture, and Metrics............66
Define Two Categories of Requirements 66
Define Your Architecture..67
Step Five: Technology Selection 68
Step Six: Addressing Critical Issues and Gating Factors 70

Organizational Issues 70

Budget and Resource Constraints 71

Technology Issues 71

Step Seven: Developing a Three-Tiered Roadmap for Immediate and Future

Deployments 72

Six-Month Roadmap (Tactical Implementation Plan) 72

One-Year Roadmap 72

Two-Year Roadmap 73

Step Eight: Review Progress and Milestones 74

Summary Takeaways 77

SECTION 3   AWARENESS AND GOALS

CHAPTER 5   **IT in Transformation: What's Going On and Where Does**

That Leave the CMDB? **81**

How Has the Model for IT Changed? 81

What Does It Mean for IT to "Show Value"? 82

Looking Ahead 83

Cloud and the Extended Enterprise 84

Data Sharing and the Extended Enterprise 86

Agile and Mobile: Changing Dimensions in CMDB System Possibilities 86

Agile: When DevOps and ITSM Collide 86

Mobile: Diverse Endpoints, Diverse Consumers, and New Challenges

for the CMDB System 88

Business Service Management (BSM):IT and Business Alignment and Its

Dramatic Implications for CMDB Systems 88

The Move to a Cross Domain IT Organization—And Why It's More Needed

(and Real) Than Ever 90

Even if Cross Domain Is a Need, Is There Any Real Progress Taking Place?

What's the Justification for Calling "Cross Domain" a Trend? 91

Is ITIL Enjoying a Rebirth as Another "New Trend"? 93

Given All This, and More, Are CMDB Systems a Reemerging or an

Aging Trend? 94

CMDB Systems for Optimizing Service Delivery over Cloud:

From Database-Centric to Service Modeling-Centric 97

Wrapping Up 97

Summary Takeaways 97

CHAPTER 6   **Getting Your Executive Team on Board: How to Sell CMDB**

to Your Organization **99**

The Executive Imperative 100

Stakeholder Buy-In 102

Distractions, Resources, and Communication 103
    A Lesson from the Field 104
Reaching Your Executive(s): A Few Thoughts on "Executive Perspectives" 105
    Executives, Cloud, and Other Trends 105
Failures and Successes Can *Both* Be Valuable Resources 107
Executive Dialogue Across the Eight-Step Ladder 108
    Margaret's Service-Centric IT Asset Management Initiative: One Happy
    Example of How the Ladder Can Help You Engage the Executive Suite 108
Summary Takeaways 114

CHAPTER 7   CMDB System Use Cases: Carving Out the Right Place to Start 117
What's Most Popular? What's Most Successful? 117
The Use-Case Landscape: A Kaleidoscope of Values 120
    Change Impact Management and Change Automation 121
    Asset Management and Financial Optimization 127
    Service Impact, Performance, and Capacity Optimization 131
Two Additional Use Cases: Security/Compliance and DevOps 137
    Security/Compliance 137
    DevOps 138
Summary Takeaways 139

CHAPTER 8   Making Your Initial Assessment Work 141
Whom Should You Talk To and What Should You Ask Them? 142
What Are You Solving For? 144
Toolset Issues: Sprawl, Redundancy, Possessiveness, and Mistrust 146
Inventory, Data Quality, and Issues 147
    Data Breadth: How Much Is Enough? 148
Data: Power, Possession, and Ownership 149
Process Issues 149
    Staffing 150
    The Hamster Scenario 151
Communication 151
    The Executive Factor, Again 152
Communication: Vehicles and Approaches 153
Use-case Audits 154
    Change Impact Management and Change Automation 154
    Asset Management and Financial Optimization 156
    Service Impact Management and Capacity Optimization 159
Pulling It All Together 160
Summary Takeaways 160

CHAPTER 9 **Maturity and Readiness: A Four-Phase Evolutionary Assessment**..**161**

Cyclical and Opportunistic 161

　Technology...162

　Processes..164

IT Organizational Evolution: A Closer Look 166

　How IT Views Itself...167

　Other Organizational Influencers...168

The Four Stages of IT Maturity: A Closer Look 170

Reactive Infrastructure Management...170

　Comments from a Stage-One Organization Seeking to Move to Stage Two.......171

Active Operational Management 172

　A CMDB System Deployment in Stage Two 172

Proactive Service-Oriented Management 174

Dynamic Business-Driven Management 175

Salient Trends to Watch Across the Four Stages 175

Summary Takeaways 178

SECTION 4 MOVING FORWARD

CHAPTER 10 **Developing a Project Plan: From Metrics to Requirements and Beyond**..**183**

Internal and External Metrics Versus ROI...184

　General Categories for Metrics..184

　The CMDB System Is Part of a Larger Undertaking....................................185

　Internal CMDB System Metrics 186

　External CMDB System Metrics 189

ROI...193

　Examples..193

Translating Metrics into Detailed Requirements Unique
to Your Organization..195

　A Workbook for Creating a Detailed CMDB System Requirement...................196

　Architectural Requirements 201

Summary Takeaways 205

CHAPTER 11 **Finalizing Your Phase One Team**.......................................**207**

Consumers 207

Stakeholders..208

Finalizing the Core Team...210

　A Recommended Core Team Matrix 212

　Optimizing ITIL Processes 213

Staffing Challenges..214
Reporting In..214
Working with the CAB...215
Wrapping Up...216
Summary Takeaways...217

CHAPTER 12 Technology Selection **219**
Core CMDB Packaging..220
Software as a Service or On-premise?...221
Deployment and Administration..222
Some Perspectives on Deployment and Administration.....................224
Architecture and Integration...228
Scope, Outreach, and Core Interdependencies............................229
Data Import and the Federated Universe....................................230
Some Deployment Perspectives on Architecture and Integration.......232
Functional Concerns...236
Use Case, Analytic, and Automation Specifics.............................238
Visualization and Reporting..242
Use Case Perspectives on Functional Priorities...........................243
Trending, Reporting, and Visualization......................................245
An Example from One Client Engagement..245
Application Discovery and Dependency Mapping.............................247
Functional Power and Outreach..248
Trade-Offs: Performance-Optimized Versus Multiuse Case 248
Four Deployment Perspectives on ADDM.....................................250
Other Investments to Consider..251
Summary Takeaways...252

SECTION 5   RUNNING YOUR PROJECT

CHAPTER 13 Closing the Gap: Fine-Tuning Before Full Deployment..................**257**
Getting There: Moving Past the Proof of Concept.............................258
Communication at the Gap...258
Scope Creep..259
Managing Process Requirements at the Gap................................260
Modeling and CI Definition...261
Top-Down, Bottom-Up, or Middle-Layer Outward?.........................262
Too Much or Too Little?...263
One Example of a Successful Modeling Strategy from Two Perspectives..........265
How CMS Modeling Can Support DevOps....................................266
Integration, Normalization, and Analytics..268

Integration Analytics Example One: 35 Different Sources
to Support the 5 W's 268
Integration Analytics Example Two: Optimizing Insights on 2000 Services
Through Emerging CMDB Analytics...269
Federation 269
Follow-Through, Maintenance, and Workflow..270
Accountability, Objectives, and Metrics...271
Crossing the Abyss 273
Summary Takeaways 273

CHAPTER 14 A Tiered Road Map for Going Forward **275**
Core Road map Ingredients 276
One Case Example: Acme Financial Services Corporation's Three-Tiered
Road Map...277
Initial Summary and Analysis 278
Acme Corporation's CMDB System Goals..279
Approach...279
Other Issues 280
Gating Factors..281
Target Areas for Phase One 281
An Overview Graphic of Acme Financial Services Corporation's
Three-Tiered Road Map..283
6-Month Road Map for Acme Corporation 283
Creation of an Effective Core CMDB Team with Strong Management
Oversight...283
Creation of a Detailed Requirements Document 285
Technology Adoption 286
Phase-One Technology Value Targets 289
Milestones...289
Costs 290
Production Infrastructure Status at the End of the 6-Month Road Map..............290
12-Month Road Map for Acme Financial Services.................................290
Updated Detailed Requirements...291
Targeting the Right Stakeholder Team..291
Change Management at the Top 292
Tipping Point 292
Goals...292
Milestones...292
Some Implementation Specifics 293
Costs 294
2-Year Road Map at Acme Financial Services.......................................294

Analytics 294

IT Maturity-Related Goals...296

Costs 296

Wrapping Up 297

Summary Takeaways 297

CHAPTER 15 The CMDB System Moves to Cloud and Beyond! 299

Progress and Benefits...300

Issues and Advice 301

Future Directions and Plans...302

What's Happening with the CMDB System Today and in the Future: Insights
Gleaned from Four Key Research Projects..304

The CMDB System as a Foundation for Service-Aware Asset Management 305

The Move to the Cloud 308

How ADDM Can Improve the "Journey to the Cloud"..............................313

The CMDB/CMS, ADDM, Service Modeling and Advanced
Operations Analytics 318

Advanced Operations Analytics: A Closer Look 318

DevOps and the CMDB System 321

Summary Takeaways 323

SECTION 6 APPENDICES

APPENDIX A Glossary of Terms and Concepts 327

APPENDIX B Sample Request for Product Information 333

Introduction...333

Distinguishing Product Features...333

Deployment Cost Efficiency 333

Deployment and Administration...333

Cost Advantage..340

Product Strength 342

Architecture and Integration 342

Functionality..350

Some Additional Questions 356

APPENDIX C Self-Assessment: What If You're *Not* Ready? 359

Chapter 9's "One-Chapter Readiness Assessment"....................................359

Complementary Self-Assessment Test 360

Don't Think You're Ready, But Want to Set the Stage?..............................362

APPENDIX D Product Map 365

Core CMDB Capabilities Integrated with Service Desk
or IT Service Management Solutions 365

Unique CMDB or CMDB-Related Offerings 366
General-Purpose Application Discovery and Dependency Mapping
Solutions 366
Application Discovery and Dependency Mapping Optimized
for Performance and/or Other Real-time Values 367

Bibliography **369**
Question and Answer Interviews 370

Index **371**

Preface

"Failure" may well be the most common adjective applied to CMDB initiatives. If so, this is partly because CMDB failures may occur at various stages: failure to succeed in getting resources after initial planning and analysis, failure to find a suitable solution for deployment, failure to do anything meaningful after the initial CMDB deployment has been completed, and failure to move ahead from a successful first phase because of executive or corporate distractions.

We have examined and documented each of these "failures" on many occasions, along with many successes. The reasons for many these failures reside primarily in misunderstandings about what a CMDB, and the broader, federated, CMDB System, is or should be. Vendors, process gurus, industry analysts, and naive IT advocates have often conflated a CMDB System with a "thing" or simply a "database holding 'truth'" in some mysterious and undefined way. Vendor hype has also promoted many recipes for disaster, especially since most of the initial CMDB offerings were frankly primitive technologies in search of an overinflated purpose.

As we shall explain in this book, the CMDB System as it exists today and in the future is made up of not one, but multiple technologies. Its success depends on having a well-defined initial use case that incorporates insights into organization, process, and politics. Because CMDB Systems are transformational, they also require strong executive commitment to support a new way of working and thinking across IT.

The good news is that, as we shall demonstrate, those IT organizations *with* effective CMDB and application dependency mapping deployments outperform those *without* in almost every way—whether it's the move to cloud, the trend to adopt more advanced, IT operational analytics, the move toward a more agile, DevOps-ready IT organization, or simply managing IT assets across their life cycles more effectively and with more service awareness.

Moreover, in spite of the rush of negative hype, CMDB deployments seem to be quietly on the rise, as more and more IT organizations are seeking to understand and manage service interdependencies in increasingly dynamic and hybrid environments. We will provide you with data to substantiate this in the future chapters, along with far more insight into the whys, wheres, and hows.

This book is the product of a collaborative effort across Enterprise Management Associates that brings together research, consulting histories, deployment interviews, and ongoing vendor dialog spanning 10 years. As such, we have been able to witness the CMDB's rise into premature glory, the associated market confusion, the growing disillusionment, and what we might call a renaissance of technology innovation emerging in the last few years. All of these phases are captured in the dialogs and discussions here—as it is our goal to provide you with an entire landscape of options from which you can begin to assess what's right for you and why.

It is our delight, and our privilege, to bring together a full decade of work into this single book—which may serve you as a guide in both how to go about planning a CMDB System and how to learn from what many other very real deployments have achieved, endured, and aspired to in recent years. While the requirements may seem, and sometimes are, frankly daunting, the benefits can be even more dramatic and empowering.

It is our belief and our hope that this book can also contribute to the still very much needed rebirth of the "CMDB idea" from a single data store toward a true system of integrated technology options, use-case possibilities, stakeholders, and benefits.

Introduction: How to Use This Book

"CMDB Systems: Making Change Work in the Age of Cloud and Agile" is a unique combination of recommendations, industry insights, perspectives, and guidelines. Although this book does provide a significant amount of guidance and structure, it also offers up many diverse examples of how various approaches to making configuration management databases (CMDBs) and federated configuration management systems work. The overall goal is to provide you with both a landscape and a guide to help you select the options that fit your level of readiness, your most critical requirements, and your longer-term priorities.

To do this, we have drawn on past consulting experience that includes extensively documented consulting reports, ongoing vendor dialogs and evaluations of vendor offerings, and 11 deployment-related interviews conducted solely for the purpose of enriching this book. We have also leveraged 10 years of research—including quantitative data analysis and CMDB deployment-related interviews. These quantitative data summaries and commentaries from CMDB team leaders, stakeholders, and consultants complement our recommendations regarding process, organization, and technology. In many places throughout the narrative, the book is designed to be much like a journalistic documentary capturing many different first-person perspectives on issues, benefits, and recommendations for success. Such a rich and diverse set of sources sets this book apart from all other books on the market today.

In Chapter 1, we define the CMDB as a "central data store of critical IT environmental information with links to such information stored in other systems to document the location, configuration, and interdependency of key IT assets, both physical assets and applications. The CMDB can support the change process by identifying interdependencies, improve regression testing by capturing insights surrounding these interdependencies, and help diagnose problems impacted by changes to the IT environment."

As we will make clear in subsequent pages, we use the term "CMDB System" to indicate that way of combining the notion of a core CMDB with yet broader requirements for federated sources, integrated automation, analytics, reporting, and visualization that make the larger project come alive with real benefits. However, since there are many different approaches to doing this—given unique IT environments, changing requirements, and improving technologies—we have chosen to use the plural "CMDB Systems" in the title. (A more complete definition is given in Chapter 1 and elaborated on in Chapter 3—*CMDB Foundations*.)

HOW TO USE THIS BOOK

As this book is both a guide and a landscape of options and insights, it is designed to encourage you to create your own individual road map optimized to your needs and your environment. You can supplement our structural recommendations with the many lessons learned from others "in the trenches"—who have struggled with and overcome the many diverse obstacles to CMDB success. Indeed, there are times when CMDB deployment narratives do seem to evoke stories from a war zone in which combatants are besieged as much by political and attitudinal issues as they are by technological frustrations. But once a "tipping point" for delivering benefits is reached (usually about 6 months out), the values can become enormous. This is true because rather than being simply technology deployments, CMDB Systems are active catalysts to promote the transformation of IT organizations from being "cost centers" to becoming "business partners" and "value providers."

In order to prepare you to create your own CMDB System road map, this book is designed around the following structure:

1. The introductory sections look at challenges and benefits overall. These sections are narrated in large part by voices reflecting actual deployment issues and successes.

2. The second section provides foundational preparation for going forward. This includes a chapter focusing on process guidelines and technological foundations (*CMDB Foundations*) and a chapter (*CMDB Deployment Stages*) outlining our proven methodology: the Eight-Step Ladder to CMDB Success.

3. The third section targets self-awareness and goals. This alignment is deliberate as the two are inseparable: You need to be self-aware to set appropriate CMDB-related goals, but having well-communicated initial objectives can spur further awareness of stakeholder priorities, technology gaps, resource requirements, and other issues. This section begins with a look at trends impacting IT more broadly, such as cloud, agile software development, mobile computing, and the "consumerization of IT." It continues with recommendations for effective and ongoing executive dialog, CMDB use case audits, and IT maturity/readiness assessments.

4. The fourth section describes how to move forward by soliciting and documenting requirements and generating metrics to guide your deployment and measure your progress. This includes creating effective and realistic plans for expected benefits, including return on investment benefits, and establishing detailed requirements to meaningfully align your goals with CMDB System specifics. We include a section on the skill sets that make for an effective core CMDB team and how you should expect to work with stakeholders and customers.

5. This section will take you through how to run your project with details on technology selection for core CMDB and Application Discovery and Dependency Mapping (ADDM) investments. The next step is "closing the gap" between proof of concept and actual deployments by fine-tuning your requirements as the realities of team resources and technology investments are established. This will allow you to create a tiered road map for going forward looking at 6-month, 12-month, and 2-year stages. Included in this section is a discussion of service and data modeling and relevant standards for federating a CMDB System.

6. In "assessing your success," we look at real-world perspectives at the tipping point of value for CMDB deployments—including lessons learned and priorities for going forward. We then address some of the most compelling opportunities for next-phase CMDB growth in terms of service-aware asset management, cloud, analytics, and agile software development.

7. The appendices include the following:
   a. A glossary of terms
   b. A sample RFP for core CMDB technology selection
   c. A guide on how to use this book for a readiness assessment (are you ready for a CMDB?)
   d. A partial list of relevant CMDB and ADDM vendors with a summary of their offerings
   e. A bibliography of consulting, research, and other sources

TIME LINE

Throughout this book, we refer back to the Eight-Step Ladder to CMDB System Success as a series of stages and talk about a 6-month window on showing initial benefits. The 6-month window is our estimation of how long you'll have before executive enthusiasm begins to wane—based on our experience from consulting and research. The expectation here is that at least steps 1-7 can be achieved within that window and some major project milestones are achieved. The hope is that initial production-level deployment of at least some components of the CMDB System can be accomplished within the first 6 months, as you approach what we call the "tipping point" in demonstrating value to your stakeholders (see Figure 1).

However, it would contradict the spirit of this book to assume that each CMDB initiative will follow the same time line and hence that the time line guidelines indicated below are absolute or one-size-fits all.

FIGURE 1

The Eight-Step Ladder to CMDB System Success, introduced in Chapter 4, is used throughout this book to help punctuate a critical set of decision points directed at optimizing CMDB advantages across technology, process, and cultural/organizational considerations.

The actual vagaries of real deployments constantly show otherwise. And while our 6-month window is not a best-case scenario—we have seen even far more aggressively successful deployments—a 6-month time line does assume solid support throughout, a full-time committed CMDB team leader, and reasonably consistent stakeholder cooperation.

First month: Even given these parameters, step one is hard to measure. In almost all cases, it will have actually begun months and maybe even years before, as the CMDB team-leader-to-be begins to consider the value of a CMDB System in context with his or her actual environment. The actual step one kickoff would begin with some initial executive dialog, time commitment, and a very high-level plan to go forward into an assessment (step two). Step one would also of necessity include several assessment-relevant interviews at the executive or management level and ideally include a few key stakeholders to support the initial formulation of the plan.

Next 3 months: Once the assessment or audit is under way (step two), it will naturally evolve into an evolutionary assessment (step three) as well. A normal expectation for this should be about 2 months, assuming, once again, a fairly full-time team leader able to focus on these activities. Another month could then be devoted to requirements and project planning and phase one team formalization in preparation for technology selection (step four).

Next 2 months: Technology selection (step five) can be exceedingly fast if, for instance, the CMDB-to-be is already present and embedded in an active service desk. On the other hand, it can take months and sometimes even years—especially when it hinges on "promised functionality" that's still yet-to-be. Here, we've taken an admittedly optimistic 2 months to go through vendor selection and proof of concept. It's important that as you narrow the field, you continue to do the "closing the gap" assessments (step six) needed to set up the final planning and road map development.

Six months to one year out: Your three-tiered road map (6 months/1 year/2 years) (step seven) should be largely a process of assembling what you've already documented into a single cohesive package. Our hope would be that at 6 months out, you've been able to get some level of CMDB-related functionality into active deployment and hence can begin to show some external and project-specific benefits. Our discussion of milestones and review (step eight) is actually projected 1 year out, after real phase one values should become more evident and hence a true tipping point has been achieved—so that you're now ready to more aggressively plan ahead for phase two in your CMDB System evolution.

WHO'S SPEAKING: THE MANY VOICES IN THIS BOOK

We have deliberately used a large number of quotes and comments from various sources to provide unique and individualized insights into CMDB System initiatives. We hope that these "voices" provide useful insights while also reinforcing the varied nature of CMDB-related deployments. For longer Q&As, speakers are identified through context, role, and vertical only. For shorter quotes, speakers remain even more fully anonymous so as not to distract from the flow of ideas. However, to eliminate any mystery, there are three general categories for the many voices in this book:

1. *CMDB team leaders*: These speakers provide the majority of the comments coming largely from research and consulting. While the speakers' actual titles may differ, ranging from VP, to manager, to architect, to other roles, they all play central roles in planning and managing their CMDB System initiatives.

2. *CMDB System stakeholders*: These speakers provide insights on issues and requirements. Stakeholder comments are taken almost exclusively from consulting engagements beginning in 2006. The speakers may be active stakeholders using the CMDB System or potential stakeholders interviewed to establish requirements and objectives.
3. *Q&A CMDB team leaders*: Because of their more extensive contributions to the book, these speakers are identified in terms of role, vertical, and organizational specifics (unlike those speakers in the first category). Otherwise, they remain anonymous. Most of these interviews were conducted exclusively for this book. In many cases, the interviews have been provided through vendors that offer CMDB solutions. These vendor sources are identified both in chapter footnotes and in a master interview list in bibliography.

WHO/WHAT IS ENTERPRISE MANAGEMENT ASSOCIATES?

As already mentioned, most of the insights gained in this book have been achieved through research, consulting, and industry dialogs over nearly 10 years done under the aegis of Enterprise Management Associates or EMA. Headquartered in Boulder, Colorado, with a strong East Coast presence and an office in Portsmouth, New Hampshire, EMA is a mid-tier analyst and consulting firm focused primarily on the challenges and opportunities of managing and optimizing IT services—from network and systems performance; to application lifecycle management; to IT service management, asset management and financial optimization, security, endpoint, and mobile; to business intelligence.

The more formal EMA summary is as follows:

Founded in 1996, Enterprise Management Associates (EMA) is a leading industry analyst firm that provides deep insight across the full spectrum of IT and data management technologies. EMA analysts leverage a unique combination of practical experience, insight into industry best practices, and in-depth knowledge of current and planned vendor solutions to help EMA's clients achieve their goals. www.enterprisemanagement.com or http://blogs.enterprisemanagement.com.

About the Authors

Dennis Nils Drogseth worked in technology for more than 30 years. He has been an analyst with Enterprise Management Associates for 16 years, where he currently supports EMA through leadership in Business Service Management (BSM), CMDB Systems, automation systems, and service-centric financial optimization. He also researches changing organizational dynamics in IT, such as issues between the service desk and operations, and the emergence of a cross-domain, "service management" organization in more mature IT organizations. He has been widely published in columns and features in trade publications such as *APM Digest*, *Network World*, and the *CSC Executive Forum*.

His extensive involvement in CMDB Systems dates back to 2004 where he pioneered unique research with distinctive industry insights during the formative years of the initial CMDB upsurge in the United States. Since then, he has spoken to hundreds of CMDB System deployments for research, and/or to provide advice and guidance. He has also supported EMA's CMDB consulting efforts by providing added insights and guidance to EMA's consulting team, as well as by participating in on-premise and phone consulting with EMA clients.

Rick Sturm has over 30 years of experience in the computer industry. He is CEO of Enterprise Management Associates (EMA), which he founded in 1996. EMA is a leading industry analyst firm that provides strategic and tactical advice to major corporations and government agencies on the issues of managing computing and communications environments and the delivery of those services. Prior to founding EMA, he worked in senior IT roles at US West and A.C. Nielsen. He was cochair of the IETF Applications MIB Working Group that developed the standards for managing application software with SNMP.

He has authored hundreds articles about various aspects of enterprise management that have appeared in leading trade publications, including *Network World*, *Information Week*, *Computerworld*, *Network Computing*, *Data Communications*, and *Internet Week*. He was the technical editor of *The OpenView Advisor*, and has also coauthored four books: *The Foundations of Application Management*, *Foundations of Service Level Management*, *SLM Solutions: A Buyer's Guide*, and *Working with Unicenter TNG*.

Dan Twing has over 25 years of IT experience including outsourcing, Software as a Service (SaaS), software development, and operations. He is President and COO of Enterprise Management Associates (EMA). He joined EMA in 2005 and leads all analyst, research, and consulting activities across all IT management and business intelligence disciplines. Prior to joining EMA, he was CEO of a payments and secure messaging software company and VP of Financial Products for EDS eCommerce Services where he created online home banking and bill paying services for the banking and telecommunications industries.

He has led dozens of CMDB and other ITSM consulting engagements for large- and mid-sized organizations. These include several top banks, investment firms, insurance firms, large retail, and state and federal government agencies. He has been a regular columnist for NetworkWorld Fusion on Outsourcing.

For more insights and companion materials, please visit: <http://www.enterprisemanagement.com/cmdbsystems>

Acknowledgments

In preparing this book, we have drawn on a wide range of sources and talents.

- First of all we would like to thank the EMA consulting team, which has developed the methodology used throughout this book. Our consultants have also provided significant reference materials in the form of reports and presentations that have contributed largely to the book's narrative content. In particular, we would like to thank consultants Chris Matney, Carlos Casanova, and Stewart Cole for their careful planning and their dedication to supporting and clarifying unique IT requirements.
- This book would also not be possible without the considerable time and consideration given to us through ongoing dialogs with CMDB team leaders regarding their successes, failures, and recommendations. These literally hundreds of conversations have helped to inform this book more than any other single factor. In particular, we would like to thank the 12 sources—in Europe and North America—who gave their time for unique Qs and As during the course of writing this book.
- In parallel, we would like to thank the hundreds of individuals from the service management vendor community, we have spoken with for their insights and updates, and their willingness to engage with us about present directions and future plans for CMDBs, application dependency mapping, analytics and automation so central to this narrative.
- In developing "CMDB Systems," we have also drawn on many published sources from the EMA library, including joint research with Axelos on IT Infrastructure Library[R] (ITIL[R]) adoption.
- No book on CMDB guidance would be complete without reference to ITIL processes and service management insights, and we have drawn from the ITIL 2011 libraries (as referenced in Bibliography) in discussions of process and best practice.
- Critical other sources include seminal works in terms of CMDB planning—most notably "The CMDB Imperative" by Glenn O'Donnell and Carlos Casanova; and thought-leading insights on the role of IT in the current business environment—most notably "The Quantum Age of IT" by Charles Araujo.
- In terms of production and editorial support, we would thank Lee Korak for his ongoing creative contributions in graphics and design, and Cecilia Kiely, Susi Juckas, Kacie Crowe, and Alison Jepsen for editorial assistance.
- We would also like to thank Steve Elliot, Ben Rearick, Punitha, and Kaitlin Herbert from Elsevier for chaperoning the project and their care and attention in production.

FAILURE IS NOT AN OPTION

THE ODDS ARE AGAINST YOU

John was looking to leave his legacy for George Washington Surgical Manufacturing (GWSM)—a mid-range company headquartered in the Midwest struggling to keep pace with dramatic changes in the healthcare industry. The IT organization and the manufacturing organization were closely intertwined with sometimes disastrous results, as changes made to a suite of in-house-developed applications turned out to cause disruptions on the manufacturing line. Even worse, ineffective change management was seriously degrading the performance of the wholesale access application supporting partners and suppliers—the very heart of GWSM's business!

In his role of Change Process Manager, John wanted to deploy a CMDB—unifying change management across IT with insights into where and how application and infrastructure modifications impacted service performance. However, he knew the odds were against him. Creating a 'single source of truth' in managing change, planning capacity and enabling more effective triage would challenge siloed ways of working and require solid executive support from the top down.

Hoping to beat the odds, John had done his homework. He'd learned from reading about past mistakes. He'd spent time identifying critical stakeholders, engaged them in dialog, and collectively evolved a plan for going forward. He understood the importance of readiness and enthusiasm in mapping this initiative to areas of value and collectively charted Phase One metrics for evaluating his CMDB's success. This required breaking some barriers between operations, the service desk, and development.

So far John's success in getting everyone to pull together was mixed. But at least he'd built up some momentum. He felt that if he could move the project forward, he might reach a tipping point when enthusiasm might finally outshine skepticism.

In the process of doing and documenting these stakeholder dialogs, John eventually got the support of his immediate management team. This required about three months of meetings in which he was able to articulate not only his plan, but existing gaps in terms of technology and process in GWSM's current environment. The management team especially wanted to better understand the chasm between development and operations in making effective handoffs—as development was so often rushed to make changes that operations never fully understood; while in parallel development made assumptions about available infrastructure capabilities that were more often wrong than right.

The support of his immediate management team helped John to escalate his plan all the way to the CIO—a formal gentleman who was change resistant and risk averse and was all too evidently fighting for his job. After another month of meetings, the CIO also bought in—once he realized that a CMDB System might become a way to remedy the currently poor reputation of IT, and so to salvage his own imperiled legacy.

John had gone through a lot of meetings and a lot of dialogs, but he finally thought he had enough momentum to go forward. Like a seasoned skier at the top of a familiar hill, John was ready to take the glide down: to implement Phase One of his CMDB initiative. It had taken him four months of planning, discussion, persuasion and revisions, but now he was now ready. All that seemed to be missing was deploying the software that his chosen vendor had promised. The vendor's CMDB was supposed to work with many of GWSM's other investments for managing change on a more siloed level. Best of all, the vendor's salespeople had spent countless hours with him, promising to listen to his requirements and even shape their product around his needs.

About five months into the process, John had a proof of concept done—albeit with a beta version that seemed to require more attention than ideal from vendor consultants to meet his requirements. But all the features were promised as a part of 2.0 release. John was reassured.

This was going to be the easy part.

Yet, the very next morning after the CIO signed off on John's deployment plan, he got a memo from the vendor apologizing for delays. Six months later, John and his team were still without a solution. With this delay, the delicate underpinnings of executive and stakeholder commitment began to fade, while development's "I-told-you-so" attitude was beginning to eat away at John's self-confidence.

Eight months later, the CIO left, and the new CIO remained indifferent at best. A year later, everyone knew the truth: The vendor-promised CMDB would never ship—and John would have to scramble to find a new role at GWSM.

(Although admittedly fictional, this story is based upon actual client experiences. For insight into the others, read on.)

CMDB OPINIONS

With war stories like the one above circulating the industry in high volumes, skepticism and confusion abound. And with so many different opinions about what Configuration Management Databases (CMDB) and Configuration Management Systems (CMS) are, have been, can be, and should be, it is no surprise that the topic has become controversial, generating often wildly contradictory views. Needless to say, this confusion is also a setup for failure—especially when it occurs, as it so often does, within a single CMDB initiative, as the voices of vendors, consultants, executives, CMDB administrators, and other stakeholders merge in a cacophony of impossible expectations and siloed priorities.

That leads, of course, to the obvious questions: What is a CMDB? What is a CMS? Moreover, what is this strange hybrid, CMDB/CMS, that we'll refer to throughout this book as a "CMDB System"?

One very high-level definition of "CMDB System" might be as follows: *An enabling set of software-delivered capabilities to discover, reconcile manage, and optimize critical IT service interdependencies in the face of change. CMDB Systems are multidimensional in benefits that over time can support the full IT organization while providing a foundation for more effective alignment between IT and the business or organization it serves. CMDB Systems generally require attention to process, culture, and communication and technology to achieve their full value.*

Technologically, the CMDB System is a means for reconciling multiple "trusted sources" to capture physical and logical service interdependencies. As such, its roots have been in data management and service modeling. This is evolving to become more inclusive of discovery, automation, analytics, and other technologies, as we shall see in Chapter 3.

The core CMDB might be defined as *a central data store of critical IT environmental information, with links to such information stored in other systems, to document the location, configuration, and interdependency of key IT assets, both physical assets and applications. The CMDB can support the change process by identifying interdependencies, can improve regression testing by capturing insights surrounding these interdependencies, and can be helpful in diagnosing problems impacted by changes to the IT environment.*

No doubt that the CMDB and, in particular, the CMDB System may sound like tall orders, and of course, they are. However, their benefits can be substantial, even transformative, and surprisingly relevant to the changing landscape of IT—from cloud, to agile, to the consumerization of IT services—as we shall see more directly in the next chapter.

A more concrete checklist for going forward with CMDB Systems should include the following considerations:

- Process is key, as the CMDB System is an enabler for any number of use cases, all of which involve superior levels of effectiveness in terms of how IT professionals and their management teams provide value to their service consumers.
- Dialog, therefore, is also critical.
- Organization, culture, and, frankly, politics will play a role as they always do when an organization seeks to improve its effectiveness.
- The CMDB has often been called a "single source of truth"—somewhat erroneously, as truth, both poetically and in reality, is often elusive and changeable. We recommend thinking of the CMDB System instead as a "system of relevance"—a more modest but more useful concept, reinforcing the idea that the CMDB System requires "what's relevant" to enable a given use case—from Change Management to asset management and service impact management, among others. When applied to CMDB-related data, truth—pure, abstract, and eternal—may often turn out to be a bit of an overreach.

WHO SHOULD CARE ABOUT A CMDB SYSTEM?

Or, in other words, who should read this book?

A very short answer would be the ready, the willing, and the curious. A somewhat more granular answer might include the following:

- Those in IT who have tried a CMDB initiative *before and failed*. This could include everyone from a CIO, to a VP of operations, to a manager, to an architect, to a change process management owner (as in the case of John just described)—or any other title relevant to taking a lead or promoting a CMDB deployment. In our experience, having failed in the past at a CMDB deployment can often pave the way for future success—as some of the "lessons learned" can become valuable signposts for steering you in the right direction in the future.
- Those readers interested in trying a CMDB System *for the first time* because managing change, optimizing assets, and/or assuring services across a complex set of interdependencies has become a serious challenge.
- Those readers with *strong ITIL (Information Technology Infrastructure Library) roots* who are ready to help lead their companies toward a more complete configuration management strategy.

- *Any IT executive* who's tired of mysterious breakages, finger pointing, and ungoverned Change Management. Or conversely, any IT executive seeking a platform to enable superior business alignment and a more service-aware way of working.
- *The curious and even the skeptical* who are not yet sure what a CMDB System is or how a new book on this topic might just turn out to be relevant to them. You might just be surprised with what you find out by reading this book!

CMDB SYSTEM DNA

In Chapter 3, we'll examine what we call the CMDB's two parents—process and technology—in more depth. Suffice it to say for now that the **process roots** for the CMDB and the Configuration Management System (CMS) arise from the Information Technology Infrastructure Library (ITIL) and its best practices for service management with a history that goes back as far as 1989. Understanding ITIL's vision for the CMDB and the CMS can be a powerful ally in making CMDB-related initiatives work. In spite of some current negative press, research[1] shows that most IT organizations (including those moving to cloud) view ITIL as likely to grow in importance—in large part because of the need for more effective service-relevant and cross domain processes and dialog across IT.

The **technology parent** for CMDB Systems is rapidly evolving in diverse ways that can often be confusing, especially given vendor hype and pro- and anti-CMDB rants. CMDB Systems may include—over time and in phases—the following components: a core CMDB, investments in application dependency mapping, more effective and reconciled investments in other discovery and inventory solutions, investments in analytics, automation, and visualization. You should also consider good project management and more progressive forms of social media to promote IT dialog as a possible part of the picture. Many of these investments may already exist prior to making the leap to a core and distributed CMDB.

A CMDB IS NOT

- A silver bullet
- A single technology investment
- A single physical database for every bit of configuration-related data across the entire IT spectrum
- A software deployment—that is, put it on a server, get it up and running, read the manual, and you're done
- A generic, and hence pure, embodiment of Change Management processes
- A generic answer to generic problems
- A "one-use case" solution

OK, SO ARE THE ODDS REALLY AGAINST YOU?

Depending on how you calculate it, the odds may be still probably against you when you compare initial expectations to final results in CMDB System initiatives—especially if you try to please too many people and take an absolutist approach to your results. In fact, our consulting experience suggests that

---

[1]Custom joint Enterprise Management Associates (EMA)/Axelos research on ITIL adoption, Q4, 2013.

22%	1.	Staff buy-in
16%	2.	Staffing and budget
14%	3.	Detailed requirements
12%	4.	Executive management support
10%	5.	Follow through
7%	6.	Process
7%	7.	Managing expectations
6%	8.	Resistance to change
3%	9.	Integration
3%	10.	Auto discovery

FIGURE 1.1

Planning, communication, and commitment are the leading factors that derail CMDB System deployments based on EMA consulting experience.

more than 75% of all strategic initiatives (CMDB or not) fail to meet at least initial expectations across IT organizations. This is often due more to inflated expectations than categorical failure.

Figure 1.1 averages out multiple factors impacting CMDB success from various consulting engagements. Getting commitment, facilitating communication, setting expectations, and combating resistance to change are all issues that dominate the two technology issues at bottom: discovery and integration. This reinforces the need to view the CMDB System deployments at least in part as a "conversation" where technology, process, culture, and politics all come into play.

Earlier consulting and research—conducted in 2006 when CMDB deployments were often first hitting their strides—show another relevant take on critical CMDB System issues. Resource and budget, data management (including currency of data and security and access concerns), and politics dominate the list of critical issues. Eight years later, these issues are still surprisingly relevant (Figure 1.2).

VOICES FROM THE INDUSTRY, VOICES FROM THE TRENCHES

There's no question that the media headlines have often turned sour. Like an up and coming politician tainted by scandal, the CMDB in particular has become an easy target for analysts, media, and vendors with axes to grind. Nevertheless, the voices behind the cacophony of CMDB-driven fear, uncertainty, and doubt are worth presenting right up front—before you seriously get started. This is partly because if they scare you off, you may not yet be ready and partly because behind each assertion and complaint highlighted in this chapter, there is a seed of insight that can ultimately help you to succeed with your CMDB System initiative.

The voices in this chapter are largely taken from naysayers in consulting engagements, who are deliberately kept anonymous.[2] Other sources cited here, only slightly modified for the sake of anonymity,

---

[2]In preparation for this book, EMA has synthesized data from seven major CMDB-related consulting engagements in North America (the United States and Canada) between 2006 and 2014 and 18 EMA research projects that include, collectively, more than 300 individual interviews. (See Bibliography for more detail.)

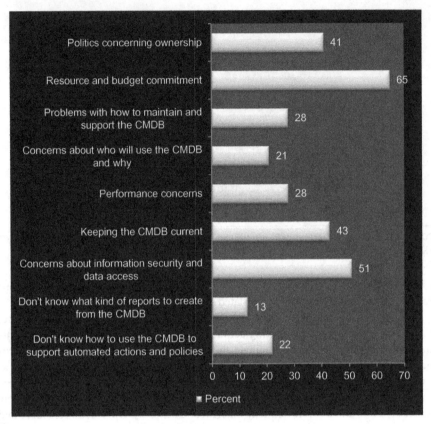

FIGURE 1.2

Another take on critical issues surrounding CMDB System deployments from eight years before, also drawn from EMA consulting and research, shows how little has changed in terms of roadblocks and concerns. What has changed for the better is a growing awareness of the problems and sometimes dramatic improvements in CMDB-related technologies.

include blogs and other commentaries posted by vendors, self-appointed analysts, and others. We've brought these together, grouping them by themes that may reflect real (and perceived) issues with making your CMDB System initiative a success.

NO VISION OR STRATEGY

OK, so you've "bought" a CMDB and want to get it deployed. Sounds simple, right? Sad to say, it's not—especially if you think of it as just that: a piece of software to get deployed. Here are some comments that arise out of what one might call a "mixed-message" initiative that, if left to itself, is destined to fail:

- "We are starting with a CMDB tool for lack of a plan."
- "Sixty-three percent stated that there was no strategy for the CMDB, 25% felt that a CMDB strategy was being developed, and only 13% believed that the CMDB strategy was well defined."

NOT UNDERSTOOD AND NOT COMMUNICATED

Now, let's say someone does have a vision—or maybe there are several people who have a vision of what they want to accomplish. But maybe, they don't agree. Or maybe, they do agree but think that one e-mail a month is sufficient for making the team all pull together. Here are some telling comments from consulting:

- "Each group is looking at its own CMDB because we couldn't come to agreement."
- "Fifty percent of all interviewees stated that information dissemination was a problem."
- "You understand only if you are involved."

LACK OF CONFIDENCE

Given that such poor communication is common, it is not surprising that some IT organizations feel that they no longer have the heart to go forward—at least not with all the real pitfalls and all the negative hype. Add to this, past failures and the "lack of confidence factor" can be daunting:

- "We have a low confidence in our ability to deliver on our CMDB strategy as shown in a survey of IT management."
- "Here we go again!"

NO RESOURCES AND HIGH COSTS

If the CMDB System seems like an impossible dream, doesn't devoting largely nonexistent IT resources sound, at best, problematic? Optimizing resources is one of the reasons we advocate proceeding in phases that bring relatively quick value and help to reinforce CMDB System benefits within three to six months:

- "We are currently at 100%. The CMDB will just be competing for resources we don't have."
- "Some people here think you can just "pop" the CMDB in. But I see it as a resource drain."

RESISTANCE TO ITIL CAN ALSO BE A FACTOR

Given the CMDB's and the CMS's ITIL roots, negative opinions about ITIL can also be a deterrent to success. We generally recommend viewing ITIL as a critical resource in planning CMDB System initiatives and building process awareness. However, sometimes, it becomes a cause for excessive "religiosity" on the one hand and partisanship on the other:

- "ITIL is not for me."
- "So here we have the initiative of the day. Before, it was Six Sigma that came and left with our last CIO."

SHAKY SENIOR MANAGEMENT

We would be lying if we suggested that CMDB System initiatives could be done exclusively from the bottom up. Experience consistently shows that strong executive commitment is key. This makes sense given the fact that CMDB Systems can be as much about positive cultural change as they are about deploying new technologies.

Nonetheless, senior management is not always the Rock of Gibraltar when it comes to standing watch over CMDB System initiatives through phase one completion:

- "Our executives are just trying to keep everybody happy. We need more direction and need to avoid management by committee."
- "Constant reorganizations make the organizational structure confusing for our CMDB initiative. This is getting better, but it's still a problem."

VENDOR FAILURE

Now, here's a twist: The problem isn't really with IT or ITIL or with management or stakeholders—it's because no vendor has created a viable CMDB System package, yet! To some degree, even though things are really beginning to improve on many fronts, the truth is that CMDB technologies are rapidly evolving out of necessity and sometimes doing so outside the traditional boundaries of what vendors market as "CMDBs."

The following comments were taken from CMDB-related consulting and research:

- "You can buy wonderful products, but they are quite complex. Time is money, and all the complexity creates standstill—especially when your vendor doesn't have time to address your problems."
- "We need a solution that is quick, nimble, and cheap."
- "There is no perfect software. Only perfect salesmen."

BACK TO THE DRAWING BOARD?

If you haven't been frightened off by now, read on! The very next chapter will show how and why CMDB System deployments are becoming increasingly valuable in the "age of cloud and agile"—just as they are becoming, in many respects, more diverse in terms of use case, technology choice, and outreach.

To some degree, the likelihood of CMDB success is improving thanks to enhancements in technology. But many of the more dramatic areas of technological progress are often missed—in large part because the industry still likes to think in linear terms about just what a CMDB is. Marketers and salespeople generally don't like to talk about multidimensional interdependencies or systems that are optimized to assimilate multiple brands outside their own. Similarly, many analysts prefer to seize on discrete technologies rather than multiple interrelated technologies—since they build their practices around market sizing discrete technology buckets.

Moreover, "failure," as it applies to CMDB System deployments, is both a relative and a subjective term. Pretty much all our research shows that depending on whom you ask, even within a single IT organization, you'll usually get significantly different answers. For instance, IT executives tend to be more bullish about the success of CMDB deployments than nonmanagers and other IT professionals. Stakeholders with particular objectives may be all over the board depending on whether or not their particular interests were addressed in phase one or phase two rollouts.

On a surprisingly upbeat note, recent research[3] on IT Service Management (ITSM) adoption indicates that CMDB deployments are generally viewed positively. Fifty-seven percent of respondents

---

[3]IT Service Management in the Age of Cloud and Agile, EMA and CXP, 2013.

regarded their CMDB deployments as "successful" or "very successful," and only five percent viewed theirs as "unsuccessful." These data, albeit based on respondent opinion, are also consistent with other Enterprise Management Associates (EMA) research efforts in recent years.

FRAMING THE CMDB SYSTEM CONVERSATION

Although it was written in 2009, this passage from an EMA consulting report still does a good job setting the stage for framing your initial CMDB System project plans:

> While vendors have taken great liberty with the concept of the CMDB as initially defined in the ITIL specifications, the true purpose of the CMDB is to empower better decisions and manage organizational knowledge. A CMDB underpins knowledge management and decision support.
>
> It is very important to understand that the core CMDB by itself does very little by way of delivering the promised benefits. It is only through gathering, organizing, managing, and using the information and knowledge—taking action—that CMDB benefits appear. This is a critical distinction and one of the single most important items to remember. This is even more important when you consider the requirement for process surrounding the use of the CMDB—something many people take for granted or skip altogether.
>
> A CMDB is therefore not a "thing," but rather a cornerstone to a larger "system." There is no such thing as standalone "CMDB" regardless of marketing statements made by over-zealous vendors. Rather, the CMDB System consists of a collection of logical and physical constituents. How these constituents come together as a decision support system requires strong process control.
>
> The scope of the CMDB System touches all facets of IT, providing benefit to all users of IT data. Like the vendors, users see the value of the CMDB based on the specific requirements that they have for its use.

Indeed, the CMDB System, at least as we refer to it here, is not a "thing" but a true "system" that can only evolve through a conversation that includes a wide range of technologies, processes, and cross silo dialogs, all of which have a place in optimizing CMDB value for any given IT environment. We have chosen the word *conversation* deliberately because at core, that's what's required to embrace both the challenges and the opportunities implicit in CMDB-related projects. And dialog—not traditionally a long suit within IT when it crosses routine or siloed boundaries—is in a sense what a CMDB System is all about, especially when it's empowered by unique levels of visibility, insight, automation, and analytics.

ON THE OTHER HAND, CAN YOU REALLY DO WITHOUT A CMDB SYSTEM?

The answer is "no" if

- you want to meaningfully combine Change Management and performance management into a consistent set of processes, insights and analysis;
- you want to extend that continuum to support financial planning across IT assets, OpEx-related costs (e.g., lifecycle asset management), and costs for the delivery of IT services;

- you want a truly service-aware IT organization;
- you want a stronger voice at the table in answering business pressures and responding to business demands;
- you're just tired of things "breaking" for no apparent reason—and want a better way not only of fixing them but also of preventing the problems from occurring to begin with;
- you want to optimize business services across hybrid cloud and noncloud environments with clear insights into relevant interdependencies, including cloud service provider interdependencies;
- you want to have a cohesive foundation for bringing development and operations together in planning, developing, delivering, and retiring application and business services.

SUMMARY TAKEAWAYS

The CMDB System has (at least) two parents—one is ITIL and process-centric and the other is a range of interrelated technologies. This very dimensionality has challenged both the market and real IT deployments where linear thinking, industry hype, and shaky planning and commitment have too often been a recipe for disaster.

Some of the reasons for caution are documented above. They include the following:

- Lack of vision
- Poor communication
- Lack of confidence
- Resources, costs, and issues of relevance
- Resistance to ITIL
- Shaky senior management and executive leadership
- Vendor failures to address complexity, integration, and other issues

In spite of these challenges, current research data show not only a modest resurgence in CMDB deployments but also an upswing in successes as well. Given all of the potential challenges, how is this possible? Some of the answers begin to unfold in Chapter 2.

WHY BOTHER? THE CASE FOR A CMDB SYSTEM

Volumes have been written, and no doubt will continue to be written, about the fact that IT organizations find themselves in the crosshairs of change—and how that's both potentially good and often threatening. There are many factors behind this, but to understand the context for valuing a CMDB, or almost any other IT investment, it's worth taking a few moments to consider the storm that's already beginning to engulf IT.

Research, dialogues, and consulting all suggest that the role of IT is itself shifting from being a primarily back-office operation shrouded in technological obscurity to becoming a more front-office-aligned resource for driving new levels of business efficiencies. These, significantly, include the enablement of new business and organizational models.

Consumer-driven IT, mobility, and the fact that 12-year-olds can provision applications (or at least applets) while standing on line at the movies—along with the "shopping mall" of cloud and shadow IT—are among the dominant contributors to this change. In parallel, more agile software developers are attempting to be responsive to business unit demands with sometimes thousands of changes per month to a single application service.

So, IT organizations are facing far more dynamic times—in which what they do is much more visible to their consumers, exposed by their customers, and yet still largely misunderstood by executives and practitioners on both sides of the IT-to-business divide. Moreover, while EMA research indicates that overall IT budget dollars are growing, IT resources are continually being challenged—just as expectations for delivering value are often going through the roof.

This is a fundamental shift away from a purely cost-driven IT culture toward a value-driven IT opportunity, which is still barely in its infancy. As an immediate corollary to this, IT must recognize that it is now fundamentally a "product" provider with much keener eye than ever before on its consumers' shifting priorities and needs.

In such a rapidly changing world, an investment that takes many years to pay off has no real place. In other words, the classic CMDB deployment, at least as it has been characterized by many in the industry, no longer makes sense.

What does make a huge amount of sense, however, is a "system of relevance" to capture critical service interdependencies across both internal and extended resources (cloud service providers, telcos, etc.) that's current, dynamic, and optimized to support both business value and IT efficiencies.

Enter the CMDB System as it is evolving to support IT's "new age."

We've chosen to end Chapter 1 with a summary of why you should care about a CMDB System in "Framing the Conversation." We discussed its enabling value, why it's a system not a thing, and how it can potentially support everyone within IT. Then, we continued by referencing the unique power of the CMDB System in meaningfully bringing together Change Management and performance management, extending those insights into optimizing IT assets, OpEx efficiencies, portfolio values and costs, its growing support for DevOps and cloud, and its transformative values in enabling a more service-aware

IT organization. In this chapter, as well as in Chapter 7, we'll look at these benefits in more dimension and depth.

A FEW INITIAL DATA POINTS

CMDB adoption appears to be on the rise. According to research from Q4 2013,[1] a majority (68%) of respondents in 13 countries either owned or were about to purchase software that would allow them to implement a CMDB. Other data collected in 2013 show similar figures—52% for those involved in IT Service Management initiatives, while for those directed at moving to cloud, 30% had CMDBs deployed, 39% claimed a federated Configuration Management System (CMS), and 44% had application dependency mapping directed at managing change.[2]

This isn't an attempt to define a hard and fast global percentage for CMDB adoption for market share or market sizing, in part because we do not believe that the CMDB, let alone the CMDB System, can be understood as a discrete market. Moreover, as reasonably consistent as these data are across multiple research studies, it is still not intended to reflect an absolute metric. For one thing, the answers you are likely to get depend on just whom you ask. For instance, CIOs are substantially more likely (often 1.5 times more or better) to be aware of CMDB initiatives than are managers or other IT professionals.

CMDB SUCCESS RATES REVISITED

How successful are these adoptions? The data first cited in the Chapter 1, and shown here in Figure 2.1, may seem surprisingly bullish.[3] Fifty-seven percent view their CMDB adoptions as either "successful" or "very successful"—albeit only 8% are in the "very successful" category. Perhaps most surprisingly, only 5% saw their CMDB deployment[4] as "unsuccessful."

Just as the standards for "failure" can vary based on how it's measured and whom you ask (as we saw in Chapter 1), gauging success for CMDBs and CMDB Systems can be potentially even more challenging. For that very reason, evaluating the success of a CMDB System deployment will represent a substantial part of this book.

When the same respondent base was examined to find trends across the research more broadly, some further indicators of "CMDB success" came forth. EMA analysis showed that successful CMDB System owners were

- spread fairly evenly across company size, which is different from in the past when CMDBs were almost invariably the exclusive domain of large enterprises;
- nearly 1.5 times more likely to receive an increase in IT budget compared with those without a CMDB System;
- fifty percent more likely to be aware of critical IT Service Management metrics, such as the volumes of incidents and problems their organizations face in an average month;

---

[1] Custom research with Axelos done in Q4, 2013, inclusive of 380 respondents across North America, Europe, APAC, and Latin America looking at shifting perceptions of ITIL and ITSM.
[2] IT Service Management in the Age of Cloud and Agile, EMA and CXP, 2013; Ecosystem Cloud, EMA, 2013.
[3] Ibid.
[4] EMA and CXP, op. cit.

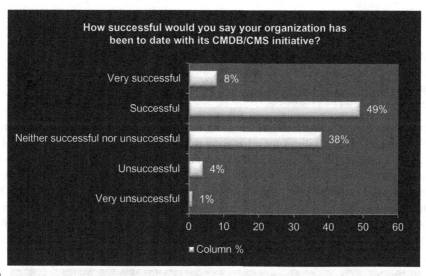

FIGURE 2.1

Based on recent global data on CMDB System adoption, success rates appear to be higher than what many industry naysayers claim, which of course leaves open the question what is success for a CMDB System and how can it best be measured?

- significantly more likely to be proactive in integrating their service desk with operations;
- more than twice as likely to be very or extremely satisfied with their service desk deployment;
- more than twice as likely to have the following integrated with their IT Service Management investments:
  - Application Discovery and Dependency Mapping
  - Integrated service desk/operations for SLM and performance management
  - Integrated Change Management
  - Integrated service catalog
  - Integrated application life cycle management
  - Integrated IT business intelligence warehouse

Are these signs of advancement and maturity because of the CMDB investment, or is it the other way around—that is, are CMDBs being deployed primarily by more progressive IT organizations to begin with? Both experience and common sense should lead you to the conclusion that both are true and each factor is supportive of the other. A CMDB System can empower an IT organization to support added levels of process efficiency, automation, integration, and overall accountability in managing and optimizing its critical business services. Conversely, CMDB adoption is, in itself, favored when IT organizations have already made advances in process, technology, and culture.

SOME SHORT ANSWERS

Consulting experience has validated the following reasons for why you should go ahead with a CMDB System—although it is hardly a master list, it is still worth noting:

A CMDB System will do the following:

- Decrease time to resolve technical problems
- Break down barriers between technology silos
- Allow automation and advanced analytics to be implemented
- Facilitate an enterprise IT dashboard
- Reduce long-term costs of IT services

Another way to look at "CMDB drivers" can be seen in Figure 2.2. Research results from as far back as 2007[5] prioritized "capabilities for integrating data across multiple sources" followed by "support for Change Management"—two fundamental tenants in planning CMDB System adoptions.

Current adoptions have evolved to focus on the use cases we will examine in detail in Chapter 7. The data in Figure 2.3 from Q4 2013[6] show a surprisingly high valuation for service impact and performance management and a not-so-surprising rise in focus on support for Security and Compliance audits. However, it should be pointed out that this question was asked twice—the first time, it was presented as in Figure 2.3, where respondents could pick multiple options. The second time, the question

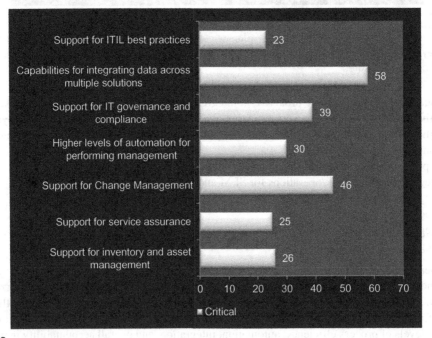

FIGURE 2.2

Early CMDB adopters viewed their investment primarily as a capability for assimilating and reconciling data from multiple sources. While this is a technology-centric focus, it is also telling. It suggests the need for a better way to optimize existing investments by bringing cohesiveness to silo-driven fragmentation.

[5] Winning Strategies in CMDB Adoption: What's Working in the Real World, and What Isn't, and Why? EMA, 2007.
[6] EMA and Axelos, op. cit.

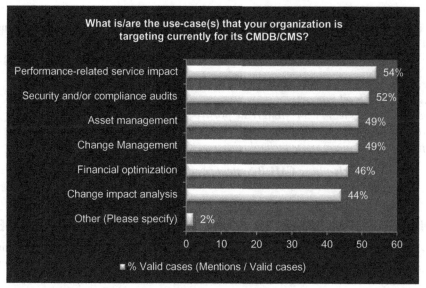

FIGURE 2.3

Current CMDB adoptions show a rise in service impact and service performance, as CMDB-related technologies evolve to become more dynamic and adaptable in nature. However, Change Management was the number one option when respondents were asked to select a single dominant use case, with security and/or compliance audits in a near tie.

asked for only the *single dominant* use case, and then, *Change Management* jumped to the fore, echoing the 2007 research results.

The takeaway from all this is twofold: Firstly, Change Management is a central enabling benefit for virtually all CMDB-related use cases; and secondly, CMDB Systems are evolving into more dynamic resources for operations with a wider range of critical use cases, including service performance and security.

RETURN ON INVESTMENT

While pure "return on investment" (ROI) is a complex discussion when it comes to CMDB System deployments, the industry is making significant strides. A few examples from past EMA research and consulting include the following:[7]

- A US financial service company reduced mean time to repair (MTTR) by 70% by providing consistent services mapped to asset inventories updated nightly.
- A US manufacturing service provider was able to reconcile disputes regarding infrastructure spends that tallied $9 million spent over 3 years, with a net gain of $2.5 million.
- A US healthcare organization reduced MTTR, downtime, and outages by 40% by implementing a CMDB. Savings returned 300% ROI over several years.

---

[7]These data are pulled from interviews across multiple EMA research reports as itemized in Chapter 1—footnote 2.

A documented evaluation of CMDB System[8] vendors showed that while most "best case" ROI fell between 6 and 9 months for CMDB deployments, one instance delivered ROI for a significant CMDB investment in as little as 2 weeks!

If there's a simple formula for quick time to value for a CMDB System, it's the following:

Mature levels of process awareness
+Strong executive level support
+A ready and willing team with strongly supportive stakeholders
+Clearly defined and ready phase one use case
+Carefully selected, appropriate technologies

All this = Powerful early-phase CMDB System results

REASONS FOR GOING FORWARD: MORE VOICES FROM THE TRENCHES

The following comments begin to illustrate not only drivers and values but also the actual dimensions of CMDB-related benefits as they may apply to you in planning your initiative. (*All the quotes below come from a mix of consulting engagement, interviews, and research dialogs.*)

DROWNING IN (SILOED) DATA?

One common driver for CMDB Systems is optimizing "trusted sources," a process that's at times as political as it is technological. The values can be enormous, but once again, they require meaningful dialog and often substantial executive commitment to override the "my tool or else!" conflicts that so often threaten the effectiveness of IT. The following quotes show the importance of communication and executive support:

- "From a CMDB perspective, a very clear need exists for correlation, automation, and reconciliation of enterprise data. A key theme when we assessed our own requirements was, 'We are drowning in data. We have lots of data, but little information.'"
- "We had many silos of data and many different repositories. All over the world, everyone was doing their own silo of work in sometimes redundant or even conflicting ways. So we needed one central book of record, and that's why the CMDB was so important for us."
- "We had $20 million in redundant data. We had redundancies in our discovery tools. SMS was used in some places, network discovery in others. One business unit used its own tools. Another business unit used a different set. The CMDB initiative is enabling us to reconcile these differences, and consolidate and optimize our toolsets for the first time ever."

OPTIMIZING IT OpEx EFFICIENCIES IN THE FACE OF RISING COMPLEXITIES

This benefit, although often difficult to measure in hard numbers, is central to successful CMDB System adoptions. Moreover, it's a benefit that depends on a true mix of improved processes, well-chosen

---

[8]CMDB/CMS Radar: the Move to Federation, EMA, 2012.

technologies, and improved levels of communication across IT. The following comments help to clarify some of the many potential dimensions of this critical value:

- "We have determined that our prior approach to managing change would not scale with the increasing complexity of our SW and HW infrastructure requirements, including Web Services and SOA, given our limited staff resources. Our CMDB System will empower both superior process and decision-making efficiencies."
- "In reducing complexity and its associated risks, we are achieving
  - reduced manual efforts and providing more consistency to keep IT operations up and running,
  - faster implementation processes and provisioning more flexibly,
  - lower overall IT costs and reduced MTTR."
- "Our current level of OpEx efficiency cannot support our business growth. We anticipate growth of 30-50% over the next 5 years. This represents a significant growth in volumes of data that we must handle effectively. From what we have already seen, our CMDB System will be the critical difference in optimizing our efficiencies to meet these requirements."

CHANGE MANAGEMENT AND CHANGE IMPACT ANALYSIS

Perhaps, more than any other use case, *Change Management* is the very heart of the CMDB System value set. Based on consulting and research, some specific use cases that are less self-evident for Change Management and change impact analysis include

- governance and compliance,
- service availability and performance,
- data center consolidation,
- disaster recovery,
- facilities management and green IT,
- support for provisioning new application services.

The comments below provide just a few examples of how CMDB Systems can empower change:

- "We had an opportunity to reinvent Change Management in our organization and go from a project management approach that was very ambivalent when it came to execution to a much more enforceable approach that supported clear ownership and led to increased levels of automation."
- "By having both preproduction and production in the system, we can easily prioritize issues, so we know when the impact is hitting many of our customers or conversely when systems are down and none of our external customers are impacted."
- "Generating compliance reports is a core value. We're audited twice a year and needed to generate detailed configuration histories to comply with government regulatory requirements. Our CMDB helps us to put all this together in a meaningful and timely way."

ASSET MANAGEMENT AND IT FINANCIAL OPTIMIZATION

While Change Management is arguably the most central CMDB System use case, it is not always the first phase in many deployments. Asset management is more often than not a critical component of phase one deployments, in part because it tends to be less time-sensitive in terms of data currency and in part because just getting a handle on what you have, who owns it, and how it is being managed is a natural place to begin.

However, investing in a CMDB System provides added dimensions to traditional approaches to asset management—by showing interdependencies between services and their hardware (HW) and software (SW) asset dependencies, so that relevance and critical vulnerabilities can be exposed.

Key aspects of CMDB-related asset management values include

- asset and inventory analysis,
- asset life cycle management,
- compliance audits,
- financial optimization.

A few testimonials further clarify some of the more tangible dimensions of value here:

- "The CMDB allows us to see—here's how everything's connected. We can approach life cycle asset management from a very problem-oriented perspective."
- "We use our CMDB to manage our inventory. If a piece of hardware fails, it's important to understand whether the failure is an anomaly or part of a trend. Tracking such incidents therefore enables the agency to spot trends to help it better manage its environment."

SERVICE IMPACT, ROOT CAUSE ANALYSIS, AND TROUBLESHOOTING

While CMDBs were initially developed with a focus more on process control than on performance management and real-time actions, both technology advances in CMDB System design and trends such as cloud computing are changing the game dramatically. Operational professionals with concerns such as mean time to repair (MTTR) and mean time between failure (MTBF) can benefit greatly from a "reconciled view of truth" including the impacts of change on performance—which is ultimately dependent on a dynamic CMDB System foundation.

Some of the more prominent use cases here include

- a reconciled view of truth across multiple monitoring and other sources,
- reflexive insights into change and configuration for diagnostics,
- validation that a newly provisioned service is performing effectively (or not),
- incident and problem management automation and governance.

The comments below should help to clarify these benefits further:

- "One of our key use cases for our CMDB System is root cause analysis. We are still largely working here in silos. Whenever we want to solve an incident and we don't know what might be the root cause, we connect to the CMDB and apply its cross domain perspectives. We can also determine if there is a change that just occurred that might have an impact."
- "We have terrific synergy between our CMDB and our core service performance monitoring and management solution—with run-time, or real-time, currency across service interdependencies."

THE MOVE TO CLOUD AND VIRTUALIZATION

While some industry pundits have decided that CMDBs are old hat in the face of new technologies like cloud and virtualization, research data suggest just the opposite. In fact, the data are more than

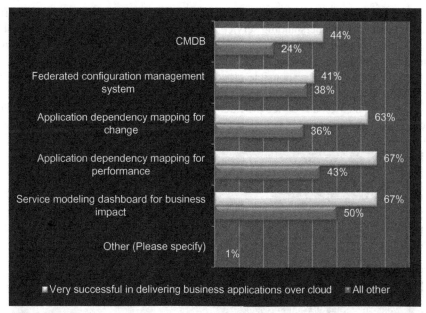

FIGURE 2.4

The power of capturing interdependencies with service modeling turned out to be a true game changer in cloud adoptions. As can be seen above, those IT organizations with CMDBs or application dependency mapping solutions directed at Change Management are nearly twice as likely to be "very successful" in deploying critical IT business services over cloud as those without a CMDB or ADDM investment. Those with application dependency mapping for performance were more than 1.5 more likely to be "very successful."

suggestive; they are almost a slam-dunk indicator that insights into service interdependencies are more relevant than ever given the vagaries and variety of public and private cloud options.

In Figure 2.4 from a 2013 research[9], the power of service modeling in various contexts is mapped to an IT organization's effectiveness in delivering business services over cloud and hybrid environments. These included internal (private) and external (public) cloud resources and full variations on cloud options—from software as a service (SaaS), to infrastructure as a service (IaaS), to platform as a service (PaaS). The goal was to address how IT organizations are seeking to manage critical IT business services across a wide range of application types in context with the full cloud mosaic.

We evaluated a number of critical technology investments, from analytics and automation, to discovery, to CMDB, Application Discovery and Dependency Mapping, and service dashboards, as can be seen in Figure 2.4. All turned out to be advantages, but few showed as striking a correlation with "very successful cloud deployments" as CMDBs or ADDM solutions for Change Management.

There are many reasons for this. In fact, an entire book could easily be devoted to CMDB Systems in the context of cloud adoption. Clearly, these CMDB-related capabilities have to be sufficiently dynamic to support changes at more accelerated tempos such as vMotion. They also need to be focused

---

[9]EMA, Ecosystem Cloud, op. cit.

selectively on relevance as opposed to simply being dumping grounds for on-premise and off-premise (when accessible) data. But understanding service management interdependencies is critical for managing and planning for cloud and *intelligently*, as opposed to *blindly*, applying the automation necessary for optimizing cloud choices with currency and conviction.

In other researches targeting responsible cloud computing adoption, respondents indicated by a two-to-one margin that having a CMDB with shared data insights would bring them greater confidence in working with their cloud service providers[10]. The reasons for this are indicated in Figure 2.5. Security, compliance, and Change Management took the lead, which is no surprise. More surprisingly,

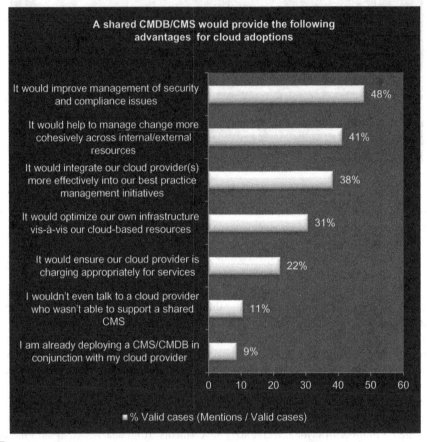

FIGURE 2.5

Having a shared CMDB System for the "Extended Enterprise" insofar as it applies to cloud service providers was a two-to-one favorite in our research. The reasons indicated above (security, compliance, change, etc.) aren't surprising and indicate a growing need to enable insights, define processes, and better assess cost and value beyond the confines of a single IT organization. It's worth noting that 11% might see a failure to support shared data in a CMDB System as a reason to say "no" to a cloud service provider.

[10]Responsible Cloud, EMA, 2010.

9% claimed some level of CMDB-related data sharing with their cloud service providers already. This may seem like science fiction, but in fact, other researches substantiate the value, and the desire, for more sophisticated IT shops to reach inside the cloud for governance along multiple lines—from performance monitoring, to application dependency insights, to cost, asset, and change optimization.

This raises bigger issues in terms of establishing collective processes for sharing data, determining configuration item (CI) ownership, and managing business services across their full life cycles inclusive of partners, suppliers, and service providers (cloud and otherwise). It is an area that we are actively researching, as CMDB Systems for the "Extended Enterprise" will likely become increasingly important in the coming decade—posing unique challenges to process, technology, and, admittedly, politics.

BRINGING THE ORGANIZATION TOGETHER

In summing up CMDB System values, it seemed appropriate to key on "bringing the IT organization together." You might argue that this is another chicken-and-the-egg dilemma because successful CMDB System deployments typically do require some improvement in process and organizational unity just to succeed in phase one. Yet, here as well, both research data and logic would dictate that this is instead a case of one hand washing the other. CMDB Systems as they evolve provide a powerful context for unifying and streamlining IT decision making, enabling automation, and promoting more advanced levels of service awareness and maturity.

The quotes selected below from EMA consulting speak for themselves in adding insight and perspectives on this single, perhaps most important, benefit for driving forward with a CMDB System initiative:

- "Our goal was to enable a systematic process in which information about IT resources and their interdependencies are well managed, and the related information about IT functions is gathered, managed, and utilized to serve our rapidly growing business needs."
- "I would say that as a fundamental, achieved benefit to date, we have finally gotten the entirety of IT to work together instead of being stuck in a siloed mentality. We've only just begun this journey, but we've gotten all of IT to pay attention to it."

The following observation by Charles Araujo, founder and CEO of the IT Transformation Institute (and author of "The Quantum Age of IT" referenced in Chapter 5), provides an excellent summation for both this section and this chapter as a whole:

"Executed effectively, a CMS/CMDB is one of the most valuable resources an IT organization will ever have at its disposal. It is fundamentally a context engine allowing the organization to see its vast array of assets in relationship to and in context of both each other and the value they have been organized to deliver to the business processes they are designed to support. It is in the vastness and complexity that IT organizations get lost. They lose sight of what is most meaningful to the organization at any given moment and in any given circumstance. A properly scoped and well executed CMS/CMDB provides a mechanism to continually seek and find clarity of relevance as we seek to deliver optimum value to our customers."

SUMMARY TAKEAWAYS

IT is going through a difficult transition from being a "cost-driven" organization to being a "value-driven" organization, in which service awareness and business relevance trump introverted and siloed ways of working. This transformation places CMDB System adoption in a new context—with increased demands for dynamic awareness and business benefits.

As can be seen from both consulting and research, the values and benefits of embarking on a CMDB initiative can and should be manifold as the CMDB System evolves over time.

The critical benefits outlined in this chapter include

- *reconciling often discrepant data while optimizing and consolidating toolset investments;*
- *optimizing IT OpEx efficiencies;*
- *dramatic improvements in Change Management, asset management, service impact analysis, and diagnostics;*
- *Supporting the move to cloud and virtualization for more effective, efficient, and consistent service delivery;*
- *Bringing the IT organization together in a more service-aware way of working—that is, the CMDB can become a true enabler for the transformation of IT.*

This is nonetheless a partial list. As you read ahead in this book, many more insights into CMDB values and benefits should become apparent.

In the next chapter, we'll examine both the *process* and the *technology* foundations of CMDB Systems in more depth, as they provide a baseline set of resources for going forward with any CMDB-related initiative.

THE BASICS

CMDB SYSTEM FOUNDATIONS

3

Given the manifold debates about issues and values in CMDB Systems, it should be no surprise that few topics in IT today are as confusing and misunderstood as the CMDB. Some define the CMDB and the CMS by their strict Information Technology Infrastructure Library (ITIL) definitions; others use one the many descriptions given by the CMDB vendors in the market. Still, others see the CMDB as a homegrown collection of data that never quite found its way into being of use.

One common misconception is that a CMDB contains only configuration information on servers and devices in the infrastructure. Depending on the particular deployment, a CMDB may also contain information on applications, middleware, documentation, people, processes, providers, and other relevant data in addition to infrastructure components.

In this chapter, we'll examine the two foundations—or "parents"—for the CMDB System: ITIL processes and associated CMDB-related technologies, as shown in Figure 3.1. These two parents are not always understood from a common set of balanced perspectives. Processes are often favored by one set of stakeholders, while other stakeholders may be fully consumed by technologies, integration issues, and architecture. If there's a single central idea behind optimizing CMDB System deployments, it's the need to promote balanced attention to both process and technology and facilitate dialogue across these areas.

Indeed, CMDB implementations rely on effective processes that cross IT silos more heavily than many other technology initiatives. Just how this is achieved in actual deployments often becomes a microcosm of IT organizational, technology, and process challenges in general—exposing a storm of issues surrounding IT efficiency, effectiveness, and business alignment that need to be resolved, in any case, if IT is to enhance its value and adjust to changing business needs. Emerging from this storm with an intelligent, well-socialized plan with clearly defined metrics is—perhaps ironically—one of the greatest benefits of CMDB initiatives, even though it is at least partially realized before a single piece of software has been deployed.

CMDB FOUNDATIONS PART ONE: PROCESS
WHY IT'S GOOD TO GET TO KNOW ITIL FIRST

In spite of some of the claims to the contrary, as expressed in Chapter 1, the value and the relevance of the ITIL are certainly holding firm or may even be on the rise—based on data from multiple research reports. In our most extensive global research on the topic, 46% of respondents felt that ITIL's value was growing in the face of new technology trends like cloud and agile development; 49% felt it would remain the same, while only 5% felt it was in decline.[1] Moreover, those IT organizations favoring

---

[1]Custom research between EMA and Axelos, Q4, 2013.

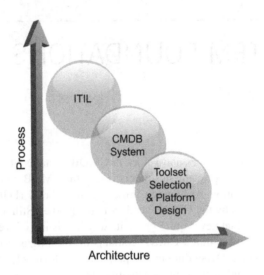

FIGURE 3.1

The CMDB System's "two parents." Understanding how to optimize process and technology together and in meaningful stages is the single most critical key to success.

ITIL showed not only more progressive approaches to service management but also higher levels of maturity and effectiveness in managing and delivering critical business services over heterogeneous cloud infrastructures.[2]

ITIL may not be perfect—and it's categorically best if viewed as a "departure point" rather than a holy writ, a doctrine, or even an ideology (as some might claim). But ITIL offers well-thought-out guidelines that also pose questions that can spark valuable analysis as IT managers and practitioners seek to adopt ITIL recommendations within their own unique environments.

ITIL is

- a common lexicon for disparate disciplines,
- holistic—a place where the full IT process mosaic can come together,
- a high-level set of recommendations for what processes should be in place,
- a valuable catalyst.

ITIL is not

- a standard,
- completely prescriptive,
- a perfect answer for a perfect world,
- a panacea for all of IT's ailments,

---

[2]Ecosystem Cloud, EMA, 2013.

While we are not insisting that every CMDB System deployment begins with ITIL and, in fact, at the end of this book, we'll visit a CMDB initiative that began in development with a focus on Scrum, ITIL is the industry's single best source for understanding the roots of the CMDB, its process dependencies, and its native values. ITIL also provides excellent guidelines for mapping, planning, and measuring a CMDB deployment once it's underway. Needless to say, we've drawn heavily from these and integrated them with our own experience in the field, our own research, and our own focus on CMDB-related technologies, politics, and cultural issues.

A (VERY) SHORT HISTORY

As infrastructures grew in complexity in the 1980s, the UK government looked across its IT organization with the objective of finding better ways of using IT services and resources. A collaborative set of IT best practices evolved into a library of books based on the experiences of enterprise IT organizations and management vendors. As these best practices matured, commercial organizations began to adopt them as well. The ITIL is the result of that effort. In order to define processes for the broadest possible audience, the ITIL is somewhat abstract, but ITIL 2011 has made real advances in translating its abstractions into actionable ideas.

Originally owned by the UK Cabinet Office, ITIL was acquired in 2013 by Axelos in a joint venture with Capita, a United Kingdom-based consultancy leading in business process management. Axelos brings ITIL best practices for service management together with a number of other best practices, such as PRINCE2 for project management and Management of Portfolio (MoP) for prioritizing investments across organizations, programs, and projects. Appropriately, "Axelos" is derived from the French/Greek philosopher, Kostas Axelos, born in Athens in 1924 and known for "uniting old and new with games and openness." See www.itil-officialsite.com for more information on ITIL and http://www.best-management-practice.com/ for insights across all Axelos-related best practices.

The ITIL framework is based on a service life cycle and consists of five life cycle stages: *Service Strategy, Service Design, Service Transition, Service Operation,* and *Continual Service Improvement.* Each of these stages has its own supporting publication. There is also a set of complementary ITIL publications that provide guidance specific to industry sectors, organization types, operating models, and technology architectures.

A HUMAN FACE TO SERVICE MANAGEMENT

Too often overlooked in assessing ITIL is its very human face. For instance, ITIL tends to see service as supporting customer needs and priorities while freeing them from the burden of unnecessary costs and risks. When it comes to IT service specifically—the core of its raison d'être—ITIL generally defines it as a blending of technologies, processes, and the people who utilize them. In ITIL's view, a customer-facing service should directly empower more effective ways of working, and should have service-level agreements associated with those objectives.

ITIL'S LIBRARIES

Refining the idea of organizing IT around services, ITIL V2 was introduced in 2000. ITIL V3 was introduced in 2007 and condensed ITIL V2's seven libraries into five while introducing the critical concepts of the federated Configuration Management System (CMS) and Service Knowledge Management

FIGURE 3.2

ITIL V3's library of five volumes offers a rich life cycle approach to service management with carefully drawn interdependencies across processes, roles, and even high-level technology requirements.

System (SKMS) as described in more detail later in this chapter.[3] These ideas were further enhanced with the current ITIL version: ITIL 2011 (Figure 3.2).

A rough sense of the life cycle approach for ITIL 2011 can be seen in the following overview of the five different publications:

ITIL Service Strategy—This volume sets the stage, in many respects, for the other four books in terms of providing an overarching strategic foundation. It includes[4]

- strategy management for IT services,
- service portfolio management,
- financial management for IT services,
- demand management,
- business relationship management.

ITIL Service Design—This volume provides guidance on how IT services can be more effectively created and introduced to optimize the strategic goals defined in service strategy. It includes

- design coordination,
- service catalog management,
- service-level management,
- availability management,
- capability management,
- IT service continuity management,
- information security management,
- supplier management.

ITIL Service Transition—This volume addresses the need to introduce, manage, and retire services in a manner that meets requirements specified in *Service Strategy* and *Service Design*. It is also at the center of the CMDB and CMS story—and is perhaps the most central to the narrative here. It includes

- transition planning and support,
- change management,

---

[3]ITIL© Service Transition, The Stationery Office (TSO), UK, 2011. ITIL definitions have been taken from *Glossary.*
[4]Ibid.

- service asset and configuration management,
- release and deployment management,
- service validation and testing,
- change evaluation,
- knowledge management.

ITIL Service Operation—This volume might be most directly associated with what many people think of as "operations" in general: ensuring that services are effectively delivered and performed in accordance with both IT and business objectives. It includes

- event management,
- incident management,
- request fulfillment,
- problem management,
- access management.

ITIL Continual Service Improvement—The idea of "Continual Service Improvement" is a distinctive ITIL value that can be critical to the overall optimization of IT's performance in support of its broader goals. *Continual Service Improvement* addresses the need to target shifting business needs while continuing to identify and document areas of improvement in IT's overall performance. It will

- identify the strategy for improvement,
- define what you will measure,
- gather the data,
- process the data,
- analyze the information and data,
- present and use the information,
- implement improvement.

While the CMDB System has its most direct roots in *Service Transition,* it can deliver underlying values in supporting the full service life cycle as described in all five ITIL volumes.

In recent EMA research conducted jointly with Axelos,[5] respondents were asked to rank the values that their IT organizations have enjoyed by leveraging the ITIL; Figure 3.3 shows the results. It is emblematic, and highly relevant to this book, that the number one statement was *"IT helps me work more effectively with others in unified processes."*

ITIL'S CONFIGURATION MANAGEMENT DATABASE (CMDB)

ITIL generally refers to a Configuration Management Database (CMDB) as a database that stores critical IT service-related elements, or configuration items (CIs), throughout their lifecycles. A Configuration Management System (CMS) is made up of one or more CMDBs, each of which should capture CI attributes, relationships and interdependencies. A few key words here are "relationships" and "lifecycle" and of course, "configuration item." This configuration item is anything that needs to

---

[5]EMA and Axelos, op. cit.

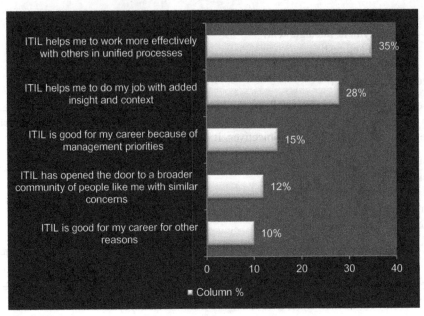

Sample Size = 257

FIGURE 3.3

In ranking values for ITIL adoption, "Supporting more effective ways of working 'with others'" received top billing. This is key to ITIL's value, especially when applied to cross silo initiatives, such as CMDB Systems, where dialogue and processes so often tend to be broken.

be managed to successfully provide an IT-related service to a client. CIs can include a wide range of materials including people, software, hardware, IT services, process paperwork, and SLAs. Defining, managing, and optimizing CIs and their interdependencies are at the heart of CMDB System deployments—as we'll examine in a little more detail below.

The dimensionality and range of *configuration items* open up a whole world of interdependencies and insights for which ITIL should be given a great deal of credit. We are no longer talking about just managing things—we are talking about managing IT services in their full human, as well as technical, dimensions.

THE CONFIGURATION MANAGEMENT SYSTEM (CMS)

In understanding the real impact of the CMS, it's best to stay focused on the term "system," as ITIL's "Configuration Management System" includes both a sense of federation and potentially more dynamism than a single standalone CMDB.

ITIL's definition of a Configuration Management System (CMS) refers to a system that supports configuration management through effective data assimilation and toolsets that track, aggregate, analyze, and showcase critical information regarding configuration items and CI relationships. The CMS may extend to provide insights on releases, problems, incidents, known errors, and changes. A well-evolved CMS can support virtually all ITIL-defined service management processes.

This definition of CMS allows for more flexibility with "releases, problems, incidents, known errors, and changes." As such, it can become a foundation for empowering virtually any IT process or requirement, which increasingly includes both operations and even development—well beyond ITIL's traditional service desk roots.

The end of the ITIL CMS definition basically indicates that CMS is used in all ITIL-defined service management processes. In the real world, this is a statement of potential that needs to be addressed in phases. Remember that despite its potential to bring about huge benefits, the CMDB System is not "a single magic bullet."

> Most people think of ITIL as a 'best practice.' But the follow-on question is, 'What do you do about that best practice?' In my mind a best practice is just a set of advisories. You should follow it based on your understanding of your needs, your environment and your maturity levels. However, I see some companies trying to follow ITIL by the book as a definitive set of standard procedures, and I think this can carry some unintended consequences.
> —**CMDB Team leader from a mid-tier financial services company based in North America.**[6]

In its entirety and in real deployments, the CMS represents a much more streamlined, systemic, and dynamic approach than the market stereotype for the traditional CMDB, in which service modeling and discovery are beginning to take center stage, supplanting data storage as the true "spine" of the system.

The Definitive Media Library (DML)
Another critical component to the CMS is the "Definitive Media Library" (DML), which was called "definitive software library" in ITIL V2 but was expanded in V3 to represent more diverse media (video, voice, etc.) in order to capture a more complete array of IT-delivered services. The DML includes "authorized versions," along with associated "licenses and documentation," and may be collected in one or multiple locations even if it remains a "single, logical storage area."

In other words, the DML becomes a common resource for empowering and clarifying the development-to-operations dialogue and processes that's rightly becoming such a priority today in many IT organizations.

THE SERVICE KNOWLEDGE MANAGEMENT SYSTEM (SKMS)

ITIL's definition of CMS brings up yet another term, the *Service Knowledge Management System* (SKMS), which may be ITIL V3's single most visionary idea. If the CMS can house multiple CMDBs optimized for different levels of detail and relevance, the CMS is, itself, an enabler for this even larger vision—the SKMS.

The SKMS is a resource that encompasses the Configuration Management System along with other databases and information repositories. It is a true service management system that can acquire, analyze, update, store, and display all of the information that an IT service provider needs access to in order to offer the most complete and precise IT services for their customers across what ITIL calls the *full lifecycle of IT services*.

---

[6] All quotes are taken from EMA research and consulting. For this particular quote, see the Q&A in the next chapter.

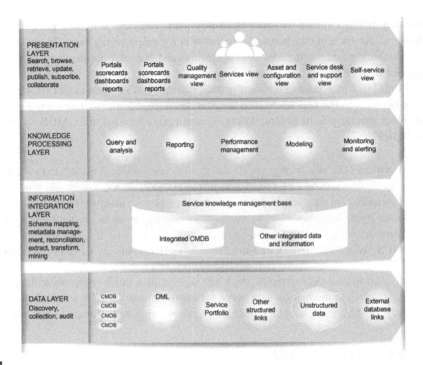

FIGURE 3.4

The primary goal of ITIL V3's SKMS is to improve efficiencies by minimizing the need to rediscover knowledge. This is a key foundation and driver for CMDB/CMS initiatives, which are fundamental to the success of the SKMS. This illustration offers a parallel view to what EMA calls "The Two CMDBs" in Figure 3.11.

Now, we are really getting somewhere when it comes to really optimizing your CMDB System investments! The SKMS is far from being just about collecting data and storing it in a single physical database—it's a system that facilitates the *analysis* and *presentation* of knowledge to support the "full life cycle of IT services." If you want to achieve value through your CMDB System and you completely ignore the need for analyzing and presenting knowledge—not to mention automation—you will never optimize your efforts.

Figure 3.4 shows an advanced logical architecture in which a core or "integrated" CMDB is federated with multiple CMDBs optimized in content and granularity for separate stakeholder groups. (EMA's term for this is "citizen CMDB.") This enables the full IT organization to enjoy a cohesive and reconciled view of services and their interdependencies.

ITIL does an excellent job of articulating *logical requirements* for integration into the broader SKMS. As you shall see in Figure 3.11, we also provide a design based on current product offerings with clear technological foundations. Both illustrations are meant as departure points for evaluation rather than literal descriptions of perfect, generic deployments (suited only for a perfect, generic world). But collectively, they also suggest a much larger landscape of value than any single data store could provide.

CMDB DEPLOYMENTS UNDERSCORE ITIL'S RELEVANCE

It's worth noting that ITIL-aware respondents who are deploying—or are about to deploy—CMDBs are considerably more bullish about the future of ITIL in the face of trends like cloud and agile than are other ITIL-aware or trained respondents (see Figure 3.5).[7] In other words, those with CMDB deployments are significantly more committed to ITIL's value. This reinforces the connection between process and technology—of the kind that we are championing in this book.

> We did approach ITIL as a standard set of best practices. But we recognized that everyone had to interpret it to meet the needs for their group, their function, and their region. So, did we follow ITIL to a 'T'? Absolutely not. Nevertheless, it was a foundation and a guide for us. For instance, we'd start with, 'What is the definition of a CMDB?' Eventually we built towards a consensus using ITIL as a departure point. And then we'd ask, 'What is a CI?' etc.
>
> —**Large North American Manufacturer**[8]

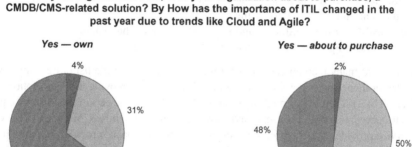

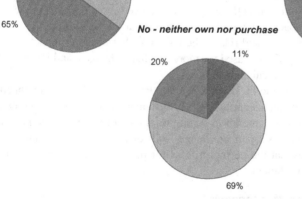

Does your organization own, or is your organization about to purchase, a CMDB/CMS-related solution? By How has the importance of ITIL changed in the past year due to trends like Cloud and Agile?

Sample Size = 380

- ITIL is becoming less important
- ITIL remains at the same level of importance
- ITIL is becoming more important

FIGURE 3.5

CMDB deployments underscore the value and relevance of ITIL in part because they are so process-dependent in addition to requiring strong service awareness and cross domain support. These data also reinforce the fact that bringing technology and process together is the best way to optimize investments in both.

---

[7]EMA and Axelos, op. cit.
[8]Footnote 7, op. cit.

A FEW CRITICAL ITIL PROCESSES

Process is at the very heart of ITIL's value. A few examples are worth singling out for discussion here in order to better understand the broader set of requirements for CMDB Systems.

Change Management

ITIL generally refers to the term *change management* as the system that ensures any and all changes to IT services are ultimately valuable changes that do not interrupt the quality of service. As such, change management is a logical system of governance that addresses very relevant questions that include the following:

- Who requested the change?
- What is the reason for the change?
- What is the desired result from the change?
- What are the risks involved in making the change?
- What resources are required to deliver the change?
- Who is responsible for the build, test, and implementation of the change?
- What is the relationship between this change and other changes?

ITIL puts forward many recommendations for making this very simple list of questions effective and enforceable. One of them, so often associated with CMDB-related deployments, is the notion of a Change Advisory Board (CAB). The CAB is made up of individuals from all aspects of the IT service process who work together to survey, schedule, prioritize, and allow changes to IT services. Members of the CAB can be from the IT service provider, the organization being assisted by the service provider, and third party groups.

However, it should be pointed out that ITIL recognizes the need for a tiered approach to address changes with different levels of impact and complexity—starting at the top with a *business executive board* for major changes with high costs and risks. The less risky but broadly impactful changes are managed by an *IT steering group*; the *CAB* is used for more localized changes; and lowest risk changes are addressed by a change manager or local authorization.

Critically and relevant to the dynamic IT environments today, ITIL recognizes the need for *standard, preauthorized changes*, which can accommodate, for instance, the thousands of content changes made to critical business applications per month in certain retail and other environments. While ITIL doesn't say much about automation in support of change—our own experience is that automation is central to making change work, so that the tiering process for reviews and planning can become increasingly focused, optimized, and efficient.

Service Asset and Configuration Management

The 2007 version of ITIL refers to "configuration management" separately as basically the steps that are taken to maintain configuration items data, including relationships, while the data is current and relevant so that IT services can be provided. Configuration management is a key component of ITIL's service asset and configuration process. ITIL 2011's Service Asset and Configuration Management (SACM) provides a more comprehensive look at how service-related assets are controlled, including the data, configurations, and the relationships of those assets. In other words, SACM is at the very heart of a Configuration Management System. Moreover, for ITIL, these IT assets have very human and technology-aware dimensions, including *management, organization, process, knowledge, people, information, applications, infrastructure, and financial capital.*

SACM objectives require effective identification, control, reporting, and management of CIs throughout their life cycles. This includes attention to the proper authorization for changes; historical, planned, and current state data; and support for the various roles and stakeholders involved in true cross domain service management.

> ITIL is needed to give us repeatable, measured, improved processes. We need to use process to make tools more efficient.
>
> **(From an EMA consulting engagement)**

Capacity Management

While ITIL places capacity management in *Continual Service Improvement* as opposed to *Service Transition,* in our experience, it is, in fact, very often associated with more advanced CMDB System deployments—often through integration with other analytic tools. CMDB Systems can provide meaningful insights into a whole host of service interdependencies, making them natural affiliates for capacity planning analytics. This is a growing trend, in part due to the impact of cloud and the need to migrate data centers from physical to more virtualized environments. Moreover, managing change responsibly means making capacity-related insights an integral part of the decision-making process.

ITIL regards capacity management as a process associated with ensuring that cost-effective and time-sensitive capacity levels are allocated for IT services and the software and infrastructure associated with them. Tellingly, ITIL then divides capacity management into business capacity management, service capacity management, and component capacity management.

Note the very deliberate tiering of this process, from "business capacity," to "service capacity," to "component capacity." Understanding these interdependencies is especially valuable in the volatile world of cloud computing and agile development.

ITIL also envisions a capability dedicated to capacity management that parallels the CMS—something it calls the *Capacity Management Information System,* or CMIS. The CMIS combines management tools with data and analysis to enable more effective capacity management. This makes perfect sense as CMDB System support for capacity management and optimization invariably requires integrations that combine capacity data and analytics with core configuration insights into service interdependencies. The actual technologies relevant to capacity management available in the market today will be explored later in this chapter and in more detail in Chapter 12.

Release and Deployment Management

Another ITIL process to consider is release and deployment management which focuses on business-relevant releases, particularly on all steps of building, testing, and deploying those releases, while ensuring current processes and services are not hindered. Release management is best done with software tools that support high levels of automation and include a level of configuration granularity for device or software entities that often exceeds what should go into the core CMDB itself.

These processes combined are shown in Figure 3.6, which provides a simplified but useful map of how *change management, capacity management, configuration management,* and *release management* can all work together.

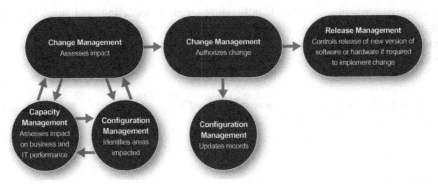

FIGURE 3.6

In this simple schematic developed for a consulting client, the overarching relationships between change management, configuration management, capacity management, and release management are represented at a summary level. As such, they provide a logical process roadmap for managing, accounting for and affecting change across all of IT, from DevOps to infrastructure updates.

> We are weak at process. We rely on people's knowledge. This is lost when people leave. ITIL will help us to manage this problem.
>
> **(Comment from a prior consulting engagement)**

Other ITIL Processes

ITIL offers many other processes beyond those described above. Figure 3.7 shows the results when respondents were asked to select the top four they were most personally involved with—and not surprisingly, a focus on operations currently dominates given the day-to-day workings and priorities of most IT organizations.

Nevertheless, as they evolve, CMDB Systems can support a wide variety of processes and stakeholders, as indicated in Figure 3.8. Taken from a specific consulting engagement, this diagram shows how one client's CMDB deployment is mapped to ITIL workflows. As complex as this may seem, it is nonetheless only a very high-level map.

CMDB DATA AND CONFIGURATION ITEMS: A SECOND LOOK

Understanding and managing CMDB-related data and CIs is central to CMDB System success. ITIL V2 grouped CMDB-relevant data into the following logical categories:[9]

Technology data include asset data, such as costs, locations, hardware and software configurations, related contracts, software licenses, and maintenance and support histories; physical and logical topology data; and operational data, such as availability, performance, and capacity.

---

[9]EMA and Axelos, op. cit.

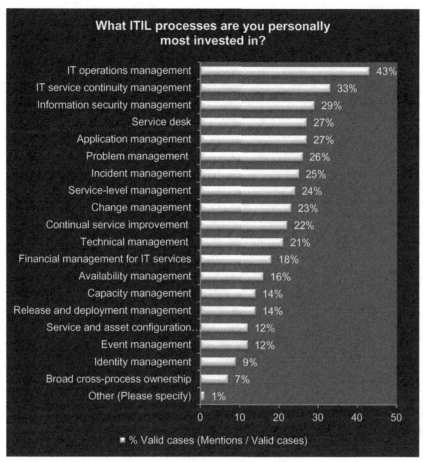

What ITIL processes are you personally most invested in?

Process	%
IT operations management	43%
IT service continuity management	33%
Information security management	29%
Service desk	27%
Application management	27%
Problem management	26%
Incident management	25%
Service-level management	24%
Change management	23%
Continual service improvement	22%
Technical management	21%
Financial management for IT services	18%
Availability management	16%
Capacity management	14%
Release and deployment management	14%
Service and asset configuration...	12%
Event management	12%
Identity management	9%
Broad cross-process ownership	7%
Other (Please specify)	1%

■ % Valid cases (Mentions / Valid cases)

Sample Size = 380

FIGURE 3.7

In Q4 2013, 380 global respondents selected the four ITIL processes with which they were most personally involved. Not surprisingly, operations is at the top of the list, with Change Management near the middle and the core processes surrounding CMDB development reflecting a smaller and in some respects more elite set of skills.

ITIL Service Transition, op. cit.

Process data include service models that map assets to services, business process models that map services to business processes, and IT Service Management process workflows.

People data include asset-to-user mapping and user information, such as roles and responsibilities. They also include IT staff member data, such as asset-to-support mapping (indicates which IT staff people support which assets), which is useful for incident escalation.

Provider data include when, and under what conditions service providers are engaged.

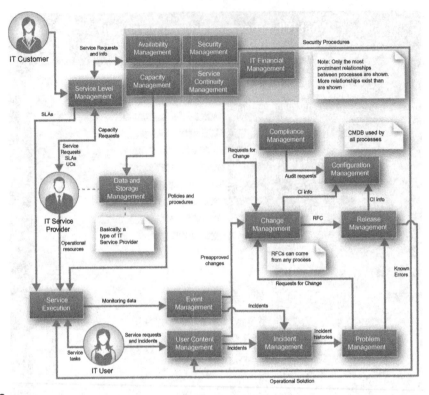

FIGURE 3.8

A mapping of one company's CMDB deployment to ITIL workflows. In spite of its apparent complexity, it should only be viewed as a high-level sketch.

ITIL 2011 also refines how to better understand CIs and CI categories beyond broad categories of hardware, software, buildings, people, documentation, etc. For example, ITIL 2011 also includes the following:

Service Life cycle CIs—including business case, release documentation, and test plans.
Internal CIs—comprising those required for individual projects internal to the IT organization.
External CIs—such as external customer requirements and agreements, releases from suppliers or subcontractors, and external services.
Interface CIs—those required to deliver the end-to-end service across an ecosystem of multiple service providers, for example, an escalation document that specifies how incidents will be transferred between two service providers.

This last category is especially intriguing as it shows how ITIL is setting the stage for the very real and growing challenges of managing services across many separate political entities—which nonetheless may constitute a true business ecosystem of partners, suppliers, and service providers of all varieties.

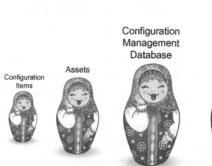

FIGURE 3.9

Russian nesting dolls may not look very technical, but they can be a useful analogy for appreciating the relationship between CIs, assets, the CMDB, and the CMS.

Figure 3.9 provides a broader, albeit light-hearted, look at how CI's map to assets, CMDBs and the larger CMS.

Another key foundational concept from ITIL is the *CI attribute*, which is essentially data about a configuration item, such as the price, version, name, or position. This configuration item data is captured in a CMDB and becomes a part of a CMS.

In real CMDB System deployments, CI attributes can extend to multiple sources through a consistent service modeling system—as described in the following section on technology—to support unique use case requirements, from capacity, to performance or state, to financial data.

A FEW FINAL POINTS

ITIL libraries and resources have a lot more to them than can be shared here. ITIL also offers certification and training and events and print and digital libraries. ITIL's website contains case studies, white papers, glossaries, and lists of events, trainers, classes, etc.

Finally, ITIL 2011 addresses a number of valuable insights including the need for communication, how to manage stakeholders, organizational issues, and even some capability-centric guidelines for technology priorities.

Since process is an intrinsic part of CMDB System preparedness, ITIL will resurface in comments and guidelines from time to time throughout this book.

But to wrap up for now, here are the key summary talking points for bringing ITIL into your broader CMDB System initiative:

- Do not plan ITIL in an ivory tower.
- Use ITIL as a starting point, not the end goal.
- Modify ITIL processes to your business, not vice versa.
- Map roles, artifacts, and scenarios carefully.
- Understand how your current tools function in your process model.
- Understand ITIL's broader possibilities, but proceed in stages—*Big Vision, Baby Steps.*

CMDB FOUNDATIONS, PART ONE: PROCESS—SUMMARY TAKEAWAYS

CMDB Systems have two "parents"—process and technology—with process being central to both the CMDB's heritage and real-world issues in deployments.

The ITIL arose out of the need to manage IT services more effectively and consistently in the late 1980s, but it wasn't until more than a decade later that ITIL became a major force in the United States. In spite of some industry claims to the contrary, ITIL is becoming more important in many IT organizations as cloud, agile, and the need to show value more effectively for IT services are all factors driving the IT landscape toward a more cross domain, service-centric universe.

ITIL 2011 offers a life cycle approach to service management, which includes *Service Strategy, Service Design, Service Transition, Service Operation,* and *Continual Service Improvement.*

The key concepts introduced in this process-oriented section of this chapter are the following:

- Configuration Management Database (CMDB)
- Configuration item (CI)
- Configuration Management System (CMS)
- Definitive Media Library (DML)
- Service Knowledge Management System (SKMS)
- Change Management
- Change Advisory Board (CAB)
- Service Asset and Configuration Management (SACM)
- Capacity management
- Release management

CMDB FOUNDATIONS PART TWO: TECHNOLOGY

Trying to understand, prioritize, and evaluate CMDB System technologies is inherently a challenge—made all the worse by industry and market forces as each vendor tries to define market requirements around itself. This section provides a foundational overview of CMDB-related technologies. Threads of this discussion will continue throughout this book—with an in-depth look at technology selection in Chapter 12, high-level guidelines for an RFP in Appendix B, and a list of some key CMDB System vendors in Appendix D.

The fact is that the CMDB System is *not* a single technology, which in itself has become a major source of confusion. Sadly, the CMDB, and to a lesser degree the CMS, has largely been defined by various constituencies according to what's most convenient for them. These include vendors that develop (or attack) CMDB/CMS-related solutions and technologies, consultants and systems integrators with processes and game plans associated with CMDB-related deployments, analysts seeking to cram the "CMDB" into a two-dimensional technology market, and even IT executives and professionals who have narrowly construed wishes for a magic bullet tailor-made for them.

EMA often refers to the challenge of CMDB-related deployments as an issue of the blind men and the elephant—each man sees just one dimension of the beast. And while these siloed perspectives usually include debates between those wedded to process (sometimes too religiously) and those who see the CMDB System primarily in terms of technology, the analogy can just as well be applied to the confusion and prejudice arising from the relevant technologies alone.

CMDB SYSTEM TECHNOLOGIES: A CLOSER LOOK

Critical CMDB System foundational technologies include the CMDB itself, Application Discovery and Dependency Mapping, other discovery and inventory tools, automation, analytics, dashboard and visualization, and other investments.

Configuration Management Database (CMDB)

The CMDB's core functions are to assimilate and reconcile critical data sources through manual population, bulk updates, or automation—informed by policies, dialogs, and, increasingly, by analytics. In turn, CMDB-supported modeling can help to articulate, access, and promote the critical service interdependencies that will ultimately make the CMDB investment worthwhile. How the CMDB evolves should correlate directly with careful IT planning that targets a phased approach based on use case priorities, such as *change management, asset management, service impact management,* and even *performance management.*

The CMDB—whether a federated "citizen CMDB" or core, "integrated CMDB"—is not a "data warehouse" optimized for high-volume data analytics. Rather, it is a resource aimed at capturing critical service interdependencies, relationships, and device and software configurations. Currently, few vendors offer the CMDB as a standalone solution but typically embed it in other systems such as service desk with asset and change management or service performance solutions vendors where CMDBs are optimized for more real-time usage.

Application Discovery and Dependency Mapping (ADDM)

The central value for all ADDM solutions is to discover, in as automated a fashion as possible, application-to-infrastructure and infrastructure-to-infrastructure interdependencies so critical for both the CMDB System and for effective service management overall. Cloud and virtualization have challenged and continue to challenge, ADDM solutions to become more dynamic and adaptive to real-time, or near-real-time, changes.

ADDM solutions may be either agentless, agent-based, or a combination of both. The varied approaches represent vendors' best efforts to get beyond thorny security issues and even reach into public cloud environments (Figure 3.10).

ADDM typically falls into either less real-time, configuration-centric capabilities more traditionally associated with CMDBs or more transaction-aware, real-time capabilities with roots in performance management. Both are relevant for a CMS optimized to empower a true SKMS, and both are becoming more and more pervasive and effective in CMDB System deployments. Moreover, as the ADDM market evolves, we anticipate a gradual merging of ADDM values—in which real-time performance insights can directly become supportive of configuration and even asset interdependencies.

Other Discovery and Inventory Tools

Discovery and inventory tools can be correlated with CMDB deployments either dynamically or manually. In some cases, they are integrated with ADDM solutions to feed the CMDB System as a single package. They can range widely based on domain and use case, from network discovery, to PC inventory, to security, to capacity planning, to monitoring tools that "discover" key pieces of infrastructure and/or applications in support of event or performance-related analytics. We have identified more than 50 discovery sources in some enterprises, while those with multiple geographic

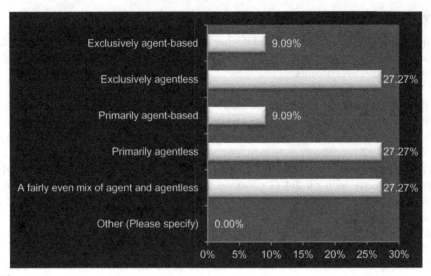

FIGURE 3.10

Many ADDM solutions are either primarily agentless or a balanced mix of agent and agentless, with 64% of solutions providing some mix of agent-based discovery and agentless discovery. This mix may overall provide the greatest versatility and reach in dealing with security, cloud, and other issues. However, primarily agentless deployment options are growing in popularity due in part to cloud and other factors.

presences and localized buying preferences can escalate this number into the hundreds. How to prioritize what, where, and when to integrate these sources into the larger CMDB System will once again depend on use case priorities as evolved through the eight-step methodology proposed in Chapter 4.

Automation

Little could be more critical to CMDB success than proactively phasing in automation—both in populating and maintaining the CMDB and in optimizing CMDB System insights in managing change, service performance, and even life cycle asset values. Automation comes in multiple flavors, ranging from what the market would call "configuration tools," to runbook and IT process automation, to triggering events based on shifting CI attributes for remediation and alerts. A partial list of options to consider—*for phased priorities over time*—might include

- PC configuration, patch management, and audit capabilities;
- system configuration, VM provisioning, and patch management;
- network configuration solutions;
- service desk workflow;
- development-centric simulation and design automation;
- automated application provisioning (DevOps) typically associated with cloud and virtualization;
- manifests for transitioning development models into production;
- security-related identity and access management solutions;

- runbook or IT process automation for stitching multiple automation capabilities together;
- load balancing and other performance-related capabilities;
- other cloud-specific or virtualized automation surrounding a whole new array of packaged solutions, including software-defined data centers and software-defined networks.

Analytics

If the CMDB System is above all about insight—that insight needs to be fed and optimized through good analytic tools. These tools may have a range of capabilities, from advanced reporting to truly advanced heuristics, including self-learning algorithms, transaction analytics, and "big data" in various forms. "Big data for IT" and "operational analytics" have become buzzwords—but in some respects, they do not do justice to the breadth and variety of analytic choices that can contribute meaningfully to CMDB-related initiatives. The following are just a few categories to consider:

- Self-learning predictive analytics, some of which already use service modeling to correlate performance anomalies with CMDB-related interdependencies
- "Big data" in the form of integrated data warehousing and data mining ranging from visualization and search to more advanced trending over time for capacity, performance, and other insights
- "Big data" in terms of integrated data warehousing and data mining for IT financial planning and optimization for CapEx investments and OpEx efficiencies
- Transaction-centric analytics that may look not only at IT service performance but also at user behaviors and business outcomes, including user experience insights

All of these analytic options are already being actively mapped to service modeling and integrated with CMDB Systems in some deployments. Most analytic integrations favor ADDM over core CMDB for a variety of reasons, chief among them being dynamic currency. Some analytic tools already have ADDM-like modeling built into them.

Dashboards and Visualization

Dashboards and other forms of visualization may be directly or indirectly affiliated with any of the above technology choices. And as anyone in IT knows, good visualization is where IT harvests and shares its insights both within silos and, even more importantly, across domains.

Other Relevant Investments

Enabling and empowering the full CMDB System across multiple phases and use cases may well involve other technology investments beyond the general categories listed above. Two examples are *project management* and *social IT*—both of which ideally support better stakeholder planning and dialog. Another relevant investment, the *service catalog*, deserves special attention as an outwardly facing expression of CMDB modeling to empower automation and governance in provisioning (or enabling self-provisioning for) new IT services.

A REMINDER: "BIG VISION, BABY STEPS"

What you've seen so far in this chapter, and in particular what follows, is indeed a "big vision." The goal here isn't to suggest that you should go out and invest in all of it at once for a phase one CMDB deployment. Nothing could spell disaster faster than that. The goal instead is to map out a checklist of resources for how, where, and why you might want to begin—in this case, from a technology adoption perspective.

The simplest thing might be to say, "Just get the core CMDB deployed and go from there." In reality, however, simply getting the CMDB up and running may *not* in fact be your first technology need. Instead, your first steps may come from improved discovery, or an investment in process automation, or perhaps even a service catalog to begin to identify critical services. Indeed, some ADDM solutions in themselves are functioning effectively as phase one "virtual CMDBs"—especially when they have built-in capabilities for assimilating and reconciling multiple third-party sources.

The good and bad news are that developing a CMDB System is not a linear process with one-size-fits-all beginnings and generic ends. Above all, it requires you to consider your needs, strengths, and vulnerabilities and to plan judiciously, choosing from a wide range of options—realizing that what might be right for you might not at all be the best choice for the next IT organization.

So take a deep breath, and then, forge ahead.

A LOOK AT THE BROADER CMDB SYSTEM AND THE SERVICE MANAGEMENT ECOSYSTEM IT SUPPORTS

As shown in Figure 3.11, the potential reach of the CMDB System in supporting what ITIL would call a *Service Knowledge Management System* is rich and diverse. Indeed, even Figure 3.11 is not meant to be complete or exhaustive so much as it is intended merely as a sketch of how different technology investments can come together to harvest the power of CMDB-driven insights over time.

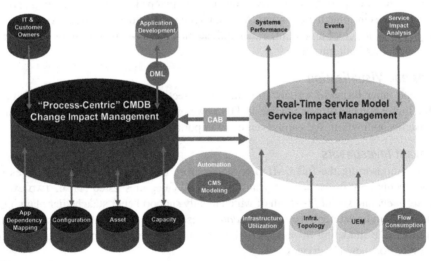

FIGURE 3.11

The CMDB System in a well-evolved deployment leverages multiple integrations to support different use cases and different stakeholders. It should be stressed that this is not a single-phase option. No deployment should begin trying to do everything indicated here. But this list does provide some guidance for selecting how and where you want to evolve your CMDB System based on readiness, need, enthusiasm, and value. (Acronyms in this drawing include DML for Definitive Media Library, CAB for Change Advisory Board, and UEM for user experience management.)

The two spheres in Figure 3.11 EMA were once labeled "the two CMDBs." The idea behind this was to show how real-time or near-real-time insights could provide strong value in concert with more process-centric systems so that, for instance, changes can immediately be understood and validated in terms of infrastructure, application service, and business outcomes. Conversely, when problems arise, insights into how and where changes were made and managed could immediately be linked with performance-related issues.

However, the term "two CMDBs" no longer applies to the current market and industry taxonomy that buckets CMDB technology as a single, physical database. So, we are now using the term "real-time service model" to suggest how CMDBs—including federated CMDBs—may access critically relevant CI-related data without necessarily moving into a separate data store. This is a critical distinction because it centers the broader CMDB System less in database technology than in service modeling capabilities with reconciled data access.

A summary of what's included in Figure 3.12 is described in more detail with the following list:

- *IT and customer owners*—This phrase is shorthand for IT stakeholders, managers, and executives who have relevance to the broader CMDB initiative and service and consumer owners outside of IT.
- *Applications development and the Definitive Media Library*—These terms apply as the CMDB System evolves to support development and DevOps requirements for staging the introduction of new application services across the infrastructure. Analytic, automation, and service dependency insights are also key here.
- *Application dependency mapping*—This concept has been discussed under "Application Discovery and Dependency Mapping" (ADDM). As CMDB Systems evolve, the combination of

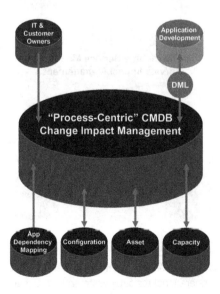

FIGURE 3.12

A closer look at the process-centric CMDB, where most deployments begin. Even as half the drawing in Figure 3.11, this still remains a superset of what you might look to incorporate in a phase one initiative. More guidance on approaching how to phase in your capabilities is provided in Chapter 7 for use cases and in Chapter 12 for technology selection.

real-time, transaction-centric ADDM tools with more traditionally configuration-centric ADDM may in some cases serve as the spine for the broader system.

- *Configuration*—This term is shorthand for "configuration automation" solutions, such as those targeting network, systems, PCs, and other devices and those that extend to provisioning new application systems. Note that here, the arrow is drawn to show bidirectional interaction so that insights into larger service interdependencies can inform more point-optimized configuration tools, while appropriate levels of detail and currency from these tools can update the CMDB based on policy.

- *Asset*—This term refers to asset-specific data, asset inventory tools, and/or an asset management database that houses financial information in greater detail than is appropriate for a core CMDB. Once again, the arrow is bidirectional so that appropriate asset-specific data can update the CMDB, while service-relevant insights can help to deliver a baseline for more effective asset life cycle optimization.

- *Capacity*—This term refers to one or multiple toolsets optimized for capacity planning analytics—again a critically bidirectional process ideally, in which capacity-related currency is maintained and service-related insights and interdependencies are shared. Going clockwise from the top left in Figure 3.13:

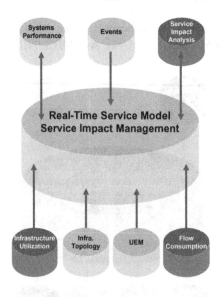

FIGURE 3.13

Service Impact Management CMDB System deployments typically arise from CMS and service modeling capabilities embedded in Business Service Management (BSM) performance-centric offerings. These often draw from a wide array of primarily operational toolset investments for CI state-related insights on performance issues and time-sensitive capacity-related issues (e.g., flow consumption and infrastructure utilization). The trade-offs for doing this will be examined more closely in Chapter 12 and the Service Impact Management and Capacity Optimization use case in Chapter 7.

- *Systems performance*—This refers to any number of systems management sources, from log files to time series data resident in monitoring and analytic sources.
- *Events*—This can come from any part of the application/infrastructure and once again typically feed analytic engines.
- *Service impact analytics*—These are link service interdependencies, change and performance data together in a common analytic thread.
- *Infrastructure utilization*—This refers to analytic tools that can harvest KPIs impacting shifting capacity requirements.
- *Infrastructure topology*—This is key for real-time awareness of the networked infrastructure (layers 2, 3, and above), either as integrated into an application dependency mapping tool or as a separate resource.
- *UEM*—This refers to user experience management and what we call "the transactional stage," which can unify insights into application and business performance and business outcomes.
- *Flow consumption*—This complements infrastructure utilization analytic with insights into how application traffic over the networked infrastructure may be impacting both performance and capacity-related issues. It may also provide insights into how and when applications are being used.
- *Etc.*—This is not meant to be a complete list, but it is a good departure point for planning.

Figure 3.14 provides a look at the intersection of the "two CMDBs" as process and governance come together with real-time awareness via a unifying service model. Key here is the balance of how the Change Advisory Board (CAB) or other change governance teams are balanced with automation for enhanced dynamic currency.

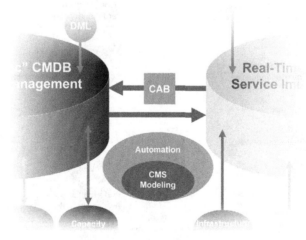

FIGURE 3.14

The Change Advisory Board (CAB) and automation are emblematic of how changes are managed, activated, and implemented and how appropriate analytic capabilities are triggered based on use case requirements. This is, in reality, an area rich in trade-offs that ideally grows to support higher levels of automation, along with more effective dialogue and review—as the CMDB System itself evolves to support more stakeholders and more use cases with higher levels of internal efficiency.

Service (CMS) Modeling: Where Logical and Physical Service Interdependencies Come Together

Figure 3.15 offers a logical depiction of *the* central requirement in the CMDB System: an adaptive service modeling system to bring together physical and logical interdependencies across the broader service landscape. This allows for data to reside in many different locations through a unified system of access. The beauty of associating logical (e.g., "customer" or "service provider") with physical infrastructure, middleware, and applications and their attributes is becoming increasingly more relevant as the extended IT organization becomes an ecosystem of partners, service providers, and, in some cases, suppliers.

So Where Do I Buy One?

As inherently valuable as this modeling capability has become, no vendor actually markets just such an animal. To be clear, service modeling is often embedded in CMDB, ADDM, and service dashboard offerings, where it's presented as critical functionality. But most vendors approach service modeling with a tree-hugging reluctance once reserved for another innovative technology: Advanced Operations Analytics. Service modeling has also gotten a bad name in many quarters due to the labors of customization so often necessary to make truly business-relevant service models appropriate for specific IT and business environments.

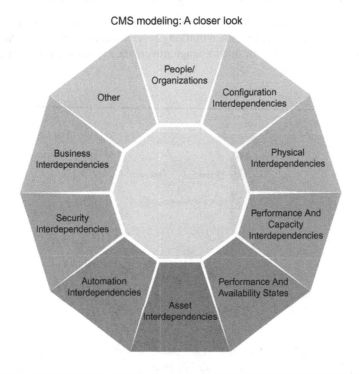

FIGURE 3.15

A versatile, flexible, and easily administered service modeling technology is at the very heart of CMDB System success. This is still an emerging area for industry attention, especially as a separate focus in itself. However, real progress is being made in creating modeling technologies with higher levels of automation and dynamic currency.

Nonetheless, some vendors have actually worked to provide a cohesive and largely automated service modeling system that can support many elements, including imported insights on CIs and CI attributes from third-party sources. Moreover, we are beginning to see a trend in some larger enterprises to adapt more fluid service modeling across multiple specific CMDB investments to create a broader unified system—a user-friendly "model of models" to help instantiate a more effective federated "manager of managers."

Just how this may evolve will be revisited in more depth in Chapters 7 and 12.

CMDB SYSTEM FOUNDATIONS PART TWO: TECHNOLOGY—SUMMARY TAKEAWAYS

The second, and often more visible, "parent" for both the CMDB and the broader CMDB System is technology—an area in which the industry is beginning to innovate in meaningful and dramatic ways.

Relevant technologies to watch include

- core CMDB capabilities for data assimilation, reconciliation, and service modeling;
- Application Discovery and Dependency Mapping solutions, which come in a growing variety of form factors to support a wider array of use cases;
- other discovery and inventory tools;
- automation capabilities (process automation, device configuration automation, and runbook, among others) that support CMDB efficiencies and profit from CMDB-related visibility to avoid "automating train wrecks";
- analytics both to help feed the CMDB System with appropriate data and to leverage CMDB System insights to better match analytic outcomes with key service-related interdependencies;
- superior visualization and reporting capabilities;
- other technology investments, such as project management, social IT, and service catalogs.

The very center of the CMDB System, technologically, is a strong service modeling system coupled with capabilities for data assimilation and reconciliation, as well as targeted data access, across a wide variety of service management investments. This is an area where the industry has largely stumbled in the past but where new offerings are beginning to provide more nimble and flexible links across multiple service management tools, including multiple CMDBs.

CMDB SYSTEM DEPLOYMENT STAGES: AN EIGHT-STEP LADDER TO SUCCESS

4

By now, you understand that implementing a CMDB System is a complex process. It's a challenge to succeed and easy to fail, but it's more than worth it when it's done right.

Now let's transition to increasing your odds for success by providing a proven methodology for planning and assessing your project. In this chapter, we introduce EMA's eight-step methodology for CMDB System deployments or what we call an "Eight-Step Ladder to Success." These steps include the following:

1. Define your objectives and consider your resources—stakeholders, budget, etc.
2. Move forward with a technology, process, and organizational audit to further clarify your resources and needs.
3. Do an evolutionary or maturity assessment (leveraging the maturity model provided in Chapter 9) to better understand where you are in the interplay of technology, process, and organizational development.
4. Clarify your requirements, further refine your metrics, and define your phase 1 architecture based on the insights you've gained in the first three steps. This is your first real phase 1 plan.
5. Following the architectural component of this plan, select and plan deployment for the right mix of new and existing technologies to go forward in phase 1 and beyond. This step includes proof-of-concept (PoC) trials.
6. Revisit critical issues and gating factors now that your team, your technologies, and your goals are all in place. Move forward to close the gap between PoC and full-production deployment. This should include identifying any integrations needed for phase 1.
7. Tune your initial phase 1 plan and use it to develop a Three-Tier Roadmap with detailed and realistic metrics directed at 6-month, 1-year, and 2-year phases. Now, you're ready to move into production-level deployment.
8. Review your progress and milestones after 6 months and 12 months—when you should begin to see a tipping point for value in phase 1.

In many respects, these stages can be viewed as an overlay to using this book, which is designed to support you in critical decision-making relevant to each phase. With this in mind, there will be a "What to Look For" box in each phase so chapter resources can be more easily accessed and applied to your program.

It's also worth noting that there are some important recurring themes throughout this eight-step methodology, reflecting decisions that will need to be revisited with increasing levels of granularity throughout the process of CMDB System deployment. These include the following:

- *Objectives and metrics:* While you will want to define an initial set of objectives in step one, these will necessarily be at a very high level. Moreover, they will invariably change and evolve once you engage more actively in dialog with stakeholders and executives. This book provides a guide for supporting the move from *objectives* to *high-level metrics* to *granular metrics*— optimized to unique environmental and stakeholder goals.
- *Team building, stakeholder definitions, and stakeholder management:* In step one, you'll begin to gather a team to support your effort. However, your team, its skill sets, and its levels of involvement should also evolve as you confirm your available resources in dialog with executives and the larger stakeholder community.
- *Executive buy-in and support:* This is hugely critical for CMDB success and doesn't happen in just one step. Executive leadership/sponsorship—ideally C-level or at least VP-level— is often the single most important variable in achieving value from a CMDB System. However, it won't be something you can achieve in a single conversation. It requires an ongoing dialog through which your objectives can be optimized across the various political and cultural obstacles that so often block real IT effectiveness with or without a CMDB initiative.
- *Process assessments and recommendations:* This is another conversation that needs to occur throughout your planning and deployments. We generally recommend using ITIL as your departure point and then doing your best as a team to match ITIL processes with real practices, technologies, and organizational structures in your own environment.
- *Technology evaluation, selection, and deployment:* As already stated, a CMDB System is not a single technology and, in its federated form, may ultimately depend even more on effective service modeling than on a single data store. Your technology choices must align with your evolving CMDB System goals based on use cases and metrics. Understanding what your relevant technology investments are (e.g., inventory and autodiscovery), identifying where your gaps are, evaluating critical additional investments and integration requirements, and deploying new solutions where and when needed—these are not one-time-only efforts.

STANDING IN THE MIDDLE OF THE STORM

Accomplishing all of the eight stages is admittedly not an easy task. It is not something that any one, or any one group, can do perfectly. It requires a well-managed team effort. The goal of this book is to support you and your team as *agents of change*—for you are nothing less than that. The actions in the Eight-Step Ladder to CMDB System Success may seem daunting, even insurmountable, but in actual practice, they have been proven to work. How much—how exhaustively—you examine each of the issues raised here will depend a great deal on your phase 1 priorities, your resources, and your unique environment with its own strengths and weaknesses.

But before even starting on the ladder, you should consider your vantage point. Much like an effective CIO, you should learn how to "stand in the middle of the storm." By this, we mean not only should

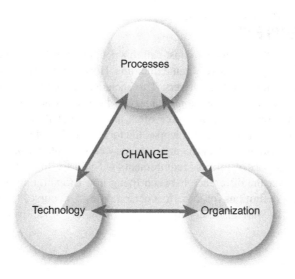

FIGURE 4.1

Delivering an effective CMDB System requires standing in the middle of the storm surrounding technology, organization, and process and optimizing communication, dialog, and interdependencies within it.

you pay attention to *process* and *technology*, but also you should also learn to map these potentially generic considerations to the specific realities of your own IT *organization*, as shown in Figure 4.1.

While ITIL provides some useful background on organizational structure and even technology requirements, the reality of dealing with the politics and cultures of individual IT organizations calls for standing in the middle of the triangle depicted below.

This means making an effort to bring conflicting priorities, mind-sets, and even "languages" together in a commonly understood initiative.

What do we mean by "language"?

Just consider how many IT organizations pay considerable sums to *process consultants*, *systems integrators*, and *organizational consultants*—each group largely oblivious to the other and each group with its own terminology for describing objects, processes, and objectives. Each group has its own perspective on the "right" way to do things. In many instances, efforts to coordinate across these groups lead to a costly merry-go-round—with circular movement as opposed to actual forward progress—often with millions of dollars changing hands.

While the industry still treats the corners of the triangle as three separate worlds with different specialists attached to each, they are, in fact, fundamentally interdependent. Technology can impact process and vice versa—making certain actions "automated" or "routine" that weren't before. Process and organization are of course closely intertwined—and need to be understood as such. Effective process definitions should be sensitive to your actual political environment, while your organizational structure may well have to evolve to support more cross-domain service awareness if you're going to succeed in the long run.

WHAT ABOUT "PEOPLE?"

One thing you might ask is, "Why didn't we just call this people, process, and technology?" After all, that's the usual formula applied to this very same dilemma. However, in our view, "people" is actually a pervasive undercurrent behind all three drivers. This includes not only process but also technology. Just ask a network techie and an applications manager whose tools are more reliable in ascertaining application-to-infrastructure issues, and more often than not, you'll get a very human, as well as technology-centric, debate. For better and for worse, the tools that IT professionals use, their workday identities, and their very sense of job security are often very closely intertwined.

"People" are also a big part of process requirements—if you try to abstract the two as separate entities, you'll soon discover the difference between living in a Utopian universe and living in a real one—with perfect process definitions for imperfect personalities. Of course, "people"—with their psychologies, skills, and quirks—are also very much a part of the organizational models you'll need to reckon with.

A CLOSER LOOK AT THE THIRD VECTOR

Within the *organization*, the dominant factor is culture—a nexus of politics, skills, business objectives, and belief systems. Culture becomes the dominant driver for IT evolutionary change through which process and technology are fundamentally enablers and influencers.

This attention to culture is not just a nice-to-have. As we examine in more depth in Chapter 9, IT organizations, their processes, and their adapted technologies are in fact evolving and must evolve. In large part, this evolution is driven by hard economic forces pushing IT to do more with less while, at the same time, increasing business impact and relevance.

As simple and basic as this idea may be, it poses an obvious and logical question: "Evolve to what?" Or as a corollary, "To what end?" Is the goal a low-cost, commoditized investment in technology as some would have it, or is it a structure for more proactive, open-ended, yet still controlled growth?

IT is truly undergoing a paradigm shift today—with pressure not only to be more cost-effective but also to behave "more like a business." Historically, this is not altogether new. To some degree, the writing was already on the wall for a cultural transformation within IT with the initial success of small e-business subgroups within organizations where online operations merged IT and marketing into one dynamic whole. Cloud, agile, mobile, and the consumerization of IT have all also factored into this shift—as IT struggles to evolve from a purely cost-driven organization to a true business-value provider.

Contrast the need for a cross-domain, service focus with traditionally fragmented organizational paradigms—where the data center wars with the network operation center and both complain about the help desk. This was (and still often is) a culture of finger-pointing across islands of isolated disciplines focused on network, systems, application, database, and other domains, each harboring its own introverted, "tribal" view of the IT world. Compared to this, the need to manage the infrastructure in support of a business service, and to optimize IT portfolios based on value creation, represents nothing less than a radical change in how IT organizations must function if they wish to be successful.

Believe it or not, your CMDB System is a fundamental enabler for just such a change. As it evolves, it can mean the difference between driving slowly on a narrow dirt road and moving ahead on a superhighway. Moreover, as phased progress is made, your CMDB System will soon begin to feed and nourish itself as an integral part of how your IT organization operates.

CLIMBING THE EIGHT-STEP LADDER TO CMDB SYSTEM SUCCESS

Figure 4.2 provides a summary of critical steps or stages that we have found to be most beneficial in ensuring early phase value for CMDB System initiatives.

Climbing this ladder requires an awareness of two general ideas:

1. The ladder is built around recognizing the need for iterative conversations around critical areas of project definition, planning, and CMDB System deployment. Leading the charge among these necessary conversations are the following:

   a. The progression from baseline objectives to high-level metrics to more granular, measurable, and enforceable metrics

FIGURE 4.2

EMA's Eight-Step Ladder to CMDB System Success is a critical reference point for planning your CMDB initiative, and in many respects, it reflects the organizing principle of this book. This ladder is based on years of experience in the field, where it has proven successful. It should be pointed out that skipping any of the steps tends to invalidate the process—as the ladder is based on informed decision-making that requires a structured and deliberate build.

    b. CMDB System team building and stakeholder engagement
    c. Executive buy-in, commitment, and leadership
    d. Process definitions and process evolution
    e. Technology surveys, assessments, evaluations, and deployments
2. Proceeding up this ladder effectively requires recognizing the importance of "standing in the middle of the storm" of *technology*, *process*, and *organization* while seeking to leverage your CMDB System to optimize the interdependencies across all three.

So now, we're ready to begin the climb.

STEP ONE: DEFINE YOUR OBJECTIVES AND CONSIDER YOUR RESOURCES

Just where you begin often depends on circumstances beyond your control. The impetus may come from a technology investment—for example, your company may have purchased a CMDB (possibly even inadvertently) as a part of its new or preexisting service desk, a Business Service Management manager of managers, or an innovative application dependency mapping solution. So you may be the lucky midlevel manager (or architect or process expert/Change Management owner or fill in the blank) tasked with making it all work. Let's call this *Scenario One*.

In *Scenario Two*, your company has a top-down ITIL initiative underway, and change and configuration management are the next processes on the list to implement—typically after other processes such as incident and problem management have received their due. You may not even have any CMDB-related software in-house, let alone deployed, but once again you agree to step up and try to make it all work.

For *Scenario Three*, let's go back to the beginning of Chapter 1. Your company is experiencing real pain. In the example given, John's company was floundering over the introduction of application releases and the ongoing disruptions they caused because of ineffective Change Management. In this scenario, you see the problem. You realize you have a chance to make a difference. And you sign up to change the world for the better. You wish to be a true *agent of change*.

Needless to say, there are plenty of other scenarios, and in many cases, elements of Scenarios One, Two, and Three come together in different combinations with highly individualized blends of personalities, executive commitment, and technology and process readiness. But believe it or not, of the three scenarios presented above, the best case situation is actually Scenario Three.

In other words, the best place to begin is with a business-relevant goal that combines process and technology—a goal in which organizational dynamics and culture will have to play a part. Sometimes, that goal can be as exalted as a top-down executive initiative to transform IT to become more business-aligned—both more effective in delivering value and more efficient in managing operational and capital costs. At other times, the driver can be quite specific. We've seen, for instance, perfectly successful phase 1 mandates directed at optimizing the life cycle management of endpoint (PC and/or mobile) systems.

In general, the leading areas of value from a successful CMDB System, examined in more detail in Chapter 7, include the following:

- Managing change (including configuration and release management)
- Optimizing assets for life cycle efficiencies
- Understanding service impact for service performance management

Other effective initial drivers can include DevOps (really a variation on managing change), Security and Compliance initiatives, disaster recovery planning, and even the move to cloud and virtualized data centers.

Just remember, don't try to do everything at once.

Even with the exalted, top-down goal of transforming IT, a phase 1 CMDB System needs to address something quite specific and ultimately measurable. Pick an area of focus where there are enough pain to appreciate a better way of working and a team willing to be open to a new way of doing things, and then, it becomes possible to deliver measurable value quickly. This can set the tone for the rest of the project, as success begets success. Have the "big vision" but proceed with "baby steps." It is critical to show value early and often along the long path of implementation.

Our consulting guidelines for step one are as follows:

Seek Senior Management Input

- *Review the history of previous IT implementations.* Past failures can go a long way to ensuring future successes. However, past failure will also carry predictable debris of emotional weight among executives and stakeholders. Your goal is to transform the pessimism into a "lessons-learned" discussion, and in the process, you're already beginning to cement your phase 1 plan.
- *Determine stakeholders (owners and users).*
- *Identify resources available for the project (financial and personnel).*

Set Objectives

- *Set strategic objectives, not tactical.* Whether Change Management-related, asset and financial, or service impact and service performance-oriented, follow the pain and the enthusiasm for change within your own organization. This is the high-level sketch you need to go forward to promote dialog and refine objectives into a more detailed, actionable, and specific framework.
- *Map technology to process and organization.*
- *Plan for phases.* Don't plan to do everything at once.

Address High-Level Issues

- *Consider cost and value up front.* It's essential to consider the impacts of costs and the available resources at this stage. You certainly won't have a fully evolved plan, but getting a rough idea of budget and staffing commitments is key. The goal is to build a plan that will deliver value over and above those commitments, and in parallel, to allocate sufficient resources based on phase 1 needs.
- *Plan for ongoing maintenance.* This should be considered from early on in the process. Bad data can lead to bad decision making and bad results. Figure 4.3 provides a simple, visual reference point for how virtually all IT processes depend on good data, and by implication, good insights into CIs and their interdependencies.
- *Be aware of time frame concerns.* You can expect no one to be patient with your deployment if you take more than 6 months to demonstrate at least some initial value.

Establish Measurable Metrics

- *Outline some initial implementation steps.* At this stage, these steps should reflect your own planning and initiative requirements as opposed to anything approaching finalized ROI or other metrics. Don't shoot for the moon here. Look at what is natively valuable and necessary to the plan at hand.

HOW DO YOU KNOW IF YOU'RE READY?

There are times when you need to recognize and accept the fact that you aren't ready for an actual CMDB deployment—at least given initial expectations and plans. One of the more common examples occurs in enterprises with global sprawl, multiple autonomous data centers, and individualized teams

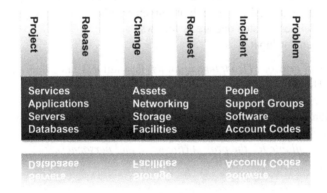

FIGURE 4.3

All IT processes need good data! The pervasive benefits of good, reconciled data across your CMDB System, whether accessed and reconciled by modeling or actually normalized in a core CMDB, are illustrated above. Processes such as incident, change and problem management may need data ranging from assets, to people, to services, to infrastructure details such as networking and storage. This "superhighway" of insights—once it is integrated with analytics, automation, and strong visualization—is what can make a CMDB System so transcendent in value.

with different toolsets, cultures, process readiness, etc. Mergers and acquisitions often represent a variation on this. Trying to impose a CMDB as a unifying force across these organizations without taking initial steps to plan for coherence in other areas is bound to fail. The software may be up and running. It may even include data from all localities. But the chances of anything meaningful being done with it are slim to none if there aren't consistent processes, objectives, and stakeholder expectations.

On the other hand, purely siloed CMDB System initiatives generally fail to show value because they are not far-reaching enough to deliver real value.

Understanding the right "baby steps" and then generating an initial plan to ensure phase 1 value is the key to step one on our Ladder to CMDB System Success.

This book is designed to support you in applying this eight-step methodology for optimizing CMDB System value. With that in mind, we are providing a short summary of relevant chapters for each step. While we strongly recommend reading this book in its entirety before starting out, here are some of the more salient sections for approaching step one:

- Chapters 1 and 2 provide overall insights and warnings to help you mentally prepare step one more effectively.
- Chapter 3 discusses the foundations of the CMDB System. With its overview on process and technology, this chapter is a must-read before diving in further with your CMDB System plans.
- Chapter 5 provides you with added insights in terms of industry and business trends that can support you in approaching your executive/senior management as outlined in Chapter 6.
- Chapter 7 gives the insights you need to select and prioritize use cases.
- Chapter 11 provides additional insights on the skill sets required for initially gathering and defining your team.

STEP TWO: TECHNOLOGY, PROCESS, AND ORGANIZATIONAL AUDIT

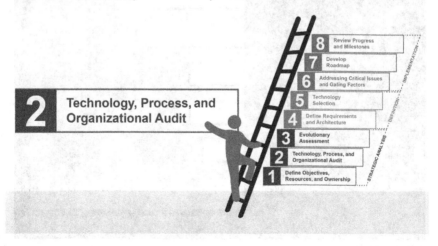

Once you've got the ball rolling, it's time to evaluate further where you are and what you need. Many organizations bypass this step with typically fatal (in terms of CMDB success) consequences. Moreover, the learning and evaluation done at this stage can be worth its weight in gold, even, if for some reason, you decide not to go any further with the initiative.

Some issues to address in this step in the ladder include the following:
Seek Manager and Engineer Input to Assess Technology Requirements

- *Identify which management tools are in place, who is using them, and where and why they are being employed.*
- *Identify redundancies and gaps in existing toolsets.* These typically involve discovery tools, configuration and Change Management tools, asset inventory, and other asset management capabilities, as well as any dependency mapping, capacity planning, performance management, automation tools, and other solutions that may be relevant to your near-term objectives.
- It's not enough just to know where your toolset gaps are. You should also evaluate where your data is currently aggregated or stored. For example, Figure 4.4 shows where asset management, financial planning and service planning data is typically kept, based on EMA research.

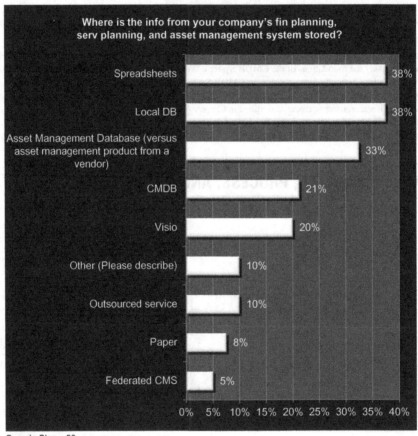

Sample Size = 80

FIGURE 4.4

Across years of research, consistent patterns have emerged in terms of the fragile threads of how and where data are managed and stored relevant to key use cases and disciplines. In this case, the question asked was this: "Where is the information from your financial planning, service planning and asset management system stored?" (Service-Centric Asset Management in the Era of Cloud Computing, EMA, 2011.)

- *Assess which tools are working and which are not.* It's no surprise that this is often a very emotional and technical discussion. You may uncover long-festering jealousies between silos and strong individual attachments to tools that, for years, have defined a person's way of working. When conflicts over mean time to innocence (aka finger-pointing) between two IT "tribes" spark what might be described as "acts of war," you have to realize that finding some resolution to just this debate can have strong positive values in itself.
- *Identify the integration requirements between existing and planned toolsets going forward.* Integration is a critical and ongoing technical challenge when it comes to CMDB Systems. While real progress is being made on many fronts, thanks to industry improvements and standards such as Web Services, knowing what will be needed to truly work together for your phase 1 deployment is critical.

Put Processes in Place

- *Identify informal versus formal processes.* Realize that whether your processes are documented or not, most IT professionals have an established way of working, and that way of working may or may not follow a documented way of doing things. Making the effort to document the undocumented—and then connect the dots between a top-down, comprehensive ITIL mosaic and what's really going on in your organization—can pay real dividends in and of itself, even if you stop short of deploying an actual CMDB.
- *Assess how well current processes work in real life.* This is an area sometimes even more fraught with politics than toolset evaluation. But if you don't evaluate these processes, you won't be doing your job, and you will be missing a chance to deliver significant value to your IT organization. Trying to be perfect or exhaustive in doing this evaluation is likely to leave you feeling imperfect and exhausted yourself. How deeply to go here should be aligned with phase 1 objectives and needs.

Review Current Organizational Structure

- *Ask how well different technology groups work together.* The good news here is you don't have to go out and hire a guy with expensive clothes just to ask this question. Remember, you're not trying to pose as a bona fide "organizational consultant," but you do need to consider how the current organizational matrix will impact the effectiveness of your CMDB System initiative.

In looking at your organizational, technological, and process interdependencies, you may also want to consider other things such as current investments (and practices) in social networking and social IT, current levels of automation and how they impact processes, and how IT operations, the service desk, and, if applicable, development share processes and dialog effectively or not.

Especially relevant to step two are the following sections:

- Chapter 7 provides detailed guidelines for a technology and process audit based on use case.
- Chapter 8 offers real examples of what to look for in assessing communication gaps, addressing stakeholder issues, managing technology assessments, and dealing with "process dissonance." It is the single chapter most affiliated with this step.
- Chapter 9 helps you to better assess the interplay of process, technology, and organization in terms of four overarching maturity levels relevant to CMDB Systems and beyond.
- Chapter 12 addresses technology requirements in more depth in context with product design in the current marketplace.

STEP THREE: EVOLUTIONARY OR MATURITY-LEVEL ASSESSMENT

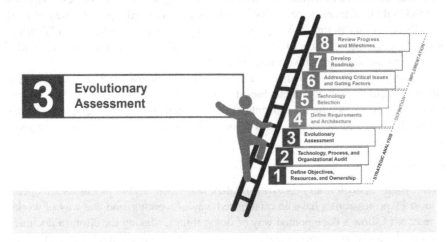

EMA's IT Development Assessment Model, examined in-depth in Chapter 9, is developed around four stages as shown in Figure 4.5. An effective maturity assessment is critical for a number of reasons—possibly the most important is to determine if you're even ready to effectively deploy a CMDB or CMDB System. Solid insights into your IT organization's maturity level are also likely to get the attention of your senior executives—and may help them to view your initiative with keener interest and relevance.

Below are brief summary descriptions of the four stages.

REACTIVE INFRASTRUCTURE MANAGEMENT

At the reactive infrastructure management level, most organizations are trying to survive day-to-day crises. Most management investments are element-centric with some domain-level investments, and domains of expertise (network/systems/application/database) are fundamentally separate and isolated from each other. Generally, IT organizations at this level are not yet ready for a CMDB.

FIGURE 4.5

Understanding where you are in terms of IT maturity is critical to planning your CMDB System deployment effectively. Those IT organizations still centered in reactive infrastructure management are generally not yet ready for a core CMDB deployment but may want to begin, instead, with consolidating and integrating their discovery and inventory investments. Conversely, if you're among those few IT organizations nearing the dynamic business-driven model and don't already have a CMDB deployed, you should select investments and processes based on higher levels of automation, service modeling, and integration with your existing investments.

ACTIVE OPERATIONAL MANAGEMENT

At the active operational management stage, IT is awakening to its own potential. Day-to-day issues are still paramount, but infrastructure management tools are more likely to be domain-focused (network/systems/application) versus element-focused (by type of server or network device), and cross organizational dialog has improved. Many CMDB System deployments begin at this stage and act as a bridge to accelerate the organization into the next stage.

PROACTIVE SERVICE-ORIENTED MANAGEMENT

In terms of organizational transformation, proactive service-oriented management is perhaps the single most important stage. Certainly, it is important within the consciousness of IT because at this stage, the separate cultural affiliations among areas of domain expertise are superseded in order to create more effective management of the total infrastructure with all its interdependencies. At this stage, a service organization, which usually grows out of either the operations center or the service desk, becomes a fundamental and consistent interface to the broader business.

DYNAMIC BUSINESS-DRIVEN MANAGEMENT

At the fourth stage, dynamic business-driven management, automation and business alignment have become so integrated with IT processes that the role of IT is able to shift fundamentally toward becoming a true business partner. Day-to-day performance and availability issues are largely managed by automation so that IT can focus on capturing business advantage and optimizing to shifting business conditions. Unfortunately, few IT organizations have reached this stage, even if there has been some visible progress over the years in this direction.

An example of a maturity placement from an actual consulting engagement directed at a CMDB System initiative is shown in Figure 4.6.

Company X is in the Early Active Stage
- Focus is on daily issues
- Change is a challenge—despite tracked metrics
- Little consideration for integration when getting new tools
- Scattered automation
- SLM generally not implemented
- Higher level analytics not easily available and manually populated

FIGURE 4.6

Understanding relevant "maturity" or "developmental" issues is key to CMDB System Success. Company X, in this case, happened to be a large retail enterprise. The very high-level checklist shown above came about through roughly 30 interviews conducted across relevant IT stakeholders and executives in addressing a phase 1 asset-oriented CMDB initiative.

Most of what's needed for an evolutionary assessment is provided in Chapter 9. However, Chapter 5 is also key to this discussion as it offers added insights into trends and dynamics impacting IT organizations overall. These trends provide a critical backdrop for assessing both maturity levels and what's most likely to impact your IT organization in the future.

STEP FOUR: DEFINE YOUR REQUIREMENTS, ARCHITECTURE, AND METRICS

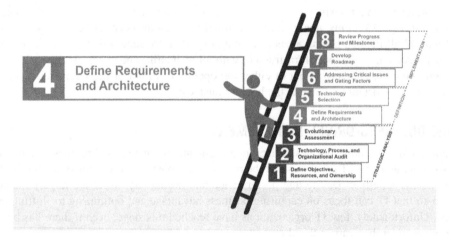

This step represents a critical watershed, but it is far more likely to be successful if it builds on insights from the past three. It requires creating the core of a true project plan, including high-level and granular metrics, as well as a defined phase 1 architecture with an eye to future growth. It is at this stage that you should also seek to finalize your phase 1 core team and stakeholder requirements. This step in the ladder should be a content-rich precursor to the tiered roadmap you'll develop in step seven.

A high-level summary of objectives for this phase is presented below:

DEFINE TWO CATEGORIES OF REQUIREMENTS

1. *General requirements*: Broad, sweeping requirements common to IT organizations
   - For example, "Improve IT's efficiency in managing changes impacting critical business application services."
2. *Detailed requirements:* Requirements specific to a particular company
   - These requirements should relate both to organizations and to individual stakeholders to help set expectations for the CMDB initiative.
   - These requirements should also span the elements of the IT organization relevant to a phase 1 plan, with an eye to broader involvement over time. Ideally, they should be socialized across the entire IT organization to promote cooperation and sow the seeds for future phased-in growth.
   - These specific requirements should help prioritize what's critical and what's "nice to have."

DEFINE YOUR ARCHITECTURE

- Revisit the work you've done in looking at your technology gaps as they map to your initial, near-term, and longer-term requirements.
- Map carefully what you need to achieve in technology to support process improvements in phases.
- Define a checklist for vendor feature comparisons—which will evolve in growing levels of detail once you commence the process. Chapter 12 and Appendix B provide a foundation for making vendor comparisons.

Some things to keep in mind in terms of objectives, metrics, and technological priorities are as follows:

- *Use case is critical*: For instance, asset management is often selected for phase 1 because it is generally the least time-sensitive and allows for more manual updates. It also provides a grounding in leveraging the CMDB System to "know what you've got" in terms of infrastructure, supporting software, and/or endpoints. In many cases, as CMDB initiatives move toward Change Management, this extends to developing a solid definition of applications—both those developed in-house and those delivered externally through service providers. On the other hand, minimizing service impacts and optimizing service performance may be the first priority for your CMDB System. Needless to say, each of these use cases will require different priorities in terms of technology, stakeholder involvement, and process readiness (Figure 4.7).

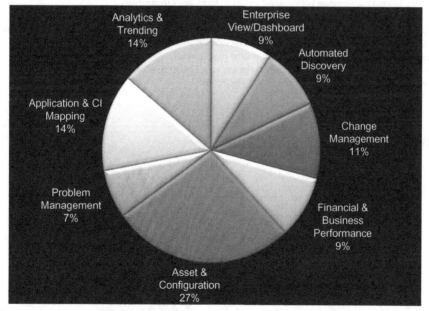

FIGURE 4.7

Use case is critical: based on interviews of more than 20 individuals in one company, we found the expectations and priorities indicated in the figure above. Note the mix of technology priorities and use case priorities—as the two here begin to inform on each other. It should be stressed that this was viewed as a useful "wish list" for implementing the next steps of vendor selection, integration, deployment, and adoption. From this, a more focused and prioritized set of objectives could be developed, socialized, and achieved.

- *Metrics need to evolve in support of your plan—not merely as a political move to get buy-in*: Creating the right metrics for your CMDB System initiative should flow naturally downward from your key objectives and upward from your stakeholder dialogs, assessments, and goal definitions. Pie-in-the-sky ROI goals pulled like a rabbit out of a magic hat will invariably come back to bite you. Optimizing ROI for your CMDB System is at least in part art as well as science—both grounded in a hard look at reality over which you're willing to apply common sense.
- *By now, your real "team" should take shape*: At this point, after the work you've done in terms of dialog and stakeholder and executive buy-in, you can expect to finalize your team membership and its broader resources. This may or may not look a lot like what you sketched out in step one. As we'll examine more in detail in Chapter 11, team membership will usually include process expertise, architectural expertise, business or managerial expertise (read "good communicator" among other attributes), and technical skills such as master data management. In many cases, vendor or other consultants will make up a part of your phase 1 team.

Many chapters in this book directly support this very critical fourth step. The chapters that are most relevant are the following:

- Chapter 3 is key to understanding both process and basic technology foundations.
- Chapter 7 provides insights into how to perform a use case audit in order to articulate metrics and outcomes.
- Chapter 10 includes an in-depth discussion on how to develop CMDB System-related metrics and requirement at all levels and how to link this effectively to ROI—with promises you can reasonably expect to keep. It is the core "how-to" chapter in this book to help you define CMDB-related requirements.
- Chapter 11 offers insights into selecting and developing your CMDB System team.
- Chapter 12 indicates what to look for in technology selection.

STEP FIVE: TECHNOLOGY SELECTION

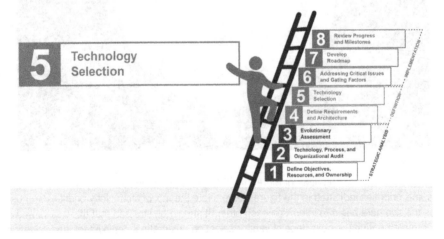

Evaluate current situation

- Gaps
  - ➤ Tools (interfaces incompatible)
  - ➤ Process (working in a silo)

- Redundancies
  - ➤ May require multiple tools
  - ➤ Avoid duplicate functions

- Other topics
  - ➤ Discovery and population
  - ➤ Automation
  - ➤ Maintenance
  - ➤ Security

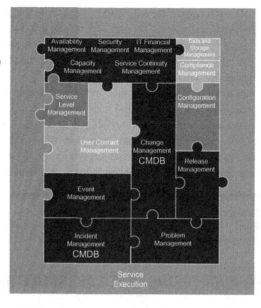

FIGURE 4.8

This matrix, albeit tuned to one specific client, looks at the overall preparedness and provides an excellent backdrop for focusing toolset selection for CMDB Systems. The color-coding combines both technology and process readiness—with white indicating strength, gray some weakness, and black a fundamental problem area.

Tool selection is typically what everyone believes, or at least hopes, will provide a silver bullet for the entire CMDB System project. It is indeed another critical step, but it is no panacea.

Figure 4.8 is a high-level evaluation matrix targeted at toolset and process effectiveness in mapping out where this client needed to go next. White indicates readiness, gray indicates marginal capabilities, and black areas are those that will need to be upgraded significantly over time.

Here are some of the more salient considerations in technology selection:

- From step four, you should already have a list of existing tools and a list of additional functions that will be required to support the CMDB project.
- As you delve further, you should consider options in terms of where and how your CMDB is or will be optimized. For instance, whether it is embedded—for example, in a service desk, a BSM performance-optimized solution, or an asset management-oriented solution—may well set the stage for what is most natively at hand for meeting phase 1 objectives.
- What skill sets are required to optimize new and existing tools, and how does your team's skills stack up against those requirements?
- Consider SaaS versus on-premise. If SaaS, what are the capabilities for on-premise integration (e.g., with automation tools)?
- How critical in phase 1 is application dependency mapping?
- Integration is always key, and often a challenge, even with innovations like Web Services. Some critical areas for integration might include discovery and inventory, service desk,

service catalog, change impact analytics, asset management and SW license management, monitoring and performance tools, and in-house developed databases or other tools.

- What are your requirements to support virtualization and cloud in the near-term and foreseeable future? The good news here is that most CMDB-related vendors already support those capabilities or are actively moving to do so.
- Automation requirements for phase 1 and phase 2 deployments should be identified and prioritized.
- Do your requirements reach beyond your own internal IT organization? What about your partners, suppliers, and even service providers? If you're serious about managing a business service in the current environment, it may become necessary to have some reach beyond your purely "on-premise shores" and to share reports and analysis with your "Extended Enterprise." Once again, the good news is that this is increasingly becoming possible with current and evolving technologies.

Chapter 12 and the RFP in Appendix B are central to step five. However, there are also critical insights in Chapter 3 for a core CMDB System technology vision, and in Chapter 13, there are insights for some critical gating factors in going forward with deployments (e.g., CI definition and service modeling).

STEP SIX: ADDRESSING CRITICAL ISSUES AND GATING FACTORS

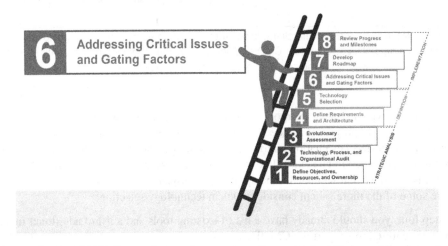

With step six, the CMDB System is just about to move forward into full phase 1 implementation. But much like the ground check on an airplane before departure, you are well advised to do a thorough, albeit 11-hour, scan for freshly surfaced issues (or potential ones) before the project is finally given clearance to take off. While Chapter 13 provides added insights from real-world deployments in terms of "closing the gap" between PoC and full-production deployment, the following summary is a useful place to start:

ORGANIZATIONAL ISSUES

- Review for a second time any previous CMDB efforts that failed. You may want to consider the following questions for each: Why did it fail? How can you avoid those pitfalls this time? Is there a history of setting poor expectations? How is that impacting you now?
- How do different roles, including executive IT and general IT, view the initiative now? What are the possible areas of dissonance? Where is enthusiasm the highest and is that a good or a bad thing (e.g., causing overinflated expectations)?

- Be advised that senior management focus wanes after 6 months, if not sooner. Once lost, that focus and support are difficult to recover—so try to scale the project accordingly.

BUDGET AND RESOURCE CONSTRAINTS

- Resource allocations sometimes change too quickly to sustain projects that don't deliver value immediately. Where do you stand now?
- Take a deep breath and look around one last time at the environment you're trying to manage. Take note of any potential factors that might impact future budgeting or resource availability— for example, pending M&A activity might radically change the infrastructure.
- Other mandates (e.g., Sarbanes-Oxley and Basel II) could cause the project to exceed budget or exceed OpEx resources. Failure to account for this can cause the project to be canceled—so try to be accurate in your forecasts.

TECHNOLOGY ISSUES

- What have you learned from the evaluations done for PoC trials?
- What toolset integrations are still pending?
- When reviewing the phase 1 system as it's intended to perform, what issues remain? What pleasant surprises, if any, have you discovered? How can you tweak your deployment to optimize the good and minimize the bad?
- To what degree are other initiatives (such as the move to cloud, virtualization, Agile/DevOps, or mobile) likely to place new constraints or requirements on your plans?
- Service modeling and CI definition are a big focus for step six. They are the wings of your airplane, the tracks for your train, and the very heart of your CMDB System.

Figure 4.9 presents one company's list of top concerns at the "gating factors" stage. While not everything on this list was easily fixable, it did provide a solid, candid, and useful point of preparation for going forward with a CMDB System.

1. Sustained executive management support (11)
2. Setting initial expectations (8)
3. Implementation of solid process (8)
4. Getting funding (7)
5. Getting buy-in (6)
6. Getting the right level of requirements to understand the value (5)
7. Resistance to change (5)
8. Identifying and maintaining application information (3)
9. Dedication of key SMEs (3)
10. Collecting too much data (1).

FIGURE 4.9

These documented "gating factors" for Company Y reflect input from more than 15 interviews. The numbers reflect the number of respondents who voted for each as what he or she felt was the preeminent concern.

Chapter 13 is devoted to "closing the gap" by addressing "gating factors." You might also want to revisit Chapter 1, which presents a litany of failures, and Chapter 8, which focuses on making the initial CMDB System assessment work.

STEP SEVEN: DEVELOPING A THREE-TIERED ROADMAP FOR IMMEDIATE AND FUTURE DEPLOYMENTS

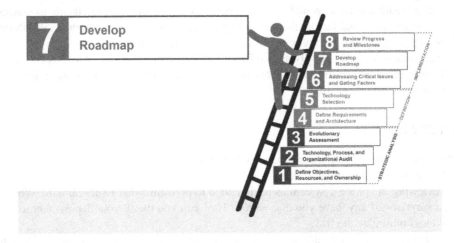

By now, you should be ready to finalize a detailed set of objectives for phase 1 and move forward. You should also be ready to look into the future and consider how you want your company's CMDB System to have evolved by the end of phase 2. A summary of things to consider in building a Three-Tier Roadmap is presented below:

SIX-MONTH ROADMAP (TACTICAL IMPLEMENTATION PLAN)

- Set hard deadlines for short, deliverable tasks.
- Conduct a review at the end with milestone comparisons.
- Complete a small step with wins every 90 days (maximum).
- Phase 1 should begin to emerge toward a tipping point in showing value with the move to production-level deployment.

ONE-YEAR ROADMAP

- Your tipping point for phase 1 value should by now become a powerful ally in supporting your CMDB System initiative.
- Consider what will be included in next tactical roadmap.
- Set expectations within IT regarding which projects will be addressed next.

- Set medium-term goals and reviews—mapping to metrics for benefits in terms of technology, process, value-based, and efficiency improvements.
- Phase 1 should be "complete."

TWO-YEAR ROADMAP

- Document a vision for a more complete CMDB effort with phase 2.
- Adjust as milestones are met and new components are made available.
- Demonstrate progress made and clearly estimate time left until completion.
- Include far-reaching future directions.

A very high-level sketch of a tiered rollout for staffing and technology adoption as derived from an actual past deployment is presented in Figure 4.10.

Step seven in this ladder is specifically addressed in Chapter 14. Chapter 10, with a focus on project plan definition, is also a good reference.

	Six–Month Roadmap (0–6)	Twelve–Month Roadmap (6–12)	(12–18)	(18–24) Three–Year Roadmap	(24–30)	(30–36)
Tasks	Core CMDB POC Citizen CMDB POC (EAD) App Mapping (OEI) Discovery (OEI) Detailed Require Doc Build CMDB Team	Core CMDB Citizen CMDB (EAD) Integration with Park and Currents Integration with Park and Acme	Upgrade Park Service Desk to Current Version Change Management	Disaster Recovery SLM	Service Catalogs	Exec Dashboard
Software & Hardware	Currents (dependency mapping) Acme Asset Management (desktops)	Acme Asset Management (servers) Park CMDB Park Configuration Manager (Patch Management) (Application Management) (Content Management)				
Staff	Team Leader CMDB Expert CMDB Expert Info Architect EAD CMDB Expert EMA Review	Team Leader CMDB Expert CMDB Expert Info Architect EAD CMDB Expert EMA Review	Team Leader CMDB Expert CMDB Expert Info Architect EMA Review			
Costs	Software: $0 Hardware: $15K IT Staff: $416K Consult Staff: $14K CMDB Only: $445K TOTAL: $445K	Software: $X Hardware: $X IT Staff: $416K Consult Staff: $14K CMDB Only: $430K TOTAL: $430K	Software: $X Hardware: $X IT Staff: $1331K Consult Staff: $56K CMDB Only: $1387K TOTAL: $1387K			

Assumptions: Fully loaded IT staff costs are $80 per hour.

FIGURE 4.10

A very high-level sketch of a three-tiered plan for staffing and technology adoption, designed to support added detail as the deployment evolves. Vendor names have been changed in order not to distract from the general flow of ideas. Note the core buckets presented here for decision-making, which include costs and technology investments, and staffing. A complete plan would also address process and organizational implications, as well as value-specific metrics.

STEP EIGHT: REVIEW PROGRESS AND MILESTONES

By 6 months and especially by 12 months out, your phase 1 CMDB System deployment is fully underway, and you're ready to leverage production-level benefits where you should achieve that critical "tipping point" of demonstrating real tangible value. No doubt there will be some surprises, good and bad, along the way on all fronts—technology, process, and organization.

You should view this step as an opportunity to begin a new assessment, beginning with step one but taking a much more empowered and streamlined approach, as you create more granular phase 2 metrics and to project CMDB System vision and benefits into a broader and changing future. Step eight is also an opportunity to realign your executive support, your resources, and your team as makes sense. Don't be shy about communicating and documenting benefits. Throughout the initiative, you must be the project's champion—its salesperson. That will be truer at this stage than at any other time in the project's life cycle.

Chapter 15 leads in supporting step eight.

CASE STUDY INTERVIEW

Introduction

Throughout this book, we will be examining individual deployments on a Q&A basis to help get a better feel for the realities behind the recommendations provided here. While some of the interviews occurred during the actual writing of this book in 2014, we have also included prior interviews from both consulting engagements and research.

This case study interview was generated by an interview at an industry event in Q2 2012[i] and provides insights into many of the ongoing discussions that are reflected in steps one to eight. In particular, look for insights on *leadership and organization*, *service modeling*, *process*, and *stakeholder politics*. From a process perspective, the quotes on ITIL first used in Chapter 3 should be familiar. They were deliberately included again here to show the broader context behind these savvy comments.

One speaker is from large global manufacturer in the food and beverage industry, and the other is from an insurance company with more than $4 billion in total assets. Both companies are headquartered in North America. The interactions were documented by EMA, and a summary of the key perspectives is presented in the following Q&A.

What Was the Driver Behind Your CMDB Deployment?

Manufacturer

"We had many silos of data and many different repositories. All over the world, everyone was doing their own silo of work in sometimes redundant or even conflicting ways. So we needed one central book of record and that's why the CMDB was so important for us—breaking through the silos and having a 'System of One' for the whole globe."

Financial Services Company

"The primary reason for the CMDB implementation was to understand the makeup of our applications and the systems supporting them. As much as was practical, we wanted to apply the CMDB and its insights to support change and configuration management requirements across the application infrastructure."

Can You Talk a Little Bit About the Politics Driving Your CMDB Deployments?

Manufacturer

"Our CIO and several executives had been involved with a CMDB before and knew what a CMDB could do. We had their support. There was some resistance at the operational level. In the past, we had a failed CMDB implementation—when requirements were constantly creeping in during deployment. Everyone had their own interpretation of what was needed—across North America, Latin America, Europe, and Asia. Apparently, there were some real fireworks back then. But on the other hand, that past effort also spread a more general awareness of the need for a common source of truth."

Financial Services Company

"We were largely driven by multiple departments wanting to come together to work more efficiently via a common solution. These were groups such as service management, storage, infrastructure management, and application support. And while we needed and got executive sponsorship, our most heated discussions weren't about whether we should do something, but how should we implement it. For instance, should we apply a tool with fully automated discovery or should we go with manual data entry? And what types of tools, or systems, should we leverage for data?"

What Was the Role of ITIL in Your Deployment?

Financial Services Company

"Most people think of ITIL as a 'best practice.' But the follow-on question is, 'What do you do about that best practice?' In my mind, a best practice is just a set of advisories. You should follow it based on your understanding of your needs, your environment, and your maturity levels. However, I see some companies trying to follow ITIL by the book as a definitive set of standard procedures, and I think this can carry some unintended consequences."

Manufacturer

"We did approach ITIL as a standard set of best practices. But we recognized that everyone had to interpret it to meet the needs for their group, their function, and their region. So did we follow ITIL to a 'T'? Absolutely not. But it was a foundation and a guide for us. For instance, we'd start with, 'What is the definition of a CMDB?' Eventually, we built toward a consensus using ITIL as a departure point. And then we'd ask, 'What is a CI?' And 'What CI attributes are most important?'"

How Many CIS Do You Have?

Financial Services Company

"Right now, we have 10,000."

Manufacturer

"We started with 10,000 CIs and now we're at more than 13,000. We're still very conservative in how we grow our deployment because we started at ground zero."

What Was Your Biggest Challenge?

Financial Services Company

"When we discussed the CMDB with different groups in our organization, each team got very excited about what they wanted to get out of our CMDB. But very quickly, we could see that many of their priorities were at least a couple of years away from implementation. So everybody's understanding of the scope was different. For instance, we had desktop people saying, 'Can I inventory my mouse? Can I inventory my keyboard and my monitor?' They all wanted to see those as CIs."

"But managing this wasn't too difficult. I asked everyone two questions: First, 'What is this equipment that you're prepared to manage from day one to its entire life cycle as a CI?' and, second, 'Do you have the resources to manage these items as CIs once they get into our CMDB?' If there were no costs associated with CI inclusion, then everyone would want everything included in the CMDB right at the start. But as soon as they begin to understand the costs, including update and data access costs, they viewed it differently."

Manufacturer

"Our core initial challenge was learning to approach the CMDB properly. Our program manager brought in vendor-provided experts to help us out and to give us a proper education because we only had a short time frame to get it deployed correctly."

"Focusing the scope was also a challenge. For instance, we had to tell people, 'No, you can't put your desktop in here for phase 1.' So for this, we relied on our service model to define how we could grow for the future."

"Finally, communication was another key challenge—with both stakeholders and executives. Even as we started to see light at the end of the tunnel, we had to manage expectations at the top as well as horizontally."

How Many People Do You Have Supporting Your CMDB in Terms of Core Team?
Manufacturer

"We have three people supporting our CMDB. One is going to be focused on discovery. Two are directed to cover our core requirements based on the data model. And we have developed processes in place to populate those classes. In our support model, according to ITIL standards, the only people who update our CMDB are the configuration management analysts. They are the gatekeepers. But our CI owners are accountable for updating those classes—not the core CMDB team."

"The policy is that if you make a change to a CI, there must be a change record. If you change a CI without changing the record, that can be grounds for termination. Also, there are logfiles that we've activated in support of our CMDB. So from our baseline, we can do delta checks. The CI owner has to also own discovery and the processes around discovery relevant to his or her CI. If discovery indicates a change, the CI owner is notified by e-mail automatically. If a change record already exists, then everyone is happy. If not, then both the CI owner and the configuration management analyst are notified and the CI owner will have to take action."

Financial Services Company

"We're still working on rounding out our core team, so I don't have a set number there. But we also want to use the principle that the owner of the information has to update the information. For instance, we have a dedicated application team that pushes the application code into different application servers. This team needs to own the relationships surrounding our applications and their components. We also have an infrastructure team building infrastructure services such as authentication, directory services, and data services. And that team will be responsible for the servers as well as the infrastructure across the various connections."

Can You Talk a Little About Service Modeling and Application Dependency Mapping?
Manufacturer

"Our top-level model is our business strategy. And below that, we have our domain classes. So therefore, we define our application dependencies by populating those classes. You may have an *application class* or a *server class*, for example. Once we have those classes populated with their CIs, we then do our relationship mapping. Having the right model defined gives you what you need for your strategic direction—the focus, the avenues, the boundaries, and the scope. You may not understand how to pull everything in at once, but having an effective model is a huge help in simplifying and staging the challenge."

Financial Services Company

"Rather than taking a top-down approach, we started by looking across multiple layers. Right out of the box, our solution gives us a rich set of types that you can import and match to—such as computers or different kinds of servers at the device level. Then, you can go above these types and look at applications. So we didn't try to build a monolithic application where all the interdependencies are included. We started by building services that perform one particular function, but which can become reusable components. You can define a specific application/infrastructure service as a service component—for instance, DNS Lookup. Then, as you go upward, you can associate that service with a business function. In other words, we tried to build our business services from the bottom up out of subordinate and reusable service components."

Do You See Your "Service Model" and the "Data Model" as Being Fundamentally the Same or Different?
Financial Services Company

"In my understanding, in the CMDB, the data model is already done for us in our solution. So it's a matter of how the data model is applied and leveraged to make it a service model."

Manufacturer

"Our service model is based on ITIL's definition, and it's all about the processes, functions, services, and technologies that we deliver to our customers. So therefore, it's a separate idea that can be applied to the data model. Our global finance team defines our business strategies company-wide. And these are of course not about a data model or technology. But that's where we started, so we can trace everything we do back to those business services."

How Did You Manage Stakeholder Expectation Setting and Incent Stakeholders to Participate in the Care and Feeding of the CMDB System?

Financial Services Company

"We started with a POC and socialized it with some of the teams to get feedback. And that worked for us."

Manufacturer

"We made sure our global stakeholders were a part of the teaching and learning around the CMDB. So we involved them in the educational process and then in defining our service model and its composition. At first, this was very foreign to many of us. But soon, we got consensus on that model around the globe—from Africa to Japan. In this case, a picture was worth a thousand words. Then, we said, 'OK, now let's look at the server class. There are three different types of servers.' Once again, we circulated these ideas and got consensus. Soon, stakeholders began to see their names associated with certain CIs. So we used modeling to socialize the scope and set expectations.

"As far as incenting stakeholders to contribute to the care and feeding of our CMDB, we had a lot of separate spreadsheets. The UNIX team had one, the Linux team had one, etc. So now, we've eliminated that. Having a single point of record across IT was a strong selling point. Now, the CI owner can profit from a centralized book of record that makes his or her job easier as well."

¹This interview was with two ServiceNow customers at a ServiceNow-sponsored event. It is one of multiple interviews in this book provided either directly through EMA research or through vendor events and other contacts. While it is not the objective of this book to provide specific vendor recommendations, vendor contexts for Q&As will be made clear throughout. In Appendix D, we will provide a partial list of vendors with solutions directed at CMDB Systems—including core CMDBs, Application Discovery and Dependency Mapping tools, and unique analytic CMDB-related offerings.

SUMMARY TAKEAWAYS

As an eight-step methodology to support you in managing and optimizing CMDB System initiatives, the "Ladder to CMDB System Success" also creates a framework for this book.

The Eight-Step Ladder to CMDB System Success includes the following steps:

1. Define your objectives and consider your resources.
2. Move forward with a technology, process, and organizational audit to further clarify resources and needs.
3. Do evolutionary or maturity assessments—as you evolve from *Reactive Infrastructure* to *Active Operational* to *Proactive Service-Oriented* to *Dynamic Business-Driven.* It's also important to remember that each of these stages reflect interdependencies across process, organization, and technology—the three critical drivers impacting your progress toward maturity.
4. Further clarify your requirements and metrics, define your architecture, and finalize your team.
5. Select the right mix of technologies you need to move forward in phase 1 and beyond.
6. Address critical issues and gating factors as you close the gap from PoC into full production.
7. Develop a Three-Tier Roadmap for phase 1 at the 6-month mark. This includes a 6-month roadmap directed at initial deployment objectives, a 12-month roadmap assessing full phase 1 progress, and a 2-year roadmap looking ahead to phase 2 and a more complete CMDB System vision for 2-3 years out.

8. Review your progress and milestones at 6 months, 12 months, and 2 years. Reassess where you are in context with internal changes, technical and business outcomes, shifting market and technology trends, and advances in CMDB-related technologies.

As a parallel process, keep in mind the key iterative conversations that apply to each step in this Eight-Step Ladder. These include the following:

- A process of refinement and adjustment should take place as you move from high-level objectives to more generalized metrics to the granular metrics inherent to your deployment. Some, but not all, of these metrics should reflect business and efficiency outcomes. Others will involve the scope and staged deployment of your CMDB System.
- Team building and stakeholder identification, dialog, and overall management should include expectation setting, metrics definitions, and processes for interactions.
- Executive buy-in and support should evolve as an integrated part of our planning, goal definition, resource allocation, and deployment.
- Process recommendations and assessments should also be addressed in context with your goals, objectives, technologies, and organization.
- Technology evaluations should be directed at what you already have and what you need to invest in, as well as any required integrations. Your technology foundations should grow with you as you build toward enhanced levels of automation, analytics, role support, and use case value.

Finally, recognize that to be successful, you should do your best to stand in the "middle of the storm" with its three drivers—*process*, *technology*, and *organization*. "People" are in fact a part of all three. "Organization" is grounded in culture and political structure—so easily ignored and yet so relevant to optimizing your CMDB System.

One last reminder: Pace yourself! What's provided in this chapter is a checklist with guidelines aimed to help you succeed. How much effort and detail you put into each area will vary based on time, resource, and focus available. Trying to do any one of these steps perfectly could cause unnecessary delay and ultimately failure. But the questions raised by each planning stage are worth considering, and "going up the steps" in sequence is critical to making your overall CMDB System deliver on expectations.

AWARENESS
AND GOALS

IT IN TRANSFORMATION: WHAT'S GOING ON AND WHERE DOES THAT LEAVE THE CMDB?

5

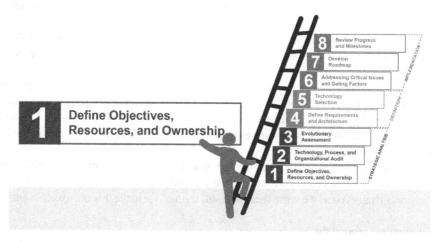

In this chapter, we consider an array of significant trends that are, directly or indirectly, impacting CMDB System adoption. These trends range from cloud, to optimizing the Extended Enterprise, to new dimensions in IT-to-business alignment, to changing views of ITIL. The chapter concludes with a brief summary of shifting adoption priorities for the CMDB itself.

These discussions draw substantially from recent research to substantiate and clarify these trends. This chapter also provides useful background for Chapter 15—in which cloud, agile, and other trends are examined more explicitly as the "next steps" in CMDB System planning and direction.

But before going any further, it's worth considering perhaps the most central question of all:

HOW HAS THE MODEL FOR IT CHANGED?

At the beginning of his book, *The Quantum Age of IT,* [1] Charles Araujo writes, "IT as we know it is dead." He then presented five key attributes of an effective IT organization. According to Araujo, IT should be all of the following: "a learning organization," "a disciplined organization," "a transparent organization," "a dynamic organization," and "an intimate organization."

---

[1] Charles A., The Quantum Age of IT, IT Governance Publishing, 2012.

While the first four of these attributes are fairly intuitive, some readers will no doubt struggle over what's meant by "intimate." However, if you think through the last few chapters, and in particular Chapter 4, nothing could be more relevant to optimizing CMDB System investments than *dialogue* and *conversations* and the "intimacy" they might engender across IT silos as well as between IT and its consumers. In many respects, a CMDB System can become a foundation for improved intimacy across IT, and between IT and the business it serves, by promoting new levels of efficiency and more accurate shared insights.

The other attributes in Mr. Araujo's list are also worth noting. Among them, "a learning organization" is key. After all, effective progress in process, culture, and technology requires a collective commitment to learning that can pay big dividends in itself. An IT organization that fails to learn is prevented from adapting to the ever-changing IT ecosystem, and without that adaptation, the organization may be faced with some form of at least partial extinction (e.g., outsourcing and departmental computing initiatives).

"Transparent" can mean many things, but in this chapter, we'd like to highlight *visibility* in terms of how effectively IT can deliver in supporting business objectives—in providing value as well as in optimizing operational performance.

"Disciplined" and "dynamic" are probably the most self-evident attributes, although "dynamic" needs to be understood beyond responding to purely technical demands—even as vastly accelerated rates of technology-related changes have brought many IT organizations to their knees. "Dynamic" can also be applied to cultural changes as IT evolves toward a more business-driven model to become more service-oriented and customer-aware.

The Quantum Age of IT also underscores the fact that the mantra of "stable and precise" no longer works for IT in the twenty-first century. However, many traditional CMDB implementations—including no doubt many occurring even as we write this—are still trying to achieve this unworkable and relatively static ideal.

So how do you get around this?

As we've stated before, the CMDB System should be viewed as a "system of relevance," rather than a "single source of truth." The burdens of relevance are at once less onerous and far more meaningful in terms of action, analysis, and automation. While "truth" implies something everlasting or at least stable, relevance suggests a far more dynamic universe.

WHAT DOES IT MEAN FOR IT TO "SHOW VALUE"?

There has been a lot of industry discussion of late about the changing role of IT toward becoming more of a broker of services, optimizing external as well as internal resources in support of business requirements. Cloud's huge array of new application options—what we sometimes call "the shopping mall of cloud"—are one of the main reasons for this change.

Being a "broker" does make sense on several levels—especially once you take into account the many options of public and private cloud for service delivery and service selection. However, a brokerage approach may not go far enough in showing value in a growing number of environments where IT is no longer just expected to deliver applications that "serve the business" from the point of view of efficiency. In these environments, IT is being asked—directly or by implication—to provide capabilities that can help transform how a business works and even help create new business models. This may be a cause for significant in-house innovation in application development and/or a much more refined tuning of how IT services can be optimized based on insights into usage, effectiveness, and business outcomes.

Moreover, given ever-present pressure to show value, all IT organizations must understand their internal and external consumers as never before—in terms of both personal satisfaction and business results. Otherwise, they will be relegated to being mere cost centers—reactive and often clumsy in meeting business demands and, as we shall see later in this book, often underfunded and underresourced.

To some readers, this may sound a bit heretical. After all, in the past, being a cost center that met the tactical needs of the organization was an acceptable role for IT. However, IT's magic curtain—separating technology choices from the consumer—has been lifted once and for all now that teenagers are provisioning applications on their way to school. As our research on User Experience Management[2] has shown, the "consumerization of IT" isn't only about technology. It's about being responsive to human beings—their appetites, needs, abilities, and roles. In the end, IT's mission lies exactly there.

So, you may ask, what does this all mean for the CMDB System (which may sound about as far away from flesh-and-blood appetite as the planet Mars is from your favorite beach)?

If IT is going to empower its service consumers, then it needs to have an effective platform for looking outward, not just inward. It must have a clear and dynamic set of insights into the technical interdependencies behind its services *as they relate to* dynamic shifts in internal business needs and external consumer behaviors. Only in this way can IT proactively help new business models to take root, evolve, and thrive.

LOOKING AHEAD

The rest of this chapter will share data from our research into trends impacting IT. This is intended as preparation for a look at broader environmental requirements for CMDB System planning, which include the following:

- Cloud, virtualization, and the Extended Enterprise
- Agile and mobile
- Business Service Management (BSM) and the move from "cost center" to "business partner"
- The need for a truly cross domain, service-oriented IT organization
- The growing relevance of ITIL and process awareness in adapting to new technologies
- The growing relevance of service modeling and the CMDB System in the face of all these trends

The goal of this chapter is to provide additional insight into the general IT landscape as it's evolving and potentially impacting your CMDB System directions—in terms of both challenges and opportunities. Some of these data should help to arm you with reference points to use when making a case for CMDB to executives or stakeholders who require being in touch with current priorities. In a sense, this chapter is a prelude to the next one—preparing you to walk into the C-level office with a better idea of your executive's potential concerns.

However, this chapter is not meant to be a complete list of trends in IT today. For instance, "big data," and in particular "big data for IT," have not been discussed here but will be dealt with in more

---

[2] User and Customer Experience Management—IT at the Crossroads of Change, EMA, 2012.

detail in Chapters 12 and 15. This trend is, actually, increasingly relevant to CMDB Systems as analytics can not only feed and support service modeling updates to CMDBs but also profit from interdependency insights in terms of data gathering and relevance.

CLOUD AND THE EXTENDED ENTERPRISE

Cloud may already be a big part of your landscape. And if it isn't yet, it will be soon. It may be public or private cloud (or a combination of both), but cloud is going to be a major part of the IT landscape for the foreseeable future. Virtualization has already become commonplace, and while simply moving to a virtualized infrastructure doesn't count as fully "cloud," this move is changing the game dramatically for CMDB Systems. Virtualization brings with it requirements for dynamic insights and flexibility in terms of capturing the impacts of changes, and managing assets, across the application/infrastructure.

While some pundits have tried to convince the industry that cloud is rendering CMDB adoption obsolete, current research has shown that just the opposite is true. We will look at that more closely later both in this chapter and throughout this book. However, at this point, the main objective is to provide a basic overview of cloud adoption in its current form and the challenges it poses for a CMDB System.

Based on data from EMA's *Ecosystem Cloud*[3] research, the following trends surfaced:

- Forty-four percent of respondents with cloud initiatives were balanced between internal cloud and public (external) cloud, while 29% were predominantly internal and 28% were predominantly public. Figure 5.1 provides a more granular look at how cloud services are being prioritized across IT and the enterprises they serve.
- Of these, 58% felt that cloud was "essential" or "important." An additional 12% were generating revenue through cloud services. Only 9% viewed cloud as merely supplemental. In other words, it appears that cloud adoption in some form is not just a nice-to-have.
- Very significantly—and adding to the relevance of CMDB Systems—45% of respondents viewed their cloud services as "considerably" or "entirely" dependent on traditional infrastructures. In fact, *everyone* claimed at least some dependence on the traditional infrastructures. This is one reason why the popular marketing term "journey to the cloud" is partly a misnomer. Rather than an end point, cloud is primarily an amplified set of resources that will have to work in a mixed world at least for the foreseeable future. The visibility and insight that a CMDB "system of relevance" can provide across this heterogeneous landscape can make a real difference in improving service quality, availability, and value.
- Moreover, cloud offers no escape from responsibility. Even in dealing with publicly delivered SaaS solutions, only 11% of IT organizations felt that problem performance and access management lay primarily with their service providers. Instead, internal IT remained on the hook for quality assurance, incident and problem management, policy-based service provisioning, and overall service governance.[4]
- Seventy percent of cloud adopters were experiencing shadow IT organizations cropping up within lines of business, sometimes in competition with corporate IT. When asked about the impact of these shadow IT groups, 63% of respondents said they found those maverick organizations disruptive and threatening to their own organization.

---

[3] Ecosystem Cloud: Managing and Optimizing IT Services Across the Full Cloud Mosaic, EMA June, 2013.
[4] EMA, custom research, Q3, 2013.

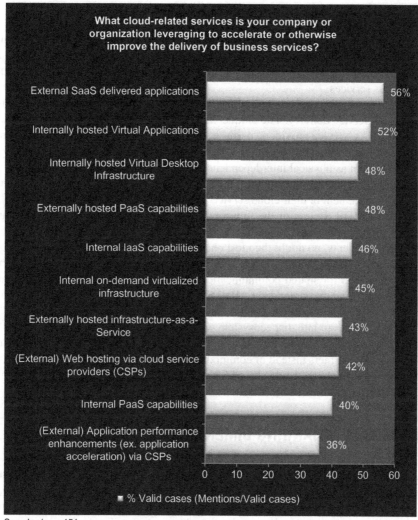

What cloud-related services is your company or organization leveraging to accelerate or otherwise improve the delivery of business services?

Service	Percentage
External SaaS delivered applications	56%
Internally hosted Virtual Applications	52%
Internally hosted Virtual Desktop Infrastructure	48%
Externally hosted PaaS capabilities	48%
Internal IaaS capabilities	46%
Internal on-demand virtualized infrastructure	45%
Externally hosted infrastructure-as-a-Service	43%
(External) Web hosting via cloud service providers (CSPs)	42%
Internal PaaS capabilities	40%
(External) Application performance enhancements (ex. application acceleration) via CSPs	36%

■ % Valid cases (Mentions/Valid cases)

Sample size = 151

FIGURE 5.1

These data show the breadth and diversity of cloud adoption in North America. Very important to keep in mind here is that even with public cloud services, only 11% of respondents depend primarily on their service providers for managing quality and appropriately provisioning access. Cloud may put the world in your hands, but in the end, it's still in your hands.

DATA SHARING AND THE EXTENDED ENTERPRISE

Cloud hasn't created the "Extended Enterprise." The Extended Enterprise was around in a major way with Web 2.0 business application systems at least as early as 2009, as businesses and organizations found that they could expand their efficiencies with partners and suppliers through a meld of interrelated application business services.

However, cloud has significantly amplified the need to see beyond IT's own boundaries to create a common context for service delivery. The unique value of CMDB-related service modeling, in which logical attributes (SLAs, service providers, partners, etc.) can be affiliated with physical infrastructure of software attributes, is a natural fit for the Extended Enterprise where organizational interdependencies are just as important as physical interdependencies in ensuring service quality.

Significantly, 73% of the respondents in our research *Ecosystem Cloud* viewed data sharing and visibility into the environment of their cloud service providers (CSPs) as "very important" or "critical." In other words, the CMDB System of the future will have to support interdependencies that include service providers, in both cloud and noncloud environments.

Given these requirements, no doubt the most challenging issue will be enabling process conversations across separate IT organizations, some of which may actually compete with each other. In other words, whenever the need for shared communication and processes arises, culture and political divisions are likely to challenge the "extended CMDB System," just as they so often do within a single IT organization.

Yet, the ability to reach out into that ecosystem with cohesive insights into service values and interdependencies will eventually become enormous—especially among those CSPs seeking to differentiate themselves by being partners instead of commodity suppliers.

Figure 5.2 shows how data are being shared for service management issues currently—placing the Extended Enterprise in a more realistic context.

AGILE AND MOBILE: CHANGING DIMENSIONS IN CMDB SYSTEM POSSIBILITIES

Agile software development, along with the invasion of mobile devices throughout organizations, represents new terrains for IT Service Management and consequently for the CMDB System, and they pose very different challenges. Agile will require breaking down the walls between development, the service desk, and operations that have been so long in place in many IT organizations.

Mobile, on the other hand, will present very different kinds of opportunities and challenges—new *opportunities* for managing and optimizing the CMDB System through more effective communication within IT and *challenges* in terms of managing mobile assets nondisruptively across an increasingly heterogeneous mix of end devices.

AGILE: WHEN DevOps AND ITSM COLLIDE

Our research[5] shows that about 65% of respondents globally are seeking to integrate application release management with their IT Service Management strategy.

---

[5] IT Service Management in the Age of Cloud and Agile, EMA and CXP, 2013.

Sample size = 104

FIGURE 5.2

Here, we can see how application service-related data are being shared across a larger business ecosystem—what we call the "Extended Enterprise."(Ibid.) Not surprisingly, while data sharing is most common within a specific IT organization and between IT and its internal customers, there are also a meaningful number for data sharing with external partners and CSPs right on through external telecommunications service providers. This need to communicate more effectively in terms of relevant service interdependencies will become a prime driver for CMDB Systems in the future.

- Forty-seven percent are leveraging their service desk as a front end for requesting new application functionality.
- Forty percent have some level of integrated release management with their service desk. Of these, 90% share known application defects and the resolution of application issues between desk agents and operations.

The implications of this down the road for the CMDB System are enormous—even if today, only a minority of IT organizations have shared application/infrastructure dependency insights between development, operations, and the service desk team.

This is beginning to change as development, which historically has tended to live in a world of "simulation," must increasingly share common ground with operations—which historically has lived in a world, for lack of a less biased phrase, of "historical reality." Once these two worlds can truly come together, insights into application/infrastructure modules will include known versus hoped-for attributes, and the daunting gap between development and operations should at least begin to close.

Throughout this book, you will see what turned out to be a surprising number of forays into DevOps for CMDB deployments—including, in Chapter 15, an example of development actually acquiring a CMDB for use and pushing it out into a less mature operations organization!

MOBILE: DIVERSE ENDPOINTS, DIVERSE CONSUMERS, AND NEW CHALLENGES FOR THE CMDB SYSTEM

The challenges of optimizing *mobile* are also very much part of the ecosystem that IT organizations must address. Consider the following data points from a recent survey[6]:

- Eighty-seven percent of all business users regularly use both a PC and at least one mobile device to perform job tasks, and the remaining 13% of business users principally use only PCs. There is no indication that tablets are *replacing* PCs for business use; however, it is clear they are largely being adopted to *supplement* the use of PCs in the workplace.
- Roughly half of all mobile devices are employee-owned, whereas 71% of all PCs are purchased by employers.

What this means for ITIL's "Service Asset and Configuration Management"—the very heart of the CMDB and its processes—is significant once you accept the fact that service delivery doesn't just happen in a data center but increasingly requires in-depth insights into end point access in terms of configuration, asset management, and performance. Once again, the versatility of linking physical components with logical (human) "owners" through CMDB-driven service modeling can provide a meaningful advantage here.

BUSINESS SERVICE MANAGEMENT (BSM): IT AND BUSINESS ALIGNMENT AND ITS DRAMATIC IMPLICATIONS FOR CMDB SYSTEMS

In ITIL, BSM and business relationship management (BRM) are a part of *Service Strategy*. They embody the critical dialogue that unites IT and the business objectives. This requires meaningful communication between IT and the business it serves—a conversation that can become significantly more effective once good data surrounding service impacts, service quality, and service interdependencies are readily at hand.

BSM may not sound like a new trend, but in fact, it has become more relevant than ever as IT choices in service creation and provisioning, and business requirements for superior alignment and responsiveness, have never been greater, as recent data show in Figure 5.3.[7]

The relationship between BSM and your CMDB System may seem less than robust at first, but in our experience there is often a strong correlation between having IT evolve to become a business partner and success with CMDB deployments. This is underscored in the following excerpt from a consulting assessment for a company we will call "Acme" for the sake of anonymity:

---

[6]Custom EMA Research, 2013.
[7]Custom research with EMA and Axelos, 2013.

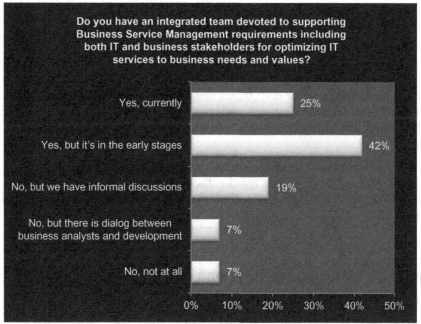

Do you have an integrated team devoted to supporting
Business Service Management requirements including
both IT and business stakeholders for optimizing IT
services to business needs and values?

Yes, currently — 25%
Yes, but it's in the early stages — 42%
No, but we have informal discussions — 19%
No, but there is dialog between business analysts and development — 7%
No, not at all — 7%

Sample size = 380

FIGURE 5.3

The data underscore the importance of BSM initiatives combining IT and business stakeholders to better align IT services with business needs, as 67% are at least in process with BSM and an additional 19% have at least informal discussions.

In a "classic" organization where IT is considered a cost center, there is a strong tendency to cut staff and minimize costs because the services provided by these core groups are invisible to IT's clients. Typically, the cost of implementing a CMDB is limited to determining initial software licensing needs and calculating installation, configuration, and integration requirements. This is done as an incremental project in terms of Acme Company budgeting. After the initial implementation is finished, however, the ongoing maintenance and support costs of the CMDB must be absorbed into the base IT budget.

In an "IT as a business partner" model, a formal chargeback system is typically adopted. Each core technology silo (network, database, etc.) provides a service to the business unit at a negotiated and measured level and associated cost. Service is provided at an appropriate level based on the needs and criticality of the applications and business units, and IT silos right-size based on the demands for their services. In the case of CMDB efforts, we have seen a much higher success rate from companies that have transitioned to IT as a business partner, especially in the long term.

In other words, not only the move to becoming a business partner is supported through insights that a CMDB System can provide, but also the resources—fiscal and human—needed to support the CMDB System on a meaningful ongoing basis are significantly more likely to be available via a business partner IT organization.

Some quotes from these client engagements directed at CMDB-related staffing and planning tend to reinforce this idea:

- "We are a cost center from a finance and control perspective and a business partner from a business analyst point of view. But this has proved insufficient. Our resources are spread thin. We are doing 20 tasks when we can really only focus on two tasks."
- "We are a cost center because we don't have a tangible product. Partly as a result [of this], we are running lean and mean. Our workload has doubled, but the IT staff has remained static. This means finding resources to support our CMDB initiative will be a serious challenge."

The transition to becoming a true business partner is critical, but just like a CMDB System, it is also multidimensional. Figure 5.4[8] provides a broader discussion of both business alignment and technological maturity. Inherent in all of these advances is the need to evolve to become a more cross domain IT organization.

THE MOVE TO A CROSS DOMAIN IT ORGANIZATION— AND WHY IT'S MORE NEEDED (AND REAL) THAN EVER

For more than 20 years, IT organizations have been seeking technologies that will allow them to operate with a more cross domain focus—starting perhaps with the advent of ITIL in 1989 and followed by the advent of the first SNMP platforms early in the 1990s. So there is indeed very little new about the need to move toward a more cross domain IT reality.

The following comments taken from CMDB-related engagements also underscore the importance of cross domain readiness for CMDB System initiatives. While the first speaker laments the siloed, or "Wild West," cultures of some IT organizations, the second comment shows a benefit realized after a cross domain approach has truly taken hold:

- "We have found a very strong commonality among IT organizations where the predominant culture is one of tactical competency with an active 'can do' approach. This tendency is borne out of necessity, as the tools and solutions available to IT professionals just a few years ago required expert knowledge in order to analyze and solve problems. This environment has led to a 'Wild West' approach to IT management, where the focus is on tactical problem solving not strategic planning. However, current philosophy across most industries has changed considerably in the last few years as IT organizations realize that the gunslinger approach does not scale well to escalating technical requirements and is susceptible to single points of failure as the technical experts retire or leave the workforce."
- "We estimate that downtime at Acme improved 60% because now that it has taken a nonsiloed approach to managing and optimizing its IT services. Cross-functional teams, as supported by its CMDB, take more pride in the difference they make to the business."

---

[8] Ecosystem Cloud, op. cit.

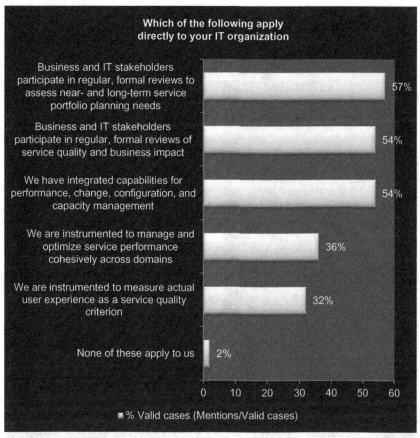

Sample size = 245

FIGURE 5.4

These options provide a template for readiness in terms of both IT-to-business alignment and true cross domain service management. CMDB Systems can help to inform business-alignment discussions; directly support integrated performance, capacity, configuration, and Change Management; help to deliver a more cohesive view of service performance across domains; and help to correlate user experience with service interdependencies in order to optimize planning, triage, and business value.

EVEN IF CROSS DOMAIN IS A NEED, IS THERE ANY REAL PROGRESS TAKING PLACE? WHAT'S THE JUSTIFICATION FOR CALLING "CROSS DOMAIN" A TREND?

We would be lying if we claimed that "cross domain IT" is a trend just like "cloud" and "agile." If it is a trend, it's certainly not getting a lot of ink or media attention by comparison. Yet, it may be the most important undercurrent behind many of these more technologically defined, and hence more heavily marketed, directions.

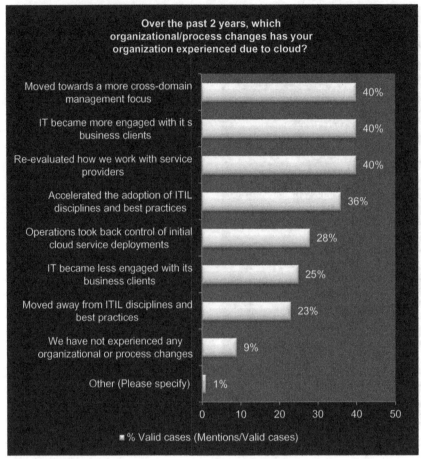

Sample size = 151

FIGURE 5.5

The data above illustrate how cloud is accelerating the move toward a more cross domain approach to IT. Cloud is also generally accelerating the need for ITIL, most probably because ITIL and cross domain efficiencies are linked, just as ITIL is linked to more effective business alignment. All these factors can play heavily in favoring a CMDB System that can focus IT toward higher levels of value.

Figure 5.5[9] takes us back to cloud and shows some interesting priorities—moving to a more cross domain way of working topped the list, along with increasing business dialogue and reevaluating vendor relationships. Indeed, other research data have indicated, for instance, that respondents overwhelmingly feel that cloud has made asset management both more cross domain (indicated by more than 90% of respondents) and more service-oriented in nature (as indicated by more than 80% of respondents).[10] Figure 5.5 also highlights priorities such as an increased appreciation for ITIL. Note that we gave them

---

[9]Ibid.
[10]Service-Centric Asset Management in the Age of Cloud Computing, EMA, 2011.

both options and those who accelerated ITIL are in a substantial majority over those who are retreating from ITIL because of cloud.

Yet, another slant on the need for a more cross domain organization is indicated in the following list, taken from research targeting the evolving role of IT Service Management. Recent data[11] show that the top five priorities for service desks highlight integration between the service desk and operations, another core variant on cross domain:

1. Improved integration between the service desk and operations for improved incident and problem management
2. Improved user experience for internal customers
3. Improved integration between the service desk and operations for configuration and Change Management
4. Improved user experience for external customers
5. Enhanced asset management strengths across IT

All of these, including improved user (internal and external) experience and enhanced asset management across IT, speak to the need for a more effective cross domain team—this time including the service desk as well as traditional, operations-defined silos.

While it may seem optimistic to put a stake in the ground and declare that the move to support a cross domain IT organization is a trend versus simply a need, IT *is* being pulled toward a cross domain structure by very real pressures from cloud adoptions, superior user management, and higher levels of expectations for IT to deliver service value. The data cited here offer just a few examples to reinforce this case. The irony is that as an underlying cultural change, cross domain may in the end become one of the most important "trends" cited in this chapter, both for CMDB adoption and for IT in general.

IS ITIL ENJOYING A REBIRTH AS ANOTHER "NEW TREND"?

Looking again at the cloud and virtualization trends, the data in Figure 5.6[12] suggest that ITIL will at least be holding its own as IT organizations make the move to cloud and virtualized environments. It is, after all, the best—and arguably the only—guide offering a truly cohesive view of IT processes as they fit together in support of creating and delivering business services. While it's true that cloud and virtualization don't often lend themselves to traditional or religious approaches to ITIL, they do require higher levels of cross domain collaboration than ever before.

Other recent research data strongly reinforce the value of ITIL in supporting BSM or business-alignment initiatives and in supporting integrated agile/DevOps initiatives.[13] Seventy-four percent of respondents saw ITIL as key for BSM, and 71% viewed ITIL as playing a substantive role in DevOps and agile.

Also intriguing is the relatively close link between higher levels of ITIL commitment and value and more advanced technological maturity. Figure 5.7 illustrates this—as 86% versus 65% of those with more technological maturity see ITIL as "very" or "extremely" valuable. More dramatically, those who

---

[11]Ibid.
[12]Ecosystem Cloud, op. cit.
[13]EMA and Axelos, op. cit.

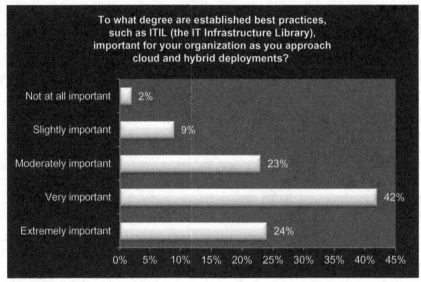

To what degree are established best practices, such as ITIL (the IT Infrastructure Library), important for your organization as you approach cloud and hybrid deployments?

Not at all important — 2%
Slightly important — 9%
Moderately important — 23%
Very important — 42%
Extremely important — 24%

Sample size = 151

FIGURE 5.6

These data reinforce the value of supporting true service-driven processes in a landscape made both richer and more complex by cloud and virtualization.

see only marginal value for ITIL are more than twice as likely to be technologically less advanced. To be clear, we mapped "technological maturity" to the variety of more advanced service management technologies in place and deployed. These ranged from advanced analytics and automation to executive dashboards to CMDB and ADDM deployments. We made the assumption that the more of these advanced service management investments were deployed, the more technologically "mature" the respondent's IT organization was.

These data also suggest that CMDB-related initiatives need to integrate technology and process as mutually reinforcing advantages. Rather than being the "chicken-or-the-egg" syndrome, real-world experience plus common sense would suggest that it's a "chicken-and-the-egg" story. As IT organizations advance in managing services, they are more likely to make deeper commitments both to ITIL and to the technologies relevant to superior service management.

GIVEN ALL THIS, AND MORE, ARE CMDB SYSTEMS A REEMERGING OR AN AGING TREND?

In doing this book, anyone would expect us to be hoping for the former—and in fact, recent data really seem to support the reemergence of the CMDB and in particular the broader CMDB System as a part of the very trends we've discussed above.

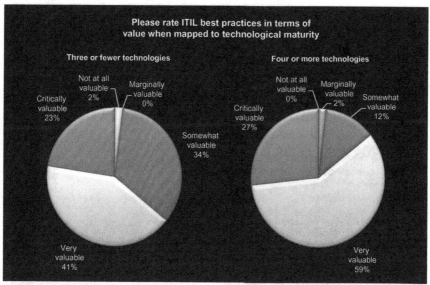

Sample size = 109

FIGURE 5.7

These two circles indicate the "chicken-and-the-egg" relationship between ITIL enthusiasm and advanced technology adoption. The circle on the left represents a low level of technical maturity with only three of the technology areas (listed below) deployed. The circle on the right is more technologically advanced with deployments in four or more of the areas listed below. As you can see, 86% of those with more advanced service technology deployments view ITIL as either "critically valuable" or "very valuable," compared to only 64% of those with fewer than four service management technologies deployed.

The technology areas presented in the questionnaire were the following:

- Service desk
- Asset management
- Workflow/process automation
- Integration with non-IT call centers or customer support
- End-user self-service portal
- Performance and availability management
- Service level management
- Service management dashboard
- Service catalog
- IT financial planning system
- Project management system
- Application life cycle management solution
- IT business intelligence/data warehouse

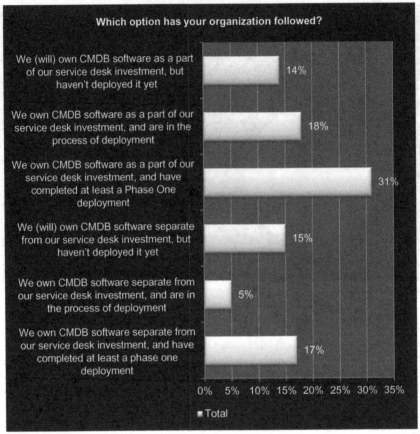

Sample size = 170

FIGURE 5.8

More CMDBs are being deployed as an integral part of a service desk than as a separate integration—most often with BSM solutions geared more toward performance or service impact management—by a margin of nearly two to one. Across both groups, 48% have completed a phase one deployment, and 23% are in active deployment.

While in the past CMDBs were more heavily favored by larger enterprises than by smaller businesses, current data suggest that this is changing. However, larger companies are not surprisingly more likely to pursue federation.

Recent research shows that more than half of those surveyed regarding IT Service Management either have already deployed a CMDB, own a CMDB, or are about to purchase a CMDB within 12 months. Of those who did not already have a CMDB System, nearly one-third planned to purchase one in the more distant future. In Figure 5.8, you can see a mix of where and how CMDBs are being deployed.[14]

---

[14]EMA and CXP, op. cit.

CMDB SYSTEMS FOR OPTIMIZING SERVICE DELIVERY OVER CLOUD: FROM DATABASE-CENTRIC TO SERVICE MODELING-CENTRIC

Now let's look at CMDB adoption specifically in the context of cloud and virtualization.

Here are a few data points taken from a recent survey of IT professionals in North America. These individuals were focused on integrating cloud resources into their broader capabilities for delivering application business services. Among these respondents, 83% were pursuing some type of service modeling, and of these,[15]

- fifty-four percent were leveraging service modeling in a dashboard for business impact,
- fifty percent had deployed application dependency mapping for performance management,
- forty-four percent had deployed an application dependency mapping solution for managing change,
- thirty-nine percent had deployed some aspects of a federated CMS,
- thirty percent had deployed a core CMDB.

One implied takeaway here is that service modeling is becoming the heart of a CMDB System—a true "system of relevance" for managing heterogeneous cloud, virtualized, and traditional infrastructures in support of business service delivery.

A few other data points from this research are also telling. Given the need to support more dynamic behavior in cloud environments, 67% of those respondents who had either CMDBs or application dependency mapping solutions supporting Change Management updated 40% of their CI's automatically—a much higher percentage than more traditional CMDB deployments in the past.

From a benefits perspective, those with CMDBs deployed were twice as likely to see themselves as "very successful" in delivering services across the cloud mosaic. But perhaps most significantly, there was a more than ten-to-one correlation between "very successful" deployments of CMDBs or change-oriented ADDM solutions and those "very successful" in deploying business services over cloud!

WRAPPING UP

The goal of this chapter isn't simply to cover newsy trends of marginal interest for planning a CMDB System. Rather, it's intended to provide you with a chance to look more closely at the very dynamics with which you and your team will need to work to adjust to changing requirements and optimize to new opportunities and, potentially, new use cases.

Moreover, this chapter should help to arm you well for the next step—so that as you move into the executive suite, you can better tie in your CMDB System initiative to some of the more critical areas of interest and/or concern for both IT executives and IT in general.

SUMMARY TAKEAWAYS

If IT as we once knew it is "dead," clearly, a new age is beginning with more options and more challenges than ever before. In this climate of change, IT must learn how to become a "business partner" with a value-driven versus purely cost-center culture. These challenges inherently favor investments in

---

[15]Ecosystem Cloud, op. cit.

CMDB Systems—in large part because of the need to capture critical service interdependencies across increasingly complex infrastructures, applications, and organizational landscapes with radically changing requirements for managing change and optimizing value.

Both the challenges and advantages of CMDB Systems are informed by research data on each of the following areas:

- Cloud, virtualization, and the Extended Enterprise
- Agile and mobile
- BSM—the move from "cost center" to "business partner"
- The growing need for a truly cross domain, service-oriented IT organization

Research data also show that as the Extended Enterprise emerges as the new norm, an increasingly diverse group of professionals—who will differ in terms of skill sets, geographic locations, organization types, and business models—will need to collaborate more effectively to manage change and optimize value for IT-related services. Such an environment allows for a growing range of benefits for CMDB Systems if they can be applied both creatively and wisely to address these challenges.

GETTING YOUR EXECUTIVE TEAM ON BOARD: HOW TO SELL CMDB TO YOUR ORGANIZATION

6

A few years ago, EMA conducted some research to see which variables most impacted the perceived dollar value of CMDB-related deployments. The analysis considered a variety of factors (e.g., company size, time in deployment, and executive commitment) and correlated them with perceived dollar value in making the CMDB a contributing part of IT.[1] Figures 6.1 through 6.3 tell a narrative that frankly surprised us, even though we knew that high-level executive buy-in was critical for CMDB initiatives.

Figures 6.1–6.3 provide a clear narrative with a clear winner. To get these data, we looked at 162 IT respondents in North America. The respondents were asked specifically to estimate dollar value contributions over the most recent twelve-month period without subtracting costs, in order to simplify the calculation for respondents.

---

[1] CMDB Systems and the Move to Federation, EMA, 2010.

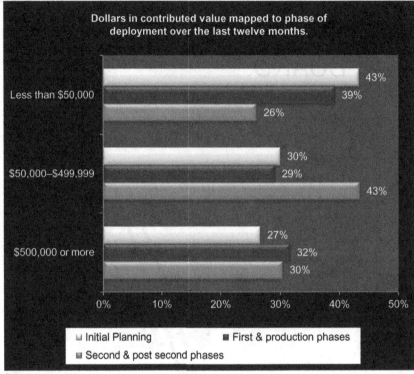

Sample size = 162

FIGURE 6.1

This figure indicates a disappointingly modest improvement between dollar values achieved based on **time in deployment**. While the top cluster—"less than $50,000 in value achieved in 12 months"—logically tiers to the "initial planning phase," then "first-phase production," then "second phase," the next two categories appear to level out. And in fact, there are no meaningful differences in high-end dollar value ($500,000 or more) based on time in deployment.

THE EXECUTIVE IMPERATIVE

The need for executive leadership was also echoed in numerous consulting engagements—putting a voice together with the data above. Here are just a few comments from clients:

- "The biggest risk is a lack of executive management visions. Our prior project failed because the CTO left during the project. There was no one to push the project forward. It was bad timing."
- "Our CIO and our CEO must be clear about the CMDB value and direction."

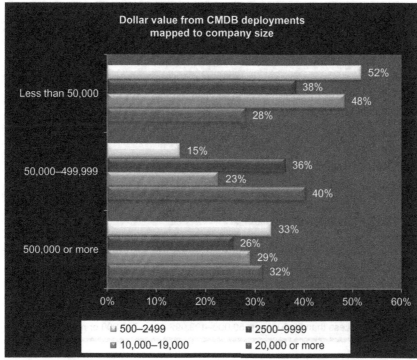

Dollar value from CMDB deployments mapped to company size

Sample size = 162

FIGURE 6.2

This figure points to **company size**—the most obvious determinant of absolute dollar value. Here, a pattern similar to Figure 6.1 emerges, with a clearer bias in "less than $50,000 in value," but company size makes surprisingly little difference once dollar value is higher. Some explanation might be found in the fact that large enterprises often have the most entrenched fiefdoms, and issues of politics and collaboration can be the most challenging there. On the other hand, progressive midtier enterprises and even smaller environments can skyrocket their CMDB Systems forward with good leadership.

From a consultant's assessment, we see the following perspectives:

Based on interviews, [conversations with] executives, and reviews of past successes, the single most important factor will be senior executive support of the project combined with a clear roadmap. The CMDB project must be sponsored and supported by the CIO. The key factors are:

- Providing clear vision and strategy for the CMDB. This will be especially important to the production staff that may be resistant to attempting a CMDB without a very clear value proposition coming from on high.
- Supporting CMDB policy in a "red action" environment when the expedient path would be to take less coordinated action. For example, we predict a strong push to "gather the data now and figure out how to maintain it later." This path would be disastrous for the CMDB efforts. But to avoid it will require clear management direction and prioritization.

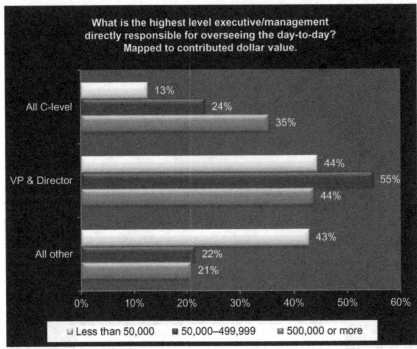

What is the highest level executive/management directly responsible for overseeing the day-to-day? Mapped to contributed dollar value.

All C-level	13% / 24% / 35%	
VP & Director	44% / 55% / 44%	
All other	43% / 22% / 21%	

Less than 50,000 ▪ 50,000–499,999 ▪ 500,000 or more

Sample size = 162

FIGURE 6.3

This figure looks at the highest level of **ongoing (day-to-day) executive commitment** as mapped to perceived dollar value of the CMDB System. In contrast to Figures 6.1 and 6.2, the data here stand out as strikingly consistent with expectation. Based on these research data, ongoing C-level commitment appears to be the single most significant factor in ensuring CMDB System success.

Note the "red action" situation, so common as an issue with CMDB System initiatives, a problem related to what one interviewee calls "the hamster scenario" later in this book, in which IT professionals keep spinning around in the same "hamster wheel" without taking the time to exhale and think about employing new processes and a better way of working. Both conditions will typically go unresolved without meaningful, top-down executive pressure.

STAKEHOLDER BUY-IN

Stakeholder buy-in across the company is probably the number one reason for getting your executive (or executives) firmly on board as soon as possible. The need for senior executive commitment is underscored by the fact that many CMDB System initiatives involve balancing enthusiasm with expectations across often territorial and sometimes competitive silos. The following example is all too typical. This excerpt is from a consulting report for a large financial organization where our consultant spoke with more than 25 stakeholders:

- Getting buy-in from everybody including LOBs outside of IT, especially around the areas of data ownership (e.g., retiring data stores and owning data), was the number one challenge. A key quote in this category was, "IT is territorial by nature, and our tech groups don't respect what others do. I only want to work on data that I own."

As it turned out, "getting strong executive support," with 15 votes, was top of a list that included a number of other criteria. The top half of the list of criteria deserves a look, both because it serves as a good reference in itself and because it helps to shade the need for executive leadership in CMDB context. The following are the top five concerns indicated by the 25 stakeholders, with the items strongly dependent on strong executive support in **boldface**:

1. **Strong support from a senior executive** (15 votes)
2. Getting the right level of requirements to understand value (13 votes)
3. **Getting sustained executive management support with a clear vision and no ambiguity.** (Several individuals cited examples of projects that started and stopped regularly on a quarterly basis.) (11 votes)
4. **Setting initial expectations correctly**, putting together a roadmap with short-term wins, and identifying the right pilot project. (11 votes)
5. **Getting funding (especially ongoing funding after the initial project finishes).** (This response included funding concerns about stretching an already busy staff, understanding the total cost of the project up front, and conducting initial risk and impact assessments.) (7 votes)

Another comment from a consultant at a different client engagement targets *culture*—since cultural factors, in their full humanity, are primary indicators of CMDB System success or failure.

> • The most significant challenge in adopting a CMDB will be cultural and management issues. More than 90% of the issues identified by interviewees focused on cultural and management areas (organizational follow-through, communicating the value proposition, etc.).

DISTRACTIONS, RESOURCES, AND COMMUNICATION

These are three areas in which strong and sustained executive buy-in is critical. Two of these themes—resources and communication—have been already touched upon in the quotes above. But each deserves a closer look in preparing for executive suite interactions.

Distractions: Too many concurrent IT initiatives will distract from, and may even derail, a CMDB System initiative. This in itself tends to require executive attention, as major IT projects usually have their priorities driven by the executive suite.

The following comments from a consulting report highlight the importance of focus, prioritization, and consistency from executive supporters—by showing that it is often lacking:

> • A common theme among those interviewed was that the "strategy" is much too focused on high-level initiatives. Currently, there are 16 major initiatives in place. And there appears to be little, if any, prioritization. There are two general issues with this approach. First, the initiatives should support the IT and CMDB strategies, but so many active projects may distract from going forward. The problems with this lack of prioritization are summed up in a quote from the interviews: "We have 16 nonprioritized, unfocused, broad-scope initiatives. How do we keep the CMDB project from being ignored? Without prioritization, IT simply works on the projects it wants to, and the difficult tasks never get addressed. We need to have clearer marching orders from the top." Another, possibly even more emphatic, comment was, "Projects just happen with no advanced warning." Needless to say, the lack of a clearly prioritized CMDB strategy initiative represents a significant risk factor for the CMDB project. It's also worth noting that 16 major initiatives are far too many; most midtier enterprises may have three to five simultaneous IT initiatives at the highest level.

Resources: Executive buy-in is essential if a CMDB initiative is ever to have a hope of *adequate resources* in terms of both funding and organizational/headcount support. Guidelines for these will be examined more closely in Chapter 10, but suffice it to say here that resources, like the CMDB System itself, will need to evolve and grow, and this requires an ongoing and substantive level of executive commitment. Moreover, even organizational models may sometimes have to change. None of this will happen without a firm executive hand.

Communication: Another critical factor to consider is how executive priorities are communicated. Needless to say, this is not all on your executives' shoulders—a lot will depend on you. But a planned venue for sharing executive priorities in support of the CMDB System rollout is critical, and this requires ongoing dialogue with relevant executives. Ideally, you should walk in with some ideas for a communications plan and then modify it based on executive perspectives. Even when the support is already there, failing to set up clear channels for communication can have negative consequences—as can be seen in the following consultant comments:

- Twenty-five percent of all interviewees said that strategy dissemination across IT was a problem. Strategic information is pushed down two levels. After that, it falls off.
- One theme that was echoed by several interviewees was, "Our executives need to be less reactive and more proactive with their communications."
- We recommend that senior management clearly establish ownership of the CMDB initiative with an early mandate to provide clarity and definition around what constitutes the CMDB System. This information should be published through internal communications channels and be available for review by management and staff on a regular basis.

A LESSON FROM THE FIELD

In one consulting engagement, the CIO of a major corporation supported a CMDB project and, somewhat grudgingly, agreed to the assessment our consultants were doing. However, he didn't see why he needed to be interviewed by us or why we were doing 30 interviews. We explained to the CIO that the interviews not only were necessary to paint a picture of the common practices, environment, and requirements but also helped to create a common understanding and facilitate clear communication about the project. Interviewing *him* was key to understanding his thinking about the project so it could be shared during the other interviews.

The CIO reluctantly agreed to participate, but commented, "I sent an email. People know why we are doing it and that it is important."

After conducting the 30 interviews, which provided more than sufficient data for us to make our recommendations, the CIO asked us to do 40 more. We explained that we had all the information we needed and that more interviews would only be redundant. It would also increase the cost of the assessment project by 40% and add weeks to the process of finalizing the report.

The CIO said he would happily wait the extra time and pay the extra cost because the interviews were helping everyone better understand the project, the process, and the benefits. He really wanted to get this right.

We conducted the additional interviews. Though they did not change our recommendations, these conversations further set the stage for success. By doing the interviews, the vision behind the CMDB initiative became more widely known and understood throughout the IT organization. Moreover, people felt like they had input to the process—and that gave them a sense of ownership and involvement.

REACHING YOUR EXECUTIVE(S): A FEW THOUGHTS ON "EXECUTIVE PERSPECTIVES"

In general, our research and dialogues with stakeholders have shown that executives are more inclined to support a well-thought-out CMDB System initiative than one might assume given the mix of bad press and day-to-day stress that many C- and VP-level executives face. The CMDB System addresses executive concerns about routinely running amok when changes are made by providing a coherent and credible approach to overcoming this and other problems—such as service availability, asset audit failures, loss of control in the move to cloud, and any number of other related instances.

- "Our CIO declared, 'I have no place I can look to see who's responsible when we find out we're having a problem.' Then he declared the CMDB into existence."
- "Overwhelmingly, [our IT staff is characterized as] smart, tactical people who excel at execution but fail at service-aware process. One of our executives commented, 'We have availability through raw, brute force. We need a system to help us move to the next step.'"

The good news is that data from multiple research projects over the last few years show that, compared with other IT professionals, CIOs have shown a stronger predilection for viewing CMDB-related initiatives *as important* and likely to bring value.[2]

This trend is reasonably consistent with other IT executives and midlevel managers, who fall in between rank-and-file stakeholders and CIOs in sustaining the CMDB faith. CIOs are also more likely to view CMDB deployments *as successful* than the rank-and-file.

There are many possible reasons for this bullishness. Probably the chief among them is the fact that the cross-domain value of the CMDB System can be threatening to domain-centric stakeholders, on one hand; while once stakeholder enthusiasm begins to rise, CMDB progress and the benefits it brings are bound to frustrate some, even if it delights others. After all, no one likes to feel left out of a good thing, and no one likes to feel martyred by a struggling initiative. The executive view should reflect the bigger picture in terms of scope, time, and value—a view that should also favor his or her support for your CMDB System.

Figure 6.4 shows very positive and consistent data from the research cited above regarding director-and-above-level views about the importance of the Information Technology Infrastructure Library in the face of trends like cloud and agile.[3] Executive commitment to more effective processes falls in line with their favored view of CMDBs. In fact, in our experience, it was often the advent of a process-aware CIO that sparked some of the more effective CMDB rollouts.

EXECUTIVES, CLOUD, AND OTHER TRENDS

Executives, particularly C-level executives, also tend to be more attentive to other trends rocking the status quo—providing both new opportunities and new challenges. The impacts of public and private cloud adoption are excellent examples of this—as shown in the following research findings[4]:

---

[2]These data are consistent across at least four recent EMA research projects, including Ecosystem Cloud and IT Service Management in the Age of Cloud and Agile, EMA and CXP both in 2013.
[3]Custom research between EMA and Axelos, Q4, 2013.
[4]EMA and CXP, op. cit.

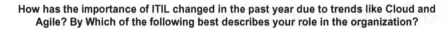

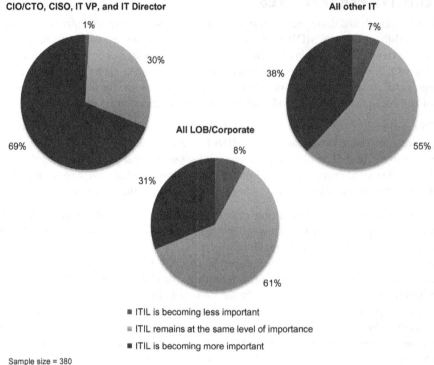

FIGURE 6.4

These data show that the executive community is nearly twice as likely as the rank-and-file IT community to see ITIL growing in importance in the face of trends like cloud and agile. Both attention to process and the need to move to a service-centric versus domain-centric organization continue to be escalating executive concerns.

- CIOs are nearly twice as likely as other IT professionals to see cloud as an opportunity for expanding service desk capabilities.
- CIOs are also more than twice as likely as other IT professionals to see cloud as shortening review change. And they are almost three times more likely to see accelerating attention to DevOps.
- IT professionals are twice as likely as CIOs to claim no impact from cloud.
- CIOs are twice as likely to say cloud drives "improved support for vendor governance" and "enhanced social media for IT efficiencies" as other IT professionals.

This isn't just a caffeinated love of what's "hot"—but a real awareness that cloud and other trends like mobile, user experience management, and the need to transform IT into a value-driven organization are impacting IT as never before. This awareness can be a significant advantage for a CMDB System initiative if these factors are taken into account as the plan is formulated.

FAILURES AND SUCCESSES CAN *BOTH* BE VALUABLE RESOURCES

While past successes can provide models for how to proceed with your own planning and executive dialogues, don't be afraid to also leverage past failures, especially if you can show that your plan builds on "lessons learned" and provides new and better options. In fact, our consulting experience shows that often the best CMDB initiatives come out of past failures. Some of our most successful clients have had not just one but two CMDB-related failures under their belts. These clients considered the CMDB valuable and wanted to implement one, and they understood just how difficult a deployment can be. Their initial failure helped them to be open-minded enough to more accurately assess their current environments and to understand the importance of culture and communication. In these organizations, the executive team was generally more open to new ideas about how to stay involved and express their commitment.

In other words, past failures can provide ripe environments for gaining the resources and commitments for success.

Two comments from a client engagement highlight two sides of value from the same coin: a past initiative that was in some respects both a *failure* and a *success*. First, the more positive perspective is as follows:

- "Disaster recovery is a great example of how to sell a big project. It is our most successful project. It shows how we can play to our CIO's concerns with risk."

Now, the more guarded perspective from a consultant's perspective, highlighting what to do differently, is as follows:

- The disaster recovery team gathered a complete list of applications and the mappings of those applications to the infrastructure. This task required two full-time headcount 16 months to accomplish. While it was successful at capturing a "snapshot" of the environment, there were no provisions made for automated refreshes of data. The reason for the manual approach to the application mapping is summed up by an interviewee: "There was no executive sponsorship for keeping original application mapping updated. We didn't know how to justify the ROI in terms of headcount savings, and yet, we still spend a lot of human resources just to collect this data. Now, we can come back and show better value with newer, more effective, and more automated application dependency mapping tools."

One of the subtexts of the discussion above is the question of risk—both in terms of the appeal of disaster/recovery and in terms of justifying investments for automation that might, in the end, have saved the company considerable dollars. If there is one salient negative (albeit understandable) quality of the mind-set within the executive suite, it is *aversion to risk*—especially when it involves shaking up the existing order for something less certain.

In one sad episode, a client cut its CMDB budget by several million dollars—as it struggled to venture forth into what executives perceived as still unfamiliar territory. At the same time, this company invested nearly 7 million dollars in far more "familiar" consulting fees for a corporate-wide IT audit. The net result was data that were useful once but obsolete as soon as the consultants left the building. For less than half the price, this same company could have had an automated, longer-term solution with far more multidimensional options for delivering benefits beyond audit compliance.

EXECUTIVE DIALOGUE ACROSS THE EIGHT-STEP LADDER

One of the many ways to approach the Eight-Step Ladder to CMDB System Success is to see it as a road map for executive dialogue. Certain stages will require direct executive dialogue and sharing of ideas. Other stages will deliver on the data gathering and insights you'll need to promote your ideas and drive the executive conversations forward.

A summary of where and how you might focus is indicated in Figure 6.5, which divides the steps into two categories: steps that require direct executive interaction (in bold) and steps that are more focused on fact-finding, data gathering, and overall preparation. (This doesn't mean that there is no need for executive dialogue in steps 2, 3, 5, and 6, but rather that they center more on assessments and planning as opposed to direct executive communication.)

MARGARET'S SERVICE-CENTRIC IT ASSET MANAGEMENT INITIATIVE: ONE HAPPY EXAMPLE OF HOW THE LADDER CAN HELP YOU ENGAGE THE EXECUTIVE SUITE

To help flesh out this eight-step process and see how executive dialogue can play a positive role, let's imagine that Margaret, who manages a small (10-person) cross-domain service management team, is driving a program for phase one deployment. Her CMDB System phase one priority is targeted at enabling a more effective and service-aware approach to asset management so that IT assets can be not only accounted for and managed for compliance but also optimized throughout their life cycles in support of service delivery. It's a tall order, and Margaret knows that she needs full executive-level support both to get the needed resources and to help ensure that stakeholder participation is as it should be.

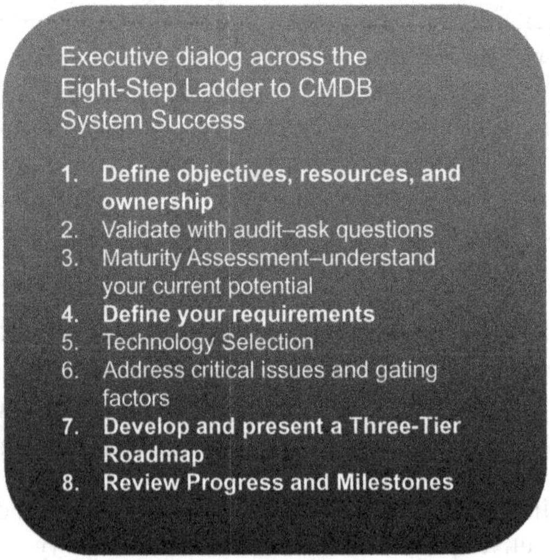

Executive dialog across the
Eight-Step Ladder to CMDB
System Success

1. **Define objectives, resources, and ownership**
2. Validate with audit–ask questions
3. Maturity Assessment–understand your current potential
4. **Define your requirements**
5. Technology Selection
6. Address critical issues and gating factors
7. **Develop and present a Three-Tier Roadmap**
8. **Review Progress and Milestones**

FIGURE 6.5

Executive communication is valuable throughout the Eight-Step Ladder to CMDB System Success but is most critical in steps 1, 4, 7, and 8. These conversations help to engage the executive community in your decision-making, promote better communication with stakeholders and the IT community at large, and solidify support as you go forward.

In **step one**, Margaret will need to develop an initial sketch of requirements and objectives and share these with the relevant executive before even beginning. To do this, she must tie the initiative to a requirement that she knows the executive cares about, such as a failed audit or poor asset utilization with resulting cost and service availability issues. Of course, it helps if her executive has already requested some action in this direction—even if it's not explicitly for a CMDB System. "Don't let this happen again!" can be enough to move forward if her plan is sound and credible.

In this case, Margaret's CIO has watched costs spin out of control and his credibility tailspin into the mud—trying to justify a picture of how he's governing IT when even he can't connect the dots to see the image of "what's out there" clearly. Margaret's plan for an ITAM-centric (IT Asset Management-centric) phase one CMDB System is a first step in climbing out of IT darkness, mandated in part by her own management, even if the details, for now, are her own.

She knows she has to follow the step one guidelines provided in Chapter 4:

Set objectives:

- Seek senior management input.
- Review history of previous IT implementations.
- Determine stakeholders (owners and users).
- Identify resources (financial and personnel) available for project.
- Set strategic not tactical objectives.
- Map technology to process to organization.
- "Big Vision, Baby Steps."

Address high-level issues, including the following:

- Cost and value up front
- Ongoing maintenance
- Timeframe awareness

Establish measurable metrics:

- At this stage, measurable metrics should center on the efficiency of the CMDB System rollout, with some higher-level insights into true business value that will be fleshed out later by climbing the Eight-Step Ladder.

The dialogue goes well. As it turns out, Margaret's CIO is foundation-level Information Technology Infrastructure Library (ITIL), so he doesn't need to be told, at least in theory, what a CMDB is. Margaret's commitment to building a federated CMDB System takes a little more explanation, but once the CIO can see it in terms of a Configuration Management System, he's fully on board. He makes positive suggestions for prioritizing the initial scope for phase one that Margaret is comfortable incorporating into her plan. He also supports her request: one additional full-time support person to work with her in gathering the data needed to evolve a more complete assessment. As far as any capital expenses, though, he's less certain. They already have a CMDB embedded in their service desk—won't that be enough? Margaret can't be sure yet, but she suspects that they'll also need to make some investments in better discovery and inventory tools.

With this basic level of support, Margaret is off to pursue **steps two** and **three**—asking questions, helping to build stakeholder involvement, and, in the end, performing a maturity assessment using the model provided in Chapter 9 of this book. She has also created a web page for both critical stakeholders and members of her executive team, which allows updates to be shared across the entire organization. Finally, Margaret and her one-person staff have, with management and executive support, organized workshops for CMDB-related dialogue that include relevant service desk and operations personnel. She is lucky that her CIO has made these meetings mandatory, not optional "if you can spare the time" meetings.

But Margaret knows that they still have to deliver. First of all, she needs to find a credible organizational phase one partner to work with her own group—the new *service management team,* which reports to the VP of operations. The service management team was created to support a more holistic, cross-domain approach to managing services in terms of day-to-day incidents and problems. Margaret's immediate manager saw real value for his organization in stepping up to the CIO's dilemma with a CMDB System. But he reports to the VP of operations who has even more cross-domain clout. So Margaret has to ask, which group is most likely to drive a cross-domain ITAM program effectively?

After considering some relevant research, she sees that the data suggest a fairly diverse list, though they are still led by operations (see Figure 6.6).[5] So after several conversations, Margaret finally persuades her manager to get his boss (the VP of operations) to "own" the initiative. Reviewing the list, she also solicits strong stakeholder support both for IT procurement of the infrastructure and for the service desk team for end points (PCs and mobile).

This research also gives Margaret some advance insight into the leading factors in strategic IT Asset Management (Figure 6.7). She makes sure that her executives appreciate the fact that "executive commitment" sits at number two in rank, missing number one on the list by only a single percentage point.

1. Operations as a whole
2. IT procurement
3. Enterprise procurement
4. Financial accounting across IT and the enterprise
5. Data center operations
6. Cross-domain Service Management Group
7. Service desk/ help desk
8. Service planning/ customer planning
9. Telecommunications
10. Financial planning within IT
11. NOC
12. Applications portfolio planning

FIGURE 6.6

Which organization is most likely to drive a cross-domain ITAM initiative effectively? While IT operations clearly won out, this list also highlights both the diversity of IT assets and the fractured nature of how they are managed in many organizations.

[5]EMA, 2011—also applies to Figure 6.7.

Sample size = 290

FIGURE 6.7

Not surprisingly, success factors for strategic, or cross-domain/service-aware, IT Asset Management map similarly to success factors for the CMDB System as a whole. In this case, however, the priorities are fairly close together, with only an 11% difference across the top six.

She uses the opportunity to get executive buy-in for parallel support of IT procurement, which requires an executive nudge, and the service desk, which is already happy to participate.

Margaret doesn't stop there. She knows that generic issues and those within her own organization are two different things. She uses the initial research data as a template to find out what's really concerning to the stakeholders as she talks with them. Canvassing 25 stakeholders across operations, procurement, and the service desk, Margaret and her assistant work from a well-thought-out list of questions and topics, which include the following:

- *Size of asset management team*
- *Identification of how asset management is conducted today*
- *Planned obsolescence*
- *Equipment upgrades/identification of equipment*
- *Maintenance of current lists*
- *Process to add server*
- *Approvals and justifications for addition of assets*
- *Load on equipment*
- *Which tools are in place?*
- *What is missing from the current approach?*

- *What pain does the customer experience from processes or lack of processes?*
- *What processes exist to deal with software asset management?*
- *What is the need for asset management?*

As she does her assessment, Margaret comes to the conclusion that her organization is currently at the *active operational* level of maturity but is seeking to move toward *proactive service-oriented* stage with the rollout of the CMDB System in phases one and two. She socializes this with her executive team members, both to get their agreement and to help them evaluate their IT organizational priorities going forward. This communication proves to be critical in further consolidating executive commitment and enthusiasm, and—in a most fortunate arrangement—Margaret's report is circulated across IT to everyone director level and above.

Margaret is now ready for **step four**—defining requirements. In dialogue with her executives, she finds that their top six priorities for ITAM as enabled by the CMDB System dovetail reasonably well with her own thoughts and those of many stakeholders—some of whom nevertheless have very personal or silo-driven priorities. Now that she's invested the time and effort in listening to stakeholders across her IT organization and documenting their concerns, socializing phase one and phase two priorities is less controversial, even if some stakeholders still feel left out. The list that Margaret comes up with is as follows:

1. *Reducing costs via effective software asset/license management*
2. *Justifying costs by measuring value*
3. *Supporting the move to virtualization and cloud*
4. *Improving the accuracy of inventory records*
5. *Managing service providers as integrated resources*
6. *Consolidating silo-based asset management into a single service-centric view*

These are very generalized objectives, not all of which can be honored in phase one, so Margaret and her assistant work hard to create a more granular set of metrics leveraging the guidelines in Chapter 10. Executive review is solicited for the final set of metrics so that executive expectations and priorities for phase one are more clearly aligned. Once this is achieved—after some back and forth—the list of objectives is sent to all relevant stakeholders, and a summary list is circulated across the entire IT organization.

Now, with firm executive support, Margaret gets a bigger team to work with—including an architect and a process expert. She also has a modest capital expense budget to invest in new discovery tools.

Step five: Technology selection begins. Ultimately, Margaret has to persuade her executive team to make three investments: a better inventory tool, an Application Discovery and Dependency Mapping tool that can be shared with operations for service impact and problem management, and a superior answer for software license management. This would stretch the dollar amount Margaret is allotted, and the budget remains fixed. So she finally decides to defer the investment in new software license management but has just enough to take advantage of a SaaS-based service in the interim.

Margaret's team is ready to go forward with **step six**—addressing critical issues for closing the post proof-of-concept gap. There, they dig down into documenting all the various data repositories, spreadsheets, and Visio drawings that will have to be assimilated into a cohesive set of assets and services over time. They also document more granular process changes that need to occur for IT to work more effectively in optimizing its hardware and software assets in phase one.

Margaret's team is now ready for **step seven**: in which she'll develop and socialize her three-tiered road map. The good news here is that the executive team has been on board right along. Margaret is no longer in the business of "selling" the value of what she's doing so much as engaging executive sentiment in tuning and optimizing the initiative. Their ongoing commitment now seems assured—at least for the next six months—and this means support for corralling those stakeholders who have either too little enthusiasm or too many expectations and helping to promote much needed process and cultural changes.

Needless to say, Margaret is pleased—and the initiative moves forward, even if she knows she and her team are also working within a time-sensitive landscape. If they did their homework correctly, they'll all be ready for positive executive interaction in **step eight**, when they intend to ask for an ongoing versus just a project-level commitment to the CMDB System as it evolves—making it a line item in the annual budget. This way, it can become an embedded part of the way the IT organization works, grows, and improves, much like a transit system in a city.

INTERVIEW WITH A US-BASED PROVIDER OF HEALTHCARE SERVICES

This Q&A was taken from an operations-oriented service impact initiative in which service modeling plays a role. However, it is not a conversation centered on a core CMDB. Nonetheless, it offers some excellent insights on how executive, organizational, and process issues can come into play and provides some useful takeaways on how to prepare IT stakeholders for cultural as well as technological change.[6]

Can You Describe Your Role Vis-à-Vis Your Overall Initiative?

"I joined this company about three years ago in part because I wanted to work in the healthcare vertical. My former CIO transferred around the same time, which made the transition easy.

"Our initiative targeted converged infrastructure management, including application performance management. Our CIO wanted me to assess the health of our infrastructure, and we wanted to move from a technology-centric, siloed organization to a service-based organization. Basically, we needed to achieve higher levels of business alignment and operational efficiency—to support business growth without increasing headcount or incurring additional IT costs.

"As a healthcare services provider, we provide claims processing and administration on a state-by-state basis as a kind of ASP (application service provider), and we also fully support more than 30 clinics throughout the United States. We have more than 400 full-time employees working within the United States, and then we also have about 300 offshore contractors to support our application development efforts."

Can You Say More About Your Application and Infrastructure Environment?

"Because much of our work involves government contracts, it's critical that our data are very secure in order to comply with HIPAA and other requirements. As a result, our infrastructure is largely a private versus public cloud.

"Over the last three years, we have moved toward a largely virtualized environment. We have more than 8000 virtual machines, with a very big storage footprint since we have to keep patient data forever. Right now, we are about 90% virtualized and our goal is to become 95% virtualized or better. We've also deployed a number of other application services, including MS Exchange, SharePoint, Web Services, and others.

"From an overall business application perspective, we're supporting two types of business models. For our clinics, we provide support for electronic medical records (EMR) as well as basic administration. Pretty much all healthcare information is electronic now, including doctors' charts and prescriptions—which saves a lot of paper. In those states where we're serving as a claims processing application service provider, we're deploying claims processing software, and we also provide substantial call center support."

What Was the Overall IT Environment Like when You First Joined This Healthcare Services Provider?

"To be honest, it was something of an eye-opener for me. I had prior experience working in companies where the IT organizations were very mature. This included both mature processes often with ITIL certification and a mature approach to engineering and toolsets. This gap in process awareness was one of the concerns of our CIO as well.

"When I arrived here, they were very siloed, and their toolsets reflected this. They had largely domain-focused tools. The processes were also very broken. The server team didn't talk to the network team, and the network team didn't talk to storage. So, incident and problem management best practices just weren't there. The people weren't trained to share information, and the toolsets they had couldn't support the cross-domain root cause. If you monitored storage, you didn't know or care about how your system might be affecting the server, so it was hard to get even a temporary fix, let alone an effective resolution of ongoing or recurring problems."

What Are Some of the Benefits You've Achieved from Your Initiative?

"We've seen high levels of availability (above 99.9%), strong savings on storage, and 60% lower costs overall. This includes a 50% reduction in our cabling footprint and 30% reduction in power costs. Overall, we're enjoying better than 60% [reduction in] alarms, a 70% reduction in trouble tickets, and a nearly 60% reduction in mean time to repair. About 40% more problems are now resolved by level 1. When it comes to supporting new application service requirements, we've reduced the time from two to four weeks to just one week or less."

What Have the Impacts of This Been on Your Organization?

"Organizationally, I've also been able to achieve new levels of efficiency by breaking down technology silos. When I started, we had more than 200 full-time employees just dedicated to operations tasks, and I've been able to reduce that number significantly. Right now, rather than having everyone broken up in separate domains, we are organized by process with cross-functional skills in each group. With executive support and commitment, we have a service operation team dedicated to maintenance and overall monitoring. We have a service delivery team dedicated to provisioning, capacity planning, and installation. This team also provides support for very complex problems and incidents. And we have a service design team—a small group of engineers that just do design and optimization of the infrastructure and provide technical consulting services."

What Advice Would You Give Someone Seeking to Lead a Similar Effort in IT Transformation Toward a More Cross-Domain, Service-Centric Organization?

"We are very pleased that we have been able to do this type of transformation—and do it at a true enterprise level. I've not seen it very often outside of some high-tech companies where the core culture is inherently more supportive. But for most IT enterprises, it's hard to do in part because of politics and job security [concerns].

"Of course, we did have some turnover, but I think we were ahead of the game because my direct reports and I initially took a hard look at the skill sets of the people who worked for them, and then we developed an engagement strategy. We had a workshop for six weeks on the IT transformation initiative. Each director would conduct his or her workshop and share directions and listen to each employee. We asked them to think about where their individual talents and passions might lie in the new organization—and that helped us a lot. Overall, we ended up with an enthusiastic, high-performing team.

"I've been through many reorganizations in the past decades, and most involving a big transformation are poorly communicated and shock the people who are going to experience change. This is always a negative. But if you have strong executive support and if you engage the people early on and tell them what you're planning and get their voices heard once the reorganization gets under way, the result is much more positive."

What Are Some of the Next Steps?

"We're starting to focus more aggressively now on service modeling with a common view of how our applications and systems are interconnected. We also have service delivery managers who serve as the liaison to the business and work actively with business stakeholders. They are resident in different states where we are providing claims processing services and help to communicate local requirements back to us at the data center.

"Right now, development is largely separate, so bringing greater attention to integrating development with Change Management and operations is another future step—probably further in the future."

⁶Interview with a midtier healthcare services company based in the United States using CA Technologies' Service Operations Insight.

SUMMARY TAKEAWAYS

Getting the executive team on board is critical to the success of your CMDB System initiative. Research bears this out—showing that more than *time in deployment*, *maturity of deployment*, and even *company size*, *ongoing C-level commitment* is the number one factor in bringing tangible CMDB-driven value. What we call the "executive imperative" can cut through stakeholder reluctance and siloed politics, as well as help to mitigate the impatience and frustration of wannabe stakeholders who feel left out of phase one objectives. Executive commitment is also essential for getting needed OpEx and CapEx resources—which can ideally lead toward ongoing support for the evolving CMDB System as a line item in the IT budget.

The good news is that the busy and often embattled IT executive suite tends to be significantly more bullish about CMDB and ITIL values than the general IT population—in large part because smart IT executives recognize the need for a more service-driven versus silo-conflicted organization. On the other hand, senior IT executives also tend to be risk-averse and will need to see solid plans for making investments that may appear to be either disruptive or of questionable value.

The best way to engage key executives is to follow the eight-step methodology proposed in Chapter 4, weaving in clearly defined milestones for dialogue, buy-in, and developing and retuning a communications plan. It's important to stress the fact that executives should express their support as part of the communications plan. If an executive supports the project in the silence of the office, does anyone know? Uncommunicated executive support is virtually no support at all, turning what might seem to be a victory into a nonevent.

As the project leader, do not be afraid to ask the executives for their active support. Be clear that research has shown that their commitment and involvement are keys to success and you need them to participate if they want a positive outcome. You can deliver the system and the benefits they want, but you cannot do it without their active involvement and support.

While we recommend ongoing interaction with executives, the four most critical steps in the ladder for your executive conversations are the following:

- *Step one—Define objectives, resources, and ownership.*
- *Step four—Define your requirements.*
- *Step seven—Develop and present a three-tier road map.*
- *Step eight—Review progress and milestones after phase one completion.*

CMDB SYSTEM USE CASES: CARVING OUT THE RIGHT PLACE TO START

7

Neither the CMDB System nor the CMDB is by itself a "use case." One of the surest ways to fail is to approach your initiative from that perspective. It would be the crude equivalent of buying a car without first getting a driver's license, or making travel plans, and then pretending that just having the car sitting in your garage will get you where you want to go.

Not only are the stakeholders and the processes different in each use case, but also the technological priorities will shift—sometimes dramatically—based on use-case needs. Figure 7.1 highlights the need to step back and assess unique stakeholder perspectives in order to set meaningful use-case priorities for a CMDB System. This isn't to say that you shouldn't plan for building and evolving the CMDB System, but how you start needs to be optimized to your own unique environment. In other words, there is no "generic" phase 1 answer, just as there is no "generic" IT organization, no "generic" business model, no "generic" CIO, and no "generic" operations team.

The goal in this chapter is to provide a multidimensional set of guidelines for selecting use-case priorities and performing necessary top-level assessments.

WHAT'S MOST POPULAR? WHAT'S MOST SUCCESSFUL?

Media, both mass and technological, often gets carried away with issues of popularity—whether it's a superstar singer or a new option for mobile applications—to the detriment of balanced insights into real-world priorities. Nonetheless, understanding what's being more broadly favored can sometimes

FIGURE 7.1

Take off the blinders with regard to CMDB System use cases! In this critical chapter, we'll examine how to optimize your CMDB System investment by using a use-case focus. This way, you can help shed light on parochial stakeholder blindness and see big picture values, without getting lost in the vast sea of options that a CMDB System can support.

shed light on value and relevance, especially if it's placed in context with other insights. It is in this spirit that we're sharing some insights into what's "hot" and "what's flying high" in CMDB-related use cases.

Figures 7.2 and 7.3 approach the question from three different angles. Figure 7.2 describes priorities for CMDB System use cases as taken from the 2013 EMA research,[1] while Figure 7.3 provides insights into what kinds of benefits succeeded in the past with a somewhat different menu of alternatives.[2] Looking at these two figures side by side will suggest some worthwhile departure points for diving deeper into use-case planning.

Looking at Figure 7.3 in greater detail, the following can be deduced:

- The number one value actually achieved is improved operational efficiencies—which cuts across ALL use cases. This underscores the role of the CMDB System as a broadly impactful enabler.
- The second big achievement in terms of monetary value is reduced downtime. This cuts across more effective Change Management, as well as service impact and performance use cases.
- Reduced costs for hardware and software assets come in third—and reflect the general popularity of the asset management use case as a place to start.
- Reduced mean time to repair (MTTR) due to improved Change Management is tied with these in value and correlates strongly with both OpEx efficiencies and reduced downtime.

---

[1] ITSM in the Age of Cloud and Agile, EMA and CXP, 2013.
[2] The CMDB/CMS: from Database to Federation, EMA, 2009.

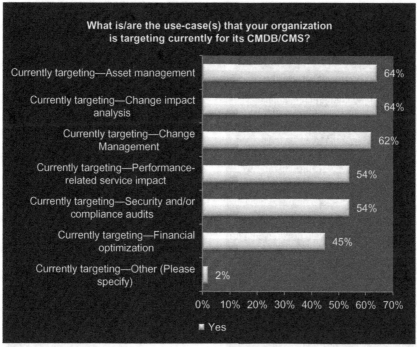

Sample size = 326, Valid cases = 326

FIGURE 7.2

Not surprisingly, asset management, change impact management, and change management lead in popularity among an IT Service Management-centric respondent base, often at the core of CMDB System adoption. However, it's important to note that performance-related service impact also plays a critical role, as does Security and Compliance. Financial optimization is in last place, as it represents an area where for the most part good analytics are still just emerging in the industry.

- Reduced MTTR by identifying the right person to fix a problem (CI owner) may sound less earthshaking than the above, but it is a core benefit in many CMDB-related initiatives. In fact, it inspired a new acronym in one client—"mean time to find someone (MTTFS)."
- More effective compliance audits are another standard value for CMDB System initiatives.
- Improved diagnostics are an area on the rise due to improvements in technology and the growing power of interrelating IT analytics with service modeling.
- Reduced costs for service-level agreement (SLA) violations are aligned with improved service availability.
- Reduced time to provision new applications is another area of CMDB-related benefit that's on the rise—as cloud, in particular, is demanding a more collaborative and dynamic handshake between development and operations.
- Disaster recovery is frequently aligned with CMDB System initiatives—and sometimes a precursor to them, as was seen in the last chapter.

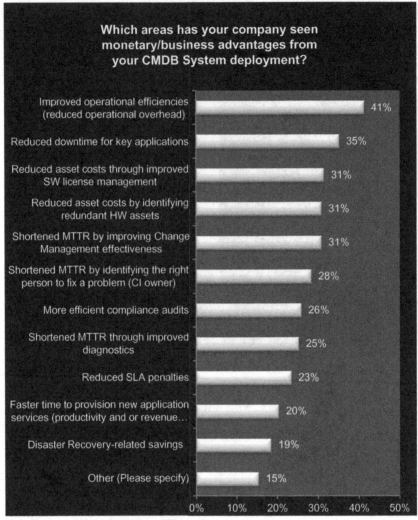

Sample size = 162, Valid cases = 162

FIGURE 7.3

This look back at 2009 is still largely relevant to where success is being achieved among CMDB-related initiatives and offers an interesting set of comparisons.

THE USE-CASE LANDSCAPE: A KALEIDOSCOPE OF VALUES

In this section, we'll examine the three leading use cases: *Change Impact Management and Change Automation, Asset Management and Financial Optimization,* and *Service Impact Management and Capacity Optimization.* Each use case will be examined for subsidiary use cases within it and will be discussed in terms of metrics for planning objectives, process considerations, issues, technology priorities, and documented benefits from actual deployments.

CHANGE IMPACT MANAGEMENT AND CHANGE AUTOMATION

Change Management is at the very heart of the CMDB System value set. Change Management includes impact analysis of changes to configuration items (CIs) and their associated services, as well as change automation for activating changes more effectively. These two use cases are very much connected. The most logical sequence to follow is to start with change impact and then proceed to change automation—in other words, get the visibility you need in place first and then automate. However, while this might not be bad as a general rule of thumb, it does not apply here. Little could be more counterproductive to successfully deploying a CMDB System than delaying automation, making it a last-phase effort. A better rule of thumb in this case would be to take a more pragmatic approach: begin with change impact management and automate whenever possible.

Why change impact management is at the heart of the CMDB System

You should also try to capitalize on the fact that change impact management helps provide a foundation for virtually all use cases here, while at the same time, it can be extended and enriched by them. For instance, change impact management can both inform on and profit from close ties to Service Impact Management as well as Capacity Optimization or conversely asset life cycle and license usage awareness. These are very fluid values in the real world, as, for instance, understanding how changes may impact service performance while leveraging a clear vision of service interdependencies for triage will both offer strong, proven benefits for CMDB Systems.

Across multiple client engagements, EMA consultants have estimated that as many as 60% of IT service disruptions may come from the impacts of changes made across the application infrastructure. A key to resolving critical performance issues is having both strong Change Management governance and a solid record of *how*, *by whom*, and *when* changes were made and *where* they might impact critical services. Planning changes for minimal service impact is also a value here and helps to empower another related use case—DevOps and life cycle application management.

Insights into capacity and CI utilization can also be invaluable in planning changes more effectively and in automating environments where optimizing capacity can be driven by both shifting business demands and impact on business outcomes.

Similarly, Asset Management and Financial Optimization can profit from being grounded in change impact management so that assets and their life cycle management requirements can be linked to IT services, and IT-related OpEx costs can be more tangibly linked to delivered services and their values.

Change automation

Change automation typically begins with workflow and often includes support from a Change Advisory Board (CAB). Beyond that, it can profit from direct ties to other types of automation such as release management automation (more commonly called "configuration automation") for actively making configuration changes to devices and runbook or IT Process Automation (ITPA) for closed-loop management of changes in response to incidents or planned requests. Often, these automation tools are combined with analytic capabilities to provide unique advantages in making more effective and consistent changes. With the move to virtualization, the ability to deliver changes in a more automated fashion with a clear eye to service impact is becoming a much-requested capability.

Some related use-case perspectives

Some subsidiary use cases of Change Impact Management and Change Automation include the following:

- *Governance and compliance:* Governance can extend to managing change to support smoother, more efficient, and less disruptive Change Management processes and also to support industry-related and other compliance-driven audits. Collectively, these can provide significant financial benefits including OpEx savings, superior service availability, and improved security and savings from penalty costs incurred when changes are made poorly. (Metrics for these will be discussed later in this chapter under the use-case *Security and Compliance.*)
- *Data center consolidation—mergers and acquisitions:* Planning new options for data center consolidation is definitely on the rise. Mergers and acquisitions often factor in as drivers for data center consolidation. The benefits here can similarly be striking as more effective Change Management can dramatically accelerate the time required for data center consolidation while also improving the accuracy and quality of the outcome.
- *The proverbial "move to cloud":* The stunning rise of virtualization and the persistent move to assimilate both internal and public cloud options make change impact management and effective change automation essential. This is definitely one area where trying for a "System of Relevance" as opposed to a "Single Source of Truth" will serve you well—as cloud is all about dynamic resources with many complex interdependencies in which "truth" in any absolute or static sense may never be an option, but where relevance is key. Cloud is, after all, the epitome of a universe that is neither "stable" nor "precise." Managing the impacts of change proactively and well is arguably the single most critical variant in optimizing public and private cloud investments.
- *Disaster recovery:* Disaster recovery initiatives may be an extension of data center consolidation or they may be independent. Automating change for disaster recovery is one of the more pervasive drivers for CMDB Systems by making DR more automated, consistent, and efficient.
- *Facilities management and green IT:* This use case requires dynamic insights into configuration and "performance"-related attributes for CIs both internal to IT (servers, switches, desktops, etc.) and external to traditional IT boundaries (facilities, power, etc.). Extending the CMDB System to support the IT and also the business infrastructure not only can produce significant dollar savings but also can promote a more prominent and respected role for IT as a whole.

The following sections provide multidimensional insights into selecting and planning an initiative for Change Impact Management and Change Automation. They include top-level discussions of

- metrics for planning, assessment, and promotion;
- relevant IT Infrastructure Library (ITIL) processes;
- technology priorities;
- examples of benefits from actual deployments.

Some high-level metrics for Change Impact Management and Change Automation

Getting started with any use case requires having some idea of what you hope to achieve. The following list is meant as a useful reference to help you to sketch out more specific Change Management values. In other words, it is a generalized list that refers to "changes" generically as opposed to changes applied to specific CIs. For instance, you may want to direct your Change Management initiative at desktops or servers in specific locations, at support for managing key application interdependencies, or at governing vendor-related changes for infrastructure-as-a-service options outside your immediate IT organization. It should be stressed, moreover, that this list of metrics is not meant to be complete, and as such, it might help you to think of other relevant metrics specific to your environment.

A good practice might be to combine ideas generated from the metrics list below with some of the more specific change impact management-related use cases previously described. The larger goal, for instance, might be to virtualize 60% of all servers by end of year nondisruptively or to deal with new data center issues from a merger or to create a specific plan for disaster recovery.

Once you begin to succeed in meeting well-defined and tangible objectives, they should help dramatically in gaining acceptance among both executives and stakeholders while also enabling you to assess your own progress in a meaningful and nondisruptive manner.

The bullets in Figure 7.4 are examples of common Change Management metrics or objectives in CMDB System deployments.

Process considerations

Many of the ITIL processes related to change impact management and to change automation have been discussed in Chapter 3. These include ITIL processes for the following:

* *Service Asset and Configuration Management (SACM)*—the process to assure that assets are properly controlled, available, effectively configured, and understood in terms of interdependencies.

* Reduction in number of unapproved changes detected
* Reduction in number of change collisions
* Reduction in number of failed changes and re-do's
* Reduction of changes made on service impact
* Reduced cycle time to review, approve, and implement changes
* Improved time efficiency to validate that changes made are non-service disruptive
* A decrease in documentation costs required to initiate changes and add new applications
* Number of changes that do not deliver expected results

FIGURE 7.4

These high-level metrics provide useful departure points for planning measurable objectives directed at Change Impact Management and Change Automation. It's important to keep in mind that these metrics should both support socializing the value of the CMDB System initiative among stakeholders and executives and provide you with useful guidelines to assess the direction, priorities, and impact of your phase 1 rollout.

- *Change management*—the process responsible for controlling the life cycle of all changes for minimal disruption. Some of the underlying questions included are as follows:
  - Who requested the change?
  - What is the reason for the change?
  - What is the return required from the change?
  - What are the risks involved in making the change?
  - What resources are required to deliver the change?
  - Who is responsible for the build, test, and implementation of the change?
  - What is the relationship between this change and other changes?
- *Capacity management*—the process responsible for ensuring effective capacity levels for IT services and their supporting infrastructure.
- *Release and deployment management*—the process for planning, scheduling, and controlling the build, test, and deployment of releases and for delivering new functionality required by the business while protecting the integrity of existing services.

Figure 7.5 provides a useful summary for envisioning how processes for change management, capacity management, configuration management and release management work together.

Some other relevant ITIL processes for Change Impact Management and Change Automation not discussed in Chapter 3 include the following[3]:

- *IT operations management*—the day-to-day management of IT services and their supporting infrastructures
- *IT service continuity management*—the process targeted at managing/minimizing risks that could impact IT services
- *Application management*—the process directed at managing applications throughout their life cycles
- *Continual service improvement*—the process directed at optimizing IT-to-business alignment by making improvements in IT services targeted at supporting current or shifting business requirements

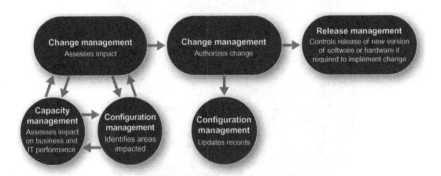

FIGURE 7.5

This synopsis of change management-related processes helps to summarize some of the interplay between change management, configuration management, capacity management, and release management. (This figure first appeared in Chapter 3 as these processes also help form the foundation of the CMDB System in general.)

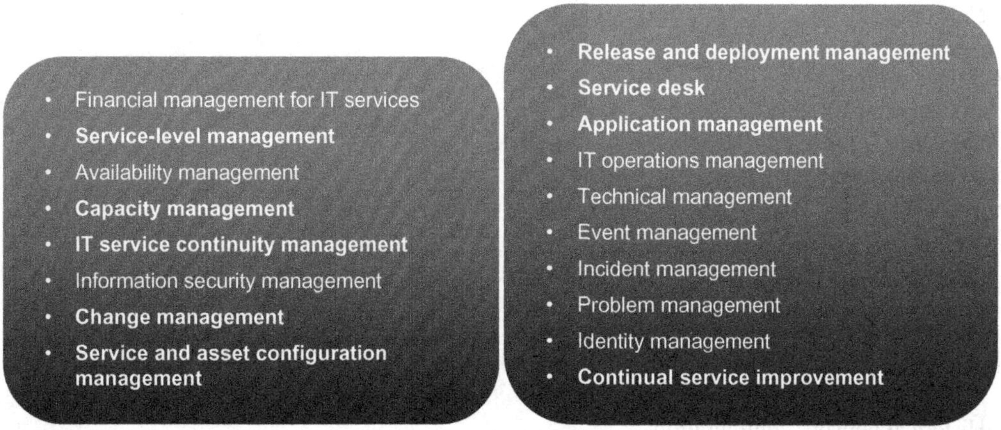

- Financial management for IT services
- **Service-level management**
- Availability management
- **Capacity management**
- **IT service continuity management**
- Information security management
- **Change management**
- **Service and asset configuration management**

- **Release and deployment management**
- **Service desk**
- **Application management**
- IT operations management
- Technical management
- Event management
- Incident management
- Problem management
- Identity management
- **Continual service improvement**

FIGURE 7.6

A list of ITIL processes with those most relevant to Change Impact Management and Change Automation highlighted **in bold**. Two of those in bold not discussed in this section are SLM, which will be discussed under Service Impact Management and Capacity Optimization, and service desk, which is a pervasive presence across all three major CMDB System use cases.

ITIL presents a cogent picture of how service processes interrelate in multidimensional ways. While this is not at all a complete list of ITIL processes related to Change Impact Management and Change Automation, it is a good place to start your thinking and planning.

Figure 7.6 highlights processes most relevant to Change Impact Management and Change Automation across the broader ITIL spectrum.

Formal change reviews versus automation

Another topic directly related to Change Impact Management and Change Automation is the role of the CAB—and formal, informal, and ultimately automated reviews. As discussed in Chapter 3, the critical point here is that ITIL rightly proposes a tiered approach to change approvals, starting at the top with the *business executive board* and going down to *standard, preauthorized changes*, where automation can come more actively into play. Defining your approval requirements, and evolving more routine changes into higher levels of automation, is a core part of creating an effective phase 1 plan for Change Impact Management and Change Automation.

Some technology considerations

Just as it's important to understand process-related objectives within your organization, it's also important to identify gaps in a toolset available for managing change. While it's impossible to honor every stakeholder's dream solution, it's important to find out what your organization feels is needed, where it's needed, and why. While Chapter 12 provides an in-depth look at toolset selection, some of the following highlights can also help focus the search for toolset gaps for change impact and change automation.

Does the system provide the following?

Change management histories
    Systems (successful versus unsuccessful changes)
    Desktops

        Network
        Applications
    CAB review support
    Desired/approved state
    Actual state
    Future/planned state
    Historical/past state
    Change impact analysis

Does the system integrate with

    service catalogs
    service impact analysis
        Real-time network configuration
        Historical network configuration
        Real-time system configuration
        Historical system configuration
        Real-time desktop configuration
        Historical desktop configuration
        Real-time storage configuration
        Historical storage configuration
        Real-time security-related configuration changes
        Historical security-related configuration changes
        Configuration changes across the real-time virtualized infrastructure
        Trending and optimization across virtualized infrastructure for service optimization

A look at Change Impact Management and Change Automation benefits

In scoping out a phase 1 initiative that targets Change Management, it's always good to know something about what other initiatives have achieved. The following quotes, once again taken from multiple IT organizations with CMDB System initiatives directed at Change Management, may help you to see the value in addressing this critical but often challenging phase 1 use case:

> - We use our CMDB in the change management process to create a snapshot after the change and validate that the change was made correctly.
> - In order to manage vMotion we got a solution that was dynamically current and automatic in modeling infrastructure and application interdependencies.
> - Our CMDB is doing a good job of supporting our migration toward a more fully virtualized infrastructure. It's also helping us to cut down on the number of management tools we need.
> - We make sure that every billing parameter—CPU, disk space, and other discovered data—is consistent with our records. We also use our CMDB when we want to plan a big change, a critical change; high impact, including the move to virtualization. We use it every time there's a critical change to plan. Instead of taking one week or more, it takes five minutes in the CMDB.

ASSET MANAGEMENT AND FINANCIAL OPTIMIZATION

Current research on *service-centric asset management* underscores the fact that IT organizations are looking for more cohesive approaches to managing assets throughout their life cycles.[4] This includes understanding how all assets (CapEx and OpEx) relate to the critical business of IT in provisioning and delivering services from a costs/value perspective. Both asset life cycle management on a component basis and effective Service-Aware Asset Management targeting interdependencies depend on a strong CMDB System foundation.

Asset management is often the first CMDB-related use case deployed, as most of its requirements are less time-sensitive than change or performance management. Providing added value for core technologies such as software asset management (SAM) and delivering meaningful insights into asset inventory and life cycle requirements can become strong CMDB-driven advantages.

Some specific use cases for asset management include the following:

- *Asset and inventory analysis:* Time and again, IT managers tell us something along the lines of "I vastly underestimated the problem of getting my arms around what I've got. I have multiple discovery systems, but still big holes, all used by different groups...." This most often comes up in broadly based asset management initiatives, but it is relevant to almost all follow-on initiatives described here.
- *Asset life cycle management:* Enabling clarity and visibility into asset interdependencies, including SLAs, maintenance windows, and service contracts, is central to managing assets effectively across their life cycles.
- *Compliance audits:* These can now be far more effectively automated and structured based on consistent policies once assets are mapped into a CMDB System.
- *Financial optimization:* True financial optimization can only occur once assets are understood in the context of the services they support from an interdependency perspective. Putting dollars-and-cents calculations into these interdependencies still remains something of a black art and to do it fully would require everything from advanced chargeback and demand profiling, to operational-efficiency-related metrics, to financial planning analytics and project planning data. However, there are some innovators beginning to chart these heretofore uncharted waters, primarily in the area of analytics. CMDB-driven asset management initiatives help to lay the foundation for capturing and analyzing these *cost and value metrics* in a substantive and contextually consistent way.

The following sections provide multidimensional insights into selecting and planning an Asset Management and Financial Optimization initiative. They include top-level discussions of

- metrics for planning, assessment, and promotion;
- relevant ITIL processes;
- technology priorities;
- examples of benefits from actual deployments.

---

[4]Next Generation Asset Management and IT Financial Analytics: Optimizing IT Value in a World of Change, EMA, 2014.

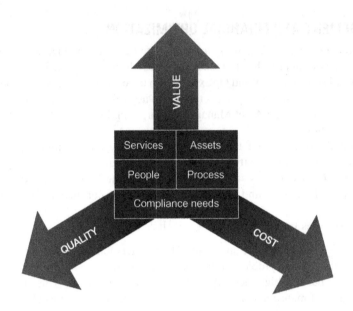

FIGURE 7.7

CMDB System-driven Asset Management and Financial Optimization, when combined with good analytics, can help to provide a backbone for running IT. This means assimilating data on IT CapEx and OpEx assets—from infrastructure to software, from applications to business services and the processes and people who manage them—in terms of both cost and contributions. The CMDB System can help to articulate, inform on, and ultimately automate the processes critical to running the business of IT more effectively.

Figure 7.7 provides a useful visual summary of how Asset Management and Financial Optimization require insights into quality, costs and value—across not only hardware and software investments, but IT services and staff-related efficiencies. The goal is to shift IT business planning away from viewing assets as static entities, to understanding them primarily as performing contributors to business value.

Metrics associated with Asset Management and Financial Optimization

As can be seen in Figure 7.8, some of the beginning parameters for planning CMDB-driven asset management deployments (e.g., *completeness of mapping of assets to owners*) target scope and initial CMDB System planning. In other words, they might be called project-related metrics. Others, such *as efficiencies in integrating or retiring assets*, can deliver strongly positive financial value and as such can play a clear role in socializing benefits that contribute to return on investment (ROI). The primary objective here, as in all use cases, should be to set metrics that can help you to plan your initiative and, then from these derive metrics, that can help to address critical business values and socialize your success.

Another way to plan for metrics and scope is to ask yourself the very basic question: What asset management capabilities are needed to satisfy your phase 1 priorities? This may sound like a silly question at first, but almost no IT organizations have a full or integrated view of how to manage all their assets cohesively in terms of value and cost. The list shown in Figure 7.9, though not meant to be complete, provides a good multiple-choice checklist from which to select your own priorities.

- Completeness of mapping of assets to owners
- Completeness of mapping of assets to customers
- Cost savings from improved compliance with SW/ licensing agreements
- Number of assets with a documented understanding of asset costs per service
- Documented improvements in the level of accuracy for costing out services to customers
- Faster ability to provision (existing/new) services to customers based on more informed insights on asset interdependencies
- Improved ability to integrate and retire new assets in terms of time efficiency, cost efficiency, and service impact (downtime)
- Number of assets mapped to appropriate security parameters
- Savings on license, support and maintenance contract costs on devices that no longer exist or need to be licensed supported.

FIGURE 7.8

This list of metrics is a useful starting point for planning asset-related initiatives for a CMDB System. These metrics are presented in general terms—so you should be clear whether the assets are desktops, servers, networked infrastructure, or application services.

Some process considerations

ITIL's process for *SACM* has already been addressed both in Chapter 3 and earlier in this chapter as a primary foundation for CMDB planning, deployment, and management. It captures the intersection of managing change and optimizing assets in context with service interdependencies.

ITIL's *financial management for IT services* addresses that complex mosaic of processes and interdependencies impacting IT service values and costs. ITIL describes this balance of value and cost as securing "an appropriate level of funding to design, develop, and deliver services that meet the strategy of the organization in a cost-effective manner."

The CMDB System can empower the delivery of critical insights into life cycle costs (CapEx and OpEx) associated with IT services and their component assets—often in conjunction with financial analytics, license management capabilities, project planning data, and/or usage-related data and analysis. This is yet another case where the versatility of associating logical and physical interdependencies for IT business services can in itself bring clarity and help to support more effective governance in furthering "the business of IT." For instance, having clear "service attribute" linkages between owners, consumers, vendor interdependencies, SLAs, usage data, business outcomes, and other attributes can help to automate a dynamic system for calculating both costs and value relevant to IT services.

1. Basic inventory for systems, desktops, and mobile devices

2. Inventory for all hardware devices including network, storage, and other devices

3. Software license management for systems and desktops

4. SW license for mobile devices

5. Lifecycle management of assets (from procurement through retirement) including change, configuration, and maintenance

6. Costing of assets based on usage and value:

    1. Desktops and end devices

    2. Applications and other services

7. Telecommunications expense management

8. Other vendor resource management

9. Enterprise assets beyond IT

10. Etc.

FIGURE 7.9

What is IT Asset Management in your organization? Phase 1 CMDB System deployments should leverage a big view of potential but key on initial priorities for delivering some tangible values within six months. This is definitely a balancing act between vision and pragmatic scope—all the more so because many IT organizations tend to take asset management for granted with a narrow domain focus, while true financial optimization of IT depends on building toward a bigger picture.

A CMDB is not ITAM

While an asset management database can easily become a part of a CMDB System, it is not in itself a CMDB. The two paragraphs below, taken from EMA consulting reports, underscore the need to separate the two.

A CMDB is not an asset management system per se. IT Asset Management (ITAM) is a great place to start, but practitioners must be careful not to fall into thinking that they must find, label, and document every asset in the IT infrastructure within the CMDB. Not only is this mentally overwhelming and nearly impossible to conceptualize, but also it is a nearly impossible task to realize. A CMDB does not contain every single asset in the infrastructure—it simply could not. Moreover, if it could, the amount of work required to keep that database current and definitive would be prohibitive.

The CMDB project must discover and bring CIs under Change Management control—not explode into an asset management exercise. There is a difference between assets and CIs.

Some technology considerations

Some of the key integrations and capabilities to consider in selecting technologies for Asset Management and Financial Optimization are

- asset inventory (integration);
- asset license/usage (integration);
- asset contract management (integration);
- financial or business-related analytics (integration);
- service catalog for indicating service costs and articulating asset values (integration);
- vendor management data (integration);
- support for desktops and mobile devices from a life cycle perspective;
- modeling to support document/contract affiliations, locations, owners and organizations, license-related Ts and Cs, and vendor/supplier SLAs and other cost-related data—as attributes for critical CIs;
- automation in support of asset-related compliance audits;
- integrations and analytics to support IT-to-enterprise planning and financial optimization.

Capabilities for change and configuration management as described in the first use case are also relevant considerations for life cycle asset management and optimization.

However, once again, please realize that eating the Asset Management and Financial Optimization elephant is best done one bite at a time. Do plan to build toward a more robust cross domain functionality with a longer-term vision but target phase 1 objectives based on realistic requirements. For instance, life cycle asset optimization for endpoints (desktops, mobile devices, etc.) represents a meaningful piece of the elephant in itself—and is more than enough to justify a useful set of phase 1 objectives.

A look at some Asset Management and Financial Optimization benefits

Here are two complementary voices to those cited in Chapter 2 to give just a few more indications of how and where Asset Management and Financial Optimization might bring value to you:

- We're doing asset management and using the system for validation of hosts to see if our applications are, in fact, residing where they're supposed to be. This will not only help us to optimize our infrastructure assets, but support us in lifecycle application planning. We're also doing integrated software asset management with our software vendor, but adding more details on who the user is, who owns the desktop, and who's paying for it.
- As a service provider, we use the CMDB internally to keep track of and account for devices in our hosting data centers for incident, problem management, and change management—especially for our more mature customers. We also use it for asset management in combination with a dedicated asset management product to keep track of all devices, purchase dates, extended warranties so that, for instance, we're not hosting a device if it's not under warranty. We run reports on a customer basis, which can help with everything from billing to infrastructure planning.

SERVICE IMPACT, PERFORMANCE, AND CAPACITY OPTIMIZATION

While CMDBs grew up with a focus more on process control than on performance management, both technology advances in CMDB System design and pressures from new trends, like cloud computing, are changing that substantially. These trends and the advances supporting them address the need for more dynamic currency in optimizing configuration interdependencies in the support of real-time service performance. Operational professionals, with concerns such as MTTR and mean time between failure, can benefit greatly from a "reconciled view of truth" including the impacts of change on performance—insights that ultimately depend on a dynamic CMDB System foundation.

We have included "capacity optimization" as part of the use case here. It draws from a convergence of performance, change, configuration, and usage insights, and as such, it could in theory belong to any of the three major use cases indicated above. However, given the increasingly dynamic trade-offs between performance impacts and capacity-related choices, the linkages are strongest in the service impact arena.

Some of the subordinate use cases here include the following:

- *A reconciled view of truth across many multiple sources:* By providing a more cohesive way of leveraging its many monitoring tools while also consolidating multiple redundant service-desk instances, one CMDB System initiative reduced MTTR by 70%, where downtime costs were estimated at $1 million a minute.
- *Reflexive insights into change and configuration for diagnostics:* Automating insights between configuration and change issues and performance issues to support real-time or proactive diagnostics is a core value of a service impact-oriented CMDB System.
- *Validation that a newly provisioned service is performing effectively (or not):* Once a service has been deployed, this type of reflexive system linking planned changes and performance gives a clear indication of its actual (versus projected) impact on the infrastructure and, even more critically, on the end-user experience.
- *Incident and problem management automation and governance:* When the CMDB System is combined with strong support for ITIL processes and other workflows, it can harden incident and problem management processes so that they become both more automated and more consistently followed.
- *Finding the owner:* Simply automating the process of finding individuals who "own" problematic CIs when service disruptions occur can in itself bring significant benefits. As noted in the caption for Figure 7.3, reducing "MTTFS" is well worth considering as a CMDB System metric. One client projected a savings of nearly $60,000 per year, just in OpEx service desk phone time applied to finding the right level 2 or 3 support.
- *Linking capacity and performance for diagnostics:* Having a clear, dynamic, and well-modeled set of insights into how capacity issues may have impacted a service performance problem can help immeasurably with both triage and resolution of the problem. This is especially true when a change causes capacity issues. Capacity issues often require that linkages to geography, CI owners, and other factors come together to paint a picture complete enough to resolve the problem.
- *Optimizing capacity for more effective service delivery:* Having a relevant and current model of how and where CI capacity trends are evolving can be invaluable in optimizing IT service values while minimizing costs. Capturing the linkages between performance, service interdependencies, configuration changes, and capacity dynamics is already producing impressive benefits in some CMDB System deployments. These insights often become all the more critical in the move to assimilate internal and external (public) cloud resources.
- *Business process and service-specific benefits*: Enjoying a more cohesive vision of "truth" can bring benefits as varied as the IT services themselves in terms of impact and relevance. Based on specific business-model objectives, these benefits may relate directly to processes as far ranging as loan processing, hospital management and admissions, and manufacturing line efficiencies, as just a few examples.

The following sections provide multidimensional insights into selecting and planning a Service Impact Management and Capacity Optimization. They include top-level discussions of

- metrics for planning, assessment, and promotion;
- relevant ITIL processes;
- technology priorities;
- examples of benefits from actual deployments.

Some Service Impact Management and Capacity Optimization-related metrics

Figure 7.10 provides a partial list of metric criteria, which are general in nature but suitable departure points for planning more specific phase 1 objectives, as well as future-phase objectives. As should be apparent, many of these metrics have the potential to show strong financial impact in terms of overall service quality and consistency.

Some process considerations

Service Impact Management and Capacity Optimization touch on a wide range of ITIL-defined processes as they require many disciplines to work together and share information cohesively, with an eye to true service awareness. Those highlighted in bold in Figure 7.11 are the most directly relevant to this use case.

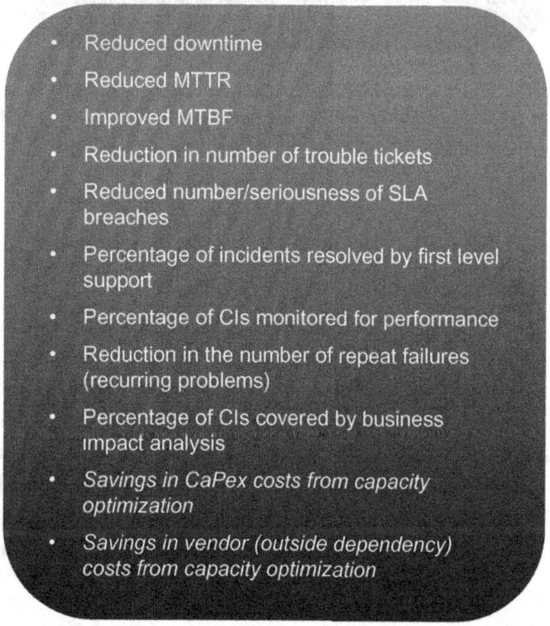

- Reduced downtime
- Reduced MTTR
- Improved MTBF
- Reduction in number of trouble tickets
- Reduced number/seriousness of SLA breaches
- Percentage of incidents resolved by first level support
- Percentage of CIs monitored for performance
- Reduction in the number of repeat failures (recurring problems)
- Percentage of CIs covered by business impact analysis
- *Savings in CaPex costs from capacity optimization*
- *Savings in vendor (outside dependency) costs from capacity optimization*

FIGURE 7.10

This list of generalized metrics targets benefits for Service Impact Management and Capacity Optimization.

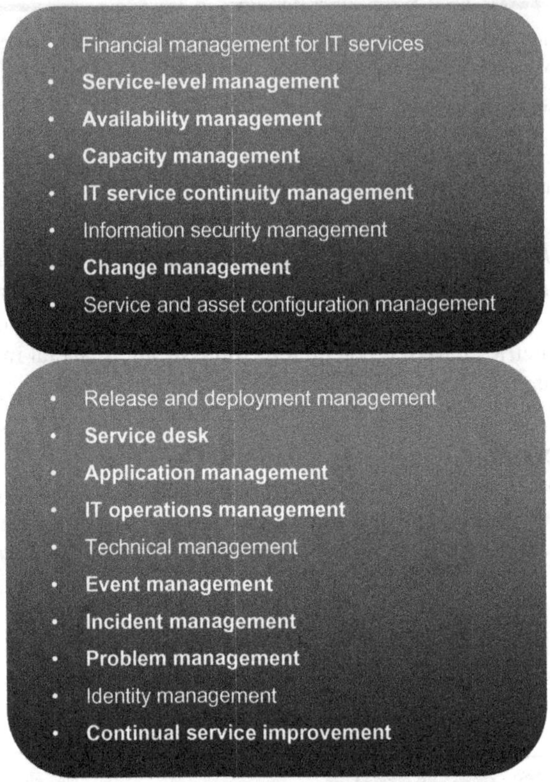

- Financial management for IT services
- **Service-level management**
- **Availability management**
- **Capacity management**
- **IT service continuity management**
- Information security management
- **Change management**
- Service and asset configuration management

- Release and deployment management
- **Service desk**
- **Application management**
- **IT operations management**
- Technical management
- **Event management**
- **Incident management**
- **Problem management**
- Identity management
- **Continual service improvement**

FIGURE 7.11

Some Process Considerations: because Service Impact Management and Capacity Optimization touch on so many different disciplines, they can be among the more challenging, as well as the most transformative, phase 1 directions for CMDB Systems.

Some of the key processes relevant to service impact and capacity optimization not yet described in this book are summarized briefly here:

- *Service-level management (SLM):* ITIL characterizes SLM as a process directly supportive of effective SLA negotiation—that includes insight into other relevant service management processes and operational level agreements so that SLAs are both meaningful and enforceable.[5] Note that this scope includes both internal and external (telecommunications, cloud service provider, etc.) interdependencies. "Operational-level agreements" help to codify how the IT organization will deliver on SLAs committed to its consumers. SLAs should not be confused with key performance indicators, such as CPU utilization, which provide useful metrics for optimizing performance, but which are inappropriate for formalized, negotiated commitments to external consumers.[6]

---

[5] Axelos, op. cit.
[6] More insight into SLM can be found in "Foundations of Service Level Management," by Rick Sturm, Wayne Morris, and Mary Jander, Sams, 2000.

- *Availability management:* ITIL's definition of availability management centers on meeting both present and future customer requirements in the ongoing delivery of IT services. The inclusion of "present" and "future" requirements makes this a much more proactive concern, hence, one more closely aligned with CMDB-related benefits and values.
- *IT service continuity management:* Here, ITIL presents a process relevant to availability management and SLM that targets potential problems that could negatively impact IT services and potential business outcomes. ITIL also makes the connection between IT service continuity management and business continuity management—an increasingly critical link in the growing list of verticals where IT services are not only redefining business operations but also enabling new business models.
- *Application management*: As already referenced, this ITIL process is focused on managing applications throughout their life cycle—underscoring an often neglected link between ITIL processes and the growing importance of DevOps.
- *Event management*: ITIL also takes a life cycle approach to event management—from initial alert through correction and validation. Insight into service interdependencies can be a significant plus in optimizing event management and minimizing event saturation.
- *Incident Management:* ITIL's focus for its incident management process is the timely restoration of IT services in order to minimize business disruptions. Although incident management has been historically centered in the service desk, it often requires a handshake with more operations-centric event management, availability management, and application management—especially in incidents that are unplanned and become "problems" impacting service performance.
- *Problem management:* ITIL views problem management as a more strategic discipline than the name might suggest at first blush. ITIL's problem management process proactively addresses root causes for problems so that incidents don't occur. Or, put in acronymic terms, if incident management is about mean time to repair (MTTR), problem management is about the more strategic requirement for minimizing mean time between failures (MTBF). The added insights and context that a CMDB System can provide help to make it a potentially a huge advantage here—especially when change, performance, and capacity issues come together in persistent and/or perplexing ways.

Some technology considerations

When looking at Service Impact Management and Capacity Optimization for service delivery, domain breadth becomes increasingly important. Below is a partial list of things to consider in terms of both domains and interdependencies as your CMDB System evolves:

Domains
Network
Network topology
Network configuration
Systems
Systems configuration
Virtual systems
Virtual cross domain
Mainframe
Mainframe configuration

Desktop
Mobile
Web applications
Web 2.0 applications
Third-party packaged applications
Custom applications
SOA applications
Browsers
Storage
Storage configuration
Database
Database configuration

Interdependencies
Infrastructure to infrastructure
Infrastructure to application
Application to application (application ecosystem)
Application component to application component (Web 2.0 application ecosystem)
n-tier application interdependencies

Relevant integrated analytics include predictive trending, data mining, correlation, and anomaly detection. In terms of automation, integration with ITPA, or runbook, can also deliver critical benefits. Finally, in terms of reports or dashboards for constituencies outside of IT, online Operations and Customer or User Experience support can also provide added value for the service impact management use case.

Benefits: A few perspectives
In large part, because these benefits are typically generated from a more "real-time CMDB," many of these respondents refer to a BSM system or a "service model" linked to their core "process-centric" CMDB. While this is not universally true, it reinforces the growing relevance of the design (shown in Figures 3.11 and 3.13) in which service modeling becomes the spine for the broader CMDB System. These service-impact benefits also underscore both the service impact management and the capacity optimization components of this use case:

- We track ATMs to see if they are in-service, out-of-service, or if their status is 'unknown.' We can also monitor and alert if the ATMs are out of cash. For just under three months, our ATM availability has trended dramatically upwards—an increase of roughly 60%. Down the road, I am looking for our BSM service model to become a point of reconciliation across multiple CMDB investments.
- We have to perform appropriate performance and capacity analysis—both to save money and to prevent any break of service level agreement commitments. Capacity analytics in conjunction with our CMS play a major role—to identify existing gaps such as over- and under-utilization of the infrastructure. We can then make appropriate recommendations and formulate some migration plans. This includes estimating the potential impact of planned changes as far as twelve to twenty months out.

> • Because our BSM System offers solid capabilities for service modeling, we can interrogate any of the areas in service management by attributes or attribute combinations in our service model, such as location, business service, or business service component. And through the service model we can interrogate relevant incidents, problems, changes, service requests, unavailability records, and our CMDB.

TWO ADDITIONAL USE CASES: SECURITY/COMPLIANCE AND DEVOPS

Security/compliance and DevOps pose some similar and yet very different challenges as can be seen in the sections below. These use cases can also build heavily on the gains from the other use cases described above such as change impact management, asset management, and service impact management. Nonetheless, DevOps in particular may be a prime driver for a phase 1 CMDB System initiative in some environments where business requirements dictate a unified view of Change Management and development-related automation.

SECURITY/COMPLIANCE

It should be no surprise that CMDB System initiatives can deliver strong value in terms of improved Security and Compliance-related governance. However, given the generally different cultural and political environments separating the security operations center from the broader community focusing on service management, this "use case" usually provides added benefits to *other* drivers, such as managing changes or life cycle governance for assets. Security/compliance can deliver critical additional potential benefits as reflected in the list of metrics in Figure 7.12.

- Percent of CIs auditable through automation (via policy, gold standard comparison, etc.)
- Percent of CIs compliant with policies/standards—more efficient SOX, HIPAA
- Reduction of incidents/problems specifically caused by noncompliant CIs
- Reduced time to perform audits for compliance
- Improved quality/effectiveness of audits for compliance
- Number of changes backed out of as a result of security issues

FIGURE 7.12

Security and governance can be a strong way to show benefits for CMDB System deployments, although it is rarely a separate use case in and of itself.

DevOps

The situation with the development community, and hence DevOps, is similar to security from a cultural perspective. However, DevOps has nonetheless recently received significant attention in a growing number of CMDB System deployments. The reasons for this are probably self-evident given the current buzz around "agile" and the pressures on IT organizations to deliver new application services and application enhancements with dramatically increasing frequency. While many of these clearly do not warrant proactive CMDB or CAB attention, their cumulative impact needs to be understood and assessed.

The following excerpts show a few of the issues relevant to DevOps that surround CMDB System deployments. The first two are issues-oriented conversations taken from client engagements. The third set of quotes includes comments taken from multiple environments in order to highlight CMDB-related DevOps benefits.

Conversation #1: DevOps as a driver

- Several significant application development issues were identified during the interviews. While the discussions centered on CMDB, 19% of the interviewees mentioned application development issues in their comments. These discussions revolved around the topics of testing and monitoring.
- We need QA and Test to play a role in Configuration Management up front. We need to understand application mapping and have better communications across the broader organization.
- Another notable topic was the inability of the development and QA groups to adequately test the impact of their applications on production. These result in 50 to 60 opened tickets, mostly around configuration issues with the network and servers.

Conversation #2: A cultural divide

- Developers do not understand the dependencies between all the services in the enterprise, but they need to.
- Development is very much done in an IT vacuum with no thought of the big picture.
- All our applications development practices are very reactive to process and data.
- We need to understand the service impact of 200 developers, especially with testing and production releases.

Conversation #3: DevOps benefits from multiple perspectives

- We have a complete approach to application lifecycle management. We leverage the system both for small adjustments in application requirements and for full-bore application deployments. By having both pre-production and production in the CMDB System, we can easily prioritize issues so we know when the impact is, for instance, going to hit many of our customers versus when none of our external customers will be impacted.
- Our system provided Development with a clear view of what their solutions would look like in production—they used the same monitoring in pre-production to test out the resilience of their solution. We're an aggressively agile shop with much more frequent releases than in the past.

SUMMARY TAKEAWAYS

This is arguably the most important chapter in this book. However, it can be summarized at the highest level with a single statement: "Let use cases drive your CMDB System, not vice versa." In other words, don't build a CMDB to end world hunger and then wait to hear the results on the evening news. Select a use case that's an optimal fit for your environment as a phase 1 objective and build from there. This is true even if the CMDB System, like analytics, is a modular investment that can and should natively expand in value once a solid core foundation is in place.

The major uses cases outlined in this chapter are

- Change Impact Management and Change Automation,
- Asset Management and Financial Optimization,
- Service Impact Management and Capacity Optimization.

Each of these can support a broad subset of use cases, and benefits often cross over from one use case to the next. For instance, there are many linkages between change impact management and service impact management, between asset management and change automation, and between financial optimization and capacity optimization. So while the CMDB System is indeed multipurpose and modular in how it evolves, proceeding with attention to effective *metrics*, *processes*, *issues*, and *technology requirements* demands a clear understanding of use-case objectives throughout.

Two other use cases were also addressed in this chapter: security/compliance and DevOps. Currently, security/compliance is largely valuable in demonstrating ancillary benefits for a phase 1 initiative driven by other use cases, such as change impact and asset management. DevOps, in contrast, is heating up in immediacy of value. In the past, DevOps has faced a similar cultural divide to that of operations and security—as application development has traditionally been indifferent to processes, technologies, and values coming from the service desk and operations. However, this is beginning to change—as should be evident through some of the interviews and comments throughout this book.

MAKING YOUR INITIAL ASSESSMENT WORK

8

Up to this point, this book has focused on critical background insights needed to address almost every rung of the Eight-Step Ladder to CMDB System Success. We've looked at what a CMDB System is and what it can be technologically. We've addressed process requirements with an introduction to the IT Infrastructure Library (ITIL). We've examined relevant ongoing trends—such as cloud, agile, and the changing culture of IT—that can both challenge and provide opportunities for a CMDB System deployment. We've discussed the whys, wherefores, and hows of getting your executive suite involved in and supportive of your CMDB effort. In Chapter 7, we presented use-case models to help you lay out a foundation for your CMDB System initiative—in phase one and beyond.

Now, we're ready to pick up where all those ideas leave off—as this chapter provides the groundwork for addressing step two (*technology, process, and organizational assessment*) and sets the stage for step three (*evolutionary assessment*) and step four (*defining requirements*). Many of the issues examined here—from data ownership to toolset sprawl to communication, culture, and process—may resurface even after you've formulated your plan and selected your technology with a proof of concept, only at a more granular level. Indeed, the demons in your IT landscape (assuming you are among the 99% that have them) won't magically disappear once you've identified them. But your relationship to them will change as you progress with your CMDB System initiative through dialog, process evolution, and, in many instances, actual organizational transformation toward a more service-aware, cross siloed model.

WHOM SHOULD YOU TALK TO AND WHAT SHOULD YOU ASK THEM?

Now, it's time to begin an intense period of dialogue across a wide range of skill sets, managerial levels, and core stakeholders. (These may change and evolve as you adjust your plan.) Generally, these dialogues will take place via a series of structured interviews. When our consultants interview IT managers and other professionals in a company, we often aim for 20 or more interviews. On several occasions, we have been asked to do as many as 40 interviews. Whether you are working by yourself or with a team, having a series of well-targeted initial conversations will provide a view of the current state of your operations.

The direction and success of your CMDB System in phase one and beyond will depend in large part on soliciting the right dialogues early on and using the conversations to develop a strategy that capitalizes on relevance as well as enthusiasm—instead of trying to please everyone.

The specific people you will want to talk to will be different for each organization. Figure 8.1 provides a useful summary of skill sets based on past research targeting IT respondents involved in CMDB Systems.[1] As you can see, the range is relatively broad, and in most initiatives, this is necessary. Your dialogues should include not only core team members but also stakeholders who represent critical data inputs, management, service desk and service management, and critical phase one consumers.

Here is an actual sampling of some of the executive management, IT management, and IT staff roles that we typically include in an interview process:

- Executive sponsor/CIO
- Line of business executive(s)
- Director of IT operations
- IT functional area managers (desktops, servers, network, service desk, etc.)
- Enterprise IT architect
- Development manager
- IT process managers (incident, problem, configuration, change, etc.)
- IT team leads (storage, Unix servers, security, etc.)

Once you've identified your full list of people to interview, here are a few guidelines for conducting those dialogues:

- We recommend that you start each interview with a brief CMDB overview. This is particularly important for those who are new to CMDB as it puts the rest of the conversation in context.
- Ask each person to bring 2-8 detailed requirements to the meeting. Guide the conversation around these requirements to get the specific information you need.
- During the discussion, the person being interviewed should focus on his or her business needs as a stakeholder or consumer (e.g., process requirements and visualization) and the interviewer should focus on the CMDB technology (e.g., integration and systems of record).
- Include *all* requirements requested. Remember that it is just as important to define what the CMDB *won't* contain as it is to define what it will. Prioritization of requirements will come later.

---

[1] The CMDB/CMS: from Database to Federation, EMA, 2009.

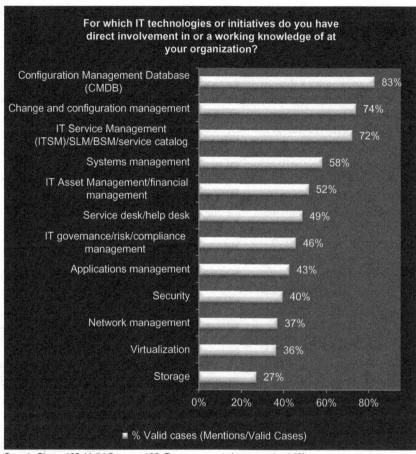

For which IT technologies or initiatives do you have direct involvement in or a working knowledge of at your organization?

Configuration Management Database (CMDB)	83%
Change and configuration management	74%
IT Service Management (ITSM)/SLM/BSM/service catalog	72%
Systems management	58%
IT Asset Management/financial management	52%
Service desk/help desk	49%
IT governance/risk/compliance management	46%
Applications management	43%
Security	40%
Network management	37%
Virtualization	36%
Storage	27%

■ % Valid cases (Mentions/Valid Cases)

Sample Size = 162, Valid Cases = 162; Responses not shown received 0%

FIGURE 8.1

Just whom you should talk to in doing your technology, process, and organizational assessment will vary based on your individual environment and needs. This figure provides a sample of relevant CMDB System skill sets based on past research.

TIPS FROM THE TRENCHES

- One-on-one interviews work best.
- Provide some added context for those who are new to CMDB.
- Technologists can be hostile if they think you're taking their tools away.
- Remind the interviewee that this is not a quiz.
- Listen well and don't criticize or challenge—you are asking for an opinion. No matter how unrealistic some opinions may seem, they still validly represent that person's point of view.
- Guide the conversation to get the detailed information you need.
- Grassroots support is critical—be honest, underpromise, and overdeliver.
- Don't get bogged down in the details—follow-up may be needed to dig deeper.

Our consultants have developed a questionnaire to help guide the discussion when conducting interviews with key CMDB project stakeholders. This questionnaire covers five key topic areas: *identification of detailed requirements, visualization (reporting), interdomain (technology and process), IT architecture, and system of record (SOR).* Here are some sample questions from a detailed requirements questionnaire:

- What key performance metrics do you use to monitor performance of this requirement in meeting the business needs? (A "requirement" in this context might be anything from patch management on a PC to introducing a major new version of a customer facing application. This will, of course, depend on who the interviewee is in terms of role in the organization. As should be apparent, some of the more strategic requirements will carry with them many smaller requirement dependencies that will also need to be documented.)
- What data are needed to meet this requirement? Where are they stored? Who owns them?
- What sort of visualization (reporting) is needed to meet this requirement?
- Do you have requirements to share data with other technology domains and IT processes?
- Overall, which components of the IT infrastructure do you consider most critical, based on change impact and service delivery?
- What performance and scalability requirements does your department have?
- Which other groups gather or keep this same management data? Why? Are the data gathered manually or through automated means?

WHAT ARE YOU SOLVING FOR?

Asking the question "What are you solving for?" brings us back to Chapter 7, with its discussion of use cases and associated metrics, as well as process priorities, relevant technology options, and benefits. That chapter is an excellent way of grounding *you* in developing and socializing an initial plan. But what happens to the road map after you have your 20 or more conversations?

Figure 8.2 is a modest example of what might be called "use-case sprawl" in a real-world consulting engagement. As you see, there was a clear focus on asset and Change Management with some technical requirements like application dependency mapping thrown in. "Enterprise view" is directed at a cohesive set of insights suitable for top-down management roles; it is also a way to drill down into insights and needs to unite stakeholders around managing change and resolving issues.

Nevertheless, Figure 8.2 still reflects a variety of key high-level priorities, not all of which can get full phase one attention. In cases like this, it will be up to you and your team to make the critical calls on what to do first and why, based on need, readiness, executive support, and "enthusiasm." When thinking about generating "enthusiasm," consider how Tom Sawyer got his friends to willingly engage in painting the fence for him. Stakeholders need to "give" in order to "get" in a CMDB System—for example, some stakeholders might be clamoring for new reports and analysis, which can pave the way for them to willingly, and even happily, commit to support superior data inputs to the system.

Figure 8.3 paints an even more complex picture of use-case options. In this example, while *asset management* remains important, there is a strong rise in *incident management,* and *monitoring* requirements make an appearance as well. (In another, yet more recent, deployment, monitoring support was even more dominant, reflecting a growing trend.) Here, *application dependency mapping* is even more critical. Other areas to note in this list are *portfolio management* (for planning and optimizing applications), *virtualization,* and role-specific needs such as *HR and finance* and *planning.*

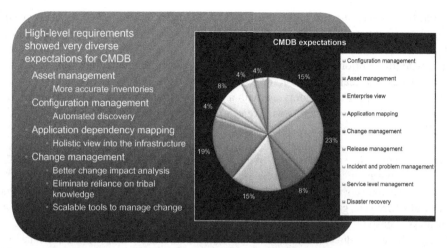

FIGURE 8.2

This shows a modest but typical "use-case sprawl" in a real-world CMDB System deployment. Needless to say, not all potential stakeholders' expectations can be met in phase one. Optimizing a plan once expectations are defined is one of the chief catalysts for CMDB success.

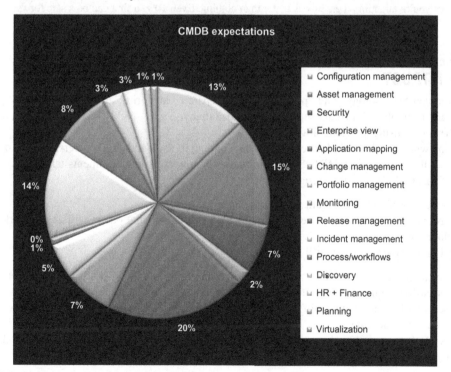

FIGURE 8.3

High-level requirements in this consulting engagement reflect even more diverse expectations. Nevertheless, knowing the priorities of both your stakeholders and your CMDB System consumers is critical in establishing the right balance for a phase one plan; it also helps the stage for next phase steps and benefits.

As should be obvious, the use cases in Figures 8.2 and 8.3 are not all of the same weight or a purely logical set of options. For instance, "retiring assets" is logically a subset of asset management. However, these requirement priorities describe what key stakeholders most want from the CMDB System. Knowing these priorities before finalizing a plan, selecting technology, and actual deploying the CMDB provides a critical foundation for going forward.

The following excerpt from an interview with a global air transportation company helps to put this idea, in perspective. The answer here was given in response to the question, *What advice would you give to CMDB System deployments going forward?*[2]

- I would propose a few key questions: 'What's your big picture?' 'Who's your audience?' 'What do you want to do with the data?'
- Look at what you've got currently and try to see how far you can go with what you have and what and where your gaps are. But also be creative about looking for new tools and solutions to help you move forward.
- Once you have your direction, you should put blinders on and attack one thing at a time. You have to think about everything unfortunately, but focus on just one use case. This gives you a track record of getting things done so you can build on your successes.
- Many people get caught up with the idea that they can have 100%—100% of the problems and 100% of the data with 100% accuracy. That just won't happen. If you can get 80% of the way for what you're targeting, then 80% is better than nothing. Even 10% at first can be a step forward!

TOOLSET ISSUES: SPRAWL, REDUNDANCY, POSSESSIVENESS, AND MISTRUST

The notion that "technology" and "people" are two separate categories, as the conventional "people, process, and technology" formula suggests, is an idea that you will quickly dismiss once you actually talk to the people using the technology.

Nothing will unearth the darker sentiments surrounding toolset (and data) ownership more dramatically than a thoroughgoing CMDB System initiative. Below are some comments taken from a cross section of past CMDB consulting engagements:

- We are territorial and don't want to replace our tools.
- We have issues with toolset ownership. There is no confidence that others will do the work. So, you do it yourself.
- Only I know how to do it; you'll mess it up.

To be clear, these quotes are taken from three separate engagements. In other words, toolset possessiveness is hardly unique or peculiar to outlier IT environments. Similar issues apply to data ownership, as we'll see shortly. The relationship between a preferred tool and its owner in IT is rarely casual and is often seen as job-defining.

Most CMDB System initiatives seek to optimize existing toolsets through reconciliation and prioritization by asking, *Which is the best source for what?* Merely posing this question can become a threat,

---

[2]Interview with a large global transportation company based in the United Sates using HP's Universal CMDB and Universal Discovery.

whether real or perceived, to those who feel their tool is sacrosanct and don't want anyone else to have any insights into how they do their job.

In contrast, one of the larger values of a CMDB System is to create a pervasive context for transparency in managing and optimizing change. If you see the potential for two psychological worlds to collide here, you're right. A less emotional discussion of how to deal with toolset sprawl can be seen in the following excerpt from a prior consulting report:

> Our studies into the number of system management tools in Fortune 500 companies have shown that typical quantities range between 30 and 60. A few examples have been found with 20 or fewer tools, and a few organizations have had 100+ tools in place. Your company is in the middle of this range. Some consolidation of systems management tools should be accomplished during the CMDB implementation process. It is not unusual for each geographic location to become an independent fiefdom with its own set of tools, some of them common to multiple locations and some unique to a single location.
>
> We recommend that tool consolidation be undertaken on a case-by-case basis as redundant tools and data are identified. Elimination of redundant tools will ease the integration efforts, although care must be taken to make sure that useful tools are not taken out of the hands of IT staff that depend on them. (Unfortunately, all too often individuals will claim a tool as essential—either because they hope it will provide some form of job security or because they have an absolute resistance to even the smallest change.) In the case where two tools collect the same data but both are considered necessary, reconciliation rules within the CMDB can be used to keep the data synchronized and updated.
>
> During the implementation of the CMDB, it will be important to have a clear and consistently-applied process for determining the system of record owner for each data field and evaluating tools that gather duplicate information. This approach mitigates this risk by establishing up front cross-domain authority to implement and enforce policies. As the goal of the CMDB is to make data more visible (not to eliminate tools), technology silos always have the option of writing reconciliation rules in lieu of eliminating tools.

INVENTORY, DATA QUALITY, AND ISSUES

Data issues and toolset issues, though not 100% identical, often go hand in hand. Good (and relevant) data are the very foundation for a CMDB System, as they are for the functioning of IT overall. The criticality of having good data quality is summarized in an excerpt from another interview targeting "advice for the CMDB System game changer:"[3]

> One thing I think I'd stress is the importance of data quality. Doing this right requires not only having a good tool, but a process in place to ensure that stakeholders are evaluating the data quality of the tools they use—so if what they see from discovery, or inventory, or systems or network management isn't as effective as it should be, they can at least begin to put a process in place to make it work. A lot of stuff is just out there and being deployed with very little attention to data quality. That of course loops back to the CMS. If what we're getting isn't good data, and no one knows it, we can't very well fix it.

---

[3] Interview with a large financial services company based in the United States using Blazent CMDB Accuracy and Intelligence.

But data quality is almost invariably a challenge. Initial-phase CMDB assessments typically unearth their share of data collection issues that are a problem in and of themselves—even without the intention of moving forward to a CMDB System. Unearthing at least some of these problems, discrepancies, and gaps is one of the benefits of the initial assessment.

Among the most pervasive examples of data-related issues are incomplete inventory and discovery capabilities—so many phase one deployments achieve real value simply by defining these problems and at least creating a plan to round out what's there. Here is a comment from a CMDB team leader in a large financial organization complaining about inaccuracies in server inventories. Due to poor levels of discovery and inventory, there was ongoing and serious contentiousness between the central IT service organization and one of the lines of business (LOBs) it served:

> • LOB confidence in IT inventories is very low. IT provided an estimate to Internet Banking with an increased cost for servers of $21M. Central IT determined the number of servers used by the LOB to be 1600. Investigation by Internet Banking found the inventory information to be off by 40% and found the number of servers closer to 400, noting that a number of servers on IT's list had already been retired or re-provisioned. After six months of auditing, the bill was reduced to $10M. This discrepancy illustrates the importance of reconciling data across IT and the LOB, and the clear need to establish source-of-record ownership.

DATA BREADTH: HOW MUCH IS ENOUGH?

Another of the challenges is the breadth of data that can apply to the CMDB System. The versatility and value of the system depends in large part on linking associations that might get lost—whether across domains, in terms of business service interdependencies, or in terms of owners, contracts, or customers, as just a few examples. This is a double-edged sword—with one side of the blade bringing value and the other bringing sheer ungovernable chaos. To mix metaphors (badly), trying to balance the breadth and depth of data inputs is a virtual Pandora's box with all but literal hell to pay if attention isn't given to setting priorities and phasing in scope, stakeholder outreach, and benefits.

To reintroduce a summary from Chapter 3 on CMDB System foundations—according to ITIL version 3—the CMS can contain the following types of data, ideally across federated data stores via both data access and data movement (copy, updates, etc.):

Technology data
Process data
People data
Provider data

The conditions for bringing all these data points together (every point from every group) will never be possible in phase one, even in the best of circumstances. Especially since the relevant data, if they exist at all, are likely to reside in any number of incongruent sources—spreadsheets, asset management databases, Visio drawings, paper documents, etc.

One very successful phase one CMDB deployment (taken from EMA research) focused on life cycle end point management, bringing critical owner, user, asset, and technical information together in an increasingly automated fashion. It was a well-understood problem across the larger IT organization, which quickly got behind the initiative. This may seem like going from the sublime to the ridiculous, but it's more like going from the sublime to the possible and the relevant.

Finally, it's worth mentioning that there are analytic capabilities emerging that can help ease the torment arising from having too many data sources with too many unknowns about accuracy, consistency, and relevance. We'll be examining these more closely in Chapter 12, but we are including this comment here to reassure you that data inputs and accuracy assessments do not have to all be done manually:[4]

- With our integrated data analytics, we're leveraging 35 different discovery tools in order to get a more cohesive 'golden record' for the CMS. When I got involved, the analytics vendor was doing a proof of concept to show us how we could have a consolidated view of all our 'trusted sources.' This included desktop, security, network management and administration, application dependency mapping, systems management and administration, asset management solutions, and BSM performance management.

DATA: POWER, POSSESSION, AND OWNERSHIP

Much like toolset ownership, data ownership is a source of power and control. Therefore, creating a system that transforms how data are collected, prioritized, and shared can create strong initial controversy. Your initial assessment will need to unearth these problems in order to promote dialogue and better manage the issues that arise. For instance, in one consulting engagement, we saw that of the stakeholders interviewed, 66% felt data sharing was an important issue at some level.

These three very blunt remarks from a different consulting engagement make a similar point while echoing concerns about toolset ownership:

- Data ownership is a big deal.
- People are very territorial. It is cultural change. We are responsible for our data. If we give up control, we can't manage it properly.
- We don't like centralized services for change control. Loss of control of change is a loss of power.

In response to these and other issues, our consultant made the following observation:

There is a common tendency in an enterprise CMDB implementation for certain data owners and domain experts to feel that their data is being compromised or taken away. The CMDB project must create a clear process to determine the system-of-record owners across the infrastructure. This must be coupled with a clear understanding that the CMDB project is an enabling technology to allow data to be shared among the staff, eliminating the manual processes, phone calls, and reliance on tribal knowledge.

PROCESS ISSUES

Believe it or not, many stakeholders are likely to be candid about process issues. These may seem less tangible and not as alarming as changes that threaten the status quo in current toolset usage and data access. In fact, these issues may actually be met with interest and support if the process improvements

---

[4]Interview with (another) large financial services company based in the United States using Blazent CMDB Accuracy and Intelligence.

can be easily understood as leading to value. On the other hand, if they seem primarily like added over-head, they are likely to be met with immediate and stubborn resistance.

The following comments from our own assessment interviews in consulting engagements show what is termed as "process candor" in three different CMDB System deployments:

- Some groups think that they are strong on process, but they are not.
- We could do better. Each silo has its own process. To provision a server, you fill out a form in Oracle Financials, and then you fill out a storage form. For other requests, you pick up the phone. There is no end-to-end process. It's frustrating.
- We are onboard with ITIL Foundation. But our processes are piecemeal—some are excellent; others are poor. It depends on the group and their pain.

One way to build enthusiasm for improving processes is to link them to very tangible areas of per-ceived (and real) weakness. This usually means targeting very specific actions that are—in the eyes of almost everyone—not going well. Redundant, and often manual, processes, such as those for collecting asset inventories, are prime causes of "process pain" in many IT environments.

The following passage from another CMDB consulting evaluation describes failed processes for server configuration and release management in an admittedly highly inefficient environment. With the advent of cloud, automation, and analytics, it is hard to imagine this level of "change management dyslexia" occurring today. But in fact, we still run these kinds of inefficiencies—usually with shorter timeframes, but sometimes at an increased scale with even more disastrous results.

Server provisioning was identified by 44% of the interviewees as a particular process that was a pain point. One interviewee estimated that more than 90 people were involved in the process of provi-sioning servers from the time a need was identified until the machine was rolled into production. This process is believed to be highly manual, with a majority of servers being "custom-built" rather than "standard issue." Furthermore, the estimated timeframe for getting a new server into production aver-aged about 3 months. Some typical comments are included below:

- "The provisioning of servers is always done as a custom build. We need a standard build with a better provisioning of servers. It takes one month to get Windows upgraded. And putting in a request is not enough. Without a system in place, we must push each step of the process."
- "We need a service catalog for building servers. 80% should be standard and 20% should be customized. This gives us the best price."
- "Development needs to agree on standard configurations."
- "We get no time estimates, no first in first out (FIFO), no prioritization."

STAFFING

Staffing is also a factor that can directly impact process. In your initial assessments, you should be alert to staffing challenges that are relevant to stakeholder participation in objectives for phase one and beyond. The following excerpt is a plea from the staffing abyss—one that needed to be brought into alignment for CMDB System planning:

- "We have about 250 servers, Windows, Unix, HP-UX, and about 10,000 desktops with pretty much every Windows OS available, along with a couple of different mobile devices. We also have two mainframes included with our CMDB. And from a networking perspective, we're a huge Cisco shop. For all of this, there's just one full-time administrator who works for me."

THE HAMSTER SCENARIO

One of the challenges in getting processes to change is that they are often matters of habit. Even when deliberate resistance to change is absent, routine often takes precedent over abstract process initiatives, especially when the initiatives are poorly communicated, rewarded, and enforced. While the following quote from an interview with a CMDB team leader may or may not be particularly useful in informing your strategy, it's bound to provoke a smile when you're faced with overcoming resistance to innovating process:[5]

* "Cultural challenges were a big factor in getting the silos to think about new ways of working together. Something like what I call the 'hamster scenario'—a hamster running around its wheel. You've got some processes in place and you're used to those processes. When do you step back and change those processes? In other words, when does the hamster get off its wheel and think it might move in other directions?"

COMMUNICATION

Step two in the Eight-Step Ladder to CMDB System Success is all about communication. It will require either you or someone on your team to learn to become a good communicator—in listening, advising, and promoting. These are nontrivial skills, but they can be learned with patience and practice. Good communication skills, aside from being helpful in a CMDB initiative, can be invaluable to you in other

---

[5]Interview with a large European-based global transportation company using Interlink Software's BSM software including the Service Configuration Manager.

ways going forward. While this book is hardly the place for "communications training," a CMDB-driven initiative can provide both a great context and a strong motive for gaining skills and confidence in this arena.

Communication issues across IT are also a part of the step two assessment, as well as a part of the CMDB System plan, and quite often, they also play a part in closing the gap between proof of concept and actual deployment. However, perceptions here can be strikingly varied, and assessing communication issues may require weighing divergent opinions among individuals and groups. For instance, these two quotes came from the very same CMDB deployment—and they refer to the same IT organization:

- Communication between silos is good. If there is a performance issue, we quickly get a group call going.
- Communication between groups is brutally bad.

If there's a nuance to work with between the two comments, it comes from what was left off the end of the first quote: "...*But it is a shotgun approach. It is reactive.*" This suggests that in assessing potential communication strengths and weaknesses, it may be more important to understand qualitative factors than to make categorical judgments that communication is either *good* or *bad*. The following comments from CMDB-related assessment interviews provide a few examples of what you might want to look out for:

- Communications is done as an informal exchange and is very ad hoc. Often, you call those who you know will say yes.
- Communication depends on interpersonal skills. It is not a lack of tools. It is all about the relationships between departments. Problem resolution is via tribal knowledge.
- IT doesn't communicate well either internally or externally. We vacillate between too big and nothing. We overpromise and don't follow through.
- Information is lost in the cascade. It is especially lost from the director level to managers.

THE EXECUTIVE FACTOR, AGAIN

Chapter 6 targeted the importance of executive buy-in, which is summed up nicely in the following quote:[6]

I think the first thing I'd stress is to get executive support. Executive support is critical, certainly, for what we're doing here. One of the reasons is that many people in the organization may have trouble grasping the benefits. So we do a lot of 'selling' and communicating. But having strong executive support behind you makes this process a lot easier.

---

[6]Blazent, first interview, op. cit.

However, the role and effectiveness of executive communication can vary dramatically based both on the leadership and on your ability to assimilate, articulate, and promote the executive role within your plan. The following concerns taken from multiple CMDB-driven consulting engagements underscore this idea:

- The big picture is very well communicated. The details are lost the further down you get.
- A lot gets lost in translation. How does this impact my job?
- You are out of the loop if you are not in management. You need to make a special effort to get information.
- The rate of change of leadership and transfers from other divisions is a root cause for some of the communications disconnects.

COMMUNICATION: VEHICLES AND APPROACHES

Communication isn't just something to document in your initial assessment and "gating factors" follow-up. As you proceed with the CMDB initiative, activating an effective communication strategy even before deployment can be a critical factor in your success. So part of the process is to listen, learn, promote, and also *do*. While the information you collect may be messy and somewhat contradictory, it should provide some insights into which venues are likely to work the best for the CMDB System initiative as it evolves. Your communication strategy should evolve along with the initiative—and therefore should be an articulated part of the overall plan.

As early as step two of the ladder, it's important to begin the communication outreach while you're pursuing the initial assessment. The need for proactively articulating the whys and wherefores of what your doing is expressed in one client's poignant comment:

- We need consistent communications updates. We are vying for airtime. We want to see some value.... We operate with a sense of urgency.

The landscape for effective communication is also evolving. In the past, most of the venues have been e-mail, telephone and voicemails, town hall meetings, and websites. But now, social IT, mobile access to data, and gamification (combining social IT with gamelike interactions) are emerging venues that are already bringing value in some CMDB System initiatives.

Here are some insights from past communications audits:

- **Good e-mail:** In general, e-mail is the preferred method of communication and telephone/voicemails are the least preferred method. However, a statistically significant number of interviewees stated that biweekly e-mail updates must be short and concise; they must be linked to relevant documentation and look forward 2-4 weeks.
- **Bad e-mail:** While e-mail is the most common method of exchanging information, a significant number of interviewees do not read every e-mail. Some estimates suggest as few as 15% of e-mails sent are actually read. Correct "framing" of e-mail was mentioned as an important factor in making CMDB communications via e-mail effective.
  - "Typically, content is not clear. Does it affect me?"
  - "There are too many e-mails, but everyone will read one from the CIO."

- **Top-down executive communications:** 100% of the interviewees feel that communication from the CIO to the management staff is desirable. Leadership forums were noted as providing an effective way to discuss goals. Scorecards and group meetings were also mentioned as helpful.
- **Town hall meetings:** Short update presentations in the town hall meetings are seen as the most effective way to "market" the CMDB and maintain visibility for the project. Generally, these updates should occur at least each quarter.
- **Websites:** A CMDB website with all the project documentation, overview, goals, schedules, progress reports, etc. is seen as a requirement to allow deeper research into the CMDB implementation on an ad hoc basis. In all cases, the key to value for communications is keeping the information fresh and updated.
- **Wiki:** A "wiki"-style website was mentioned by several interviewees as being necessary for a project as complex as the CMDB.
- **Blogs:** The service management blog was overwhelmingly seen as one of the best vehicles to communicate the type of information that must be distributed as part of the CMDB project.

Here are two additional quotes taken from interviews with CMDB team leaders:

- **Grassroots word-of-mouth leading to service catalog:** "For now we're enjoying positive word of mouth for getting interest in the CMS initiative. Eventually what we want to do is publish options for using the system in a service catalog so that people can query and request the data they need."[7]
- **Leveraging a proof of concept to help consolidate team dialog:** "We started with a PoC and socialized it with some of the teams to get feedback. And that worked for us."

USE-CASE AUDITS

Aside from these general areas of concern, it's important to frame your assessments surrounding technology, organizational, and technology readiness based on a proposed use case. In other words, while you do want to solicit input on priorities, if you go into it cold with no core shape to the project, your efficiency in honing and optimizing the dialogue will be seriously diminished.

With this in mind, we've collected the following representative comments from consulting and research dialog—targeting the three major use cases discussed in Chapter 7.

CHANGE IMPACT MANAGEMENT AND CHANGE AUTOMATION

Learning where and how your organization performs and manages changes can bring huge values in itself—and it is a prerequisite for succeeding in a change-centric phase one plan. The comments below from consulting clients are designed to reflect "findings" from just such assessments. They are organized into the following categories: *perceived impacts of change, process issues, Change Advisory Board issues,* and *technology issues.*

Perceptions surrounding the impacts of change

As is often the case within an IT organization, perceptions surrounding the impacts of changes on service delivery may range from severe to minimal—depending on whom you ask. The following comments, drawn from different CMDB assessments, were selected to illustrate a wide range of perspectives;

---

[7]Interlink Software interview, op. cit.

- Problems break down to 1/3 end-user issues, 1/3 application developers breaking the code, 1/3 configuration changes in IT.
- Management and executive management estimate the number of incidents due to change at a much lower level than the production level staff. In other words, our executives have a far more optimistic view of our ability to manage changes than our hands-on operations team. Across-the-board estimates ranged from 25% to 90% with a mean value between 75% and 80%. We have been told that this puts us below the norm. Measured against industry averages (between 50% and 60%), this represents a higher than normal impact from change.
- Changes with impact are up 50% due to both higher volume and poor testing.
- We need to use configuration management as a business advantage.

The last quote—focusing on using configuration management as a "business advantage"—is telling in that it recognizes a bigger picture and more proactive perspective on value.

Perceptions of process issues related to Change Management

The following is a medley of perspectives drawn from different IT organizations to provide insights on processes-related issues. They range from the very high-level comments to the very granular concerns. However, overall, these comments emphasize the communication issues that surround change—and the need for commonly accepted ways of working across domains versus more siloed approaches in the past:

- Change management is undocumented.
- We gather all our information from manual surveys and analysis. But these are only good until a change occurs.
- Change control needs to hold people accountable if it is to be effective. No one questions why.
- Testing changes has no standards. This is a big problem. Perception is that 90% of changes are approved. The change process is not just notification.
- Change coordinators and problem managers report through different groups and have too narrow a view.
- We are not looking at changes at the right level of detail. Table changes get the same attention as global configuration changes.

A closer look at Change Advisory Board (CAB) processes and issues in one deployment

The Change Advisory Board and issues surrounding it can become a lightning rod for flagging problems with Change Management processes in general. Tellingly, the comments that follow come from an IT organization that's grounded in traditional, manual processes without meaningful service impact insights:

- We have three change coordinator meetings per week. We review the change reports, discuss impact, look for conflict. It is very common for us to 'stop the presses' on a Friday for changes scheduled that weekend.
- There are over 5000 change requests per year, and all of them are marked HIGH priority.
- We have 400 change meetings a year in our sector. With root cause analysis being manual, there is no way to do this adequately.

- The CAB currently gets information from the service desk, but the data is manually populated.
- The CAB has only a tactical view about rolling applications into production.
- Our biggest problem is impact analysis. There is just not enough data about services, servers, and application mapping.

Some technology issues related to Change Management

The following medley of comments reflects toolset concerns across different IT organizations but are all related to a phase one CMDB initiative. These are, of course, merely a sample, but they are examples of how to begin the process of defining requirements for technology adoption, architecture, integration, and new technology investments as discussed in Chapter 12:

- We need better test facilities for determining change impact.
- We don't have trending information when making change decisions. We also need real-time data on changes and desired states.
- We need empirical evidence to understand change collision.
- We need on-demand provisioning built into our CMDB with rule-based validations, established policy-based processes, and centralized storage of processes.

ASSET MANAGEMENT AND FINANCIAL OPTIMIZATION

The issues identified in our consulting engagements that are related to Asset Management and Financial Optimization typically tend to fall into three categories: *data and dependency insights*, *process issues*, and *automation*. We're also adding a fourth category—*audit-derived metrics*—as a way to highlight how useful benefits-related metrics can evolve out of audit-related stakeholder interviews.

Data and dependency insights

Good data are a primary foundation for good asset management, just as it is for effective CMDB Systems. Understanding how broken asset-related data collection is in most IT environments can be a big boost to empowering a CMDB initiative that includes assessments of existing inventory and discovery tools. Figure 8.4 provides a list of just a few data-related KPIs taken from a consulting engagement. It's not uncommon to have many multiple tool sets address data collection for these KPIs, often without consistency in how the KPIs are named or referenced. So assessing how and where data collection is critical. These assessments can help pave the way for more consistent and more effective levels of automation:

- We are focused on solving compliance problems (SOX), but we need to know how applications relate to our infrastructure software to be able to optimize our asset investments in support of business services. At a more tactical level, we also need to get better licensing information.
- We did a comprehensive sweep of 36,000 people and 42,000 PCs and laptops. We caught maybe 85 – 90% [of the devices in the infrastructure], and we still can't crack down on non-standard configurations.
- We need a solid inventory of applications. Currently, there are no common definitions, no common vocabulary, no common places to store data.

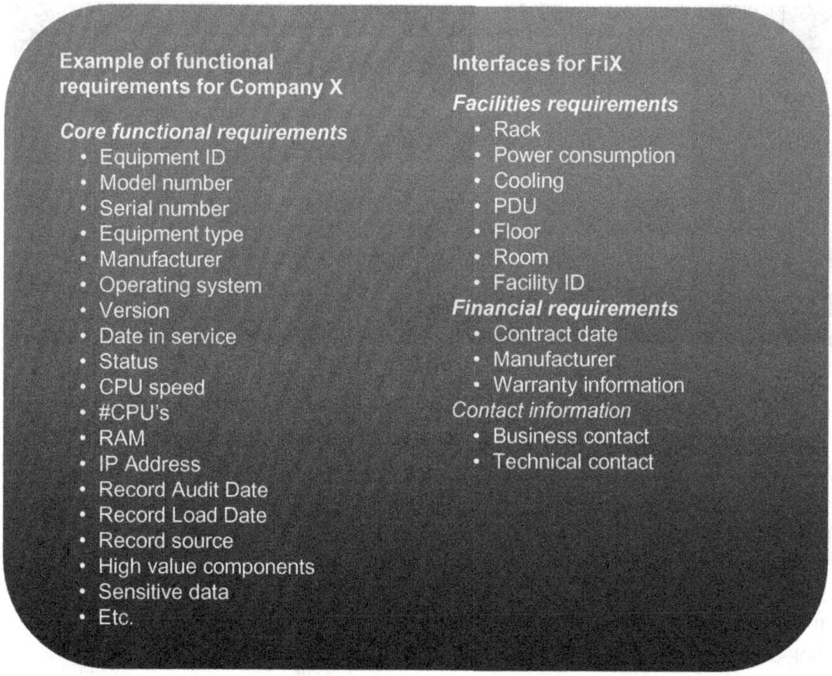

Example of functional requirements for Company X

Core functional requirements
- Equipment ID
- Model number
- Serial number
- Equipment type
- Manufacturer
- Operating system
- Version
- Date in service
- Status
- CPU speed
- #CPU's
- RAM
- IP Address
- Record Audit Date
- Record Load Date
- Record source
- High value components
- Sensitive data
- Etc.

Interfaces for FiX

Facilities requirements
- Rack
- Power consumption
- Cooling
- PDU
- Floor
- Room
- Facility ID

Financial requirements
- Contract date
- Manufacturer
- Warranty information

Contact information
- Business contact
- Technical contact

FIGURE 8.4

List of asset-related KPIs for server investments taken from a prior consulting engagement. As long as this list is, it is still not meant to be complete.

Process issues for asset management

Because CMDB System initiatives require attention to process, they can be excellent conduits for improving broken processes—especially when better technology investments in inventory, discovery, and change management help to pave the way. Figure 8.5 shows that about 50% of IT respondents link best practices to asset management—a percentage that hopefully will grow over time. The comments that follow are typical of many IT environments locked into fragmented and broken methods for capturing assets and their interdependencies and managing them throughout their life cycles:

- No enterprise asset management policy is in place.
- We do 120 asset extracts each month. We have lots of data, but the processes we currently have for collecting and managing that data are insufficient.
- Configuration and Asset Management will significantly benefit from the structure and process introduced by a successful CMDB team.

Automation for asset management

When broken processes are combined with insufficient and inaccurate data, the obvious next step is to invest in superior tools for automating data collection and discovery. The two stakeholder comments

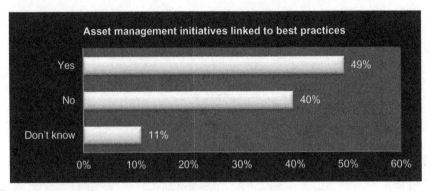

FIGURE 8.5

Nearly 50% of IT organizations say their asset management is in some way linked to best practices. ("Next Generation Asset Management and IT Financial Analytics: Optimizing IT Value in a World of Change," EMA, 2014.) Of these, 63% are tied to ITIL, while ISO 19970 -1, Six Sigma, and Capability Maturity Model Integration (CMMI) are also popular. Linking best practices with asset management indicates significantly higher likelihood of

- tracking assets and asset utilization in support of services,
- linking assets to compliance or other governance requirements,
- having automated discovery and asset systems,
- implementing asset chargeback and service chargeback.

that follow come from interviews done for a consultant assessment directed at helping clients better plan for phase one asset management-related initiatives:

- There are 13 initiatives currently underway to gather information on assets in the enterprise. This is a continuous process and provides little to negative value because there is no underlying process/tool for keeping our information current. Manual processes have been shown to be only 80% effective at best. As a result, we don't trust in the asset data. The CMDB could eliminate these surveys, freeing up headcount to take on more meaningful tasks.
- Automation is the most obvious place where we can increase the value of IT's configuration and asset management data. Manual surveys are ineffective and costly not only because they require Asset Management staff to create and collate the results, but also because the data is already out-of-date by the time the results are available for use. In addition, this type of asset data, being both incomplete and out-of-date, runs the risk of providing disinformation to our LOB clients.

Audit-derived metrics

Conducting use case-driven audits not only provides insight into process, data, technology, and other issues but also can help to set the stage for identifying very tangible, phase one metrics and benefits. These two observations from yet another consulting report help to identify unique and specific phase one objectives relevant to individual IT environments:

- Twenty percent of servers in the data center are unidentified according to one interviewee. Reducing this baseline number to 1% would be a measurable value of the CMDB and the automated discovery process.
- Improving procurement was a commonly discussed topic. With 60% of all servers built as customized solutions that do not follow standards (if these standard builds even exist), it would be a simple metric to understand how the CMDB and the associated improvements in procurement process lower the number of "custom" solutions.

SERVICE IMPACT MANAGEMENT AND CAPACITY OPTIMIZATION

The following comments highlight issues from multiple CMDB System initiatives primarily touching on service impact management. We have grouped them into two sections: Service Level Agreements section and Monitoring and Escalation section.

Service Level Agreements

- We have antiquated SLAs.
- We need SLAs tied to budget. Our SLAs need a lot of process work.
- We have approximately 150 SLAs in place, representing a very small slice (<5%) of the entire infrastructure. These are primarily focused on reporting on metrics that are convenient (i.e., already available) (such as time to resolution, logs, and end-of-the-month reports). They appear to mostly be within particular technology silos and tied to measuring specific business unit-defined metrics (e.g., determining the uptime for foreign circuits). We still do not have meaningful SLAs that measure inter-silo metrics and end-to-end processes. Our CMDB and application dependency mapping investments should help to change our SLA game.

Monitoring and escalation

- In general, each technology silo has its own monitoring tool and there are very few cases where these tools are integrated to share information. The CMDB will eventually link some of this near-real-time data together with a clearer view of service interdependencies.
- Historical data needs to be gathered not only for configuration data, but it needs to be extended to operational data such as the history of alarms for root cause analysis. We see our CMS as a complement to our analytics investments in bringing this information together in a relevant way.
- Escalation of critical issues occurs no more than once per month, and more typically once per quarter. When this occurs, approximately 30+ people dial into a call. These calls are described as 'very messy because nobody knows what the others are doing.' Using domain expertise, the incident is discussed and analyzed. The CMDB will help in providing better information and a more complete view into the incident. The CMDB will also improve the underlying infrastructure understanding and prevent these calls from occurring.

PULLING IT ALL TOGETHER

As stated at the beginning of this chapter, performing the initial assessment is an essential foundation for going forward with an effective plan. The assessment can lead to more tangible metrics and an architectural set of requirements for selecting needed technologies that are grounded in reality versus assumptions. It is also a critical baseline for socializing your initiative and a guideline for optimizing future stages, such as final *gating factors*, before deployment (Chapter 13).

In this critical step of the ladder, you are truly going "public." You are beginning the cross-organizational dialogues that will evolve with your initiative well past phase one. In many CMDB initiatives, these relationships and conversations may be the single most impacting catalytic factor in achieving CMDB System Success—both in activating the plan and in meeting informed expectations.

Moreover, your assessment should provide insights and value in optimizing your IT organization that will reach beyond the CMDB System itself. So don't be shy about communicating "lessons learned" to your executive team.

SUMMARY TAKEAWAYS

This chapter is aimed at providing you with the guidance you need to do an effective assessment involving technology, process, and organization—building on the stages of IT maturity discussed in the prior chapter. The many voices and points of view taken from real-world assessments are introduced here to help you anticipate what might actually be said when your CMDB System deployment gets under way.

Some of the key takeaways are the following:

- Don't skimp. Our consulting typically targets around 20 key stakeholders, and in some cases, that number has been doubled based on executive requests. That's an enterprise-scale level, though, so in smaller IT organizations, the number might be reduced to 10 or even fewer.
- This is your opportunity to engage CMDB System stakeholders and consumers by understanding their priorities, promoting your plan, and optimizing value and effectiveness based on dialog.
- Learning how to say "no" goes along with learning how to listen.
- Most assessments will expose a wide range of priorities for the CMDB System—not all of which can be accommodated in phase one or even in immediate follow-on phases. However, knowing what the priorities are and who holds them is one of the keys for creating an effective plan.
- Dialogues around data and toolset ownership often generate strong emotions and can sometimes expose real potential resistance to the CMDB System.
- Critical venues for communication include traditional resources such as e-mail and phone, town hall and/or other meetings (ideally including at least some that are executive-driven), and a website either dedicated to the CMDB initiative or logically affiliated with it. Wiki-like data sharing, blogs, and a catalog of options for getting CMDB-driven reports and data can be valuable additions. Newer options that should be looked at seriously include mobile access to information, social IT, and gamification.
- Assessments should be not only broad in scope but also optimized to flesh out your initial plans for phase one objectives along such use-case lines as *Change Impact Management and Change Automation, Asset Management and Financial Optimization,* and *Service Impact Management and Capacity Optimization.*

MATURITY AND READINESS: A FOUR-PHASE EVOLUTIONARY ASSESSMENT

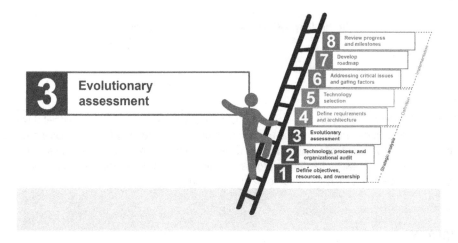

In order to move forward through the stages of IT evolution, it's important to understand how the three chief drivers—organization, process, and technology—can provide a cyclical dynamic for growth. Within this dynamic, IT can make many opportunistic choices and investments. For instance, a management solution enabling better collaboration between the help desk and operations center can positively impact process and organization.

CYCLICAL AND OPPORTUNISTIC

Artful leveraging across each of the three critical drivers shown in Figure 9.1 can become a formula for accelerating the climb toward a more dynamic and business-aligned IT organization. In order to codify the process as you move forward in your CMDB System planning, it's worth revisiting each vector briefly.

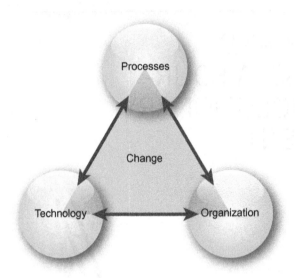

FIGURE 9.1

"Standing in the middle of the storm" as described in Chapter 4 has its upside. The three chief drivers for growth—technology, process, and organization—should be understood not only for their challenges but also for the opportunities they present. It's important to recognize that there can be cyclical handshakes across these drivers—say, between hardening process definitions, richer organizational interactions, and automation—so that each one pulls the other forward up the maturity ladder.

TECHNOLOGY

EMA created a model for IT architectures that also provides a basis for looking at IT maturity dynamics for technology adoption. The basic pieces of this model are

1. instrumentation,
2. data gathering and discovery,
3. data store,
4. integration and data sharing,
5. analytics,
6. automation,
7. visualization and reporting,
8. business alignment.

This model can be understood from an evolutionary perspective by contrasting Figure 9.2 with Figure 9.3. Figures 9.2 and 9.3 illustrate how fragmented investments can become more unified and mutually reinforcing through a more integrated system.

As an organization evolves to higher levels of maturity, each of the components described above are affected as follows:

- *Instrumentation and data collection:* Over time, element-centric data collection should evolve to reflect support across system and network platforms and across network, systems, and

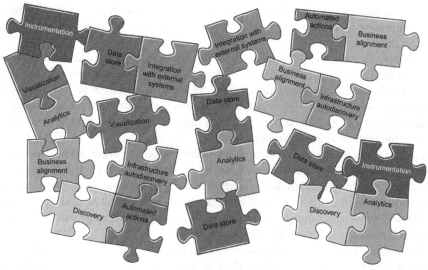

FIGURE 9.2

One way to measure the evolution of IT architectures from isolated toolsets to more mature, service-oriented, and dynamic technology investments is to consider how siloed toolset designs become more integrated through advances in discovery, data sharing and integration, service modeling, analytics, automation, dashboarding, and reporting. The move to a more cross domain, layered, and modular approach to service management continues to be one of the core definers of the industry.

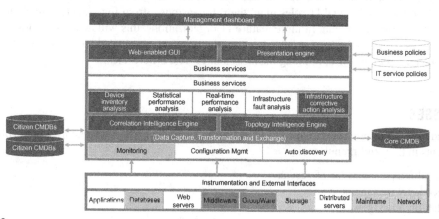

FIGURE 9.3

In contrast to Figure 9.2, here, we see what might be called an integrated Service Knowledge Management System. As part of a CMDB System initiative in which the isolated fragments indicated in Figure 9.2 come together in a more effective, and more cohesive, mosaic. The full CMDB System can exploit and/or empower integrated resources vertically, up and down this model, and horizontally, within a single layer. Current trends are making an IT analytics layer (as described in four parts above the "correlation intelligence engine" and "topology intelligence engine") far more pervasive and real than ever before. While automated actions are not singled out in this drawing, they are an integrated part of almost every part of this design.

application domains to provide insight into full infrastructure interdependencies. As data collection improves, it becomes more policy-driven and operates in support of analytics—rather than as a separate, isolated process.

- *Data store, data sharing, and integration*: Data sharing and integration are key requirements for a CMDB System, just as they are for service management applications in general. This is true both within a single brand and across multiple brands. Moreover, integration should be directed across the components indicated here—data gathering, analytics, visualization, and automated actions—for enhanced flexibility and for defining and resolving problems. The importance of integration increases as the level of automation increases.
- *Analytics*: This is one of the most critical areas of investment and differentiation among management solutions today and a growing part of the formula for CMDB System success. Analytics can range from capabilities devoted to problem isolation and root cause, to capacity planning and accounting, to performance trending, to business impact analysis, to configuration and topological awareness, among others. Analytics can also enable more automated adaptability to change and minimize deployment and administration.
- *Automated actions:* Growing in importance as IT evolves, automated actions are closely aligned with process and IT efficiencies. While in the past a great deal of suspicion accompanied the notion of automated actions, the introduction of cloud and advances in automation-related technologies have made this an area of growth fully as active as that of analytics. As IT matures, automated actions will help to minimize, and in some cases eliminate, much of the action required for routine, day-to-day problem resolution and administration.
- *Visualization, access, and business alignment*: It's important not only for data/information to be analyzed and correlated but also for it to be presented in a context that supports critical decision making. As visualization and access to management services evolve, they will do so based on an understanding of individual IT roles in all their dimensions—from functional to psychological, political, and organizational. In more mature IT organizations, this will actively combine IT and business roles—whether for customer experience management and business impact, or for strategic planning, or for optimizing business and IT cost efficiencies.

PROCESSES

The broad list of ITIL processes below can be a daunting way to approach IT maturity and evolutionary assessments in their full granularity:

- Financial management for IT services
- Service-level management
- Availability management
- Capacity management
- IT service continuity management
- Information security management
- Change management
- Service configuration and asset management
- Release and deployment management
- Service desk

- Application management
- IT operations management
- Technical management
- Event management
- Incident management
- Problem management
- Continual service improvement
- Identity management

To simplify making a maturity assessment, Figure 9.4 shows a grouping of process interdependencies as organizational teams might focus on them. This allows for efficiency and readiness to be considered team by team. This simplified approach can also be a useful reference point going forward as you evaluate organizational dynamics across the four stages of maturity:

- *Service Support*: Most IT organizations begin with some level of service support, even if it's focused on end-user PC complaints. This category also includes functions such as help desk, customer service, and client support; incident and problem management; knowledge base; and change/request management.
- *Operations*: This area includes disciplines such as real-time, predictive, and historical fault and performance management and job scheduling, business continuity management, and output management.

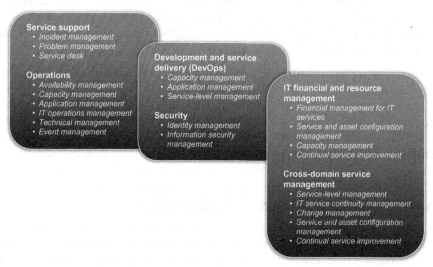

FIGURE 9.4

Clustering ITIL processes by team or organizational model can be a helpful shorthand enabling you to assess and map your own maturity levels to the four-phase maturity model in this book. The following list provides a closer look at how they map. It should be mentioned that configuration management is a pervasive presence across virtually all of these groups.

- *Development and Service Delivery (DevOps)*: The very concept of DevOps dictates a fundamental shift toward more of a business focus. The increasing prominence of DevOps is a sign of positive evolution within IT, as is attention to the core foundations for service delivery such as service-level management, service provisioning (for enabling services), and the critical handshake between advances in simulation and automation in development and advances in change and performance management in service support and operations.
- *Security*: Broadly speaking, security includes access control, identity management, and threat management. The latter also includes functions such as intrusion detection, security/event management, and virus protection. Security, which has long been a separate enclave within IT, is evolving to become a more systemic practice, becoming more tightly integrated with other management processes and non-IT domains, such as human resources and accounting. The growing role of analytics and the faster pace of change are also pushing security more and more into mainstream of operations, development, and other IT groups.
- *IT Financial and Resource Management*: This includes procurement, inventory management, software distribution and hardware release management, license management, configuration management, capacity planning, and optimization of the infrastructure, as well as usage insights for costing and portfolio planning. While many IT organizations have some level of asset management, very few have evolved to support an integrated more strategic focus here—something that a CMDB System can help to enable.
- *Cross domain Service Management*: Although there is clearly a move in this direction due to cloud and other factors, few IT organizations actually use this name for their cross domain efforts. The goal is to find a foothold in how your IT organization is evolving to support cross domain requirements and seek out those already in place—if they exist—and to engage with stakeholders in other groups. Even if the CMDB falls under a separate organization, this group more often than not will be closely allied with your efforts to both improve your IT Maturity Levels and enable your CMDB System success.

Cloud is accelerating the need for cross domain service management teams, which are now often associated with planning the move to internal and external cloud resources more efficiently. In other IT environments, this group can be associated with architectural planning and design, or with tool set selection and support, or with change and configuration management and the CMDB itself. Therefore, don't approach the title too literally. Try instead to understand how your IT organization is, or is not, beginning to move in this "cross domain service management" direction in its own unique way.

IT ORGANIZATIONAL EVOLUTION: A CLOSER LOOK

Organization is defined predominantly by culture—a mix of political dynamics, business dynamics, skills, and associated beliefs that form a basis for communication and affiliation, as well as, at times, for antagonisms and prejudice. The sum total of these cultural forces, which include individual leadership, is often the single most important driver for IT transformation, for which process and technology function fundamentally as enablers.

In the past, many processes and strategies have been built around a static concept of IT organizational structures, and at various periods in IT evolution, this seemed like a credible perspective. Even if IT organizations were changing, the change was viewed as much slower than changes in technology or management software products. Similarly, processes were often viewed as fairly constant, and best practices were often constructed in a virtually timeless fashion against a fairly constant organizational landscape. Best practices were, in the eyes of some theoreticians, the "best of all possible worlds" mapped to the "best of all possible organizations."

As a corollary to this, a fundamental organizational error often made was seeking to establish a relatively static, idealized, isolated, *back-office* state in which IT organizations were expected to function. This static approach neglects the fundamental intersection of technology, organization, and process, along with the now very visible requirements for IT to embrace requirements to become more consumer-aware, cloud-ready, agile, and dynamic. All of these factors underscore the fact that neither businesses nor IT can afford to reside in categorically different cultural worlds, each with its own languages, priorities, and assumptions.

HOW IT VIEWS ITSELF

IT's perspective on its role and mission and on the internal and external cultural factors supporting this role/identity is fundamental both to define where IT is in its evolution and to plan for change and improvement. In fact, the four phases of IT evolution outlined in this chapter can be linked to four "personas" or personality types as a useful shorthand in assessing the broader complexities of IT organizational culture. As those personalities change in mindset, IT's capacity for more effective change and adaptation also improves (Figure 9.5).

A summary of the four phases are in terms of the "personas" shown above are the following:

- *Reactive heroes*: IT is reactive to change and supported by a few "heroes" within its organization whose abilities in troubleshooting or capacity planning are not shared across the broader group. More often than not, this IT shop is elitist and feels misunderstood. It is also fragmented and likely to be divisive within itself.
- *Operationally empowered tribes*: At this stage, IT functions primarily as a collection of skill groups (network specialists, systems specialists, etc.) that have effective common processes within them and some cross group processes. Operational control is a focus. The tribal nature of domain-centric skill groups, in spite of its humorous overtones, is strongest in this stage.

FIGURE 9.5

The four phases of IT evolution can be mapped to "personas" to more easily grasp the nature of attitude and cultural change as IT organizations mature toward becoming true business partners.

That's because much like departments at a university, these organizations have evolved around common training and backgrounds. They all read similar magazines, follow similar analysts, and share common, and often prejudicial, views of each other.

- *Internal service provider:* At this stage, IT views itself as a true service provider within the broader organization and has superseded subgroup divisions for a squarely business-driven service support role. IT interfaces with the broader business as a consistent and effective unit, and customer service becomes more of a focus. This transition often represents the biggest single leap—both in mindset and in process and technology adoption. It is also a cornerstone for CMDB System success.

- *Proactive business partner:* At this stage, IT has automated most day-to-day tactical requirements and views itself as a proactive business contributor. Its role goes beyond supporting the business to informing on and actively shaping business advantage. The relationship between creating new IT services and transforming business effectiveness is understood and shared by leaders within both IT and the business or organization it supports. Ideally, a common language has evolved to promote more proactive conversations that unite IT transformation with business-model transformation.

OTHER ORGANIZATIONAL INFLUENCERS

Some other criteria influencing IT organizational maturity are described in Figure 9.6.

- *Breadth of organizational functions:* Which areas are addressed and which are not? For instance, in the early stages of IT organizations, functions are defined in purely operational terms and skill sets. As organizations evolve, more business-specific functions—ranging from service planning

FIGURE 9.6

This figure captures another set of parameters that complement the personalities described in Figure 9.5. As an aggregate, they can help to streamline your evaluations for CMDB System assessments and, more broadly, for organizational evaluations.

and business alignment to asset and investment analysis—are defined and understood. The criteria outlined from a process perspective are mapped out in Figure 9.4.

- *Organizational structure and the level of cross silo cooperation and integration from an organizational perspective:* This is one of the most critical areas for evolution. It requires moving from element-centric skills (the "hero" associated with knowledge of a single brand—e.g., a Cisco router) through domain-centric organizations (network/systems/applications) toward more effective cross domain communication based on business requirements. Cross silo integration will leverage more advanced technologies capable of providing insights across network, systems, application, database, e-business, and eventually even storage and security interdependencies.

- *Proactive versus reactive management:* There are a number of areas where it's important for IT organizations to evolve toward a more proactive versus reactive mindset, with associated processes and organizational dynamics in place. These include the following:

  - A more proactive and planned approach to making investments in both the infrastructure and the management solutions and strategies for managing that infrastructure. Making investments in a knee-jerk response to failure or catastrophe or in a purely political appeasement of external business pressures can be a short road to failure. Contributing to investment decisions with clear internal goals and rationales and insight into the impact on the broader business can elevate IT from a black hole of ungovernable technology expense to a position of respect as an informed and strategic business contributor. This is one reason for following the Eight-Step Ladder to CMDB Success rather than just assuming that deploying a CMDB will fix all your problems.

  - A more proactive approach to resolving issues in infrastructure service, performance, availability, change, etc. requires better processes and better tools—with enhanced intelligence and automation to address what heretofore has been primarily firefighting. Remember that ITIL's proactive definitions of "problem management" and "availability management" go far beyond merely responding to a crisis.

  - A proactive approach to defining and resolving personnel and cultural issues with an eye to cross domain versus siloed affiliations. For instance, individuals are often defined in terms of one-dimensional sets of skills as they fit into a traditional IT structure (e.g., network engineer). But many have richer backgrounds that may touch on everything from business development to international skills. As IT becomes more of an integrated business service, multidimensional backgrounds can become welcome sources of advantage. Current research shows a trend of supporting more cross domain skill groups and more cross domain-directed teams within IT. Once again, this change is critical to the CMDB System, which in the end will demand a more cross domain mindset to establish priorities and optimize service-related insights.

  - *Increased awareness of process:* The growing importance of resources such as ITIL and Six Sigma indicates that IT is becoming more process-conscious. If applied with attention to the specifics of your environment, this will be a positive catalyst for evolutionary change.

  - *Business alignment:* A structure for achieving enhanced alignment with the broader business is paramount if IT is to evolve toward a more strategic role. This can be facilitated in a number of ways. For example, a business liaison can be established through a senior service planner, sometimes taken from a help desk or service desk background, and used to interface with customer clients. This business planner may also have experience with e-business or other task forces. With this alignment comes a greater requirement to invest in tools and processes to measure and document value and impact to the business; these may include accounting, service modeling, and scorecards to assess the performance of IT investments (services, brand-specific devices, applications, etc.) as they track to critical business outcomes and business needs. Needless to say, the CMDB System can become a powerful enabler for relating business outcomes and needs to IT capabilities more effectively.

THE FOUR STAGES OF IT MATURITY: A CLOSER LOOK

Recent research and consulting have led to the creation of the four stages of maturity, first described in Chapter 4 and reprised here in Figure 9.7. The following section will describe each stage in more depth, with additional commentary from two client engagements for stage one and stage two. A deployment case study at the end of this chapter fits largely into stage three.

REACTIVE INFRASTRUCTURE MANAGEMENT

At this level, most organizations are trying to survive day-to-day crises. Most management investments are element-centric with some domain-level investments, and domain-specific expertise (network/systems/application/database) is fundamentally separate and isolated. There is an initial focus on basic help desk support, reacting to isolated customer problems, so that management is done reactively by incident rather than proactively by automation. Processes focus on passing problems to specialists quickly without intervening capabilities for broad infrastructure diagnostics and proactive control. This results in inefficiencies and overuse of advanced skill sets for resolving problems. Security is limited to isolated point solutions, primarily firewalls and antivirus desktops. Most management purchases are driven by crises rather than as planned investments (Figure 9.8).

From an organizational perspective specifically, the relationship between IT and the broader business is likely to be one of weak credibility and poor communication with the likely perception that IT is a black hole for investing money. When it comes to business value, outsourcing may be viewed as an attractive alternative to the fragmented and often inconclusive voice of IT.

Stage one organizations nevertheless invest in moving to stage two by improving breadth of data gathering and moving toward more effective management software, especially in the area of service support.

FIGURE 9.7

The four stages of IT maturity.

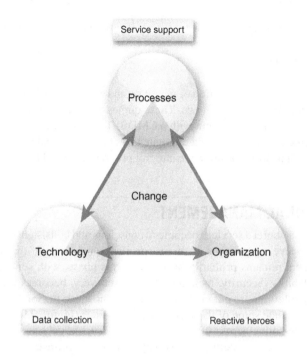

FIGURE 9.8

Dominant drivers and influencers of reactive infrastructure management.

While IT organizations locked in stage one may not yet be ready for a CMDB, let alone a CMDB System, the move to Stage Two may be empowered by addressing some of the preliminaries described in our Eight-Step Ladder to CMDB System Success—such as documenting toolset gaps and existing processes.

COMMENTS FROM A STAGE-ONE ORGANIZATION SEEKING TO MOVE TO STAGE TWO

- Right now, we call the experts to validate anything important.
- We are very reactive. How we approach each problem is based on the technical expertise of specialists involved.
- Our focus is on closing tickets. We do very little root cause analysis.
- If it takes more than 20 min to fix a problem, then we simply reimage the machine. We don't fix the components.
- As a corollary to communications between silos, there are no standardized processes between groups.
- Freeware gets added to machines all the time. This causes some problems and represents some risk to our organization. We don't have a good way to control this.
- We are terrible at prioritization and cannot say "no." We need to learn to say that it will cost you x$ to undertake this additional task.
- Tribal knowledge is used in emergencies to restore services. Other changes are rubber-stamped. We approved 992 of the last 1000 requests.

- No meaningful correlation between infrastructure components, service delivery, and business impact is available.
- The CMDB is called just in crisis situations.

These quotes reflect a common condition of reactivity and a lack of visibility that together make any initial CMDB deployment largely superfluous. These quotes—all taken from the same deployment— provide a clear example of jumping the gun with a CMDB. The goal of the consultant in this case was to establish the requirements for process and dialogue that could have made the CMDB more effective here and prepare this organization for more meaningful progress toward IT maturity.

ACTIVE OPERATIONAL MANAGEMENT

In stage two, managing outsourced services becomes a conscious and consistent effort extending beyond network-centric service-level agreements or server-specific components of the data center. However, service-level management remains primarily historical at this phase, with some real-time linkages to performance and availability. Security, including disaster recovery, becomes a primary concern, and more systemic security solutions are put in place. Ironically, the move to cloud, or the threat of moving to cloud, may serve to escalate some of the security-related issues (Figure 9.9).

At this stage, event handling across the infrastructure will be largely automated and far more efficient. On the other hand, service definitions as they map to this infrastructure will not yet be well defined. The net result will be a fast restoration of core infrastructure operation but with significant gaps in time when critical business services can fully resume online.

Stage two organizations prepare for stage three by investing more in infrastructure-wide solutions— most critically a CMDB System along with superior automation and analytics. Security will become a more cohesive, systemic investment, and asset and resource management will become more pervasive and structured for consistency and life cycle concerns. A conscious effort to promote processes and dialogue that enable better cross domain communication is also fundamental to arriving at stage three.

A CMDB SYSTEM DEPLOYMENT IN STAGE TWO

The following comments come from a maturity assessment done for an EMA client in the early active operational stage. This client had well-established domain expertise but not much cross domain capability. This company was at a point where a CMDB initiative could help to drive value, but not without added attention to process issues and cross domain investments.

- Day-to-day operational issues are paramount. Change represents a significant challenge to the organization, and a lack of visibility exists across the enterprise for both configuration and monitoring data.
- Management investments are domain-focused. There appears to be little consideration for integration when new tools are introduced into the environment.
- Domain-specific expertise (e.g., network, application, and database) is fundamentally separate and isolated.

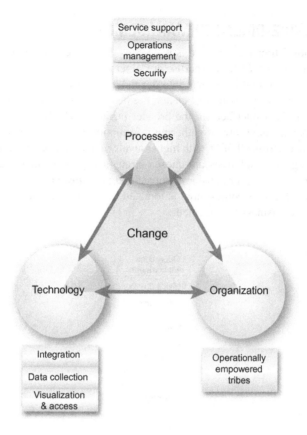

FIGURE 9.9

Dominant drivers and influencers of active operational management.

- Service-level management and higher-level analytics and intelligence engines are scattered.
- Business processes do not provide IT management layers with information on prioritizing troubleshooting or allocating resources to give the highest levels of service to business functions that provide the highest profit.
- No centralized CMDB exists for systems management data and metrics.
- IT support is reactive, and problems take longer to find and fix because of a lack of integrated, reconciled CMDB data.
- There are few measurements of true customer experience. Users may experience a degradation or interruption in service, but there is not complete enough information to tell what caused the outage. In some cases, IT monitoring may show that all underlying systems are up and available although the end-user cannot retrieve data. In many cases, there is no correlation between transaction, performance, and availability data.

PROACTIVE SERVICE-ORIENTED MANAGEMENT

In terms of organizational transformation, this is perhaps the single most important stage, because at this stage, the separate silos of domain expertise are superseded to create more effective management of the total infrastructure with all its critical interdependencies. At this stage, a service organization, which can grow out of either the operations center, the help desk, or a separate third source, becomes a fundamental and consistent interface for the broader business. The help desk begins to shift focus away from incident management toward gathering information for service planning and coordinating processes for governance across all of IT with higher levels of automation and efficiency (Figure 9.10).

In this stage, management solutions are chosen strategically rather than reactively. Priorities for analytics and visualization to capture business impact and priorities are consciously defined and proactively sought, and workflow becomes more automated to capture best practices across various processes in operational and business management.

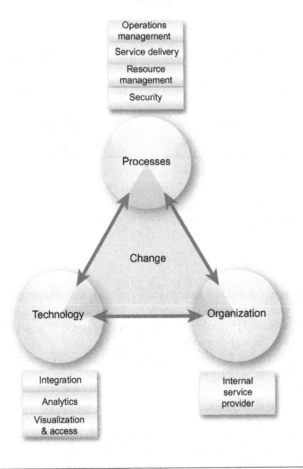

FIGURE 9.10

Dominant drivers and influencers of proactive service-oriented management.

The organization views itself as a service provider to a mixed constituency of internal, external, and business partner clients. This means an integrated face to the business with an individual or team dedicated to proactive service planning. IT also appreciates and consciously addresses the cyclical model defined in Figure 9.1, in which technology investments, process improvements, and organizational evolution are leveraged deliberately and creatively by executive IT management. IT's role vis-à-vis the larger business has become one of enhanced respect, with metrics to show both the business value and the cost of business services.

Progress toward stage four will require continued investment in self-healing and increasingly predictive analytic capabilities and an increased dedication to business alignment in all of its dimensions—from cost to security (including compliance and audit) to revenue generation and improved business or organizational performance.

DYNAMIC BUSINESS-DRIVEN MANAGEMENT

At this stage—and let's be clear that this is a stage that still lies largely in the future for most organizations—automation and business alignment have become so integrated with IT processes and organizations that the role of IT can shift fundamentally once again. Day-to-day performance and availability issues are largely managed by automation, so that IT can focus on capturing business advantage and optimizing to shifting business conditions. Planning new services and optimizing end-user and consumer experience on an individualized basis will be more a matter of focus than simply sustaining services or fixing breakages. IT data will increasingly inform not only on infrastructure patterns but also on business, legal, and security-related behaviors, which will pose both new challenges and new opportunities (Figure 9.11).

Resource management is fully focused on managing assets, capacity, and other investments as a dynamic part of IT's business portfolio. In stage four, the infrastructure can become largely virtualized so that business services can dynamically and optimally exploit available resources based on business demand. At the same time, public cloud resources are assimilated as well-understood and well-managed components of the larger whole—as an extension of (not a replacement for) IT's core portfolio. This is, in a sense, a fully integrated common ground between service management and asset management, where assets, including outsourced services, are evaluated not only in terms of cost but also in terms of performance and business contribution. Automation is a primary definer for this phase, as corrective actions, reports, dynamic service provisioning, Change Management, and other disciplines will all become foci for automation.

Proactive capabilities are achieved through investments in advanced intelligence that shift resources automatically based on observed conditions and events. Advanced heuristics might even anticipate a power problem ahead of the local utility, based on patterns in usage and performance. The linkage between business service and infrastructure will be modeled so that infrastructure restoration can be driven and prioritized by business requirements in automated fashion.

SALIENT TRENDS TO WATCH ACROSS THE FOUR STAGES

Some of the more significant trends that emerge across these four stages for IT evolution are the following:

- There is an evolution from element-centric management, to domain-centric management, to infrastructure management, to a focus on application and business services and business advantage. At each of these junctures, cultural, technological, and organizational factors must be addressed.

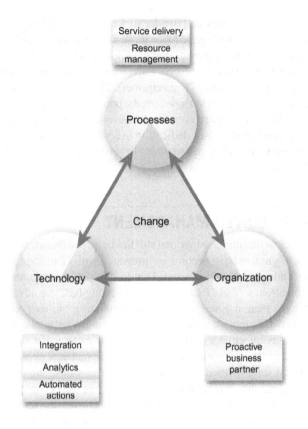

FIGURE 9.11

Dominant drivers and influencers of dynamic business-driven management.

- Early-stage dependence on heroes and highly technical skill sets in day-to-day firefighting are gradually realigned through higher levels of automation so that experts can refocus on planning, optimization, and business advantage.
- Over time, the help desk shifts focus away from problem and incident management toward a true service desk more directed at proactive customer experience and service development.
- There is a similar shift away from help desk-based incident management to more automated performance and availability management solutions typical in the operations center, which over time can evolve toward preventative rather than reactive capabilities.
- Business alignment occurs in part through the gradual emergence of a new organization that can present a single face to both internal and external customers and is focused on strategic service planning as it maps to business priorities. This organization can emerge from the help desk/ service desk, from the operations center, or from elements of both.
- The cultural-and-technology chasm dividing the service desk and the operations center in early-stage IT organizations is slowly being crossed. IT evolves toward a more integrated set of processes in support of strategic service planning, allowing the service desk and the CMDB System to play a larger, more unifying role.

- Security progresses from isolated point solutions to a more systemic approach. Similarly, there is a gradual integration of security disciplines as extensions of mainstream management services; for example, access control is integrated with service provisioning and Change Management and intrusion detection is integrated with performance and availability management.
- Asset management matures beyond segregated domains toward a more dynamic, performance-aware view of total infrastructure resources as they map to services and business requirements. A rise in the importance of accounting, usage-based analysis, and chargeback and financial analytics will accompany this trend. Applications and application portfolios will increasingly be managed as business-facing assets with clear linkages to business outcomes based largely on data from user and customer experience, usage, and other metrics rather than on merely convenient assumptions.
- The increasing importance of analytics in management technology makes it, along with the growth of automation and service modeling, among the three most dominant technology differentiators and enablers.

INTERVIEW WITH A GLOBAL FINANCIAL SERVICE COMPANY IN STAGE THREE: PROACTIVE SERVICE-ORIENTED MANAGEMENT

The following Q&A[1] sheds light on many dimensions of CMDB System deployments while also serving to represent largely stage three, proactive service-oriented, dynamics in IT maturity. Some of the other highlights include the following:

- The importance of a service-aware executive sponsor in sparking the project
- Evolution from a single use case CMDB—data center migration—to a broader ongoing resource
- A move to federation in this case based on data import
- Evolution from a regional CMS toward becoming a global CMS
- The importance of process and ITIL
- A clear focus on scope and use case

How Did Your CMDB System Deployment Get Started?

At the beginning the primary driver was to build a relationship repository of IT equipment to support a move to build new data centers. To answer questions like, 'If I turn the switch off on this rack, what happens?' Or, 'When I turn off these servers, what will be the impact to IT and to the business?' At the time, we envisioned this as a fairly linear project in scope—a finite investment, to support our migration in moving data centers from one building to another.

Then, what became clear was—that this project, the seeds of our CMS, was actually an important operational tool. We were beginning to understand many of the day-to-day interdependencies that we couldn't get our arms around before. People doing incident and particularly Change Management started to see the benefits when going through planning and approvals, because they could see the impacts of what they were doing.

We could see interdependencies at a new level of consistency and detail—from power, to hardware, to logical OS, as well as applications, database and middleware components. That was the level of scope initially, and now we're paying the price, so to speak, for our success, as we try to build our model out more thoroughly to support other areas.

Can You Say More About How Your Team Works?

We are responsible for day-to-day maintenance, as well as for integrating and federating multiple data sources. We delegate the data quality of specific sources to the domains responsible. Data quality should be the purview of the people whose day jobs depend on that data. So we have established processes in place to build a more effective approach for doing that. For instance, we have established three levels:

1. Inventory, monitoring and other federated sources and their owners
2. Service modeling owners
3. Technical owners of polices and effective execution of data federation.

How Does Your Federation Work?

We 100% import data. It is all brought in as a copy from individual CMDBs based on established policies. Where we can, we're looking at introducing dynamic API repositories to expand the scope and ultimately reduce the batch imports for all this data. But at the moment we import on a daily basis. We used to have an import schedule based on unique CI frequencies, so that some of the more dynamic CIs were updated every day, others every week, or weekends, etc. but that became too complex. So now we just import all the data for the core system every night.

How Critical Is the IT Infrastructure Library to Your Initiative?

I would say ITIL is a critical part of this initiative. It provides a supportive background in establishing service management processes and recognizing the core value of process across our organization.

Can You Describe Your Current Environment and Scope?

Currently we are focused on data center infrastructure for the CMS—we are not yet including end-user equipment. We have tens of thousands of physical devices spread across multiple data centers, and tens of thousands of logical OS instances.

We are working on bringing application interdependencies more front and center within the CMS, which brings in different ways of understanding the context for managing change. We have a program to better understand how our applications map back to IT services and Change Management processes associated with those.

What Type of Services Are You Supporting?

We have thousands of services—which we define as anything that has a "level agreement" (Service Level Agreement, Operational Level Agreement, etc.) associated with it. There isn't a hard and fast hierarchy of how we cluster services. We try to manage them based on each one's individual requirements.

The currency we operate in is IT services, and we're just beginning to relate individual IT services and processes to broader business services.

What Are Some of Your Present-Day Objectives in Expanding the CMS?

What's happening now is we're beginning to see additional benefits in supporting regulatory and compliance requirements. We're helping to ensure that appropriate levels of redundancy and other control items such as version currency.

What Recommendations Do You Have for Other CMDB System Deployments?

Both I and my team feel strongly that process is king—and that once good processes are in place, the ability to bring in good data is the easier part of the challenge. No software by itself is a silver bullet. The CMS requires dialog and planning and cooperation across multiple stakeholders.

Other advice I would give is always know your scope. Know what you're trying to achieve and the value proposition around it. Know what problem you're trying to solve. Don't just go from a by-the-book approach to ITIL in which everything imaginable might be a CI and therefore belong in the CMS. Do what's achievable and what's going to provide value. And as we expand our reach, another rule comes into play—the bigger your reach and organization quite often the shallower your coverage can be.

It's true, we get questions all the time about why don't we have this or that incorporated into the broader Configuration Management System. But as successful as we are, we still can't be all things to all people.

[1]Interview with a European-based global financial services company using Interlink Software's BSM software including the service configuration manager.

SUMMARY TAKEAWAYS

This chapter looks more deeply at how the three drivers that impact IT Maturity Levels—technology, process, and organization—interrelate. It establishes shorthand for looking at key influencers and characteristics of each. These include

- instrumentation, data gathering and discovery, data store, integration and data sharing, analytics, automation, visualization/reporting, and business alignment for *technology*;
- service support, operations, development and service delivery, security, IT financial and resource management, and cross service management for *process clusters as they map to organizations*;
- reactive heroes, operationally empowered tribes, internal service provider, and proactive business partner as they map to *organizational personalities* at each stage of IT maturity.

The four key phases of IT maturity are

1. Reactive infrastructure management,
2. Active operational management,
3. Proactive service-oriented management,
4. Dynamic business-driven management.

While many IT organizations today are seeking to evolve from the *active operational management* stage to the *proactive service-oriented management* stage, many still remain stuck in the *reactive infrastructure management* stage, in which individual heroes resist the clearly defined processes needed to share information within and across silos. Generally speaking, IT organizations still in this first stage are not yet ready for a CMDB, and as seen in this chapter, those that have jumped the gun are likely to find their CMDB ineffective.

Active operational management is an excellent stage for initially deploying a CMDB and evolving toward a larger CMDB System, once the willingness is in place among both stakeholders and executive leadership to commit to a more cross domain, service-aware way of working. At this stage, the CMDB System initiative can become both a cultural driver and a technology driver in moving into the next phase of IT maturity.

The transition into *proactive service-oriented management*, where true cross domain processes and organizational models come into being, is at once the most critical stage in IT maturity and the one that is most directly affiliated with highly effective CMDB deployments. This is because the CMDB System can become both a catalyst and a beneficiary of the move toward a more cross domain, service-oriented mindset.

Dynamic business-driven management remains a rarity except in certain high-tech and web-based business models, as it requires a unique cultural commonality between IT and the business or organization it serves, as well as strong investments in automation and analytics. At this stage, the CMDB System becomes a foundational enabler for optimizing superior levels of business alignment, automated efficiencies, and contextually driven analytic resources.

It should be stressed that—at least across the last three stages—the impacts of the CMDB deployments and their associated software investments not only represent technology advances but also can help you to move forward to achieve an even more progressive level of process effectiveness and business alignment. This is part of the "cyclic and opportunistic" thread that's so critical to optimizing technology investments in evolving IT toward higher levels of maturity.

You should take this into account when you do your evaluations at the end of CMDB deployment phases. Showing clear evidence of process and cultural improvements, as well as technological advances, is one way to ensure continued executive support for you and your initiative as you move into new phases for the future.

MOVING FORWARD

DEVELOPING A PROJECT PLAN: FROM METRICS TO REQUIREMENTS AND BEYOND

10

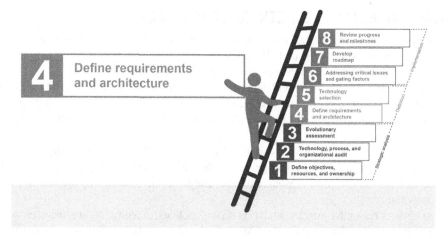

An effective project plan associated with a CMDB System initiative should address many components. Among the core ingredients are the following:

1. Use case and overall objectives
2. Metrics arising from these
3. Detailed requirements arising from these
4. Return on investment (ROI) objectives as appropriate
5. Defined milestones—typically 6 months, 12 months, and 2 years out
6. Team building and development—in conjunction with...
7. Stakeholder identification, engagement, and development
8. An effective and evolving communications plan
9. A clear definition of technology requirements—including architectural needs, where and how to invest, and where and how to prioritize technologies for integration
10. Other initiatives likely to impact and possibly redirect the CMDB System initiative—for example, the move to cloud/virtualization, mergers and acquisitions, data center consolidation, new requirements for application sourcing, development and deployment, and business model changes and business expansion
11. Cost and resource requirements from the present through an anticipated 2-3-year window

This chapter will primarily address items 2, 3, and 4 on this list (metrics, requirements, and ROI).

Building on the assessments, you've already established to create a viable set of metrics, and requirements is central to any effective CMDB System initiative. Without these, the initiative itself can become rudderless and, much like the CMDB itself, succumb to too much data and political pull, with too little relevance and focus.

The step two assessment, as discussed in Chapter 8, should provide you with solid insights into stakeholder roles and needs and help you identify communications issues, opportunities, and likely venues. Combined with a better understanding of your actual IT maturity level (Chapter 9), the step two assessment serves as the springboard for developing the metrics and requirements discussed in this chapter.

INTERNAL AND EXTERNAL METRICS VERSUS ROI

The place to begin with setting metrics and milestones with the CMDB System is in planning its phases with reasonable objectives for scope and efficiency.

This is so even if political pressures may try to steer you otherwise.

It's tempting to shoot for the moon with hard dollar value for a CMDB initiative. There's likely to be plenty of political pressure to create metrics that show the financial value. However, defining financial metrics requires a real appreciation for the specifics in your environment and a well-thought-out set of deployment-related metrics.

In fact, most IT organizations move ahead initially with a CMDB investment without a fully formalized ROI commitment as they come to recognize that the CMDB can be an enabler for many values, but just in itself, the CMDB is more of a resource than an endgame. Given this, why are non-dollar-specific metrics so important?

The most obvious reason for metrics still has to do with politics, executive commitment, cross organizational enthusiasm, and overall support for the CMDB System as it evolves. While no one expects a CMDB initiative to be a quick and easy endeavor, the people in your organization will look to see where and how it is benefiting them broadly and, in particular, how it is helping them to achieve their critical business missions.

You can hardly expect this to be otherwise.

The implementation of a CMDB System can quickly have a dramatic and pervasive impact across IT, and our research[1] underscores this with 50% of the respondents affirming that 75% or more of their overall IT organization is impacted by their CMDB initiative as you can see in Figure 10.1.

GENERAL CATEGORIES FOR METRICS

The need for the following categories for CMDB System metrics has borne out over years of consulting, dialogue, and analysis:

- Metrics directed at ensuring effective milestones in the evolution of the CMDB System itself. These metrics generally can be divided into three areas: *scope (breadth* of coverage), *accuracy* (*integrity* of information), and *efficiency* metrics documenting improvements in the maintenance and evolution of the CMDB System.
- External metrics directed at clear use cases. These metrics will look familiar as they were briefly described in Chapter 7 for core CMDB System use cases:
  - Change Impact Management and Change Automation

---

[1]The CMDB/CMS: from Philosophy to Federation, EMA, 2009.

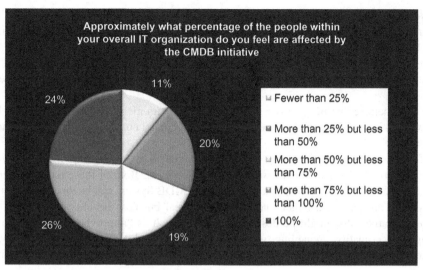

FIGURE 10.1

These data reinforce the fact that the CMDB System should support a large percentage of the IT organization—whether as stakeholders and administrators or, far more broadly, as consumers of data, analysis, reports, and even process-driven automation.

- – Asset Management and Financial Optimization
- – Service Impact Management and Capacity Optimization
- – IT governance initiatives targeted at compliance, security, and risk
- The third category of metrics fully articulates "hard" value in support of some ROI calculations. Logically, they are primarily subsets of the second group, although some hard metrics directly supportive of CMDB System project efficiencies may also be included if they can be clearly linked to OpEx values—as CMDB process efficiencies enable broader operational efficiencies impacting how IT works as a whole.

THE CMDB SYSTEM IS PART OF A LARGER UNDERTAKING

Before going further with the discussion of metrics, we'd like to introduce this quote from an EMA report, which helps set the stage for why assigning metrics to CMDB deployments requires attention to detail, flexibility of mind, and sufficient modesty, to realize that as an "enabler," the CMDB by itself cannot do it all:

> The CMDB System is an enabling technology. It provides access to IT data in a structured, reconciled, and synchronized manner from the many technology silos and toolsets spread across your organization. It feeds high-level analytics and intelligence engines that can enable new, more accurate, and more effective ways of sharing and analyzing information. However, it is NOT in itself a service desk, change management system, dashboard, etc. As such, it has little dollar value in and of itself.[2]

[2]Defining Value for CMDB Systems—Some Internal and External Metrics to Help you Get Started. EMA, March, 2008.

The single most important reason why you should bother with metrics

It may sound childlike, but the best place to begin your consideration of metrics is by asking "why?" While the first answer at the top of most adopters' minds is likely to be *because I have no choice if I'm going to sell this thing*, there really are much better reasons if you look more closely—and by setting expectations about how you're going to proceed up front, you can save yourself from a great deal of pain in the end.

We strongly believe that the best reason for CMDB System metrics—internal/external, hard, soft, and in-between—is to make sure that you are making pragmatic cost choices (e.g., tools and staffing) along the way.

Two of the worst reasons for putting CMDB metrics in place are to *justify the cost of the CMDB project* and *to provide an absolute yardstick of CMDB success.* Both of these motivators may sound good, but they create the false notion that the value of CMDB System can be directly measured. Since CMDB Systems are part of a larger undertaking, the real business benefits come from measuring those larger initiatives that might be described in terms such as "improving operational efficiency," "improving service quality," "enabling two organizations to combine more effectively through mergers and acquisitions," and "enabling new types of application services through more effective change management."

The boundaries for measuring these larger initiatives will extend beyond the immediate CMDB System endeavor. So when it comes to providing absolute yardsticks, you would be dealing from both sides of the deck if you collected only costs directly associated with CMDB and tried to map them to benefits that are also the result of many other investments in software, services, and training.

You'll find that you become much more credible once you're forthcoming about this. Ultimately, fudging numbers and trying to impute mystical values to your CMDB will come back to bite you.

That isn't to say that looking at the impact of these broader initiatives isn't valuable—in fact, most CMDB metrics designed to show external value do examine those additional impacts. But by being clear up front in developing your ROI—and by being honest with yourself, your stakeholders, and your management about how you're managing your project—you will promote better commitment and investment in the long term.

We believe that ultimately, CMDB Systems should not be viewed and measured as *projects*. Rather, they should be seen as carefully managed investments that support broader operational and business goals that become a foundational part of the IT budget.

Consider the data in Figure 10.1. CMDB Systems should be enablers for any number of benefits across all of IT. They will typically involve a number of federated resources with a wide range of stakeholders and owners. They should continue to evolve to support a broader range of objectives and changing business priorities. And they should also continue to evolve as new and improved CMDB software and technologies emerge and as your organization matures yet further in culture, process, and business alignment. Figure 10.2 shows respondent priorities for CMDB-related benefits and objectives from prior EMA research.

INTERNAL CMDB SYSTEM METRICS

The metrics presented here are designed to support you and your team if you're managing the CMDB deployment. As such, these metrics will need to be communicated horizontally to stakeholders across your organization, communicated upward to your management, and, depending on your role, communicated

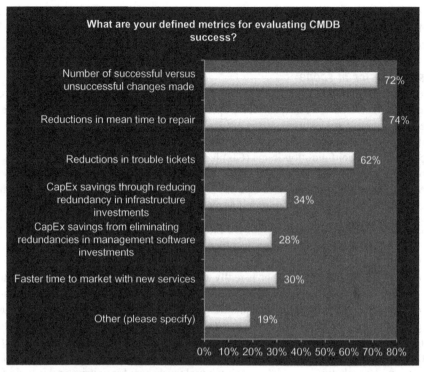

FIGURE 10.2

This shows how respondents prioritized metrics in their CMDB deployments in prior research ("The CMDB/ CMS: from Philosophy to Federation," op. cit.). *As you can see, reductions in MTTR and an improved ratio of successful versus unsuccessful changes clearly topped the charts.*

downward to your constituents. As an *itSMF* guide for metrics[3] astutely points out, "metrics are a form of communication… Designing metrics is not a technical or back office job. For metrics to work, all parties must be consulted." (This includes stakeholders and customers.)

However, the metrics in this section are not what might be called "customer-facing." They're designed to create an environment in which your team can work together efficiently and consistently. ITIL even likes to suggest that establishing some commonality among stakeholders across various metrics may promote "friendly competition" by providing a common way to see how each group is measuring up. New technologies for gamification can make this option more thorough and attractive, as has been evidenced by more than one deployment we've witnessed.

We should stress that, on the one hand, the list of metrics and metrics-related questions below is not complete. On the other hand, you can sabotage your initiative by imposing too many internal or project-related metrics at once. So, please view the sample list of metrics below as exactly that—samples. We would suggest that in total, your internal CMDB System metrics should consist of no fewer than ten key parameters (those applied to stakeholders in general) and not more than twenty key parameters.

---

[3] Metrics for IT Service Management, itSMF, Van Haren Publishing, 2006.

The following list is a set of questions around which you can build your own far more specific metrics. More fully evolved metrics and requirements, as shown later in this chapter, are typically stakeholder-specific, are far more granular in scope, and, hence, are much more numerous.

Questions for metrics of scope
- How does the committed budget map to requirements to support at least phase one objectives in terms of estimated costs in SW, services, operational overhead, and other quantifiable parameters?
- Have all appropriate stakeholders been identified and committed?
- What percentage of configuration items (CIs) have identified owners?
- What percentage of CIs are loaded and under management based on phase-relevant objectives?
- What percentage of trusted sources or sources of record have you identified and confirmed for inclusion into the CMDB System required to meet phase one objectives?

This last metric is easy to overlook, but it's often the single most challenging part of laying the foundation for CMDB Systems. It requires a cold eye to redundant toolsets, often used by competing groups across your broader IT organization.

The next set of metrics related to scope is really a holding place for multiple CMDB System *design objectives* that are in themselves going to vary based on phase one goals, architectural choices, and other factors. Fundamentally, these metrics should provide you with a yardstick to map how you are progressing in getting a federated system of trusted sources that can actually communicate with the core system. This requires identifying which CIs should be included in the phase one core and which should not. It should also address requirements for reconciliation, normalization, and synchronization across the system. As such, this becomes an architectural worksheet for metrics and in and of itself will deserve a whole separate and dedicated analysis.

Metrics for accuracy and integrity
The *itSMF* guide for ITIL metrics suggests useful metrics for accuracy and integrity under the broader heading of *configuration management*. The metrics that apply to the CMDB include

- number of failed requests for change from bad CMDB data;
- number of failed changes caused by poorly documented CIs;
- number of breached SLAs because of CMDB errors—including missing items, misleading relationships, and poor escalation because CIs are not linked to the appropriate SLA;
- number of requests for change without corresponding CI updating;
- percentage of inaccurate CIs;
- number of incidents due to inaccurate CIs.

To these, we have added the following few thoughts, most of which approach similar problems in a slightly different language:

- Number of missing or duplicate CIs
- Number of changes to the CMDB per month due to identified errors with the CMDB System
- The consistency with which CI updates are done with the right frequency to meet requirements (i.e., number of instances when updates that should have happened didn't—through either manual or automated population)

Metrics for efficiency

These metrics target the evolution and maintenance of the CMDB System. Not all of them may be appropriate for early-phase adoptions. But the general goal is to find metrics that support operational efficiency in the near and longer term. The following metrics can directly contribute to reducing the total cost of ownership (TCO) of your CMDB System:

- Percent of CIs that are discovered or updated automatically
- Percent of CIs that are synchronized and reconciled automatically
- Percent reduction in the cost of maintaining CI data
- Percent of cost reduction in extending the CMDB System to include new critical CIs or CI attributes (through improved technology choices, deployments, and/or team processes)

Figure 10.3 shows one way of graphing some of the more salient metrics in assessing the progress and effectiveness of your CMDB System. This is a summary of the metrics presented above. The horizontal axis focuses on time and the vertical on dollars/value.

EXTERNAL CMDB SYSTEM METRICS

Now, let's revisit some key external metrics that may be associated with your CMDB deployment as first introduced in Chapter 7. These *external metrics* are almost certainly going to involve more than just the CMDB investment. They are indications of the real value to operations, and ultimately to the business, as your CMDB System enables better access to information, better analysis, and better collaboration across IT—just as a superhighway enables a car to travel at faster speeds than it can on a potholed country road. While many of these external metrics may suggest dollar benefits, only a prioritized few should be developed into clear ROI benefits.

Change Impact Management and Change Automation
- Reduction in number of unapproved changes detected
- Reduction in number of change collisions
- Reduction in number of failed changes and redos
- Reduction of changes made on service impact
- Reduced cycle time to review, approve, and implement changes
- Improved time efficiency to validate that changes made are non-service-disruptive
- A decrease in documentation costs required to initiate changes and add new applications
- Number of changes that do not deliver expected results

Asset Management and Financial Optimization
- Completeness of mapping of assets to owners
- Completeness of mapping of assets to customers
- Cost savings from improved compliance with SW/licensing agreements
- Number of assets with a documented understanding of asset costs per service
- Documented improvements in the level of accuracy for costing out services to customers
- Faster ability to provision (existing/new) services to customers based on more informed insights on asset interdependencies

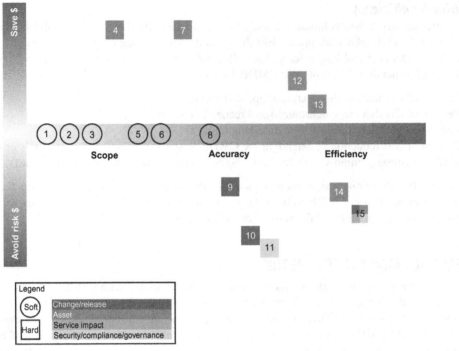

FIGURE 10.3

Metrics summary for internal CMDB System metrics. 1. Budget adequacy for scope. 2. Number of stakeholders defined. 3. Percentage of CIs with identified owners. 4. Trusted source (source of record) assessment. 5. CMDB system design. 6. Number of CIs included in the system. 7. Percentage of inaccurate CIs. 8. Appropriateness of CI updates. 9. Number of errors per month caused by erroneous changes to the CMDB. 10. Failed requests for change from bad CMDB data. 11. Number of breached SLAs due to CMDB errors. 12. Percentage of CIs discovered/updated automatically. 13. Percentage of CIs synchronized and reconciled automatically. 14. Percent reduction in cost of maintaining CI data. 15. Percent of cost reduction in extending the CMDB System to include new CIs or CI attributes.

- Improved ability to integrate and retire new assets in terms of time efficiency, cost efficiency, and service impact (downtime)
- Number of assets mapped to appropriate security parameters
- Effectiveness in meeting security/compliance audits
- Savings on license, support, and maintenance contract costs on devices that no longer exist or need to be licensed-supported
- Efficiency in managing assets across their life cycles—number of unplanned incidents

Service Impact Management and Capacity Optimization
- Reduced downtime
- Reduced mean time to repair (MTTR)

- Improved mean time between failure (MTBF)
- Reduction in number of trouble tickets
- Reduced number/seriousness of SLA breaches
- Percentage of incidents resolved by first-level support
- Percentage of CIs monitored for performance
- Reduction in the number of repeat failures (recurring problems)
- Percentage of CIs covered by business impact analysis
- Savings in CapEx costs from capacity optimization
- Savings in vendor (outside dependency) costs from capacity optimization

Security/Governance/Compliance
- Percent of CIs auditable through automation (via policy, gold standard comparison, etc.)
- Percent of CIs compliant with policies/standards (e.g., more efficient SOX and HIPAA)
- Reduction of incidents/problems specifically caused by noncompliant CIs
- Reduced time to perform audits for compliance
- Improved quality/effectiveness of audits for compliance
- Number of changes backed out of as a result of security issues

---

Below is a summary set of recommended metrics from an EMA consulting engagement with a large financial services company—combining internal and external values.

Consider including the following metrics and set targets to improve them over a realistic time frame:

- CI information (CIs, CI attributes, etc.) that is not as authorized
- Incidents and problems that can be traced back to ineffective changes
- New software requests that were not completed successfully because of poor impact assessment, incorrect data in the CMDB, or poor version control
- Cycle time to approve and implement changes as documented through the impact assessment
- Degree of conformance to current software licensing agreements
- Exceptions detected during configuration audits (e.g., when actual state is not as authorized)
- Unauthorized IT components in use (e.g., by audit, staff, or customers)
- Change in the average time and/or cost of diagnosing and resolving service desk calls that cannot be resolved immediately (on the first call)
- Change in the number and/or seriousness of incidents and problems
- Change in the number and/or seriousness of occasions when an SLA has been breached and the problem can be traced back to errors made in the change management, configuration management, release management, problem management, or service desk
- Number of changes to the CMDB per month because of identified errors in the CMDB
- Cost savings for acquisition and retirement of assets (recovering costs on software and reducing hardware expenditures is easily measured and provides value across the entirety of operations)
- New OpEx efficiencies as the reduction of redundant software reduces infrastructure complexity by eliminating moving pieces

External metrics in summary
Any astute IT executive will quickly be able to see value as you begin to show improvement on even just a few of the above metrics. It should be pointed out, however, that these metrics will take more time to achieve than those metrics only associated with CMDB System deployment.

Figure 10.4 shows a summary of "hard" metrics for assessing the effectiveness and external impact of your CMDB System by addressing many of the external metrics listed above. Those in the inner part of the circle are directly related to downtime or other costs; those on the periphery are more generally directed at savings from operational efficiency. The metrics are clustered to highlight areas of inter-relationship across disciplines.

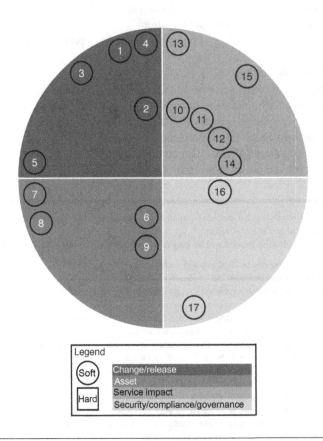

FIGURE 10.4

This shows a summary circle of values for CMDB System external impact. Metrics in the inner part of the circle are directly related to downtime and other costs. Those near the periphery are directed at operational savings. 1. Reduction in number of failed changes and redos. 2. Reduction in the number of changes with negative impact to service performance/availability. 3. Reduction in cycle time to review, approve, and implement changes. 4. Improved time efficiency to validate that changes made are nondisruptive. 5. Decrease in documentation costs required for initiating changes. 6. Cost savings from SW licensing agreements. 7. Faster ability to provision services. 8. Improved ability to integrate and retire new assets. 9. Savings from eliminating license, support, and maintenance costs on superfluous devices. 10. Reduced downtime. 11. Reduced MTTR. 12. Reduced MTBF. 13. Reduction in trouble tickets. 14. Reduced SLA breaches. 15. Percentage of incidents resolved from first-level support. 16. Reduction of incidents/problems specifically caused by noncompliant CIs. 17. Reduced time to perform audits for compliance.

ROI

While most IT organizations are ultimately willing to go forward with the CMDB investment on softer grounds with respect to ROI, our experience with CMDB consulting often exposes an understandable desire to quantify benefits in terms of cost in some way. In fact, virtually all our clients have requested some support for determining the ROI of their CMDB initiative.

The basic equation for this is as below:

$$ROI = (CostSavings + AddedValues) / CostsIncurred$$

Needless to say, in most CMDB System adoptions, neither "cost savings" nor "added values" (e.g., faster time to provision new or existing services) nor "costs incurred" is a trivial discussion.

We strongly recommend limiting costs incurred to those costs specifically for deployment, software, training, and operational overhead of the CMDB System deployment itself. This does not, for instance, include monitoring tools that are purchased once a "trusted source" assessment reveals critical gaps. Nor does it include the help desk costs, investments in analytics tools, or active configuration management (release management) capabilities. The need for any of these excluded items may be revealed by CMDB-driven assessments, but they are not native costs for the initiative itself.

As a general rule, costs associated with CMDB System software and services should be directed at data capture, transformation and exchange, and reconciliation and synchronization, along with discovery. This list can include actual discovery capabilities for topology and interdependencies, as well as application dependency mapping, and access to federated sources. Finally, it should include OpEx and CapEx integration costs to extend the system as it matures.

However, since many of the discovery capabilities may well turn out to be found art—for example, from strong network or configuration management tools that are already supporting other functions—it's best to limit the discovery costs to those specifically adopted for the CMDB deployment itself. This may seem like a step back from the larger CMDB System vision, but it's the only way to link CMDB-related direct costs into the formula without including what might otherwise become a huge percentage of toolset costs across all of IT for monitoring, analytics, configuration, automation, asset management, service desk functionality, etc.

EXAMPLES

In order to provide more substantive guidance on ROI metrics, here are a few examples taken from research and consulting, providing more context around some of the data points for ROI in Chapter 2:

- Over the past three years, we've tied the CMDB into the change process, and then made sure that it would be supportive of the financial processes and financial systems, and over the course of three years we successfully disputed $2.5M out of a $9.0M spend. In other words we are in a much better position to show our customers what we're doing and why it's costing them what it is." (US Managed Service Provider and Systems Integrator)
- Our CMDB was an attempt to achieve world class availability and at the same time control costs. With id="dq0020"M a minute in downtime for our whole ecosystem—supporting 6,000 transactions a second—MTTR and downtime reduction is critical. We reduced MTTR by 70% through the CMDB." (US Financial Services Provider)

- We were throwing money willy nilly at our service assurance effort without rhyme or reason. We have reduced outages by 40% through our CMDB system, which has brought us 300% ROI in three years." (U.S. Healthcare/Services Organization)
- We have already seen some good ROI, but I don't have all the numbers. We were carrying 30% extra operational overhead, and reduced our Service Delivery organization from 250 to 160. Moreover, 70% of the outgoing calls driven by customer issues were going from one support group to another within our telecommunications organization. The CMDB is already helping to provide a much more consistent and effective way of sharing that information." (Pacific Rim Telecommunications Provider)

One consulting report documented CMDB initiative included the following for cost-related metrics and generalized cost benefits in calculating TCO:

- $100,000—for professional services.
- $45,000—for ITIL training for thirty IT staff.
- $118,000—for twelve senior IT and business stakeholders at 33% of their time over three months for planning and implementation, assuming a fully loaded cost for a senior person at $120,000.
- Software costs were "free" based on bundling the CMDB System with another product.
- Total phase one costs: $263,000.
- *Savings* in this implementation included reduced impact of planned and unplanned changes at $330,000 per year in terms of critical business service availability. In addition, cost reductions in operational expenses for technical support tallied $187,500 per year. There were yet further savings from reduced costs in maintaining duplicate tools and resources.
- Total phase one savings (circa 12 months): in excess of $517,500.

A more detailed documentation of just *one specific* cost parameter from another consulting assessment client is as follows:

- Success metric: Reduce average resolution/routing time for severity 1, 2, 3 calls to Level 2 support
- Current baseline: 48 min per call
- Assumptions: 3120 calls in 2007, $600/IT staff average daily rate
- Projected value: 33 min per call
- Difference: 15 min per call
- Annual savings: $58,500

Again, we should stress that this is just one of more than 50 ROI-related metrics surrounding this particular CMDB System initiative. For instance, these dollar savings didn't include reduction in MTTR or downtime improvements that, for critical application services, would vastly exceed the dollar amount shown in the list above.

Words of wisdom
As one of our consultants notes, "From our experience, you can start seeing measurable returns within the first ninety days of a CMDB deployment, assuming that you have well defined success metrics and detailed requirements. The overall value is not how fast you get a positive ROI, but the fact that as the system matures, you should eventually get many multiple times the return on your investments."

Please note that while many benefits can and should be measured and tracked, others will almost certainly remain intangible. For instance, projecting what "might have happened" had the CMDB System initiative not have gone forward is a little like trying to create an alternate universe and hence may sound more like science fiction. Perhaps the best approach is to look at examples from this book—and begin to consider just what the "costs of doing nothing" might have been in a select few critical areas.

Two examples of these *costs of doing nothing* are the following:

- *Disasters avoided:* Doing nothing can lead to multiple disasters. In contrast, when automatic dependency mapping detected a production firewall incorrectly labeled as "test"—proactively avoiding a major outage—this paid in itself for the total cost of one CMDB deployment.
- *Business competitiveness:* Doing nothing can limit business growth as more efficient competitors erode market share through more effective capabilities to extend their business reach through new IT services. For example, roadblocks in SOA, Web, Web 2.0, or virtualization initiatives often get stalled because IT is still lost in fragmented silos for monitoring, tracking, and making changes to the infrastructure.

TRANSLATING METRICS INTO DETAILED REQUIREMENTS UNIQUE TO YOUR ORGANIZATION

A key step to CMDB System Success is documenting detailed project requirements. Detailed requirements clarify what the CMDB is going to do for you and, just as importantly, what the CMDB is *not* going to do for you.

A "detailed project requirement" is not simply a list of reports, configuration items (CIs), or resources to be managed. A good detailed requirement clearly links CMDB-related data with a defined process that spans technology silos and/or can enable automation for processes that are purely manual. A good detailed requirement is one that [4]

1. can be understood by everyone from the CIO to mainframe programmers,
2. can demonstrate clear value to the business,
3. can be tied to CIs in the CMDB schema,
4. focuses on current business issues and information needed,
5. is inclusive of data provided by multiple technology silos.

A *great* detailed requirement is one that can also be assigned to one or more measurable success metrics and along with an annual savings target.

Conversely, Figure 10.5 shows some examples of poorly written CMDB requirements:

As an example of a well-written detailed requirement, consider the following:

> Provide dependency mapping data for the Investment Banking application to Level 2 support staff via the Command Center Console. Currently, this is done by looking up the contact information for the application manager and calling the domain experts to determine the relationship mapping. This currently takes an average of 15 minutes per call to determine the needed information—a delay that could be eliminated through CMDB-driven automation.

---

[4]This section is taken from "*How to Define Detailed Requirements for your Enterprise CMDB Project: A Hands-On Workbook,*" EMA, April, 2008.

Poorly written requirement	Why is it poorly written?
We need the CMDB to be able to validate firewall data on input against business rules.	Because this is simply a feature of the CMDB technology, not a business-driven detailed requirement.
We need a better network database where firewall information is maintained.	Because it isn't tied to solving a specific business problem.
We need to decrease risk by 30% by reducing the number of outages due to change to our firewalls.	Because it is too high-level and needs to be more specific.

FIGURE 10.5

Three examples of poorly written requirements.

This detailed requirement

1. is clearly written and understood by the business,
2. demonstrates clear value to the business,
3. can be tied to CIs in the CMDB schema,
4. focuses on current business issues and information needed,
5. is inclusive of data provided by multiple technology silos.

So, how many detailed requirements are typical for a CMDB System initiative? In general, we have found that our enterprise clients typically end up with anywhere from 200 to 750 detailed requirements. If your list includes fewer than 50 detailed requirements, they are probably too high level. Ask yourself these questions to expand your thinking:

- Have you included all lines of business?
- Are all technology silos represented?
- What about application development?

If your list of requirements includes more than one thousand, they are too detailed. If this is your problem, we suggest combining requirements that share similar traits to narrow your list. Remember, just because you *can* gather data doesn't mean that you should.

The requirements for your CMDB System will change, so it is important to treat them as a living document. Always remember to focus on the business value—not product features—when writing detailed requirements for your project (Figure 10.6).

A WORKBOOK FOR CREATING A DETAILED CMDB SYSTEM REQUIREMENT

The time to begin to create detailed CMDB System requirements is after doing your initial CMDB assessment as well as some initial planning to identify more general objectives. Any given requirement may evolve as you move through the various rungs on the Ladder to CMDB Success—including technology selection and final gating factors. But being aware of a solid process for doing it right is critical as you move forward.

Is your requirement …	
Understandable? *Is your requirement written in a way that can be understood by everyone from the CIO to a hands-on member of the IT team?*	Yes / No
Business value? *Does your requirement show clear value to the business?*	Yes / No
Supported by data? *What data fields would be used to capture the requirement? Can it be tied to CIs in your CMDB schema?*	1. 2. 3. 4. 5.
Spans databases? *Would the data for your requirement be found in different databases and tools across your company?*	Yes / No
Success metric? *What success measurement would you use to keep track of the requirement?*	

FIGURE 10.6

A short checklist for assessing CMDB System requirements.

Figure 10.7 looks at the phone-time metric identified above and places it in a template for creating detailed requirements. It includes

- a requirement summary,
- a representation of IT Service Management impact (looking at ITIL processes),
- domain and/or silo impact,
- value proposition,
- primary CIs impacted,
- further CI details.

Part 1: Requirement overview

Figure 10.8 presents the top part of the overall template. Note that after stating the detailed requirement in the "Requirement" field, it provides a number for the requirement ("Req Number"), documents the source of the request ("Req Source"), and assigns a preliminary priority ("Priority"). For example, in the case of Figure 10.8, the priority assignment was "moderate."

Taking this as a workbook exercise…

EMA Detailed Requirement	Created: 2/7/2008
Customer: Acme Company	Modified: 2/13/2008

Requirement: Provide dependency mapping data for the Investment Banking application to Level 2 support staff via the Command Center Console. Currently, this is done by looking up the contact information for the application manager and calling the domain experts to determine the relationship mapping. This takes an average of 15 minutes per call to determine the needed information.

Req Number: 5.12
Req Source: Level 2 Support Manager
Priority: Moderate
More Details: Yes

ITSM Impact:

Incident	Service Desk	Problem	Change	Release	Configuration	Financial	Service Level	Availability	Capacity	Continuity	Security
S	S	P			P						

Domain Silo Impact:

Applications	Database	Desktop	Web Servers	Middleware	Storage	Servers	Network	Architecture	Investments	Data Center	PMO
P	S	S	S	S		S	S			P	

Value Proposition

Success Metric:	Reduce avg resolution/routing time for IB Sev 1,2,3 calls to Level 2 Support
Current Baseline:	48 minutes/call
Assumptions:	3,120 calls in 2007, $600/IT staff average daily rate
Projected Value:	33 minutes/call
Difference:	15 minutes/call. This will save 32.5 days per year.
Annual Savings:	$58,500

Primary CIs for this Detailed Requirement

CMDB_Application_Service	(i.e., Investment_Banking_Application_01)
PathName	(i.e., C:\Program Files\Acme\IBApp01.exe)
CMDB_System_Component	(i.e., Server)
SystemClassID	(i.e., 444556783921)
SystemName	(i.e., ACMES01_PROD)

CI Details

Relationships
    Investment_Banking_Application_01 is contained by ACMES01_PROD

Systems of Record
CMDB_Application_Service	Vendor A Application Discovery DB (ADPROD01) - DB2
CMDB_System_Component	Vendor B Hardware Discovery DB (HDPROD01) - Oracle

Reconciliation/Synchronization
CMDB_Application_Service	None
CMDB_System_Component	Vendor C Asset Management System DB (AMPROD01) Synchronization should be daily upon discovery

Federation/Promotion
CMDB_Application_Service	Federate with core CMDB
CMDB_System_Component	Federate with core CMDB

Integration
CMDB_Application_Service	Vendor A Application Discovery DB (should be native)
CMDB_System_Component	Vendor B Hardware Discovery DB (explore third-party)
Command Center Console	Should be native between CCC and CMDB

FIGURE 10.7

This is a template used by EMA consulting to define detailed requirements for CMDB Systems. Depending on the scope of the phase one initiative, most large enterprises should have between 200 and 750 detailed requirements as part of the phase one initiative with an eye to the roadmap beyond phase one going forward.

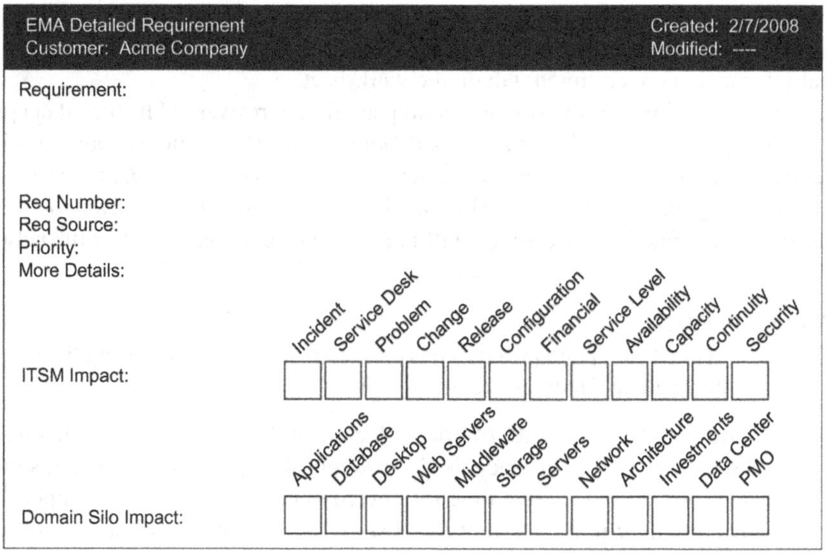

FIGURE 10.8

This presents the top of a detailed requirement template to help clarify the individual components. It can also serve as part of a workbook exercise in developing your own requirements. The categories listed for these fields should be modified to map to your organization.

Imagine an empty template for a moment—with a different requirement that you're seeking to articulate for your own initiative. Now follow these steps:

1. *Number the requirement:* Using a simple 1, 2, 3 numbering scheme for your requirements is fine. The reason for numbering the requirements is that you will be growing the list and eventually combining similar requirements. The descriptions will change as the requirements are combined, refined, and reassessed, so a simple numbering scheme will allow you to keep track of where you are as requirements accumulate.

2. *Document the source of the request:* When you combine similar requirements later, this field may include several requestors. It is important that readers can quickly scan the entire detailed requirements spreadsheet and identify the requirements that they articulated.

3. *Assign a preliminary priority:* Final prioritization will evolve and become normalized as all the requirements are gathered. But to start, just note what priority the requestor would assign to the requirement. This is useful information, even if the priority changes along the way. It is critical to note that the priority does not necessarily determine the order in which the requirements are addressed. For example, you may think the most important part of a car for your driving pleasure is the stereo. But the car is built in a logical order, and while this priority is eventually met, it is unlikely to be the first thing done. Setting the expectation of when the requirement will be met is important—and highlights the value of having a complete list of detailed requirements.

4. *Include additional details:* If the description of the requirement becomes too long or includes supporting documentation, note it in the *More Details* field and link the requirement to the additional information on a different tab on the worksheet.
5. *Estimate the impact:* Next, try to estimate the impact to both relevant ITIL (or other) processes and the technology silo in the *ITSM Impact* and *Domain Silo Impact* fields. Our consultants use a two-letter designations—"*P*" for primary impact and "*S*" for secondary impact. As you start the process, just make your best judgment. This step is important because it allows you to quickly scan the list of requirements to see which will impact Change Management or the network group.

Part 2: Value proposition

This part of the requirements template provides a critical foundation for measuring the progress of the CMDB System initiative and documenting achieved values:

1. *List success metrics:* In the *Success Metric* field, document the success metrics that will be used to measure this requirement. For instance, in the example shown in Figure 10.7, this metric is "reduce average resolution and routing time for Severity One calls to Level 2 Support."
2. *Document current baseline:* In the *Current Baseline* field, you can record the current baseline measurement for the metric *(e.g., 48 min per call).*
3. *Identify assumptions:* Document any assumptions important to the calculation of this metric in the *Assumptions* field *(e.g., there were 3120 calls in 2007 at a $600 average daily rate).*
4. *Estimate the projected value:* In the *Projected Value* field, jot down the estimated future value for the metric after the CMDB is implemented *(e.g., 33 min per call).*
5. *Calculate the difference:* Record the difference between the *Current Baseline* and the *Projected Value* for the metric in the *Difference* field *(e.g., 15 min per call or 32.5 days per year).*
6. *Calculate the annual savings:* Using your assumptions and the projected change in the metric, estimate the annual cost savings associated with the requirement and record it in the *Annual Savings* field *(e.g., $58,500).*

Part 3: CI details

It's also important to understand and document the configuration items linked to each of your detailed requirements. We recommend gathering this information in two steps. The first step is to document an example of the information that is needed. For instance, you may well know the name of the application and the name of the server on which the application runs. This might be the extent of the information available in the interview session.

The next step is to take a look at the CMDB schema for your CMDB solution. At this point, you might see a need for additional CI-related information—for example, the *PathName* for the application.

Data for this section will have to be adjusted as the CMDB System and its modeling schema evolve. Identifying and prioritizing CIs as a part of the broader service-modeling schema will be addressed in more detail in Chapter 13:

1. *Record CI relationships:* It's key to identify the relationships between the CIs and record them in the *Relationships* field. In the example of Acme Company in Figure 10.7, the relationship between the CIs is a "contained by" relationship. Realize that some of these details will be determined by your choice of technology.

2. *Identify systems of record:* This means understanding *where* the definitive data for the requirement reside. In the *Systems of Record* field, note any systems of record associated with the CIs listed for the requirement. Ultimately, you will want each CI attribute to have only one system of record—but a CI may contain many other CIs within it and may also have many associated attributes.

3. *Reconciliation and synchronization requirements:* In the *Reconciliation/Synchronization* field, you can document what type of reconciliation is needed. You will also need to know if you can update remote citizen CMDBs to keep them synchronized with the core CMDB. Finally, you will need to know the frequency of synchronization. A look at emerging analytic and automation capabilities to address these challenges will be addressed in Chapter 12.

4. *Consider federation/promotion needs:* Do you need to move the data into the CMDB or just provide a pointer to where the data live natively? Note that paper documents or flat files may require promotion of data directly into the CMDB. Document these requirements in the *Federation/Promotion* field.

5. *Document integration points:* Finally, you should discover integration points and document them in the *Integration* field. It might take investigation and research to understand what options are available. Are there common APIs or do you need to get adapters for integration from the vendor or from a third party? Make sure that these needs are well documented because integration issues can cause significant problems for the implementation team if they are ignored. A single integration should generally support multiple requirements. If not, both the requirement and the integration may not be a phase one priority.

Once you have collected a reasonably full set of detailed requirements for your CMDB System, the next step is to categorize and prioritize your requirements. Categorization of the requirements allows you to group similar or related CMDB detailed requirements. This step is important as it will allow you to quickly find a particular requirement, combine like requirements from different sources, and quickly provide an executive overview of CMDB project status.

The template and the exercise above provide you with a solid foundation for categorizing and inter-relating requirements—whether you are developing them in Excel, in project management software, or in other software with associated search criteria.

ARCHITECTURAL REQUIREMENTS

Chapter 12 not only is directed at "technology selection" but also provides a solid template for assessing architectural specifics. However, "architecture" in a broader, more strategic vein should be an integrated part of your use-case, initial assessment, metrics, and requirements planning. Probably the most important footprint for architecture is use case, where you sketch out the broader dimensions of phase one objectives.

In Chapter 7, we've given special attention to some of the technology considerations associated with each use case. Your initial assessment (Chapter 8) will expose technology gaps in data collection and other areas that will become another foundational building block for establishing meaningful architectural directions. Now, with more refined levels of metrics and requirements, you are at the point of stitching together clear architectural goals that translate into both the parameters of your modeling system and the dimensions of your phase one design.

Taking the very specific example in requirements definition above (Figures 10.8–10.10) as an example, a number of architectural requirements immediately become apparent—either explicitly or implicitly:

- The ability to link CIs to owners
- The ability associate CIs with critical infrastructure and service components
- The ability to provide clear interdependency maps and/or insights so that problem areas can be defined in context
- Reasonably real-time currency so that problems and incidents can be understood in a timely manner through the service desk and operations

Value proposition
Success metric :
Current baseline:
Assumptions:
Projected value:
Difference:
Annual savings:

FIGURE 10.9

This is a critical component of the detailed requirements template as it can provide a clear baseline for documenting progress and showing achieved benefits.

CI details
Relationships
Systems of record
Reconciliation/synchronization
Federation/promotion
Integration

FIGURE 10.10

Identifying and prioritizing CIs in context with their broader interdependencies is central to making a CMDB System come to life. Chapter 13 will provide a more extensive discussion of strategies, issues, and challenges in refining and optimizing CI definitions and interdependencies.

- Integrated support for the service desk and operations so that service desk professionals and operational CI owners have a consistent view of where and how service disruptions may reside

In other words, your broad-brush architectural requirements should be established gradually, well before diving into the details of technology selection. We recommend keeping a separate accounting of architectural needs starting at the very first step of the Eight-Step Ladder to CMDB System Success and then refining it as you move through more detailed insights into use case, gaps, metrics, and requirements.

INTERVIEW WITH AN ADVANCED CMDB SYSTEM DEPLOYMENT SUPPORTING A LARGE GLOBAL AIRLINE SYSTEM

The following interview[5] presents a very interesting picture in terms of requirements and CMDB System evolution. Although it's hardly a phase one story—just the opposite—the interviewee has evolved a federated model that requires ongoing requirements insights and dialogue. This interview highlights the fact that requirements gathering, definition, and implementation are an ongoing need, even in a successful CMDB System. This deployment is also an example of what we once called "the two CMDBs"—a classic, process-oriented system and a real-time (or near) BSM system working together in a federated CMS. Finally, it's worth mentioning the strong and still growing support for DevOps in this particular example.

How Did You Evolve Toward Your Current System?

Most people think of a CMDB in terms of a service desk. That's where you'd have the CMDB to do problem, change, request, and service management, shoving in the function of asset management, as well. Well, in our arena, we did have a service desk CMDB, but when we started working with our BSM vendor 12 years ago on event management, this vendor had its own CMDB, which included relationship information—interdependencies between a service and servers, what ran on the servers, and what they might impact. If a piece of code failed, then we could immediately see the user impact. This complemented our other CMDB where we manually populated assets for problem, change, and incident management.

Can You Say a Little Bit About Your Role and How It Has Changed?

About 18 months ago or more, I moved from the role I was in focused on the BSM CMDB to support a transition to a new service desk platform with an eye to unifying the two systems so that we could reuse some of the information on the event management side as well.

How is the Initiative to Provide a More Cohesive Federated CMS Going for You?

It's going well enough. At first we did a feasibility study, knowing that a single massive CMDB wouldn't work for our environment. We needed a federated approach. And in our environment that means leveraging many data stores as federated data sources for the broader CMS and knitting it together in a single architecture.

It's taken me a year to get full buy-in across the organization. We looked from the left to the right of the toolset spectrum, asking what tools were in place and what we could use for the broader system. There are plenty of service desk vendors that claim if you want to use our CMDB and service desk, you have to use our discovery sources. We said, 'Thanks, but no thanks.' We have a variety of solutions, for instance, just for managing our network and its subnets, or for our IP phone system.

How Are You Prioritizing Data Access for the New System?

We have a process in place that requires us to know—what are the business questions that this data can answer? What are the business uses in terms of optimizing our IT capabilities to support genuine business needs? There's no point in making data available if there's no reason to actually consume it.

One example might be we're closing down a call center in New York that might include phones, desktops, and whatever else happens to be in those offices. Can we find a way to look at a common attribute and generate a list of everything in the building, find out their relevant specifications, and find out who the main users are—or who they're going to be for that equipment in the future for planning and optimizing the move? The federated system already has most of that data and so what we need to do is make sure it's inclusive and then link it to a unique attribute associated with the move.

Who is Doing the Work and How Are You Building Your Models?

Generally, we look to the people in the organization who know where the data is, and what's trusted, to help us feed our modeling, and make sure that the current data in the system hasn't aged.

To be honest, we're not actually using a modeling studio or a vendor's modeling system. We're exploring our own database capabilities instead with a three-tiered architecture. The first tier is made up of the tools holding all the raw data about CIs. The second tier is a staging area—where we explore how we want to join the data together across silos to create the views and associates we need. Then the third tier is access. If we were using SQL, we'd have to have our consumers plumbing directly in a single CMDB. Instead, we're using a Restful Web Service API with a data map on it, so the consumer asks the Web Service for the data. All we have to do is change the data mapping in the Web Service to make sure the linkages support each new use case.

Prior to this, we were often moving from tool to tool, from source to source, with a lot of custom attribute creation, much of which was redundant. So we wanted to pull it all into the service management system to simplify the process.

What Were Some of the Drivers for This? What Led You in This Direction?

One of the current drivers was an investment process for our asset management initiative called 'Keeping it Current.' We looked at products across the IT infrastructure that were getting old or aging and falling out of vendor support—potentially causing lots of incidents, not to mention major service disruptions. The benefits for doing this right go beyond IT. They can span everything from 'I need to get off of Oracle Version 10' to helping us fuel our planes more effectively—our capability for servicing the aircraft properly depends on a current and effective IT service delivery system. As a result we're supporting a wide range of stakeholders—from Unix administrators trying to make more effective decisions right up to the manager of IT Operations for supporting business objectives, to stakeholders outside of IT.

How Large is Your Particular Configuration Team?

Right now we have two people who are more administrative and two people who are more business-requirements related—so we can better assess requirements to extend the CMS to new data sources and use cases. We also have two database administrators. This doesn't include the broader systems management team, which is largely responsible for the real-time BSM capability. As far as having someone focused on process—right now that's largely me.

What Were Some of the Challenges You Faced?

Cultural challenges were a big factor in getting the silos to think about new ways of working together. Another pressure was for a linear project plan. Some people kept asking, "why isn't there a project plan for this?" But this is an evolving system. It's not supposed to have a fixed start date or a fixed stop date.

How Are You Coming Along in Meeting These Challenges?

Right now we're stronger on the grassroots side than on the senior executive front for the CMS. Many stakeholders in the organization are seeing benefits. But I'm confident that at some point senior management will more fully recognize the value. That will have to happen in any case after a while for us to move forward. For now we're enjoying positive word of mouth for getting interest in the CMS initiative. Eventually what we want to do is publish options for using the system in a service catalog so that people can query and request the data they need."

Is There Any DevOps Direction to Your CMS Deployment?

We have this concept to help us meet the challenge of cloud called 'Agile Data Center Provisioning.' Needless to say, unless we have a good set of service interdependency insights, we can't do the automation. When someone builds a server and they choose an application for it, that information gets stored into our system through a Restful Web Service. So you can go onto a web page and see . . . the size and dimensions of an application environment that developer XYZ is building. Once approved—or once you hit the OK button—we have automation that goes off and builds the server environment required.

As another example of DevOps value—I may see that a new application resource is available, and I may want to go and leverage that application resource and its components for my service. I can now go and look to see more about similar hosts, OS, configurations, and performance histories of similar components as they've impacted my particular service, so I can better anticipate possible available and performance issues if I use those components. We hope to have that fully up and running in about five months.

Can You Say More About How You're Using the BSM, or the More Real-Time Part of the System?

This system allows us to integrate event and service performance management with the broader CMS—and we have plans to further integrate event management into our service models so that updates to the models can be generated automatically.

Do You Have any Parting Words of Advice for Someone Building a CMS?

If I had to sum it up, I would say you should understand the business need of what you're doing and bring in the data and views you need to support evident business requirements.

[5]Interview with a European-based global transportation company using Interlink Software's BSM software including the Service Configuration Manager.

SUMMARY TAKEAWAYS

Nothing could be more important to the success of a CMDB System than a well-thought-out set of metrics and requirements. As can be seen in this chapter, creating this set requires not only doing a thorough initial assessment (step two in the Ladder to CMDB System Success) but also looking ahead to prioritize values, identify critical CIs, and document clear areas of benefit with very specific and tangible objectives.

This process, however, should not be equated with return on investment (ROI). While ROI can be an important by-product of good metrics and requirements, it is far from the whole story, and if taken as a core driver, ROI can actually lead the CMDB System initiative astray. It is always important to remember that your CMDB is an enabler that can bring huge benefits that resonate across a broad set of toolsets, stakeholders, and processes—making a strict, linear case for ROI all but impossible.

One of the key takeaways here is to consider both *internal* and *external* metrics for your CMDB System. Internal metrics include those of *scope, accuracy,* and *efficiency*. External metrics follow critical use-case objectives. Metrics should be applied to support your deployment and initiative first and foremost, so that you can see how and where progress is being made—as well as measure areas of success and isolate areas that need further attention.

Detailed requirements will evolve as you move through initial assessments, technology selection, and final gating factors. Detailed requirements should also include an understanding of affected CIs and their interdependencies. Above all, promote solid stakeholder interaction with clear insights into priorities, needs, and opportunities for tangible improvement.

Finally, you should be developing your architectural requirements in parallel with metrics and broader requirements, leveraging insights from your use-case and initial assessment planning. We recommend keeping a separate tract devoted to architectural planning starting in step one of the Eight-Step Ladder to CMDB System Success.

FINALIZING YOUR PHASE ONE TEAM

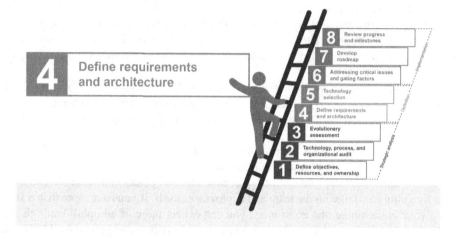

In the last chapter, we established that a significant percentage of the IT organization—in some cases, even 100%—will eventually become consumers of insights driven by the CMDB System. At the same time, there must be a far more finite set of identified stakeholders who "own" CI-specific requirements for data integrity and who directly participate in the larger CMDB System project. Then, at the core, there is the CMDB team itself.

This chapter will look at core team requirements in skill sets, expectation setting, reporting structure, and data and process responsibilities. Depending on the size of the environment and the scope of the initiative, this team may vary in size from a few part-time staff to four or more full-time individuals. But the roles and requirements will not change substantially in quality as the scale of the IT environment grows or shrinks.

Needless to say, you will need to sketch out your initial team requirements in step one of the Eight-Step Ladder to CMDB Success. You may even get an initial headcount to work with you in this process. But as you climb up that ladder, you'll gain more insight on requirements and skill set needs, as well as on consumers and stakeholders. Then, as you move toward technology selection, you'll want to ensure that at least your phase one team requirements are fully solidified, supported, and ready to move forward.

CONSUMERS

To begin, let's take a look at the meshing process between the CMDB System, consumers, and stakeholders. These constituencies make up the broader human foundation needed for any CMDB to be effective in generating value.

You may not think of "consumers" as part of your team, but in many respects, they are. They are in large part the very reason that a CMDB System exists. It's critical that the core CMDB team has a good understanding of consumer habits, perceptions, and needs. Social IT, website blogs, and other venues also provide new options for integrating the consumer perspectives with core team priorities.

The following three quotes, taken from some of EMA's research projects and consulting engagements, reflect team views on consumer scope and quality:

- We have 50 direct users and stakeholders, and about 9000 indirect users, as our CMDB supports the entire business.
- I would say that two-thirds of our 300-person IT organization are currently consumers of the larger CMDB/CMS system either directly or indirectly. Moreover, interest continues to grow as more and more people in IT begin to realize and see value in accessing information that they didn't know was there before.
- We have about 300 different types of consumers defined, including business executives, ITIL process owners, applications management, and managers and administrators for desktops, servers, mainframes, merger recovery services, and facilities planning—just to name a few.

Knowing your consumers is not a "nice to have." It will impact team operation and planning, as well as budget, resources, and ongoing future commitments.

Below is a recommendation from one of our consultants that places consumers in context with requirements for going forward with the team and deployment itself. If you have more than a 10% "holdout" among your initial phase one consumers, you can expect more of an uphill battle than is ideal. How much team time is devoted to settling disputes among existing and potential CMDB consumers with divergent wants and needs should be proactively assessed and managed.

The approach that we favor for CMDB implementations is one of demonstrating incremental value and working from a clearly defined set of detailed requirements. In this way, a well-managed CMDB implementation can gain grassroots support. However, this does not mean that the CMDB group will be immune from implementing and enforcing policies or settling disputes over data. With all projects of this scope, there will be a few holdouts who will need to be brought into line with the management "stick." This number should ideally be less than 10% of the organization. Overall, our approach has been to promote the CMDB System as an enabling technology for solving problems for both IT and the business. With strong executive leadership, this approach has been successful at other organizations in optimizing value for consumers and minimizing the burden of the core CMDB team in addressing consumer-related issues.

STAKEHOLDERS

Stakeholders play a critical role in building the success of the CMDB System—and while they are not directly a part of the core team, stakeholder management *is* very much a core team requirement. At the same time, stakeholders provide an expanding source of outreach for dialogue, communication, priority setting, and data management.

So how do you optimize this opportunity?

The following bit of good advice came from an interview with a CMDB System project manager:

> • One thing that makes our CMDB deployment work well is getting stakeholders in the game so that they're involved not just as consumers but also involved with feeding the system.

The role and involvement levels of stakeholders and domain experts may also be a gray area in the initial phases of CMDB System development, deployment, and integration—as described in the following quote from a consulting recommendation:

> On the CMDB project, there will be a need for domain experts to be brought in during various implementation phases. For example, network expertise will be required when deciding on the levels of integration appropriate for network management 'citizen' CMDBs and which of their CIs are appropriate for inclusion in the 'core' CMDB. While it is unusual for these assignments to take more than a couple of weeks, the staffing situation here suggests that these positions should be back-filled with supplementary contractors for requests of over 20 hours of a domain expert's time.

Note the *staffing issues* described regarding backfilling domain experts needed for the project. Planning for a core CMDB System team will also mean casting a broader net in terms of identifying resources, especially when it comes to critical domain expertise at various junctures during deployment.

One example of stakeholder, or CI owner, responsibilities with clear requirements for owning data accuracy is described in the quote below (excerpted from the Q&A in Chapter 4—*featuring two broadbased dialogues about CMDB adoption.*):[1]

"Our policy is that if you make a change to a CI, there must be a change record. If you change a CI without changing the record, that can be grounds for termination. Also, there are log files that we've activated in support of our CMDB. So from our baseline, we can do delta checks. The CI owner has to also own discovery and the processes around discovery relevant to his or her CI. If discovery indicates a change, the CI owner is notified by e-mail automatically. If a change record already exists, then everyone is happy. If not, then both the CI owner and the configuration management analyst are notified and the CI owner will have to take action.

"We also want to use the principle that the owner of the information has to update the information. For instance, we have a dedicated application team that pushes the application code into different application servers. This team needs to own the relationships surrounding our applications and their components. We have an infrastructure team building infrastructure services such as authentication, directory services, and data services. And that team will be responsible for the servers as well as the infrastructure across the various connections."

Realize that as CMDB-related technologies evolve, updating the "change records" as referred to in the quote above may increasingly become an automated procedure so that the CI owner remains responsible for the total system operating well in his or her domain but far less constrained by routine manual tasks. Otherwise, the incentives for going forward and evolving the broader system may get lost in burdensome administrative overhead.

Since managing stakeholders is an ongoing thread throughout this book—from initial assessment interviews, to creating stakeholder-relevant metrics, to establishing a clear tiered plan with agreed-upon

---

[1] Colloquium with a large manufacturer and a mid-tier insurance company both using the ServiceNow CMDB.

processes—we won't try to cover every aspect of it here. However, to wrap up this section, here are two comments that sum up both a caution and a value in the extended team/stakeholder management narrative:

- Set realistic expectations to everyone who could be involved in your CMDBS project. It is more complex than most people realize because you need to effectively assimilate multiple data sources.
- I would say that as a fundamental, achieved benefit to date, we have finally gotten the entirety of IT to work together instead of being stuck in a siloed mentality. We've only begun this journey, but we've gotten all of IT to pay attention to it" (from Chapter 2).

FINALIZING THE CORE TEAM

While there is not a pure, set formula for establishing a core CMDB team, there are consistent skill set requirements relevant to almost every CMDB System initiative. The following quotes from our consulting and research show the varied nature of CMDB System scope and requirements and how they impact the makeup of the CMDB core team.

- From an administrative perspective, I oversee the CMDB and I have one full-time person reporting to me. There are about 40–50 stakeholders currently.
- I have six people reporting to me directly. One of them is the Configuration Manager who validates the changes and notifies the other five. CMDB administration is not a dedicated role—probably about a third of an FTE.
- Right now the full resources specific to administration of the CMDB is about one-half of one FTE—that's me. Fifty percent of my job is CMDB administration along with being the configuration and ITIL lead for our IT organization of 300.
- We have three people supporting our CMDB. One is going to be focused on discovery. Two are directed to cover our core requirements based on the data model. And we have developed processes in place to populate those classes. In our support model, according to ITIL standards, the only people who update our CMDB are the Configuration Management analysts. They are the gatekeepers. But our CI owners are accountable for updating those classes—not the core CMDB team.

Figure 11.1, taken from our research,[2] shows how CMDB System skill sets mapped to percentages of respondents. The characteristic mix shown here for a core CMDB team includes requirements for managerial skills, architectural skills, process guidance, and stakeholder participation. Internal and external consultants typically complete the picture. As will be discussed below, *external consultants* are often either vendor-supplied or system integrator-provided, to help get the phase one deployment up and running. *Internal consultants* are typically either architectural experts brought in to help jump-start the program or domain experts keying on federated or "citizen CMDB" requirements both for integration and for prioritizing data content.

Figure 11.2 reflects average FTE (full-time equivalent) employee requirements from past CMDB deployments.[3] As averages, the numbers will vary substantially based not only on company size but also on the scope and direction of the CMDB System. The good news is that improvements in technology and automation are beginning to reduce these averages.

---

[2] The CMDB—from Philosophy to Federation, EMA, 2009.
[3] Ibid.

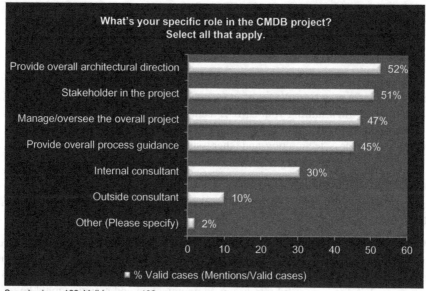

Sample size = 162, Valid cases = 162

FIGURE 11.1

This mapping of respondent numbers to skill sets reflects core CMDB team requirements fairly accurately—even if it's not at all intended as a generic standard. Data management skills, which are also key, are not separately captured here—but will sometimes fall to the "architecture" role.

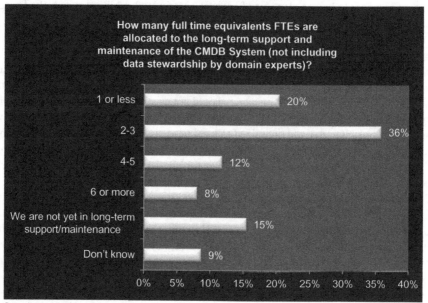

Sample size = 162

FIGURE 11.2

The average staffing requirement for a core CMDB team in this data set is roughly the equivalent of two and a half full-time employees. Technology advances are slowly beginning to reduce this number. It is interesting to note that in this same research, there was surprisingly little correlation between team staffing and the number of CIs supported—suggesting that CMDB size or scale will depend more on stakeholder resources than core team staffing.

It should be stressed that while this question asks about "full-time" employee requirements, in reality, the core CMDB team may be made up of more people who are not engaged full-time. This is important to keep in mind when staffing your CMDB team. In fact, there can be real advantages to having a core team that includes individuals with shared roles beyond the CMDB itself, as they can bring broader awareness of process, technology, and other issues to the inner workings of the CMDB System.

A RECOMMENDED CORE TEAM MATRIX

Throughout most of our consulting engagements, we have recommended a team of four full-time or part-time CMDB System "enthusiasts:"

- *Team Manager*: The team manager should be an easy-to-approach evangelist who is able to articulate the value that the CMDB brings across the entire IT organization. This is because a significant amount of grassroots education and support is required to make the CMDB initiative succeed. A focus on solid intragroup communication and service should be maintained throughout not only phase one but also subsequent phases, as the CMDB System evolves. The team manager also needs to be a good project manager, as initial success will depend on the timely completion of several key projects. If possible, this position, in particular, should be filled by a full-time employee (as opposed to a part-time employee or outside consultant).
  - *Possible associated roles for team manager*: In some deployments, it may be advisable for the team manager to have a clear set of process-centric leadership roles as well. These may include the following:
  - *Configuration manager* works with the core team to implement the organization's configuration management policy and standards.
  - *Change configuration and release (CCR) manager* might be taken on by the CMDB team manager in smaller operations with limited change and release management activities. In smaller environments, acting as the CCR manager should not necessarily require fulfilling all of the responsibilities or authorities that ITIL grants to a traditional change manager. In other words, a simplified approach to the role optimized to local needs is preferable to a role fully orchestrated in every detail. The same holds true with the release management elements of the combined CCR role as well. A broader look at CCR roles for smaller environments might also include asset manager, change administrator, and support for the Change Advisory Board (CAB).
- *CMDB Specialists*: Two CMDB specialists are typically needed for the implementation and integration of the CMDB solution. They will be responsible for working with the various technology silos to determine the initial low-level requirements, acting as a liaison for the CMDB vendor, installing software, writing reconciliation rules, adjudicating any issues with systems of records, making recommendations for tool consolidation, testing the CMDB schemas, and rolling solutions into production. Some architectural skills, with insights into broader architectural requirements across operations, can be a definite plus here. Depending on local skills and software in-house, one of the CMDB specialists may be an outside consultant with special knowledge of the CMDB-related software being deployed.
- *Information Architect/Database Specialist*: This person is responsible for categorizing and scrubbing the requirements, analyzing the data model and schema, identifying CI-level data elements (and duplication), generating updates to the website, and reporting on project progress. It is essential that this specialist has good database skills. This can be either a part-time or a full-time position.

CMDB Strategy: While primarily the duty of the team's manager, all CMDB team members should be well versed in the overall CMDB strategy and road map. In an effort that requires significant grass-roots education, it is imperative that the team is able to communicate a clear and consistent message to the IT staff regarding its goals and road map. We recommend that all team members participate in the creation, refinement, and measurement of the strategy and road map. This effort should take approximately 10% to 20% of the staff's time initially.

ITIL: We also recommend that at least one (if not more) of the CMDB team positions be staffed by ITIL-certified personnel in order to provide process support for the CMDB effort.

Data Responsibilities: The CMDB team is not responsible for the stewardship of the data itself. It's just not possible for the CMDB team to be responsible for individual data tasks that effective, domain-expert stakeholders can perform. Instead, the CMDB team is responsible for the following:

- Providing process guidelines for gathering and automating data collection
- Establishing and enforcing rules for data integrity and quality
- Setting best practices for establishing integrations with the tools that collect the data
- Drift management; reporting on the CMDB levels of accuracy, scope, and efficiency

OPTIMIZING ITIL PROCESSES

Ideally, it should not be the job of the CMDB team to instruct others in the ITIL process or define process for the groups. Rather, the CMDB team should be a reviewer and approver of these tasks—reviewing and drafting CMDB process policy as they apply to the CMDB. It's important that process documentation is understood as an up-front requirement of the CMDB project.

Additional ITIL Roles and Responsibilities

When ITIL is providing a strategic foundation for the CMDB System—and we have seen successful deployments leveraging other best practices (as exemplified in the Q&A in Chapter 15)—an expanded role for ITIL beyond the CMDB deployment itself is advisable. In this case, in addition to a core team presence, it can be a strong advantage to have another ITIL evangelist on board within the broader IT organization. This evangelist will be tasked with determining the value of ITIL in practical terms and marketing this information to relevant IT managers and stakeholders.

This individual can assist silos in reviewing their process documentation while also working with the core CMDB team to evaluate processes for keeping data updated, as data are integrated with the CMDB. By taking a "mentoring" approach, rather than using the classic "instructor/student" model, the evangelist can demonstrate the value of ITIL processes in a hands-on manner specific to each technology domain. This is yet another case where dialogue and solid back-and-forth interaction routinely trump more formal hierarchical approaches to evangelization.

Such an approach will also enable a level of consistency across the enterprise as more groups are brought online with the CMDB System. We typically recommend hiring an ITIL Master-certified employee to this position. It should be stressed that this role can bring value over and above the deployment of the CMDB System by improving IT process efficiencies.

However, it should also be pointed out that the relevance and focus of this role will depend on the specifics of the environment in terms of ITIL readiness and enthusiasm. A substantial number of successful CMDB System deployments have been able to bypass the more formal sides of ITIL process awareness—as long as there is a meaningful attempt to map out a cohesive process matrix at some level.

STAFFING CHALLENGES

While being aware of more global staffing issues won't in itself solve CMDB-specific staffing problems, it's important to keep a vigilant eye on what's realistic and what's not. The CMDB System does not emerge in a vacuum but must arise out of a real commitment to mature IT more broadly. A realistic approach always trumps an idealized approach without any legs in an actual IT environment. This is especially true as the core CMDB System team does not lend itself to environments where staffing is already so stretched that any investments in future efficiency become improbable distractions.

A few quotes taken from prior CMDB consulting work help to illustrate the issue:

- We failed miserably on a past initiative because people were too busy and things got out of control.
- Our first CMDB deployment was a good concept, very broad at the time. But only one person was assigned to the project.
- The initial project never had the right folks. This CMDB project needs the best.

Considering how to find the right team members can be just as important as agreeing on role and size. This may mean drawing from the most affected groups within IT for phase one and phase two, as well as establishing a solid balance of technical, process, leadership, and communication skills.

REPORTING IN

The core CMDB System team can't operate in an organizational vacuum. It will report into *somewhere* within IT. The data in Figure 11.3[4] confirm that while the software for the core CMDB often resides in the service desk, the service desk team rarely owns the CMDB initiative. This is true for good reason. A broader cross organizational and cross domain leadership is central to CMDB System success.

Among the more interesting categories in Figure 11.3 is "Service Management"—a cross domain team targeting broader service management goals. This relatively new organization can take many forms—some teams are focused on cloud adoption, others on operational performance management, while some take a more a strategic approach to unifying asset and service management—as well as integrating change, configuration, and other roles.

The following excerpts are two separate recommendations for the core CMDB team reporting affiliations from two different consulting engagements—underscoring the need to look at the specifics of each environment. The first environment is clearly hierarchical, while the second is an extension of already well-established responsibilities among peers.

- "How the CMDB team fits within the larger structure of the IT organization is critically important. We are recommending that the CMDB initiative be placed within under operations. As the CMDB is an effort that spans many technology silos, the team must report into the IT organizational structure in a cross functional manner, eliminating any bias based on management reporting responsibilities. Also, a certain level of authority is required to establish and enforce CMDB policies. This includes domains that might traditionally fall outside of operations, such as the application development life cycle."
- "It is common for large enterprises to have an inwardly facing infrastructure management architecture group that is responsible for establishing standards for IT management tools and evaluating new

---

[4]Ibid.

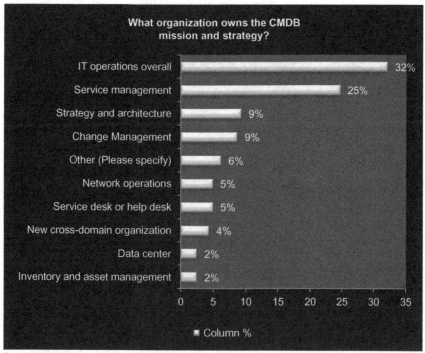

Sample size = 162

FIGURE 11.3

Broad cross domain and cross organizational leadership is key to CMDB System success. The data above generally reflect that preference.

technologies to ensure integration with the existing infrastructure. We predict that the CMDB group will, by its nature, assume some of the roles of an infrastructure management architecture group as the integration of toolsets is a primary focus for the CMDB implementation activities."

In this second case, the final reporting structure ultimately led to the broader operations organization but with strong peer synergies between the core CMDB team and infrastructure management architecture.

Wherever it reports, the core CMDB team is favored by active executive support. Figure 11.4[5] shows that the norm for most CMDB initiatives is ongoing support at the director level or higher. However, as pointed out in Chapter 6, the single biggest variable impacting CMDB System success is whether or not there is ongoing C-level involvement for the initiative.

WORKING WITH THE CAB

The CAB often has a parallel, or peer, relationship (as opposed to a hierarchical relationship) with the core CMDB team. However, it's important to proactively plan both the makeup of the CAB and how

---

[5] Ibid.

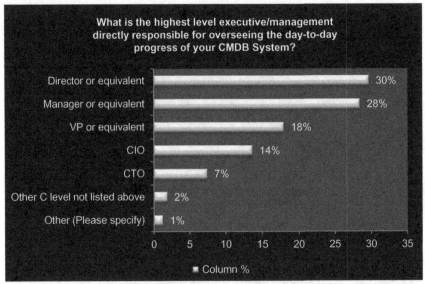

What is the highest level executive/management directly responsible for overseeing the day-to-day progress of your CMDB System?

Sample size = 162

FIGURE 11.4

Most CMDB-related deployments should expect active involvement at the director level or above. Research has revealed that the single most important variable in CMDB System success is whether or not there is active, ongoing C-level involvement. (Ibid.)

organizational interaction will occur between the two groups. This is in part the role of the process owners, as well as the team manager. There is a good discussion of CAB issues (for a dysfunctional CAB) in Chapter 7 under the Change Management use case.

The following example from another consulting engagement provides a set of recommendations for how to create this type of board (in this example, as if often the case, the CAB goes by a slightly modified name—here, it's the "Change Management Board (CMB)"):

> We recommend that the change management board consist of both management and technical experts from the major IT domains. The CMB needs to review both architectural and operational changes. The CMB should also adopt a formal ranking process for change requests, focusing on changes that have high impact or high risk. A key quote was, "We get in trouble with planned changes to environment with unforeseen impacts in scope." The impacts of change need to be tracked in order to gather baseline data. CMB performance should be reviewed on a periodic basis in order to measure progress. Dialogue between the CMB and the CMDB team leader needs to be close and ongoing.

WRAPPING UP

Creating and staffing an effective core CMDB team are central to the success of the program. This chapter provides insights and guidelines from research, industry dialogue, and actual deployments. As generally applicable as we believe these recommendations are, we would stress, once again, the need to consider your own unique environment, needs, and talent pool. While there are some fairly universal rules—for example, part-time or outsourced personnel are not optimal for leading the CMDB team—skill set priorities and staffing levels will vary based on environment size, business model, and initial CMDB System objectives.

Another thing to keep in mind is that team requirements, and especially stakeholder requirements, will have to evolve along with the scope and maturity of the CMDB System. Viewing the broader system more as a developing organism than as a static set of processes will help promote more creative and adaptive team development, as well as enable successes in other areas—ranging from technology adoption and requirements definitions to the enablement of new use cases with new stakeholders.

SUMMARY TAKEAWAYS

Team building for a CMDB System must consider the following:

- Dialogues, interactions, and responsibilities across the *broader IT community*.
- *Stakeholder* identification, development, and management—including clear and ongoing processes for data ownership and data integrity. Domain experts may also play a role in developing and supporting integrations across the CMDB System both initially and as it develops.
- *Core team* roles and functions include the following:
  - Team manager or leader—with good communication and project management skills.
  - CMDB specialists for managing and orchestrating processes central to the evolution of the core CMDB itself, as well as the core CMDB in association with federated sources, such as citizen CMDBs or other data stores.
  - An information architect—directed at governing efficiencies for the CMDB itself as it integrates with the broader system.
  - Relevant internal and external consultants (often vendor consultants with expertise in the software chosen for the core system).
  - Process expertise, and in some cases, process leadership—depending on where and how ITIL or relevant processes are being supported throughout the broader organization.
- The core CMDB team should report into an organization, such as operations or an evolved service management organization, with strong cross domain/cross silo rapport and political clout. The CMDB team should have strong, ongoing executive involvement and support—ideally at the C-level.

TECHNOLOGY SELECTION

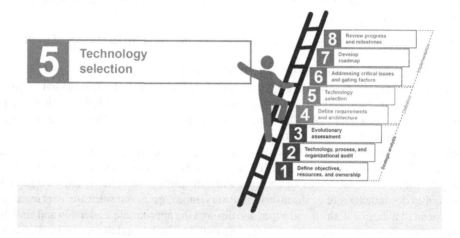

Making the right choice for a core CMDB is central to the success of any CMDB System initiative. However, there is no single answer for all environments. A great deal depends on a number of variables that you should already be in a good position to determine. These include

- use-case priorities for phase one and beyond;
- size, scale, and complexity of your environment;
- key points of integration needed to move forward and start to show value;
- key points of integration critical for down-the-road evolution;
- available resources and skill sets in terms of service modeling, CMDB, administration, integrations, etc., for the core team;
- stakeholder needs, priorities, and skills;
- other required investments (e.g., Application Discovery and Dependency Mapping (ADDM), automation, and analytics);
- existing toolset investments, which may also impact skill sets and comfort levels relevant to the adoption of new technology investments;
- preferences for software as a service (SaaS) versus on-premise solutions;
- time to value expectations for initial benefits.

This list is just the beginning. Before you begin the process of technology selection, you should have at least some insights into most of these variables from steps 1 to 4. The information provided in this chapter will help you take that background information and map it to a meaningful structure to evaluate both CMDB and ADDM choices.

The chapter ahead will address core CMDB evaluations in terms of

- packaging
- usability, deployment, and administration
- architecture, scalability, and scope
- integration capabilities
- functional advantages in terms of use-case requirements for supported analytics and automation
- visualization, reporting, and role support

Also provided in this chapter is a comparative grid between two CMDB choices taken directly from a past consulting engagement.

Next on the agenda is a summary look at ADDM selection criteria.

Finally, we will wrap up by revisiting other relevant investments, ranging from analytics, to automation, to project management and social media. However, since the core CMDB—with its support for federation—and an investment in ADDM typically form the heart of a CMDB System investment, we have chosen to focus predominantly on those.

Similarly, in planning your CMDB resource investments, we strongly recommend that you only factor in "costs" and "investments" into CMDB and ADDM choices—otherwise, you may find yourself trying to supply all of operations and beyond with new tools to meet newly exposed gaps. If there are other toolset dependencies (e.g., discovery, inventory, monitoring, and software asset management), we recommend that they be defined and expedited through the appropriate leadership and stakeholders, if necessary with executive pressure. Their value, after all, lies far beyond the core CMDB. Conversely, these tools are filling deficits critical to your IT organization even without a CMDB deployment.

CORE CMDB PACKAGING

Very few CMDB solutions are currently packaged as stand-alone options. For instance, you may already have a CMDB embedded in your service desk that's not yet in use. However, you may decide for any number of reasons that your current investment isn't the one to take you the whole distance going forward. Moreover, there are a growing number of "variations on a theme"—as some CMDBs are packaged primarily as Business Service Management (BSM) solutions optimized for service impact and performance, others target workflow and automation, and some CMDB solutions are extensions of ADDM tools.

A few questions to ask might be the following:

- What is the purchase price for the full package even if function goes beyond the CMDB itself? For example, if the CMDB is packaged in the service desk, you may want include the base service desk price. If the cost is CI-dependent, calculate costs based on a defined set of CIs. We recommend standardizing on a set a number between 1000 and 10,000 CIs and applying that to all CMDB options in contention.
- How is the CMDB licensed? Some examples might be
  - CI-based
  - user-based

- usage-based
- process-based
- server-based
- enterprise-based
- Does the vendor offer support for a proof of concept prior to deployment? Most do, so you should feel free to make that a requirement. If it is offered, how is the PoC facilitated, and does it require an additional cost?
- What does a real-world deployment approximating your own typically cost?
- What are the most prevalent factors impacting cost?
- What is the cost for maintenance?
- What is the cost for core services? (This may be critical in initial deployment, or it may not be—depending on your own in-house skill sets and the nature of the investment you're making. However, it's a definite plus to have strong deployment services available to support unique modeling or integration requirements.)
- What is the cost for consulting? (Here, you should consider consulting requirements based on phase one use-case needs. For instance, some vendors are strong in supporting asset or change management; others may be more focused in service impact and performance. Others offer very limited consulting services directly and depend on third parties exclusively.)

SOFTWARE AS A SERVICE OR ON-PREMISE?

Current research[1] confirms that SaaS and on-premise delivery models no longer belong in completely separate worlds. This is true whether the CMDB is packaged in a service desk, in an application discovery solution, or in some other context. SaaS solutions are increasingly being held to functional standards similar to those of on-premise offerings, including requirements for security in data management to meet industry compliance and other standards.

It should also be stressed that SaaS may not be an all-or-nothing choice. Your CMDB may be delivered as a SaaS capability but may still integrate with on-premise capabilities for automation, analytics, or federated data stores. This last option provides a useful alternative when certain financial or other data may not need to be directly incorporated into the CMDB but will need to be accessed selectively through the CMDB[2] System's modeling.

Our research shows that the highest values for SaaS (in ranked order) include

1. minimal administration
2. extensibility/scalability to expand resources as needed
3. OpEx cost savings
4. functional extensibility—easy to add new capabilities as needed
5. CapEx cost savings
6. accelerated deployment

Key inhibitors of SaaS typically include concerns about *data protection*, limited or too *generic* functionality, a lack of effective *integration*, and poor *performance*.

---

[1]"*The Service Desk in the Age of Cloud and Agile*," EMA and CXP, 2013.
[2]"*CMDB/CMS Radar: the Move to Federation*," EMA, 2012.

However, SaaS solutions are not all alike. Here are some key things to consider:

- Is it more than packaging? Some vendors will position their CMDB capabilities as SaaS based solely on a leasing licensing model but retain all the on-premise presence and complexity.
- How painful are upgrades and new releases? Does a SaaS approach make software upgrades and new releases relatively painless?
- Does the vendor support multitenancy? If so, what form does it offer? Support for multitenancy can mean many things. Some vendors provide physical multitenancy as well as virtual multitenancy, while others provide neither.
- SaaS resilience can vary as well. Factors such as service level agreements (SLAs) for availability, data center support for security, disaster recovery, geographic scalability, and levels of professional support will all vary based on which vendor you choose.

If you're selecting an *on-premise* CMDB solution, here are a few additional things to consider:

- Are there any hardware and/or software dependencies (e.g., server hardware and OS software) for the CMDB/CMS product to run that are not included in the base price of the software package?
- What operating systems are supported? Some examples might be
  - Windows
  - HP-UX
  - AIX
  - Solaris
  - Red Hat
  - Linux
  - SUSE Linux
  - VMware
  - appliance
  - virtual appliance
- What databases can be used in conjunction with the CMDB you're evaluating? Some examples might be
  - SQL Server
  - MySQL
  - Oracle
  - DB2
  - Sybase
  - Informix

DEPLOYMENT AND ADMINISTRATION

Making a core CMDB investment requires looking beyond packaging and bringing the CMDB System to life. The vendor you select should fit well with your team resources and use-case needs. Some key questions to ask here are the following:

- What is the average time to deploy on a "per use case" basis (asset/change/service impact)?

- What types of administrative overhead are normally required for first-phase deployment? For ongoing administration?
- What's the track record for a given vendor when it comes to versioning or updates? Are new versions provided under a maintenance agreement, or must a new license be purchased in order to receive the new version? Each vendor has a history—occasionally dark and shrouded with complaints—in this area. In recent years, optimizing version updates with minimal administrative overhead has been a major market focus for CMDB vendors across the board, however. This is an area where you should try to get answers not only from the vendor itself but also from representative deployments or third-party sources.
- What types of administrative efficiencies are offered to support deployments, maintenance, and evolution of a CMDB/CMS system? These may include, but are not necessarily limited, to
  - ease of initial CMDB/CMS population;
  - flexibility and ease of setting policies for discovery and reconciliation;
  - ease of customizing and extending the reach of out-of-the-box models;
  - ease of maintaining, updating, and validating modeled groups against discovered environments;
  - reports to support maintenance, scope, accuracy, and administration of the CMDB/CMS itself;
  - ease of entering domain expertise for CMDB updates.
- What professional services resources are provided in terms of both deployment and consulting directly and through partners? This includes factoring in the skill level of the consultants. Some consulting organizations have an attitude of "back up the school bus," that is, send inexperienced staff to a customer engagement and expect them to learn what they need to know while working for (and being paid by) the client. Checking references from other engagements is one way to get some sense of this.
- How responsive is the vendor to customer issues?
- What types of customer support groups, if any, exist? Are there regional or national groups? Do they have periodic meetings?

Looking at an evaluation that EMA did recently[3] provides a few more granular examples of what to expect when examining these different deployment issues. Average responses for initial population (presented in Figure 12.1) highlight the fact that while the population of the CMDB occasionally can be automated, **initial population** is likely to require input from a wide variety of sources, including preexisting data stores and Excel spread sheets, as well as discovery. Moreover, the eclectic nature of CMDB population will likely continue to be a requirement as the CMDB System grows in value—as functionality and sources expand, new geographies become included, or new requirements occur from mergers and acquisition.

The barrier between native support for CMDB (administration, maintenance, and management) and CMDB-related functionality is a thin one at best. In fact, understanding what's naturally supported in maintaining your CMDB will be a solid foundation for anticipating its optimal use cases. Figure 12.2 shows a range of options as mapped across an average of leading CMDB vendors to help underscore this very important point.

---

[3] *"CMDB/CMS Radar: the Move to Federation,"* EMA, 2012.

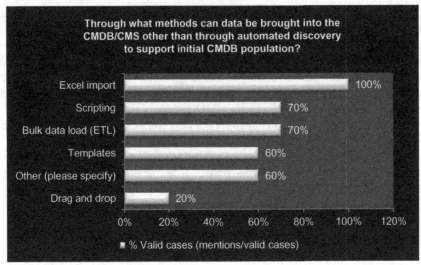

Through what methods can data be brought into the CMDB/CMS other than through automated discovery to support initial CMDB population?

Sample size = 11, valid cases = 10

FIGURE 12.1

These data present an average across 11 leading CMDB vendors and underscore the eclectic nature of **initial CMDB population**. The flexibility and ease of updating a CMDB System will also require periodic inputs from data sources that may not yet be automated or even fully integrated as the system expands to support more use cases, geographies, locations, and constituencies. As you can see, Excel Import was the most common method for capturing data for initial CMDB population.

Modeling support is also key for CMDB administration. Strong service models that can easily be adapted to changing requirements and conditions can be a dominant factor in the eventual success and breadth of a CMDB System. Figure 12.3 highlights options for a service modeling studio that 10 of the 11 participating vendors supported.

Getting back to very basic table stakes, there can be a wide range of options for how vendors will support you and your CMDB System in terms of responsiveness and type. For instance, in addition to phone support, some vendors provide online support, on-site support, and/or customer forums. Professional services also vary dramatically by use case. All 11 of the surveyed vendors offered direct support for deployment services, for instance, but only six provided direct support for asset life cycle management. Figure 12.4 highlights a related requirement—insight into guaranteed time of response when a business-critical service problem occurs.

SOME PERSPECTIVES ON DEPLOYMENT AND ADMINISTRATION

The following comments from past research and consulting have been selected to help provide added context for the decision making process in making a product choice. The vendors have been kept anonymous for a number of reasons—one of them being that these are snapshots in time and may not reflect the current state of a given vendor solution when this book is being read. These comments reflect postdeployment experiences targeted at CMDB System usability.

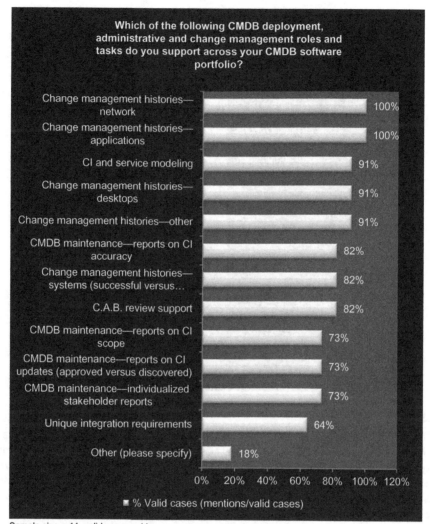

Which of the following CMDB deployment, administrative and change management roles and tasks do you support across your CMDB software portfolio?

Category	%
Change management histories—network	100%
Change management histories—applications	100%
CI and service modeling	91%
Change management histories—desktops	91%
Change management histories—other	91%
CMDB maintenance—reports on CI accuracy	82%
Change management histories—systems (successful versus...)	82%
C.A.B. review support	82%
CMDB maintenance—reports on CI scope	73%
CMDB maintenance—reports on CI updates (approved versus discovered)	73%
CMDB maintenance—individualized stakeholder reports	73%
Unique integration requirements	64%
Other (please specify)	18%

■ % Valid cases (mentions/valid cases)

Sample size = 11, valid cases = 11

FIGURE 12.2

These insights into CMDB administrative support cast a bright beam as well on use-case readiness. The question as asked in our research specified checking only those capabilities supported "without unique services." This is key because many CMDB providers will market based on purely service-enabled functionality. The other side of the coin in examining these criteria is asking what in-house skill levels are required for CMDB maintenance and administration.

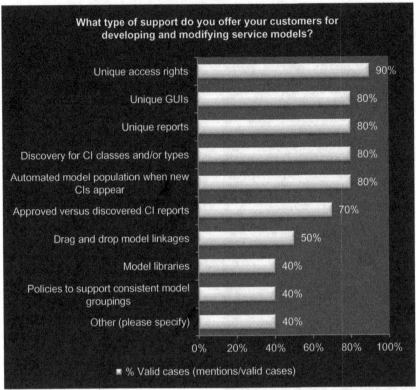

FIGURE 12.3

Modeling Studio capabilities should also be a criterion for choosing a CMDB. Note that "discovery" and "automated population" for service models and model classes are supported by 80% of the respondents here—implying native integrations with discovery and, in some cases, ADDM tools. However, the levels of automation and the administration associated with these can vary dramatically based on vendor and integrations. The beauty of service models is their ability to address both changing physical conditions and logical associations. So having a well-designed capability for model creation is paramount.

Versioning: Two experiences, two vendors

- Versions are generally smooth unless they've changed a class model that we've customized. The vendor has finally come out with a versioning wizard to tell you in advance what's probably going to break.
- You are notified of the enhancements you're not getting when you go through the updates and [given] a chance to preview what's going to be changed—right down to which lines of code are changing.

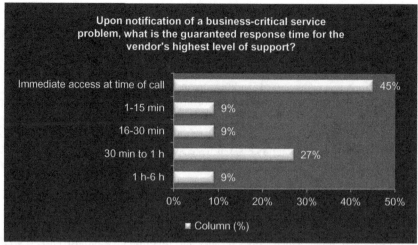

Sample size = 11

FIGURE 12.4

While hardly rocket science, it's still good to know ahead of time how responsive your CMDB provider can be when the unexpected occurs and demands quick attention. It's important to note that the question asked here was, "What is the guaranteed response time for your HIGHEST level of support?"—which leads to the next question, "What's the price?" In a few cases, it may actually be free but in most cases it will not be. Basic maintenance fees average between 19% and 22%.

Overall administration

- We dumbed down the CMDB to make it more consumable. Now our customers are accustomed to defining their own applications inside the system. Actually one thing I'd like to see in the industry is dumbing down the CMDB so the average person can use it.
- Administration and deployability are very good. We basically went from nothing to designing our data model and imported all of our current CIs and Assets, retired our asset DB, and had our CMDB up and running our CMDB all within six days!
- One of the mistakes our vendor made was [this]: five years ago, when they sold us the CMDB, they told us it could do anything we wanted it to do. And while this was true at some level, it was largely a false promise. The technology wasn't really there yet. But a lot of progress has been made since then.

Documentation and services

- I would love to see the vendor improve on its documentation—to explain more than just the 'how' but also the 'why'—more about the philosophy and guidelines for creating a successful CMDB/CMS deployment using their technology.
- In the first three months we had three consultants from the vendor. They orchestrated a learning session as well as training for our own administrators. Vendor consultants also helped us develop and customize the CMDB for our use.

Process, design, and workflow

- Our prior solution didn't have the same process-design capability that our current CMDB has. They required more investments in consulting. And there was more effort in creating the actual CMDB objects and getting those objects populated.
- I have used the change management workflow in another area—a completely different workspace from core CMDB administration. For instance, if an employee joins the company and needs to get access to email or files, we can set up a workspace to create workflows with forms provided through the CMDB, just like we might for a trouble ticket. Each workflow may require a different approval process, but it's easy to customize quickly to include the right manager, HR information, and security requirements.

ARCHITECTURE AND INTEGRATION

Just as administrative and maintenance values project into functionality and use case, CMDB architecture and CMDB functionality are very closely intertwined. However, it's useful to group the two discussions separately—with one focusing on scale, coverage, data reconciliation, and integration under the rubric of "architecture" and another looking at analytics, automation, visualization, and use-case specifics under "function." Architecture targets foundational values that should translate well into any use case. The following list includes a few salient questions to consider:

- *Scalability*: What is the highest number of CIs the solution is architected to support? What is the largest actual deployment? What is the largest number of users supported? What examples can the vendor share with you? (What is the vendor's definition of CI—i.e., how granular or not?)
- *Range of discovery*: Can the solution you're evaluating, either natively or through third-party integrations, support discovery for network (layer 2 and/or 3), systems, applications, application components, third-party applications, Web and Web 2.0, storage, database, desktops, mobile devices, and virtualized environments? Can it discover configuration details for any or all of the above?
- *Application dependency*: Does the solution support ADDM, or dependency mapping in general, as either an automated and/or manual process? Does this include application-to-application, infrastructure-to-infrastructure, application-to-infrastructure, and/or application-to-application components? Is this done directly and/or through third-party integration?
- *Reconciliation and normalization*: Does the solution you're evaluating reconcile, normalize, and/or synchronize data from multiple (in-brand and third-party) sources? Can it support weightings for "trusted sources"? That is, can it prioritize one source over another for a certain CI? Does the solution provide effective workspaces, analyses, and reports for you to support data reconciliation and normalization? Does it offer any integrated analytics for more effective reconciliation and prioritization—including meaningful data on which trusted sources are most accurate and where?
- *Integration scope*: What types of management data repositories (MDRs) can the solution access? Does it support just the vendor's own portfolio or can it also collect data from third-party

sources? These sources might include other MDRs, text records, Excel files, service catalogs, service desks, performance management tools, security tools, asset management tools, and other configuration management tools.

- *Integration enablement*: What standards are supported to enable these integrations? How are they enabled otherwise (e.g., Web Services application programming interface [API])? What policies, if any, can be applied to federate other sources for data access? What dashboard integrations are provided to extend the reach of CMDB service modeling?

SCOPE, OUTREACH, AND CORE INTERDEPENDENCIES

Not all CMDB investments scale as well as others—so especially for large, complex environments, it's important to ensure that scope is sufficient for your needs. Purely CI-volume limitations are increasingly less likely, but it's worth getting a sense not only of what the vendor claims is possible but also to at least ask for the largest validated deployment if scope is a key concern. Figures 12.5 and 12.6 highlight the difference between "architectural" and "actual" historical reality when it comes to scalability based on CI metrics. It's also important to find out what the vendor is including in the term "CI"—as the term often gets applied to device or application components. In other words, a single systems device may have 10, 20, or many more associated CIs in some cases, not including extensions through virtualization.

As can be seen in Figure 12.7, domain reach is another critical factor in assessing CMDB scope. The data here still don't reflect in-depth support for a given domain, so more granular drill-down evaluations are absolutely necessary for completing this assessment.

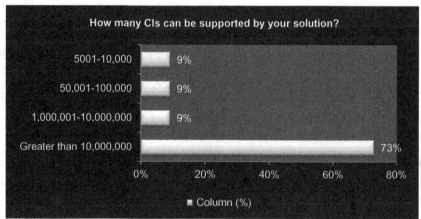

Sample size = 11

FIGURE 12.5

These show averages across 11 vendors in terms of scalability based on architectural CI count. This should just be one parameter for assessing scalability, since CIs can be counted very differently, referring to a single physical systems or network device, or one of many components within that device, or an end point PC or mobile device, or—in contrast—an entire business application system, which may include thousands of CIs.

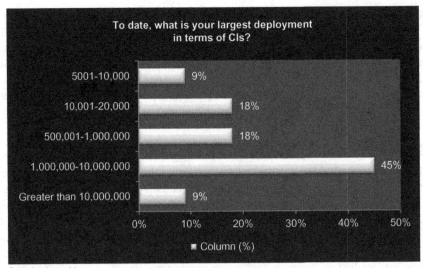

FIGURE 12.6

These show averages across 11 vendors in terms of scalability based on deployed CI count. This should just be one parameter for assessing scalability, since CIs can be counted very differently, referring to a single physical systems or network device, or one of many components within that device, or an end point PC or mobile device, or—in contrast—an entire business application system, which may include thousands of CIs.

Most CMDB vendors provide some support for ADDM, and virtually all provide at least some level of manual application dependency mapping. We'll take a closer look at ADDM later in this chapter as a separate investment. The data in Figure 12.8 reflect core CMDB capabilities for Application Dependency Mapping, while Figure 12.9 provides a more detailed look at discovered ADDM components primarily achieved through integrations.

DATA IMPORT AND THE FEDERATED UNIVERSE

Another way to look at scope is by examining the range of third-party sources that can provide data to the CMDB. You should consider integrations that are native to the vendor's own portfolio as well as those achieved through a third party, which as shown in Figures 12.10 and 12.11 may reflect different priorities. As a general rule, most CMDB providers will try to address the most common integration requirements within their own portfolio while turning primarily to third parties for less requested integrations. However, in reality, you are best served by having a broad set of choices for both third-party and vendor-provided integration options. In fact, depending on the vendor's portfolio, third-party breadth is often the more valuable choice—in terms of both range of options and freedom of choice.

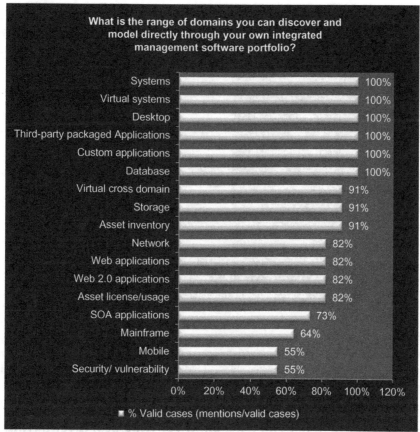

FIGURE 12.7

This figure shows a broad reach of domains supported for the 11 CMDB vendors based on what they can do via their own portfolio—in other words not including third-party integrations to flesh out weak spots within their own capabilities. However, these data do not address the level of depth within each domain, which is one of the reasons why these vendors can claim to at least touch upon so many different domains.

The trend has been increasingly to leverage Web Services instead of prepackaged adapters for CMDB integration. Web Services enhance the breadth of integration choices and can also allow for data access as opposed to actually moving data. While not all the standards shown in Figure 12.12 are focused on integration, many are—and it's clear that Web Services-related standards, such as XML, SOAP, and WSDL, are dominant. The CMDBf, while once emerging as a standard for federation through address registration, now shows reduced support as a more eclectic approach to Web Services overall is becoming more pervasive. (Chapter 13 will provide a further discussion of Web Services in context with service modeling options.)

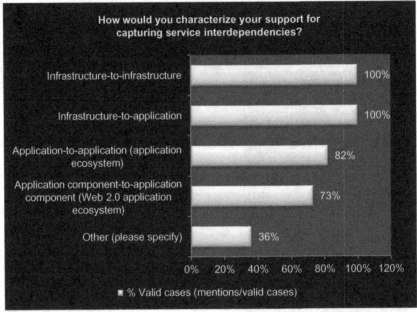

Sample size = 11, valid cases = 11

FIGURE 12.8

Virtually all CMDB vendors offer some capability for mapping applications to the infrastructure, as well as for looking at infrastructure-to-infrastructure relationships. The data above come from core CMDB solutions, most of which leverage additional investments for more automated and complete ADDM.

SOME DEPLOYMENT PERSPECTIVES ON ARCHITECTURE AND INTEGRATION
Scope and phased growth

- The vendor we chose not to go with was very service desk–centric compared to the vendor we chose, which was more grounded in IT management as a whole—including operations integration for monitoring and event management.
- In looking at our current CMDB provider, what we like is strong support for VMware and vMotion as well as good support across the network for Layer 2 and 3 components. What we're missing is storage. We're about halfway with the implementation.

Integrations and data sourcing

- Our CMDB leverages open standards and open languages. These allow us to write our own discovery pattern without professional services—all the other companies require armies. It is a very open system, which is good and bad at the same time because it leaves so many options on the table—but mostly good.

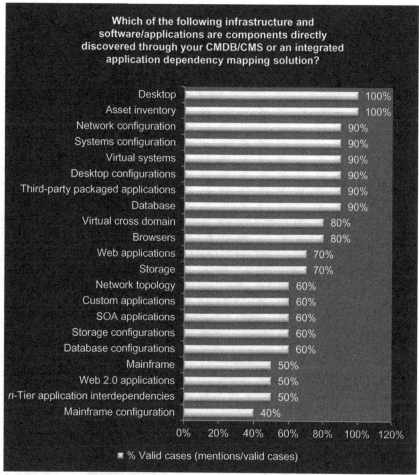

Which of the following infrastructure and software/applications are components directly discovered through your CMDB/CMS or an integrated application dependency mapping solution?

Desktop	100%
Asset inventory	100%
Network configuration	90%
Systems configuration	90%
Virtual systems	90%
Desktop configurations	90%
Third-party packaged applications	90%
Database	90%
Virtual cross domain	80%
Browsers	80%
Web applications	70%
Storage	70%
Network topology	60%
Custom applications	60%
SOA applications	60%
Storage configurations	60%
Database configurations	60%
Mainframe	50%
Web 2.0 applications	50%
n-Tier application interdependencies	50%
Mainframe configuration	40%

■ % Valid cases (mentions/valid cases)

Sample size = 11, valid cases = 10

FIGURE 12.9

This more detailed assessment looks at ADDM capabilities achieved primarily through integrations with vendor-provided or third-party tools.

- When we're integrating our CMDB with the vendor's own portfolio, the vendor's gone to great pains to make the integration of all tool sets relatively easy. But when doing third-party sources it's more of an uphill battle. So integration's a double-edged sword.
- We have a custom tool for mashups that allows us to reach into a whole bunch of sources. It's especially popular among our NOC users. It allows us to bring up historical insights that we can process through our CMDB reporting engine across the entire application infrastructure.
- We weren't going to win the political battle to get people to give up their tools for just one centralized solution. So we needed a CMDB that facilitated and reconciled data from many different sources, many different brands.

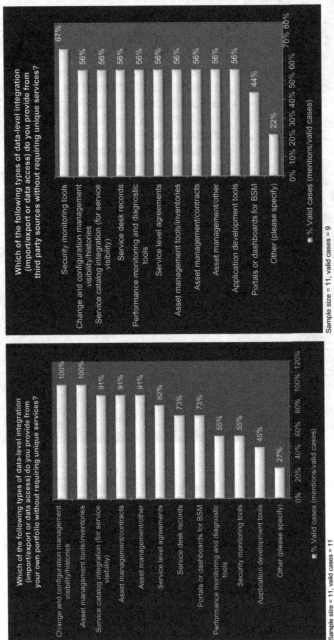

Which of the following types of data-level integration (import/export or data access) do you provide from your own portfolio without requiring unique services?

Function	%
Change and configuration management visibility/histories	100%
Asset management tools/inventories	100%
Service catalog integration (for service visibility)	91%
Asset management/contracts	91%
Asset management/other	91%
Service level agreements	82%
Service desk records	73%
Portals or dashboards for BSM	73%
Performance monitoring and diagnostic tools	55%
Security monitoring tools	55%
Application development tools	45%
Other (please specify)	27%

0% 20% 40% 60% 80% 100% 120%

■ % Valid cases (mentions/valid cases)

Sample size = 11, valid cases = 11

Which of the following types of data-level integration (import/export or data access) do you provide from third party sources without requiring unique services?

Function	%
Security monitoring tools	67%
Change and configuration management visibility/histories	56%
Service catalog integration (for service visibility)	56%
Service desk records	56%
Performance monitoring and diagnostic tools	56%
Service level agreements	56%
Asset management tools/inventories	56%
Asset management/contracts	56%
Asset management/other	56%
Application development tools	56%
Portals or dashboards for BSM	44%
Other (please specify)	22%

0% 10% 20% 30% 40% 50% 60% 70% 80%

■ % Valid cases (mentions/valid cases)

Sample size = 11, valid cases = 9

FIGURES 12.10 AND 12.11

Figure 12.10 denotes functions prioritized based on integrations within the same vendor's portfolio and Figure 12.11 denotes functions prioritized based on integrations with other vendor (third-party) offerings. These figures show different priorities in terms of integrated sources for core CMDB investments, as vendors will tend to prioritize the most requested use cases themselves. However, the best offering will provide well-supported capabilities for both its own and third-party sources—with third-party outreach generally being the most valuable for both range of options and freedom of choice.

Discovery

- When [we] first started, 95% of the discovery patterns were custom—now, thanks to many vendor improvements, we only write about 1% of the discovery patterns.
- The key is that updating the CMDB can't be a manual process. We must have autodiscovery.

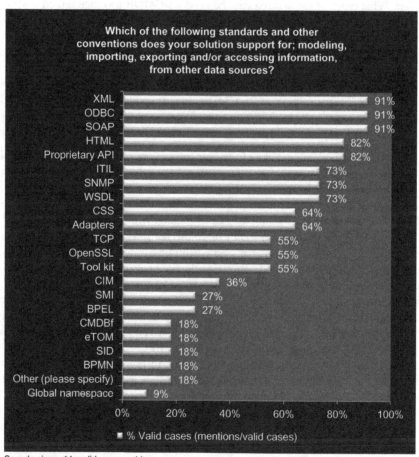

Sample size = 11, valid cases = 11

FIGURE 12.12

Standards may not often be a primary concern—but in current CMDB/CMS offerings, it's definitely worth paying attention to Web Services capabilities such as XML, SOAP, and WSDL.

FUNCTIONAL CONCERNS

The questions you should pursue for functional evaluation fall into four main categories: *Modeling and metadata*, *Analytics*, *Automation*, and *Visualization*.

- *Modeling and metadata*: How versatile and extensible is the vendor's modeling to support various CI relationships, types, classes, subclasses, attributes, and states?
- *Analytics*: What kinds of analytics does the vendor offer, either directly through the CMDB or indirectly through your own portfolio or third-party integrations, to support use cases primary to phase one and beyond? This might include if/then change analysis, correlation, data mining, or trending among other heuristics. Analytics are most often integrated into the CMDB System via ADDM—given the need for dynamic currency and versatility across the full, federated system.
- *Automation*: What types of automation can the vendor's CMDB leverage directly, with or without human intervention, including automation from its own and third-party sources? This includes, but isn't limited to, workflow, change (release) management, diagnostics, audits, etc. If the vendor's offering can trigger automation directly (without human intervention, e.g., events and Web Services), how is this done?
- *Visualization*: What visualization technologies are supported—such as portals, scorecards, Web access, and widgets? What roles does the CMDB support inside and outside IT? What kind of reports for stakeholders, CAB, etc.? Visualization is a natural for demos and proof of concept evaluations—something you should actively seek to assess from any serious CMDB candidate.

A closer look at modeling and metadata from past research provides insight into how relationships are being supported among CIs. We've seen fewer than five and as many as several hundred CI relationships being supported "out of the box." However, since the CMDB System is all about capturing relationships for most environments, more is generally better. Figure 12.13 shows some of the predominant CI relationships—each of which may be associated with use-case values without stretching the imagination too far. For instance, *adjacency or connected to* is useful for activating configuration automation, assessing the impacts of change, and performing triage, among other values. *Monitored by* is extremely valuable in managing and optimizing the life cycle of a CI as well as assessing the CI's health. It can also be useful in assessing gaps—what critical CIs aren't monitored at all? *Owner of* can be an individual or organization, if there is a fairly fixed relationship between a CI (device, service, etc.) and its human organizational owner. If the relationship is more fluid, CI "owners" may be better mapped in terms of *attributes* instead of *relationships*. Most vendors can support more than 1000 CI attributes natively, while at the low end, it may be less than 100.

CI states are another critical area of interest. Figure 12.14 highlights some of the more prevalent options. Each state can have critical value in supporting various use cases as well as populations. For instance, in managing change, it's important to be able to contrast "actual" or "discovered" state with "desired" or "approved" state. While there are some exceptions, most CMDB vendors will have some support for looking at both—however, the nature of that support in terms of enabling reporting and analytics will vary dramatically. At minimum, you should expect to be able to compare approved configurations with discovered configurations as discovery occurs for manual review. In some rare cases, a fully fluid navigation back in time is enabled—so you can literally scroll back and forward to see changes in configurations and application interdependencies over time the way you might look at a

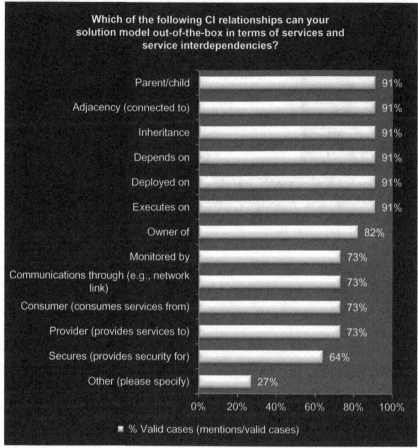

Which of the following CI relationships can your solution model out-of-the-box in terms of services and service interdependencies?

Relationship	%
Parent/child	91%
Adjacency (connected to)	91%
Inheritance	91%
Depends on	91%
Deployed on	91%
Executes on	91%
Owner of	82%
Monitored by	73%
Communications through (e.g., network link)	73%
Consumer (consumes services from)	73%
Provider (provides services to)	73%
Secures (provides security for)	64%
Other (please specify)	27%

■ % Valid cases (mentions/valid cases)

Sample size = 11, valid cases = 11

FIGURE 12.13

Relationships are what a CMDB System is all about. These are some of the more prevalent. We have seen vendor offerings with fewer than five and more than 150 CI relationships supported "out of the box." CI attributes are more fluid and can significantly extend the service modeling reach. Attributes are especially well suited to more fluid data access.

movie. While uncommon to say the least, this feature has already emerged into the market and is even a known requirement for some of the more leading-edge CMDB providers.

Another consideration is trending and historical snapshots in time—with "historical" or "past" state support. Other CMDB solutions may also support "future" or "planned" states from approved production-level conditions. This can be especially valuable in supporting DevOps requirements. Finally, we have seen parallel CMDB Systems evolve to support various groups across IT, development, and beyond so that "desired" and "approved" states in preproduction can be mapped back to production-level conditions through parallel CMDB deployments.

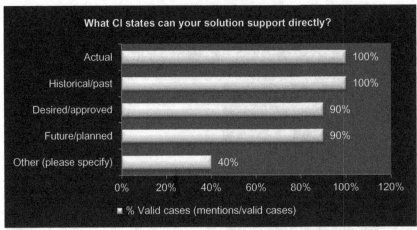

Sample size = 11, valid cases = 10

FIGURE 12.14

State support for CI is telling and critical in selecting a core CMDB solution. While the data above indicate meaningful differences in state support across leading CMDB vendors, the fact is that not all state support is equal. In some cases, the vendor may merely provide manual contrasts at the time of discovery between "actual" and "desired." Other vendors may provide far more fluid trending and analytic capabilities.

USE CASE, ANALYTIC, AND AUTOMATION SPECIFICS

It's worth revisiting use-case criteria here in context with broader technology selection issues. Once you've assessed a solution's foundation with modeling, core integration capabilities, state support, and discovery, the next step is to bring visualization, reports, and/or analytics—which are all inherently use case-related.

Figure 12.15 maps out change impact analysis in terms of domain, real-time, and historical values. The range of selections, though broad, does not separate basic reporting and visualization from more in-depth analytics capabilities—so a next step inquiry is advisable before finalizing a choice. Nonetheless, the checklist in Figure 12.15 offers a useful guide for what you might look for in terms of change impact scope of your CMDB investment. This is especially important because change impact, while most closely associated with Change Management, can contribute to all CMDB use cases you might consider (e.g., performance management, DevOps, and life cycle asset management).

Figures 12.16 and 12.17 provide a dual view of analytics support associated with core CMDB investments. Figure 12.16 shows analytic options associated directly with the core CMDB package as opposed to a separate toolset investment. The range is broader than you might expect, largely because CMDBs today are generally packaged as an integrated value with a larger investment such as a service desk platform or a BSM capability. Figure 12.17 shows extended values in analytics from integration with other vendor-provided toolset sources. You should also consider third-party integrations for analytics, which similarly extend the reach of the CMBD.

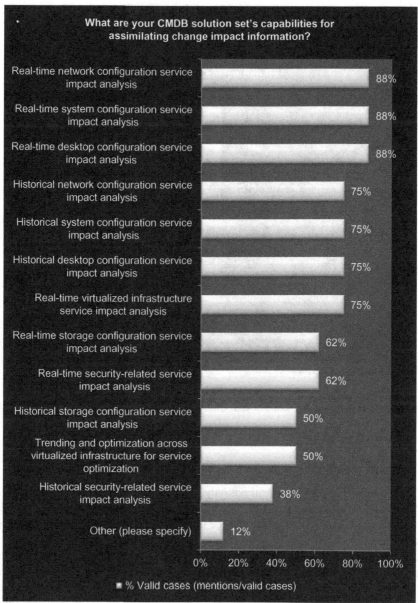

FIGURE 12.15

Change impact breadth and reach, both in real-time and in terms of historical trending, is a cornerstone not only for Change Management but also for almost all CMDB-related use cases including life cycle asset management, performance management, DevOps, and Security and Compliance. The data here show broad support across many environments among leading CMDB vendors—which may range from basic reporting and visualization to more evolved analytic support.

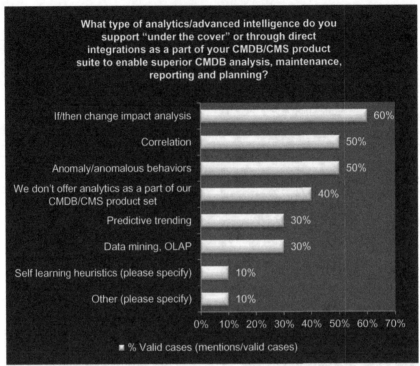

What type of analytics/advanced intelligence do you support "under the cover" or through direct integrations as a part of your CMDB/CMS product suite to enable superior CMDB analysis, maintenance, reporting and planning?

If/then change impact analysis	60%
Correlation	50%
Anomaly/anomalous behaviors	50%
We don't offer analytics as a part of our CMDB/CMS product set	40%
Predictive trending	30%
Data mining, OLAP	30%
Self learning heuristics (please specify)	10%
Other (please specify)	10%

■ % Valid cases (mentions/valid cases)

Sample size = 11, valid cases = 10

FIGURE 12.16

Analytics can considerably extend the value of your CMDB investment and should be taken seriously.

A short summary of values based on the data above would include the following:

- *If/then change impact analysis.* Critical not only for managing change but also for minimizing service disruptions, this analysis should allow you to not only view where and how a service might be disrupted but also add insight into the impacts of change on critical IT-delivered business services.
- *Correlation.* Most often associated with event management, correlation is important as a growing number of CMDB providers are enabling events to map to their service models to trigger actions—from diagnostics to change. Correlation may also be applied to analyzing CI-related data for more effective CMDB maintenance and accuracy or for more quickly assessing the potential impacts of unapproved changes to the IT environment.
- *Anomaly/anomalous behaviors.* This is most often associated with analytics for performance and security-related management issues that may map directly to CMDB service modeling— triggering faster time to resolve issues and generating significant OpEx efficiencies.
- *Predictive trending.* Whether it's an advanced analytic that can search across many undefined variables, or a less advanced analytic that cleanly projects past history into the future from

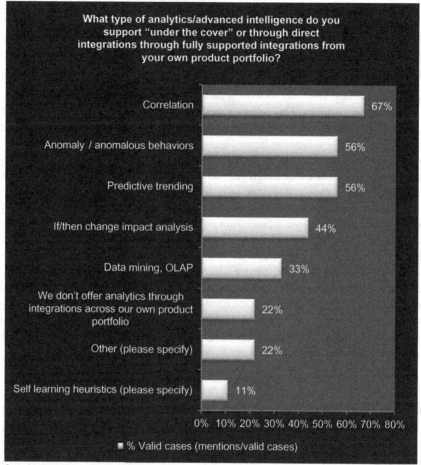

What type of analytics/advanced intelligence do you support "under the cover" or through direct integrations through fully supported integrations from your own product portfolio?

- Correlation — 67%
- Anomaly / anomalous behaviors — 56%
- Predictive trending — 56%
- If/then change impact analysis — 44%
- Data mining, OLAP — 33%
- We don't offer analytics through integrations across our own product portfolio — 22%
- Other (please specify) — 22%
- Self learning heuristics (please specify) — 11%

0% 10% 20% 30% 40% 50% 60% 70% 80%

■ % Valid cases (mentions/valid cases)

Sample size = 11, valid cases = 9

FIGURE 12.17

This figure shows analytics-related options based on integrations outside of native CMDB packaging but within the vendors' own portfolios. To get the complete picture of any CMDB investment, you should also seek out integrations with third-party tools to extend your CMDB's analytic reach.

a set of predefined parameters, predictive trending is of value for performance capacity planning and optimization, IT governance, and optimizing the business of IT—as the CMDB System contains not only critical data but also critical data relationships needed for optimizing IT as a whole.

- *Data mining or online analytical processing.* This is often used as shorthand for flexible and powerful query-based reporting and trending, often with a Cognos back end. However, some CMDB vendors also integrate with true data mining tools at the back end, where CMDB and business performance data can be brought together for common analysis.

- *Self-learning heuristics.* Although still rare, these are emerging with increasing frequency, primarily in the area of performance management—as some solutions can dynamically assess massive amounts of data, can "learn" normal behaviors based on time, and can trigger alerts or actions based on significant deviations. When mapped to service modeling in the CMDB System, these values can become especially powerful.

Automation is also key. One way to look at automation is to consider the core CMDB System as a primary investment in visibility. This includes analytics, which can enrich that visibility in terms of power, time sensitivity, and scope. Suddenly, you might say, the world is at your doorstep because you can see it all!

But then, the question becomes, *What do you want to do about it?*

Automation helps to translate that insight into active power and optimize the CMDB to the dynamic nature of current IT environments. Automation is also essential for evolving your CMDB investment more efficiently in terms of maintenance, updates, and extended reach in scope. For instance, embedded process automation can become a powerful enabler for unifying your stakeholders in addressing CI updates and managing change consistently. Figure 12.18 shows the range of automation supported within each vendor's CMDB offering package. You should also ask about automation capabilities via integrations with both vendor and third-party tools.

The true value comes from unifying "visibility" with "action." There are many vendors in the market that would love to sell you very siloed forms of automation—without the rich investments in context, impact, interdependencies, and other insights. While these solutions may offer value within a limited domain, they won't scale well to supporting broad business service requirements. Our phrase for the all-but inevitable collisions that may occur is "automating train wrecks."

VISUALIZATION AND REPORTING

Visualization is the most demonstrable value as you can actually "see" a vendor's capabilities during proof of concept. Along with automation, it is the crowning value for your core CMDB and broader CMDB investment.

One way to address visualization is to ask what roles and use cases are supported. For instance, Figure 12.2 provided insight into roles and tasks support for administering and extending the value of the CMDB itself. For more general usage, some of the roles you should consider include ones that are domain-specific: for example, network, systems, desktop, mobile, security, service desk, applications, and development. You need to also include roles that are cross domain, for example, engineering, architecture, service delivery, change management, asset management, financial planning, and user experience management. A third set of roles that you need to incorporate are ones that are enterprise-/non-IT-related: for example, financial planning, non-IT executives, online operations, and partner management.

Another way to evaluate a vendor's visualization and reporting capabilities is mapped out in Figure 12.19. "Executive dashboard" is a clear role-related use case. "Widgets" and "mash-ups" by contrast are technologies to enable added integrated values in enriching dashboard or GUI content, as well as enabling greater administrative flexibility extending the need for customize content. Widgets, and especially mash-ups, may be especially valuable in accessing CI-related data without actually

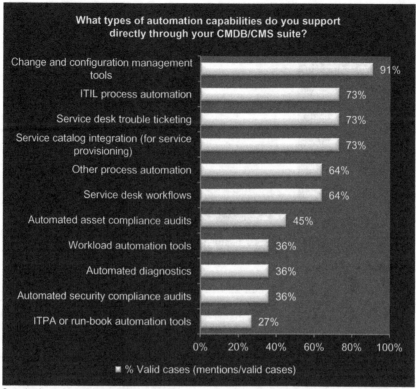

Sample size = 11, valid cases = 11

FIGURE 12.18

Here, you can see how the power of the CMDB System, with its integrated analytics, is harvested for action. These data reflect automation packaged with CMDB vendor offerings. You should also ask about automation via vendor and third-party integrations.

moving into the core CMDB. Similarly, "templates" provide strong administrative value and ease of customization, while "scorecards" can add value to measuring IT or service performance in any number of ways—from optimizing IT efficiencies in managing change to service quality and business impact indices.

USE CASE PERSPECTIVES ON FUNCTIONAL PRIORITIES

The following quotes on technology selection are taken from a mix of consulting and research reports—spanning perspectives on modeling, CI state support, and trending and visualization. These are three telling areas of CMDB differentiation to complement and round out other functionality requirements addressed in this chapter.

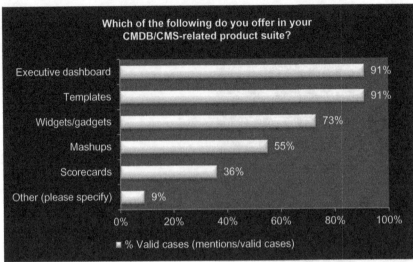

Sample size = 11, valid cases = 11

FIGURE 12.19

Visualization capabilities are, with automation, the crowning touch of your CMDB System and core CMDB investment. Above, you can see a few options that should be considered while making a core CMDB choice.

Modeling

- One thing our vendor has that others don't is a modeling UI.
- Our CMDB vendor provides a pretty well defined universe with 7000 pre-defined objects, and a schema that's 99% of what we need. Great functionality out of the box.
- One of the reasons we decided on our CMDB vendor was the highly customizable data model. I gave [the vendor] a list of all the fields we wanted to store. One of their engineers quickly turned it around into a data model for us so we didn't have to limit ourselves to [the vendor's] data model. We were up and running in a flash.
- One of the things we loved was that their CI types are versionable—so updates to the version can be easily accounted for in our CMDB. When we discover a new version we can automate the reconciliation process and easily assign a new version to the CI.

CI state support

- Our vendor supports the ability to generate and maintain snapshots of configuration in time, allowing us to better isolate and understand how application and infrastructure components affect each other. This streamlines troubleshooting and diagnostics.
- We maintain three CMDB instances: the production environment, a simulation environment, and a test environment. Our vendor's Configuration Management Database can accommodate all three instances.

TRENDING, REPORTING, AND VISUALIZATION

- One of the things I like about our CMDB is the accessibility of the information and the capability to create multiple views from multiple perspectives. This is core both to supporting a broad array of stakeholders [and] facilitating the maintenance and administration of the CMDB itself.
- One of the things I like about our CMDB's dashboard is that it integrates with our service catalog. Our vendor is also going to be shipping integrated project management in a few months, and I'm very much looking forward to that.
- The dashboard is great—good tabs, good search options, and good presentation—and a great way to drill into data.

AN EXAMPLE FROM ONE CLIENT ENGAGEMENT

An EMA consultant was asked to evaluate two options for core CMDB investments for a large public sector client in North America. The comparisons that follow are useful in showing the kinds of questions asked and how judgments might be made. The actual content for each vendor should be viewed as a snapshot in time—not a present-day statement about functionality. Both vendors and the client have deliberately been kept anonymous since, as explained earlier in this chapter, product functionality changes rapidly.

	Vendor A	Vendor B
Configuration items	CMDB A gathers and stores CIs of many different IT components including network, systems, IT assets, security policies, user information, service management history, asset financial information, SLAs, additional CIs, IT relationships, and interdependencies. The CIs and their relationships are not hard-coded. They are extendable and editable. Predefined CIs allow users to work as editors instead of authors	The following categories of CIs are supported in CMDB B: computer systems, Web servers, routers, application servers, switches, service desk records, storage devices, firewalls, load balancers, software modules, power switches, phones, PBXs, operating systems, database, software patches, well-known applications (PeopleSoft, SAP, Siebel, etc.), organization, users, business services, business applications, accounts, file services, directory services, physical characteristics, location (room, floor, building, zip code, country, etc.)
CMDB population	CMDB A provides out-of-the-box content configured with detailed attributes for over 50 CI families, 140 CI classes, and 70 CI relationship types. These definitions represent popular IT service components enabling rapid implementation of a fully functional CMDB. If customer requirements go beyond the out-of-the-box definitions, an administration utility can be used to easily configure the families, classes, and relationship types.	Out of the box, CMDB B includes an agentless discovery solution for discovering application dependencies, deep configuration details about servers, installed software, and network connectivity including layer 2 (data link in the OSI model) devices.

	Vendor A	Vendor B
Data schema and logical relationships	All IT infrastructure asset and relationship data that can be federated (sourced) from vendor A and third-party data sources. As well, CMDB A allows organizations to enter, manipulate, and manage custom IT information that cannot be sourced electronically. Universal federation adapter imports from any source. Heavy reconciliation and analysis is a powerful feature of the solution	Additionally, the CMDB B supports an XML format for loading data from virtually any source, be it a vendor B product, ISV product, customer database, or spreadsheet
	CMDB A defines relationships as either provider or dependent relationships. Provider: a relationship in which functionality is provided to other IT components. Dependent: a requestor and consumer of provider services. A drag-and-drop tool is used to modify the data schema and push the definition down to the database	CMDB B is designed based on DMTF/CIM standards with extensions added to support additional IT object types and services. CMDB B schema provides hierarchy of object classes to enable containment as well as peer relationships. The objects can be extended to support additional attributes without requiring advanced skills
CMDB maintenance	CMDB A ships with multiple consumer views that include a common asset viewer, visualization, and CMDB manager that allows users to craft, manage, and manipulate CMDB information. Additionally, CMDB As federation and reconciliation engine provides ongoing automation and data assurance to keep CI information and relationships current and relevant	Installation and scripting tools are provided to instantiate the schema and GUI is provided to extend it. Further, the GUI can be used to create, read, update, and delete objects. Existing database management tools can also be used to provide low-level functions, such as indexing and archival
Management data repository	CMDB A ships as a stand-alone product—requiring no prerequisite vendor A product installation. The initial release will support Windows/SQL. The second version will support Oracle and the UNIX operating platforms as well as Ingres	Supports Oracle and DB2 UDB. License for DB2 UDB is included in the purchase price of CMDB B
Federation	A federation adapter provides the ability to load data from multiple non-vendor A sources enabling CMDB customers to access and load data from virtually any third-party data source including vendor B. An SMS federation adapter is specifically designed to import data from Microsoft's SMS environment into the CMDB A repository. Additionally, CMDB A ships with a relationship importation adapter allowing the sourcing of discovered relationship information from non-vendor A solutions	CMDB B uses federated data architecture to connect with various data sources including Microsoft. It also provides "real-time" federation via the WebSphere Information Integrator technology, which allows us to federate with virtually any data source and fetch the data on demand. Additionally, vendor B has announced, in conjunction with other management vendors, a standards initiative around CMDB data federation. While CMDB B does not ship out-of-box integration with the vendor A products at this time, integrations using vendor Bs published interfaces have been done with similar products
Open access	Via Web Services API. CMDB A also supports XML data structures	Via Web Services API. Launch-in-context GUI or an XML-formatted file

	Vendor A	Vendor B
Integration	A federation adapter, which provides the ability to load data from multiple non-vendor A sources enabling CMDB customers to access and load data from virtually any third-party data source	CMDB B enables seamless data and process integration using Web Services interfaces and XML data format specification
Remediation and reconciliation	Vendor A products are integrated out of the box with CMDB A repository or share common asset tables and are by definition reconciled with one another. Third-party data reconciliation is done through an algorithmic mechanism and numerous identifiers to uniquely identify and determine if the external data CI being introduced to the CMDB repository is already represented. If the CI is new, it is added to the repository; if it exists, then attributes of the CIs can be overwritten or new ones added at the customer's preference	The common data model defines the naming rules to be used for each CI that is to be loaded into the CMDB B. These naming rules define the specific attributes that are required for that CI type. The naming rule attributes are used to identify unique instances of CIs as they are created within the CMDB
Performance and scalability	Performance and scalability is done through an n-tier architecture	CMDB B architecture can support up to about 100,000 devices. This equates to potentially millions of associated CIs (applications, business systems, network devices, etc.). This is done through an n-tier architecture design.

APPLICATION DISCOVERY AND DEPENDENCY MAPPING

In some cases, you will want to be sure to have an integrated ADDM package with your core CMDB. In other cases, it may come at a later time as a separate investment. However, for an effectively federated CMDB System, one or sometimes multiple ADDM investments are generally a preferred option. In fact, depending on use case and overall readiness, an ADDM package may be the right starting point for growing your CMDB System in phase one even without a core CMDB.

The ADDM market is evolving rapidly and in multiple directions at once. While this can be confusing, it is overall a good thing. Through this diversity, vendors delivering ADDM capabilities are, as an aggregate, seeking to be more responsive to a yet broader set of constituents, requirements, use cases, and roles than ever before. This includes requirements emerging from internal and external (public) cloud, the Extended Enterprise across ecosystems, agile application development and DevOps, and a dramatic upswing in currency, ease of deployment, and modularity.

For example, there has been a lot of focus on deployability across the ADDM market. In recent research,[4] most vendors indicated 0.5-1 FTE for initial setup supporting a single application with an average of 1-1.5 FTEs for expanding ADDM support for 15 applications.

---

[4]Interview with a large technology services organization based in the United States regarding their deployment of IBM's Tivoli Application Dependency Discovery Manager (TADDM).

Cost and packaging trade-offs are also worth keeping in mind—especially given the rise of SaaS-based options. One of the key trade-offs for ADDM mentioned earlier is the choice of agent-based discovery, agentless discovery, or a mix of both. Most solutions will offer some choice, but many will be primarily agent-based or agentless. Having both can sometimes be ideal, as this provides a good combination of extensibility and deployability as well as support for mixed hybrid (public/private) cloud environments where permissions and accessibility may favor a diversified approach. ADDM investments tend to be directed at mid-tier and larger enterprise or service provider environments where complexity and scope are natural challenges. As a result, they tend to scale well, with CI counts that range from less than 50,000 to more than 10 million. Domain breadth is also key as ADDM support for any core use case can profit from enriched insights into domains. Figure 12.20 provides an indication of domain breadth across 10 ADDM vendors sampled in Q4 2013. Figure 12.20 reflects native domain outreach; however, in many cases, additional domain support can come from integrations with other vendor-provided or third-party sources.

FUNCTIONAL POWER AND OUTREACH

One testament to the strength of the ADDM vendors surveyed is that most of them can discover more than 50 third-party applications out of the box and the great majority can discover more than 100 third-party applications without customization. Support for custom or in-house-developed applications varies significantly by vendor, and if this is a priority, it is something you should seriously seek to evaluate in a proof of concept.

Frequency of updates is also improving with nearly three-quarters of those surveyed supporting near-real-time updates and 100% able to support run-time changes based on policy-triggered updates, such as those from vMotion occurrences. Automation is also key for the ADDM environment, both empowering actions and triggering alarms and process automation for remediation and governance.

TRADE-OFFS: PERFORMANCE-OPTIMIZED VERSUS MULTIUSE CASE

Multiuse case: ADDM first became an area of intense innovation almost 10 years ago with the initial tidal wave of interest in CMDB deployments and the need to capture service-related interdependencies more effectively. That initial crop of companies was largely acquired and became foundational technologies for leading platform solutions with native CMDB integrations. As a group, these ADDM pioneers were focused on capturing configuration-related changes as well as application-to-infrastructure residency, with updates most frequently on a 24 h basis. More recently, some of these solutions, along with newer entrants into the multiuse-case class, are evolving to support more real-time requirements, including performance management.

Performance-optimized ADDM: About 5 years ago, the industry began to see a new crop of ADDM solutions more focused on performance interdependencies, transactional awareness, and more real-time dynamic currency. Many of these also supported CMDB integrations; all were highly automated and, to some degree, were complementary to ADDM-related investments from the first wave. Vendors in this category are raising the bar on in-depth transactional awareness, dynamic, operational insights into application-to-application and application-to-infrastructure interdependencies, and higher levels of automation in terms of discovery and currency.

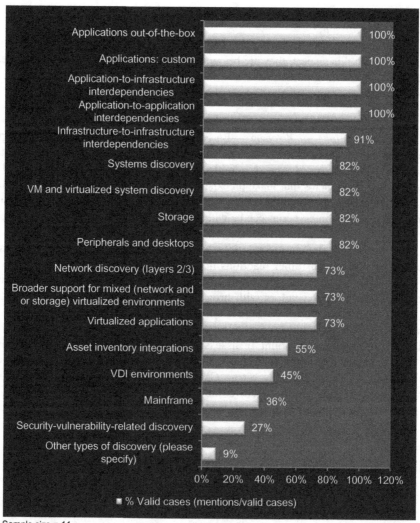

Sample size = 11

FIGURE 12.20

Domain-related reach across the ADDM vendor community not surprisingly focuses on applications first and then infrastructure, with strong support for systems, virtualized infrastructure, and solid storage and network outreach. (Note that "network" was limited by requirements for layer 2 discovery, which are not as broadly enabled across all vendors.) This chart reflects native domain outreach as opposed to outreach achieved through integrations.[5]

---

[5]"*Application Discovery and Dependency Mapping Radar*," EMA, 2013.

A summary of ADDM solutions in both camps is provided in Appendix D.

Which one is right for you?

As the ADDM market progresses, we are increasingly seeing both groups harvesting strengths from each other, and in this respect, they are becoming more alike. On the other hand, at least for the foreseeable future, there will be numerous situations where a complementary relationship between two separate ADDM packages may well be the right choice.

Trade-offs: All-in-one ADDM versus ADDM plus integrations?

All-in-one versus integrations for discovery—Based on dialogues with real customer deployments, little pleases users more than an ADDM solution that can take advantage of preexisting investments and bring added value across the board. This is, admittedly, partly a psychological benefit, as IT organizations like to see new investments that make preexisting solutions look smarter. It can also be a political benefit in terms of getting stakeholders on board more easily, especially when truly cross domain insights are required. These integrations can be within a single portfolio, with third-party solutions, or with both.

On the other hand, fully integrated solutions that "do it all" themselves also have unique benefits and can draw positive customer reactions in terms of speed of deployment and consistency in value. Not surprisingly, there is more likely to be a focus on harvesting third-party investments among multiuse-case ADDM vendors with broader cross domain and more varied stakeholder concerns.

All-in-one versus integrations for function—Since ADDM solutions are primarily enablers, functional integrations are paramount in assessing each solution on a "per use case" basis. Analytics, for instance—whether for change-, performance-, capacity-, or asset-related insights—are paramount for actualizing a true CMDB System. On the other hand, many of the performance-centric ADDM products will come prepackaged with strong performance, and to a lesser degree change impact and analytics, and in that sense will bring unique value for those particular use cases.

FOUR DEPLOYMENT PERSPECTIVES ON ADDM

- We started with a list of about 20 different companies. It turned out that application dependency mapping became the killer criterion. A lot of companies fell off because of that.
- We went with three copies of our vendor's ADDM tool and tuned it to three different environments—one for workstation discovery, one for monitoring the data center and our applications in financial management, and one for our pre-production, application testing environment.
- Our systems configuration capabilities were a mess before we invested in application dependency. It was so bad that our CTO went out and spoke to the server manager after looking at the reports of misaligned configurations and incomplete data. Once we switched over to a broader, more cohesive set of application dependency insights we suddenly got rave reviews—and almost immediately prevented 23 potential outages.
- In terms of asset management, we were pretty disconnected—we had incomplete views and no way to prioritize impacts. Now, with application dependency we can see how everything's connected and we can prioritize how to optimize our infrastructure assets.

AN ADDM Q&A

The following is derived from an interview targeting ADDM technology adoption. We chose it because it provides useful insights into some of the broader issues and expectations surrounding many "classic" ADDM implementation, targeted at multiuse-case values and CMDB integration. However, it is also very much its own story, as are all our Q&As, and so it's not meant as a generic example of all ADDM selection processes.

How Did You Select Your ADDM Solution?

We had a proof of concept evaluation with several different vendors and picked the ADDM solution fit in well with what we already had. Our focus at that time, three years ago, was a combination of incident, problem, change and configuration management.

How Did Your Deployment and Administration for ADDM Go?

The deployment was very straightforward, although managing credentials for access across the infrastructure was sometimes a challenge. As for administration, there are four of us involved in supporting and optimizing our ADDM solution for change impact analysis primarily, including me—but it's not a full time responsibility for any one of us. For instance, it takes about 25% of my time.

What Is the Scope of the Environment You Support?

We have about 800 internal business applications as well as many other smaller, more targeted applications—and most of our applications have been developed internally. It's been an ongoing process to bring on all 800. We started with the production environment and mapped the applications to servers and the infrastructure more broadly. We're getting into middleware now and have aggressive plans for more granular application mapping in the near future.

How Would You Describe the Solution, in Terms of Use-Case, and Functional Likes and Dislikes?

One of the things we like is the ability to go in and create our own rules for capturing the full business application maps. This is especially important given that most of our applications are custom as opposed to third party. Now we're automating processes for currency to keep track of all 800 applications. Our solution is also discovering more in the middleware layer, IS Web Servers, databases and other key components and is pulling them together in application fingerprints. It's also supporting us in automating our monthly configuration management audits. Our ADDM solution integrates well with our CMDB. It allows us to limit the data fed into the CMDB so we can say only populate preselected CI types.

What Is Your Leading Use-Case Focus?

From a use-case perspective we're primarily directed at change impact analysis to support our Change Management process. We have another asset management tool, so there it's a dual process. We see the applications and the infrastructure from ADDM and can then map the more detailed asset information to that model.

OTHER INVESTMENTS TO CONSIDER

Optimizing a full CMDB System goes well beyond a core CMDB investment and even beyond ADDM. That's a primary reason why other integrations are so important for maximizing value.

Below is a short list of other valuable technology considerations that, while not a direct part of the CMDB investment, can add strong value to the total effort:

1. *Data Optimization Analytics*: Of all the categories here, this is the most directly linked to value in optimizing a CMDB System. However, it is a new category, not yet truly a market. It provides a proven analytic framework for assimilating and reconciling "trusted sources" including gaps in coverage (such as in monitoring and security) and ranking contextual efficiencies for a given inventory or discovery tool. For instance, *Which inventory tool brings in the best coverage for Windows desktops?* In some cases, these capabilities can be directly integrated into a CMDB for automatic reviews or updates. Data Optimization Analytics is an investment that is particularly important in larger or more complex environments where the

CMDB should ideally harvest data from many different sources. We have seen examples of CMDBs with over 50 sources and some with more than 100 sources.

2. *Social IT, Gamification, etc.*: This is another emerging technology area that can deliver benefits in terms of promoting better processes, commitment, and dialogue among key stakeholders. Even as solutions in this area evolve, many are already providing strong values in a CMDB System context.

3. *Project Management*: While hardly limited to supporting a CMDB System, project management can be a strong plus, especially for managing and planning initial phase deployments. This is true even though, as we've stated earlier, the CMDB System as a whole should not be viewed as a "project" with a specific beginning and end date but as an evolving investment and resource—something like a year-round garden with plenty of grounds to expand. Therefore, for CMDB deployments, you should seek out project management capabilities that are nimbler and less hierarchical than some of the more traditional brands. You might also seek out those vendor offerings with a more eclectic view of tasks, so that smaller day-to-day requirements can be integrated with more strategic project goals.

4. *Service Catalog (including for cloud)*: Ideally, a service catalog, or even a service portal, should be a natural extension of the CMDB System, with consistent modeling and insight into relevant interdependencies. This is just as true for those catalogs that include cloud-based services as it is for in-house delivered services, as it's becoming increasingly important to understand dependencies outside IT's physical walls. In the end, your customers will view you, not your suppliers, as responsible for the quality and consistency of all services whether you specifically create and provision them or not. Viewing the CMDB System as a "system of relevance" as opposed to a "single source of truth" should help you navigate the nonlinear boundaries across the internal/external cloud and noncloud mosaic without getting buried in nonessential details.

SUMMARY TAKEAWAYS

Investing in a core CMDB and investing in a solid ADDM capability are two decision points that have a fair amount in common. Both will require a serious look at support for integrations, dynamic updates, visualization and reporting, and extended capabilities to harvest analytics and automation. Moreover, both vendor groups are evolving along parallel lines—as both the CMDB and ADDM markets include classic solutions typically associated with core CMDB processes for managing change and assets, as well as those solutions adapted to more real-time service impact and service performance requirements. This exemplifies the vision presented in Chapter 3—that the broader CMDB System should reflexively unite both "worlds"—of service desk and process with real-time operations and ultimately with development, as well.

This chapter has taken guidelines from recent research in evaluating vendor strengths and weaknesses. A generic RFP also based on this research is available in Appendix B.

In summary, key areas to address are the following:

- Packaging, pricing, and maintenance costs—including time to value and, if it can be substantiated, representative times for achieving ROI.

- Ease in moving between versions.
- SaaS or on-premise? (or options for both?)
- Services and consulting options available—both for core deployment and planning and for use case-specific needs (e.g., asset management, performance and service-level management, and change management).
- Ease of deployment.
- Ease of administration.
- Scalability—in terms of generic outreach (number of CIs supported, for instance).
- Breadth of domain support overall and in-depth domain support for unique use-case requirements.
- Ease of integration with other tools for discovery, analytics, automation, and other values.
- Modeling capabilities—including CI relationships, types, classes, and families supported.
- State support for CIs—e.g., discovered, desired, and planned.
- Ease of creating and customizing service models.
- Ability to access as well as import data.
- Visualization and role support.

Other capabilities to consider include Data Optimization Analytics, social IT and gamification, project management, and service catalog support.

RUNNING YOUR PROJECT

CLOSING THE GAP: FINE-TUNING BEFORE FULL DEPLOYMENT

13

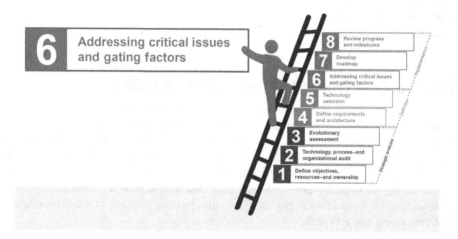

Developing an effective CMDB System is an iterative process. Challenges of communication will persist, just as will process acceptance and planning, use case and scoping, modeling CIs to fit new requirements, assimilating new discovery and other sources, and federating to extend value and reach. Following through, adding automation, defining new metrics, and redefining existing metrics will also continue as ongoing areas of attention.

However, closing these gaps takes on a new life once your core technology selection is complete and you're ready to move beyond proof of concept into phase 1 deployment. Once you've made your core technology investments, you're ready to deliver your most critical phase 1 values.

But before jumping ahead beyond a proof of concept (PoC), it's important to pause, take a breath, and reassess just where you are now that you know the native strengths and limitations of your chosen CMDB-related software capabilities.

We define "the gap" as that critical transition from initial PoC to actual deployment, when you know what your investments are for phase 1 and what they can do.

"At the gap" is the phrase we use to denote that pivotal point—which you might view as alternately standing at the edge of an abyss or on top of a rise overlooking a beautiful view. Moving forward into that splendid valley below requires fine-tuning on multiple fronts, which is what we're addressing in this chapter.

This chapter will provide a narrative of guidelines and recommendations taken largely from recent deployments and will also examine some of the questions and answers that surfaced most frequently. More specifically, this chapter will address the following:

- Getting there—moving past the proof of concept
- Managing scope creep
- Addressing process change, including ITIL at "the gap"
- Service modeling and CI definition
- Integration, normalization, and analytics
- Moving toward federation
- Workflow and follow-through
- Accountability, objectives, and metrics for going into deployment

GETTING THERE: MOVING PAST THE PROOF OF CONCEPT

The Eight-Step Ladder to CMDB System Success focuses on qualitative steps. Depending on the size, scope, readiness, and complexity of phase 1 objectives, quantitative time frames can vary hugely—so it's impossible to say exactly when you will be at the gap after PoC. Time frames can become even more elusive once you realize that some of the thinking that goes into making a CMDB System work may be done informally, in background moments without full-bore team support, as you begin to move forward on your own, setting the stage for more visible, active, executive-driven involvement.

The following quote from a past deployment provides just one example of what this might look like in terms of time frame and approach:

- We spent about nine months planning for this—defining CMDB strategy, looking at vendors, defining what CIs would be. We did all that and looked at multiple vendors before we selected one based on a proof of concept. Now we're preparing to implement that solution and integrate it with our broader service management investment. We chose an Application Discovery and Dependency Mapping solution from one vendor and our core CMDB as an integrated part of the service desk from another vendor.

What's most telling in this "closing the gap" moment is the combination of strategy, planning, vendor selection, proof of concept, and integration. The fact that it took nine months to get to this inflection point is not unusual, especially in larger enterprises, but it's not generically applicable. Toolset efficiencies have significantly improved in recent years, and the need to show value sooner than later has accelerated, so if anything, time frames have become more condensed. If asked, we'd recommend planning on a 5- to 6-month window to move from that first CMDB gleam in your eye to the actual deployment—especially given executive impatience to show value sooner than later. This includes the time required to solidify your Three-Tiered Roadmap as will be described in Chapter 14.

COMMUNICATION AT THE GAP

Communication is an ongoing requirement. Now that you've got your toolsets aligned, there will be a need for continued dialogue, stakeholder involvement, and expectation setting based on this yet more tangible and specific foundation for your CMDB System.

The quote below underscores the value of a rich and diverse communications strategy to empower "closing the gap" and facilitate the move into deployment:[1]

> - We've tried every possible communication channel to get to this point. There's no single approach that does it by itself. In other words, we need multiple approaches. These include a formal steering committee, as well as ongoing peer-group dialogs. We've set up workflow streams to channel dialogs around each process (such as configuration, change, incident, or asset management) to facilitate better peer-to-peer communication. We are also leveraging SharePoint and brown bag lunches to help smooth the process as we move beyond proof of concept toward full Phase-One implementation.

The next quote provides a very insightful recommendation for closing the communications gap before full deployment by socializing your final phase 1 objectives:

> - I have experience with doing this before—and experience with seeing implementations not go very well because they didn't bother to engage the 'consumers.' Once you've done your proof of concept, you have to put out a strawman—a clear representation of how you see Phase One coming together. If you just leave your stakeholders with a blank slate it will promote going off on tangents, taking your deployment in far too many directions at once. Instead, you should let them know—'Here's something you can work with. What do you think of it? How can you best make it work for you.' Explain what they should get out of it and guide the conversation.

Another consideration in closing the gap with communication reflects what we described in an earlier chapter as the "Tom Sawyer effect." The goal is to persuade your stakeholders that it's in their best interest to help you "paint the CMDB System fence"—the more they pitch in, the more they stand to profit from the deployment:

> - We've worked to show our CMDB stakeholders that the more you buy in, the more you get out of it. The whole theory behind how to market this after PoC is a push-and-pull process. The first stage is a PUSH—'I need you, you and you for the next six weeks.' You should target the stakeholders most prepared to show value, and at least potentially the most enthusiastic. After that, once you do show value, others will come to you! They'll see the value of pitching in and supporting the growth of your CMDB System.

SCOPE CREEP

Unfortunately, one of the things that may often emerge from just such enthusiasm is scope creep. Having an impossible list of objectives will present a theoretical burden earlier in the process, but once you've selected your software and are ready to deploy, it can become deadly. You will no longer be dealing with charts and PowerPoint—but with actual software, service modeling priorities, integrations, automations, and tangible expectations. If you plan on pleasing everyone at this late phase, you might as well just sit back, relax, and wait for the project to fail.

---

[1] All quotes in this chapter are taken from prior EMA consulting and research. Only one-on-one interviews done specifically for this book will be footnoted separately.

Here are some comments that underscore the problem of scope creep and provide some insights into how to redirect it:

- The biggest issue now is scope creep. Trying to make everyone happy at this point is like trying to rebuild the Titanic from the bottom up.
- We're managing scope creep by being incremental in how we're driving our deployment—going forward with small steps on a regular schedule.
- When we discussed the CMDB with different groups in our organization, each team got very excited about what they wanted to get out of our CMDB. But very quickly we could see that many of their priorities were at least a couple of years away from implementation. So everybody's understanding of the scope was different. For instance, we had desktop people saying 'can I inventory my mouse? Can I inventory my keyboard and my monitor?' They all wanted to see those as CIs. Handling this wasn't too difficult. I asked everyone two questions: first, 'Is this equipment that you're prepared to manage from day one through its entire lifecycle as a CI?' And second, 'Do you have the resources to manage these items as CIs once they get into our CMDB?'[2]

MANAGING PROCESS REQUIREMENTS AT THE GAP

Process and ITIL commitments also need to be solidified at this stage—before actual implementation. This is directly related to scope creep, which can quickly transform into a kind of "process creep," along with "integration creep" and "stakeholder creep," and in so doing pretty much doom the CMDB System at its incipience.

If you're following an ITIL trajectory, which we recommend as a general rule, it's also important to put ITIL in context with the specifics of your own environment (organization, requirements, etc.). The following statement arising from a CMDB deployment vacillating at the gap underscores just why this is so critical:

- I had an ITIL assessment done on based on some problems we had in supporting our environment. But we weren't sure of our own goals—what did it mean to enable ITIL soup to nuts? We tried to bring in a vendor to 'build it for us' as an extension of our CMDB deployment, but first we had to define our own processes. We couldn't build what we didn't understand to begin with.

On the other hand, undirected improvisation regarding ITIL and best practices can also disrupt a CMDB deployment:

- One of the things about a company our size is the level of arrogance you get among organizations. ITIL is nothing more than a collection of best practices, but then everyone goes off and tries to create their own.

Perhaps, nothing sums up this attitudinal issue regarding process and best practice better than this very succinct and candid statement—taken from a CMDB deployment assessment interview:

- I believe in standards, as long as they're mine.

---

[2]Colloquium with a large manufacturer and a midtier insurance company both using the ServiceNow CMDB.

The following interview segment reflects a healthy approach to how ITIL support evolved to support a CMDB initiative moving into and then beyond initial deployment:

> ITIL is reasonably well received here. As we evolve from a mainframe-centric to a more distributed infrastructure, we've become more consistent about not making changes without approvals—so much of ITIL change management, for instance, is ingrained. And our engineers are also becoming more proactive—getting beyond incident management to the more proactive approaches in ITIL problem management.

MODELING AND CI DEFINITION

Perhaps nothing is more native to CMDB System DNA than the notion of modeling—to capture interdependencies and relationships and optimize data based on context. This immediately sets up another discussion—what exactly are you supposed to model?

There are two fundamental approaches to making your CMDB System come alive through modeling. The first is the *data modeling* capabilities that should come largely defined based on your choice of CMDB vendor. This isn't to say that you won't customize or extend what the data modeling can do, but here, indeed, simplicity is key. Data modeling is an enabler—not an end game. Its goal is to facilitate the flight of your CMDB System into territories unknown without carrying the weight of too much unnecessary administrative overhead.

The second dimension to modeling within the CMDB System's "double helix" is *service modeling*. Service modeling is the heart of CMDB value delivery—optimized to use-case needs with support for federated data sources and automated insights. If data modeling is the pigment set you have to work with, service modeling is the landscape that you can paint to optimize insights and values unique to your world.

The following comment from an IT manager, taken from a panel discussion about CMDB deployments, makes the point quite succinctly:[3]

> Our Service Model is based on ITIL's definition, and it's all about the processes, functions, services, and technologies that we deliver to our customers. So therefore it's a separate idea that can be applied to the data model. Our Global Finance team defines our business strategies company-wide. And these are, of course, not about a data model or technology. But that's where we started, so we can trace everything we do back to those business services. Now, in our CMDB, out of the box, you do get a robust data model with many different classes—but how we relate those classes together in service context is based on our business model.

One thing, therefore, to consider in selecting your CMDB vendor is its data modeling options and how they may map to your service modeling requirements. A way to help you evaluate this is to ask for use-case reference points in environments similar to yours. As mentioned in Chapter 12, you will want to consider a breadth of options in terms of relationships, classes, and attribute support—just as you'll want to consider ease of administration.

---

[3] Ibid.

TOP-DOWN, BOTTOM-UP, OR MIDDLE-LAYER OUTWARD?

Implied above is that service modeling should begin with the business service as a top-down perspective. However, that doesn't always work for all environments and use cases. The following quote describes building the model in more of a layered or componentized approach. This won't provide an ultimate end game for the CMDB System, but it can be a useful stepping-stone to getting there:

> Rather than taking a top-down approach, we started by looking across multiple layers. Right out of the box our CMDB gave us a rich set of types that we could import and match to—such as computers, or different kinds of servers at the device level. Then we could go above these types and look at applications. So we didn't start out by trying to build a monolithic application where all the interdependencies are included. We started by building services that perform one particular function, but which can become reusable components. We defined a specific application/infrastructure service as a service component—for instance DNS Lookup. Then as we went upward, we associated that service with a business function. In other words, we tried to build our business services from a middle layer of subordinate and reusable service components.[4]

However, there can also be a danger in starting too "small." While a true bottom-up approach—focusing on a single domain—may have its appeal initially, it will soon create issues. In the quote below, service modeling was defined by the systems administration community, which happened to be leading the charge for the initial CMDB deployment:

> We kept it simple. Whatever our discovery tool saw, we brought into the CMDB. We developed a series of nested relationships starting with the server or systems as the parent and all the capabilities it supported as well as all of its internal components as children.

This approach may appear to work if you care primarily about systems; however, the problem in this case is that the networking and application communities felt, and in fact were, disenfranchised. The right answer here would have been not only to keep the nested relationships in systems required for their life cycle management and optimization but also to recognize that they, in turn, participate in a larger ecosystem of application and business services that live across the networked infrastructure.

Here, you can see the inherently political nature of modeling: each silo sees the world differently and would prefer to have relationships captured from its perspective alone. Needless to say, this defeats the whole purpose of the CMDB System, which requires integrating worldviews so that, for instance, system life cycle and application life cycle management can be performed more cohesively and efficiently, with far less risk of creating downtime or impacting business performance.

In one consulting engagement, EMA provided the following structure for orchestrating CI interdependencies supporting a basic, e-mail service (Figure 13.1). The map below is a useful generic look at aggregating CI groups into a meaningful service model, without eliminating the options for more detailed insights into each CI, its components, and their unique interdependencies.

---

[4]Ibid.

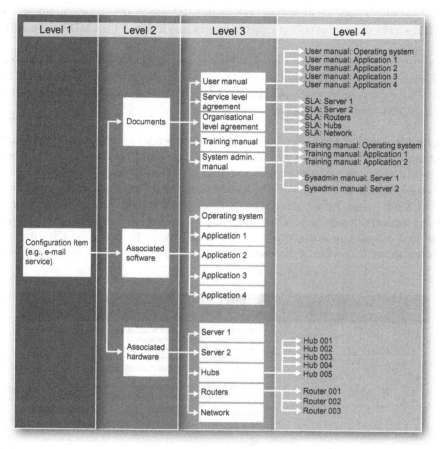

FIGURE 13.1

The CMDB configuration item hierarchy.

TOO MUCH OR TOO LITTLE?

Modeling will set the stage not only for achieving value but also for evolving and growing the CMDB System itself. If you remember our recommendation to approach the CMS as a "system of relevance" rather than a "single source of truth," you'll be better prepared to adjust and evolve your service modeling priorities. Another way to say this is that modeling provides a reflexive look back at managing scope creep—a veritable mirror of where you are in scope and direction:

> We realized that we needed to prioritize—not overpopulate. We pulled in as little data as we needed to get the job done for the first phase. It wasn't a question of what data is out there, but rather what data did we really need. If our stakeholders saw a list of 50 things they'd say that we should pick them all and build models to support them. But we asked them, 'What do you need?' Once you understand your use case and map that to available data, that drives both modeling and discovery priorities at the lowest level.

There is, of course, a trade-off to be made. Prioritizing "relevance" over "truth" in any absolute sense still doesn't take away the need to collect valuable information to enrich the CMDB and help it evolve:

> One issue I'm struggling with at the moment is the level and depth of detail to go to. I know there is a lot of advice that says 'don't go too deep,' but I then question whether the value of a CMDB is fully realized. Plus, the discovery tools tend to give you a deep level of information, so how do you balance that with the "don't-go-too-deep" advice?

It's impossible to answer this question generically. It all depends on what you're trying to achieve and what you need to achieve it. The best recommendation we can make is to be selective and then plan to aggregate more data as your use cases expand—while keeping in mind federation and data access (as opposed to data duplication) as alternatives. The levels of automation, analytics, and overall efficiencies in updating the CMDB System are also relevant touchstones as to how much data to include at a given point.

Having a process for assessing how you will accept new CIs both initially and in the future is also key. Figure 13.2 provides an example of a well-defined process for accepting CIs into the system. Not all CIs require formal review of this nature, but having a process in place with this rigor is a good

Step	Responsible role	Action
1	CI requestor	• Submit a new incident using the appropriate CI request template • Request: Create new hardware CI • Request: Create new software CI • Request: Create new relationship between CIs • Request: Delete obsolete CI or relationship
2	CI requestor	• Complete the provided CI request details spreadsheet and attach it to the remedy incident work log before saving the request
3	Configuration managers	• Determine whether the new CI replaces any existing CIs or changes the relationship of any existing CIs. If necessary, create a new product categorization. If further discussion is needed, change the status of the request to "In Progress" and hold off on making any changes to the CMDB
4	ITS managers, configuration managers and change administrators	• Review any CIs or relationships that require further discussion and plan changes to the CMDB accordingly (typically in the weekly CMDB review meeting)
5	Configuration managers	• Create or retire the CI and associated relationships. For retired CIs, change the CI status from "Deployed" to Obsolete and delete all the relationships
6	Configuration managers	• Change the status of the CI request to "Resolved." Send a "New CI" or "Retired CI" e-mail notification to the following recipients: • CMDB ITS managers • CMDB configuration managers • Change administrators • Any support groups responsible for changes to the new CI
7	Configuration managers	• Change the status of the CI request to "Closed"

FIGURE 13.2

This chart captures a fairly rigorous process for accepting and integrating new CIs as they occur. This level of rigor will not be required for all CIs, but it will provide a good foundation for going forward—as you begin to see which CIs need less review and which continue to require a full-bore review process such as the one above. You should also assess automation and analytics capabilities that are becoming available, which provide parallel insights into this very process with minimal to no human intervention.

foundation for going forward. Applying automation may take time and experience in assessing which CIs really don't need review and which do. And in fact, there are emerging on the market capabilities in automation and analytics that parallel this very process, but with minimal to no human intervention!

Extending data models and attributes

Even though you need to have a clear phase 1 set of parameters and to be strict about it with your stakeholders, your CMDB System needs to be designed for growth. One way to do this is to extend the reach of vendor-provided service modeling through customization. How much of this is facilitated through in-house capabilities or consulting support depends on the skill sets available to you. But we would recommend trying to stay aligned with your own "skill set comfort zone" as much as possible to facilitate the inevitable need to accommodate changing needs and new opportunities.

This is one of the many areas where honesty is the best policy. Try, especially, to be honest with yourself. Don't try to go beyond your abilities. It's fine to be challenged and stretched, but if you go too far, you're risking disaster. If you don't have certain required knowledge or skills, find someone who does and add them to the team. That person may be another employee in your company, a new hire, or a consultant.

The following comments reflect two proactive approaches to extending service modeling through enriching the data model to support use-case and growth requirements:

- We extended our vendor's data model by adding 25 fields. The majority of them were related to financial and asset management requirements. Very few were technical. But most of the fields were designed to support superior financial tracking.
- We customized our own attribute extensions—creating a dictionary model of sorts whereby attributes for CIs could become extensible on the fly—so that the values and the definitions were stored in discrete tables to support relationship types, CI types, etc. Right now we're aggregating about five to 15 attributes for a server CI type.

ONE EXAMPLE OF A SUCCESSFUL MODELING STRATEGY FROM TWO PERSPECTIVES

The following two interview excerpts highlight two different aspects of creating effective modeling strategies—both are, in fact, from the same deployment. The first addresses CMDB/CMS modeling in context with overall administration in a federated universe. The second provides insight into how CMDB-related modeling can be extended to support DevOps requirements. This initiative is well beyond "the gap" period just prior to full deployment—but it helps to provide useful insights into the core modeling discussion in this chapter.

How modeling empowered the growth and administration of a successful CMS at a global air transport corporation[5]

About a year-and-a-half before I got here, they had deployed a CMDB, but they didn't know what to do with it. They were pulling in everything from everywhere, but no one really understood what the CMDB was or how to use it.

---

[5]Interview with a large global transportation company based in the United States using HP's Universal CMDB and Universal Discovery.

I brought in a more object-oriented analysis and design approach so the system could capture the interdependencies across objects and their logical attributes, with increasing levels of granularity as it evolved. It's really about understanding how to leverage a top-down model so you can better understand where things are and what they are.

This also helps establish a foundation for better communication. Different IT professionals understand different things about a server, and they often speak different languages. So we use the CMDB to help them both in their own role and point of view and to better see context and commonality across siloed perspectives.

Administration

In terms of administration, we have high levels of automation in capturing third-party commercial applications. Our ADDM tool can model commercial applications very well, with effective out-of-the-box models for those apps. The challenge is custom developed applications and business application services that bring together multiple applications. For these, someone has to go in and manually create the model.

The master business service model has to be manually created and can't simply be mapped out-of-the-box. So what we've done is to make that process very easy—starting with a high-level meta-model that includes an application server, a Web server, and a database as starting points. Those components can be assigned to pre-defined instances of SQL, or Oracle, or fill in the blank. The last step is to tie it all back into the actual infrastructure.

Application team

The application team has created enrichment rules for this transition, so that two servers are identified as supporting this application for Q/A and five support it in production. Most application owners don't care what else is running on their boxes, they just want to understand their own application map, and that gets shipped up to our BSM performance management system.

HOW CMS MODELING CAN SUPPORT DevOps[6]

One thing we do have is a catalog of services—so, for instance, development can request a server for a specific application. That request gets recorded, and it gets integrated into our BSM modeling system. Or they may request a database or a Web server. Development can create that initial tree very quickly inside our modeling system. Once the resources for the new application or new sub application get approved, a new API is created, and it gets pushed out into the broader BSM system so that everyone can use it as it moves from development into test and into production.

---

[6]Ibid

Another way to look at this is we are bringing the data that we've collected in operations down into the development factory. We want the developers to use our operations tools while they're developing their code, so they can better understand what it's doing. And of course that makes it an easy transition for going back into production. You can see things like, for instance, how individual VM instances are consuming resources across their parent box, not just as it would map to a simulated development environment, but as it would map to our real-world infrastructure.

One of the things we're looking at doing is extending our automation capabilities to create a build from a developer's manifest. You know you'll need a load balancer, X servers, etc., and IIS all configured a certain way, and automation can grab that build. We are also looking at automating the linkages between performance thresholds and scaling application resources up or down so that, for instance, a critical application is not impacted by added activity from a new marketing campaign.

THREE STANDARDS-RELATED RESOURCES TO CONSIDER FOR INTEGRATION, FEDERATION, AND/OR MODELING

Standards in the purest sense haven't fully matured for optimizing CMDB System requirements. In fact, with the exception of the CMDBf standard, very little that is specific to the CMDB System world has even begun to come of age. However, there are foundational capabilities that really have made a difference, such as the Distributed Management Task Force's (DMTF's) Common Information Model (CIM) and in particular Web Services capabilities. It is, in fact, Web Services that have begun to make options for a truly federated CMDB System come alive. Finally, there are emerging standards targeting cloud for now—out of the OASIS Topology and Orchestration Specification for Cloud Applications—that may eventually reach beyond cloud and provide a foundation for that most elusive of entities: a standardized format for a declarative service model capable of supporting multiple CMDB and ADDM investments.

The following list is a high-level reference to help orient you as you begin to examine the relevance of standards in CMDB System context. Some other sources with more detailed discussions of standards relevant to the CMDB System are listed in the bibliography:

- *Common Information Model (CIM)*—CIM is the basis for most DMTF standards, including the CMDB Federation (CMDBf) standard described below. CIM is a conceptual schema that defines how managed CIs can be represented as a common set of objects and how relationships can be consistently represented between them. CIM is extensible to support individual product requirements. CIM is based on the Unified Modeling Language adopted as a standard by the Object Management Group. Many established CMDB vendors have leveraged CIM as a departure point—but all vary in how CIM is realized within their solution.
- *CMDB Federation*—In Q4 2007, the CMDBf Working Group submitted *CMDBf* to the DMTF. The CMDBf is a group of six companies (BMC, CA, Fujitsu, HP, IBM, and Microsoft) missioned to develop a standard architecture and specifications for CMDBs. The CMDBf standard describes interfaces for Configuration Management Databases and management data repositories (MDRs) to share data through federation. While the CMDBf specification promotes new query and registration services, it still requires more work for convenient use in actual deployments. In some cases, that work will fall to the vendors. For instance, the vendors selling core CMDBs will need to develop capabilities (and code) to query other CMDBs and MDRs that support that service. In other cases, the work will fall to IT organizations. For example, IT organizations with MDRs developed in-house will need to develop and code the capabilities to support the registration service.

To the degree that this specification becomes widely adopted, IT organizations will have broad and deep access to integrated data across technology domains such as network, systems, and applications, as well as tool types such as monitoring, fault, performance, and Change Management. IT organizations continually mix and match components and data sources from different vendors to meet the needs of the businesses they serve. In a CMDB environment, this will involve registering MDR data from a variety of vendors, as well as homegrown applications, with a federating CMDB. So far, however, adoption has been modest to mixed, in large part due to the emergence of other options, most of which also leverage Web Services.

*   *Web Services*—Web Services is becoming the industry's best answer for federation, especially where data need to be accessed without actual duplication. However, this is hardly the place to explain Web Services in-depth as there are so many other resources to do it better. Suffice it to say that a *Web service* utilizes Extensible Markup Language (XML)-based communication as developed by the World Wide Web Consortium. XML favors simplicity, generality, and usability and allows for Web service connections to be identified and linked on demand. Web Services function on a service "consumer" and "provider" basis, sometimes including a "broker" to register services and requests (e.g., updates on CI status or attributes). Hypertext transfer protocol provides a foundation communications protocol, such as Simple Object Access Protocol, between producers and consumers and provides a Web Services Description Language for broker interactions. Even though integrations typically require attention to individualized implementations, Web Services are ideal for updating CI attributes and sharing data on a request basis without duplicating it, as in a truly federated model. When model-driven access to CI status and CI attributes are required on a near-real-time basis, dashboards with Web service-enabled mash-ups are increasingly being applied to support visual access to federated data sources.

INTEGRATION, NORMALIZATION, AND ANALYTICS

Deciding just *what* you should integrate into the core CMDB and *where* you should federate is just as important as investing in the right capabilities to do it. Proceeding effectively from proof of concept to deployment will depend on both being selective and investing in the right capabilities to enable growth and breadth.

One approach is to target only CIs that need to be managed for change. This is classic ITIL common sense but still needs to be understood in terms of use case. If you're focusing on asset management, then changes can involve license optimization issues and actual configuration changes. If your focus is performance, you'll need to address shifting CI states and associated impacts including customer/ consumers and owners.

The two interview segments below from two different deployments highlight new options in analytics for assimilating and integrating different data sources across the federated CMS.

INTEGRATION ANALYTICS EXAMPLE ONE: 35 DIFFERENT SOURCES TO SUPPORT THE 5 W's[7]

Our Phase-One objectives center on asset and configuration management. Until recently, we had more limited data feeds and the results were incomplete and not as reliable as we wanted. Each discovery tool has its own idiosyncrasies in terms of what it captures and how it works. This impacts both our ability to manage it and our ability to optimize our hardware and software asset investments in terms of utilization and licensing. With our integrated data analytics, we're leveraging 35 different discovery tools in order to get a more cohesive "golden record" for the CMS.

[7] Interview with a large financial services company based in the United States using Blazent CMDB Accuracy and Intelligence.

We are now accelerating our deployment schedule—in part due to management pressure—bringing in change records and automating change validation through our CMDB so that, for instance, if there's a proposed record for turning on a new server or upgrading memory, we automate a process to validate—"did that change occur?" We're also linking incident and problem management-related attributes to our CIs and seeking to integrate those with release management so we can better understand when a change might have impacted availability.

I like to see our data answer the five W's—who, what, when, where, and why. Who owns or is impacted by the CI? What is it? When was a change made, or when did an associated incident occur? Where, in terms of location or configuration/component or application ecosystem? And why did the change occur? If it's disruptive, what caused it, and how can it be fixed?

INTEGRATION ANALYTICS EXAMPLE TWO: OPTIMIZING INSIGHTS ON 2000 SERVICES THROUGH EMERGING CMDB ANALYTICS[8]

We have about 2,000 of what we call "applications" in the CMS—most of which are more technical services than business applications. An application might be 'incident management,' or 'network configuration,' or 'DNS services,' as well as core business services that are used by our customers for functions such as credit card processing and account management. About 75% of those 2,000 applications are technical services, which means we have about 1,200 functional owners. My team works with them to assess data quality and relevance on an ongoing basis, and once a year we go out to them to do a thorough quality audit.

I would estimate that we have about 30 – 35 automated different sources currently, and we are adding more through our new analytics investment that adds about 15 new sources and improves data quality for five of the current sources. Over time we intend to expand the number of capabilities that we're feeding through that analytic system. The system will improve not only data quality but also CMDB governance—so we can see more clearly where we really do have coverage and where we don't. We can also use that analytic tool to evaluate new discovery, inventory, and other options from the perspective of coverage and data consistency. After all, you don't know what you don't know. You may think you're at 100% data quality because you don't have any evidence to the contrary—until it's too late.

We have extended our core CMDB functionality to support a more automated approach to population. We're updating the system on a daily basis. Some types of sources are in fact manual—such as certain applications and services. For instance, we can't autodiscover our business functions.

FEDERATION

Federating the CMDB System can mean many different things. Strictly speaking, federation means that data can be accessed and core CMDB System modeling can be updated without having to duplicate or

---

[8]Interview with (another) large financial services company based in the United States using Blazent CMDB Accuracy and Intelligence.

move data. However, many deployments treat federation as having multiple resident trusted sources that are aligned with a core CMDB and update the system based on policy, largely through data duplication.

Pragmatism and a focus on relevance can help in charting this critical path. As indicated in "Three Standards-Related Resources to Consider for Integration, Federation, and/or Modeling" box earlier in this chapter, some federation can be purely visual, as long as it is done through a modeled context of CIs and CI interdependencies. For instance, you may well want to view software license Ts and Cs associated with a CI for managing change, but that doesn't necessarily need to be lodged in the same physical location where you keep core insights into changes across services and service components.

If you can navigate through the CI to "see" license status and maybe even automate an alert to indicate that the CI is at risk, you have the CI attribute data you need to manage change. Similarly, you would hardly want to replicate the complex data sets that inform on transaction performance and usage within a core CMDB, but you may well want to have immediate, CI-driven visual access to critical state information when business service performance is disrupted and generate an alert that might even trigger a configuration management change.

In fact, in most cases, it's best to federate detailed configuration information outside of the core CMDB in toolsets optimized for automating detailed configuration updates on a device-specific or VM-specific basis. As trends such as software-defined data centers become more reality than hype, federated resources for automating configuration change will become increasingly cross-domain in themselves—and no doubt represent a parallel system still integrated within the larger CMS.

Federation is a natural way for your CMDB System to grow. Even in phase 1, as you're "closing the gap" in moving to deployment, you will at least want to consider establishing a federation strategy based on use-case priorities and longer-term growth options. We'll revisit federation in Chapter 15, as it's also an excellent focus for phase 2 deployments as you plan to go forward and build out your CMDB System.

FOLLOW-THROUGH, MAINTENANCE, AND WORKFLOW

While follow-through, maintenance, and workflow are three separate ideas, they do come together once you realize that CMDB follow-through and maintenance are closely aligned. Workflow helps to codify follow-through and, at least to some degree, automate it as well. Workflow isn't the total answer—but it is one of the core capabilities to ensure that, for instance, CI owners consistently and formally review a critical change for accuracy.

Looking more specifically at requirements for ongoing maintenance follow-through at the closing-the-gap stage, one of our consultants wrote the following to a client:

It is common in large, complex IT organizations for large-scale projects to fail if short-term, six-month deliverables are not met. This company is no exception, as past projects have suffered from this same malaise. Specific to the CMDB project, interviewees mentioned concerns about post-installation training and long-term maintenance. You can mitigate this risk initially with both a dedicated team assigned to the CMDB project and a roadmap approach that drives milestones and deliverables on a six-month timeframe. This is critical in closing the gap from technology selection into deployment. Long-term maintenance and support issues will be handled by the CMDB team.

Maintenance and managing changes as they occur go hand in hand and often transition into discussions of workflow, as the following comments confirm. Setting up effective workflows in the "gap stage" and as you progress further into phase 2 can sometimes, in itself, make the difference between success and failure with your CMDB initiative:

- We've hired a change librarian or administrator to look at changes and the affected CI and confirm that the asset has changed. We still have instances of irresponsible changes, e.g. people putting memory on the wrong server. Eventually we're going to automate this process with templates and workflow.
- Workflow is very important. We equate workflow with smart automation. The more we can build it in, the less reliant we will be on inconsistent 'human' behaviors. We can become more efficient and more effective once workflow and CMDB governance are aligned.
- When you first set up the CMDB, it's important to already understand how you're going to maintain it. For this, workflow is critical. It is the lifeblood for maintaining efficiency and productivity. It is also one of the first places that you can show productivity gains via the CMDB deployment.

ACCOUNTABILITY, OBJECTIVES, AND METRICS

Without committed levels of accountability and associated objectives, follow-through, and maintenance, the actual deployment of your CMDB is likely to stall. Effectively closing the gap from proof of concept to deployment depends on this. Tuning commitments and objectives here also helps to prepare you for the next critical step—finalizing a roadmap that should take you past phase 1 and into the future.

The following recommendation from a past consulting engagement shows the importance of putting operating-level agreements in place even before deployment begins:

By definition, the CMDB has multiple consumers of its output. The configuration management process has to maintain the integrity of the CMDB and its output. Often overlooked, but critical to success, is the implementation of operating-level agreements with specific metrics. Operating-level agreements are required in order to establish expectations of performance and interaction between the configuration management process and the functional groups were processes that consume its outputs. Major processes requiring operating-level agreements include

- the Service Desk function (for reporting CI errors),
- the incident management process (for storing support artifacts),
- The problem management process (for creation and maintenance of the knowledge base),
- The change management process (to streamline impact assessment),
- the release management process (to assure the integrity of the infrastructure after the changes complete),
- availability and capacity management (to store operational and performance-related artifacts),
- service-level and financial management (to provide a service catalog and support demand management for IT services).

All these cases require formal operating-level agreements and associated management reporting.

Closing the gap requires a tuning that combines vision with near-term reality. In other words, it's time to refine your metrics now that you know more tangibly what you've got in the way of CMDB-related investments, core team and other resource support, phase 1 objectives, and "gap-level" stakeholder dialogue. With that in mind, we thought it would be helpful to provide a few examples from the field of early-phase objectives as proof of concepts emerge into real deployments:

- For our early success, we're expecting to be able to eliminate constant asset surveys that continually burden our organization.
- We're going to start with service management metrics—how we can reduce workloads on service management people, such as help desk professionals, change managers, and problem managers, by defining a service and automating the association of relevant data. We're hoping for reduced trouble tickets at first, and the more specifically quantifiable ROI metrics—such as MTBF and MTTR for critical applications. We're going to then look for service owners to step up and help us define which applications are most critical. We want to do a cost-benefit analysis so we can prioritize what services are most critical and what are the most critical CIs and attributes we'll need to target in Phases One and Two.
- One thing we're looking at—I don't see many people talking about this—we'd like to press down the level of people who do tech support. You can hire a lot of rocket scientists and spend money, or you can simplify things so that people with lower-level skills can handle them. But to do that, you really have to have a way of visualizing dependencies and understanding how something somewhere in the system is affecting something else.
- The goal is to achieve fewer than 30 hours of unplanned downtime per critical application per year. We have about 143 critical applications.

But sadly, not every deployment begins with a well-established sense of objectives or metrics. If you haven't done at least some of the work to document where you've been, it's hard to assess how much you've progressed:

- We don't have defined metrics. The only way you could define them is if you had a baseline. If you really knew how you were doing in incident, problem and change, etc.—how many fewer incidents are occurring.

This last quote underscores the value of establishing at least some baselines before starting out. These can be hard metrics or best-guess assumptions if need be. Moreover, having some metrics about current operational efficiencies provides a value in itself with or without a CMDB.

We'd like to close this section with a quote that describes phased metrics moving from CMDB maintenance and currency to more broadly business-impacting and "saleable" metrics:

We have linked a set of metrics to each one of the processes, but most of them right now are targeted at growing the system and looking at data accuracy. Soon we'll be able to also measure how successful we are in minimizing unauthorized changes and other efficiency and value-related metrics. It's a phased deployment, a phased rollout, so the metrics will have to evolve and grow along with the broader CMS.

CROSSING THE ABYSS

Closing the gap between the visions and the actual CMDB/CMS deployments requires attention to tuning insights learned all along the Eight-Step Ladder to CMDB Success. "The Gap" is the critical moment when what has heretofore been theoretical becomes tangible. This can be both scary and exciting—or less dramatic admixtures of these two extremes. Scary because it's a moment when failures may start to become visible and real. Exciting because it's the time when the CMDB ship moves from dry dock into water and sets sail—to bring real benefits to real people.

The other side to this coin, however, is that the CMDB System is an evolutionary process, and crossing this singular moment is just one part of that evolution. As the system continues to grow and improve in scope, efficiency, and benefit, there will be many launches and extensions through integrations, federation, and—in all probability—new software deployments.

As a part of this evolution, *closing the gap* should depend on well-documented insights from prior dialogues, assessments, and evaluations. It is NOT the time to begin a primal, existential examination of what a CMDB is or should be. If you've done your homework, closing the gap can actually be fun as you refine and retune what you've already established and begin to turn planning, once and for all, into action.

SUMMARY TAKEAWAYS

The goal of this chapter was to provide you with guidelines for handling that critical moment of exhalation for fine-tuning process, planning, commitments, and expectations as you move from predeployment proof of concept toward true, production-level CMDB deployment. It also helps to set the stage for finalizing the tiered roadmap we'll discuss in Chapter 14.

In part, because actualizing CI definitions, service modeling, and data modeling are intrinsic to this stage, we have chosen to focus a large part of this chapter around these requirements—including the difference between "data model" as enabler and "service model" for capturing IT service and service component interdependencies.

We've looked at a top-down approach to service modeling that focused on global dialogue in one example and a more modular, component-centric approach from another deployment. The key lesson learned in both cases is that establishing service modeling priorities can and should become an excellent venue for dialogue, socialization, and expectation setting—including not only what goes into the CMDB but also what phase 1 benefits should become paramount. Service modeling can also become a foundation for managing and containing scope creep—which often arises once you try to close the gap and actualize what you've planned.

In addition, this chapter provides insights into technologies and strategies for federation—in which data are not duplicated but accessed in context through CMS modeling. Standards such as the DMTF's CIM, the CMDBf standard for integrating federated data sources, and Web Services more broadly were introduced. It is recommended that strategies for federation begin in phase 1, even if initial actualizing federation becomes more of a phase 2 or phase 3 priority.

Finally, this chapter also highlighted emerging analytic technologies for assimilating, normalizing, and reconciling data from multiple sources, as well as provided tangible examples of planning for follow-through, workflow, and accountability for phase 1 objectives.

A TIERED ROAD MAP FOR GOING FORWARD

14

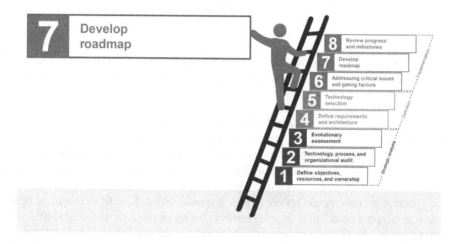

Any strategic IT initiative will require a long-term commitment with a sustained focus. This is certainly true of a CMDB System initiative, where a growing set of stakeholders must learn how to work together to optimize benefits.

However, it's impossible to sustain such an effort without clear signs of progress in short-term activities. Even on long-term projects, management focus typically wanes after 6 months. For this reason, we recommend a tiered road map with tangible objectives. At the end of each 6-month or 12-month period, a comprehensive review should be performed where milestones are compared to the road map and the road map is adjusted and enriched.

From a time perspective, following the Eight-Step Ladder to CMDB System Success, the initial 6-month road map should ideally be first drawn up after about 5 months of work—including assessments, technology selection, and process evaluation. As such, it is both a forward-looking and backward-looking document, codifying preexisting assessments and plans, while laying the foundation for what should follow. The initial three-tiered road map drawn up after 5 months should include the following (Figure 14.1):

- *6-Month road map.* This plan sets hard deadlines for short, deliverable tasks. Since this road map is usually pulled together about 5 months into the CMDB initiative, it will largely reflect what has already been achieved by the CMDB team. Therefore, the 6-month road map involves

---

*Most of the data in this chapter have been taken from multiple consulting engagements. As such, the content maps to real targets with real clients. The goal is to provide you with a narrative summary of an actual three-tiered road map with clear roots in a real CMDB System deployment.

FIGURE 14.1

The three-tiered road map helps you look both backward and forward as you move into core CMDB deployment toward the creation of a phase one CMDB System. Like pieces of a puzzle, each tier of the road map informs the next.

a look back at many of the things already discussed in this book, including modeling, technology selection, and formation of the CMDB team with clearly defined levels of executive support. However, it should also define a clear path for full production deployment and anticipate any near-term "tipping point" benefits once production deployment is under way and stakeholders begin to harvest real CMDB System advantages.

- *12-Month road map.* This should reflect a more matured look at CMDB deployment benefits as the phase one "tipping point" in delivering benefits becomes more pronounced. The goals and milestones here will be directed primarily at delivering value through stakeholder interaction with the CMDB System itself. The 12-month road map will help to provide a foundation for defining what should be included in the 2-year road map—clarifying expectations regarding which projects (and stakeholders) will be addressed next. Throughout this book, the combination of the 6-month and 1-year road maps is referred to as "phase one" of the deployment.
- *2-Year road map.* This 2-year view should provide a vision for a more completed CMDB System that supports initial high-priority use cases. This is not to suggest that your CMDB initiative won't evolve further, support future stakeholders, or expand in use-case values to support additional business and/or technology requirements (e.g., the move to public/private cloud, extensions to support the mobile environment, or renewed attention to DevOps). Like the first two stages, this part of your road map should be adjusted as milestones are met and new components are made available.

CORE ROAD MAP INGREDIENTS

In the beginning of Chapter 10, which targeted metrics and requirements, we reviewed the critical ingredients of an effective project plan. These include

1. use-case and overall objectives;
2. metrics arising from these objectives;
3. detailed requirements arising from these objectives;
4. return on investment (ROI) objectives as appropriate;
5. defined milestones—typically 6 months, 12 months, and 2 years out;

6. team building and development;
7. stakeholder identification, engagement, and development;
8. an effective and evolving communications plan;
9. a clear definition of technology requirements—including architectural needs, where and how to invest, and where and how to prioritize technologies for integration;
10. associated/related interdependencies and initiatives likely to impact, and possibly direct, the CMDB System initiative—e.g., the move to cloud/virtualization, mergers and acquisitions, data center consolidation, new requirements for application sourcing, development and deployment, and business model changes and business expansion;
11. costs and resources requirements from the present to an anticipated 2-to-3-year window.

In this chapter, we'll look at how all these pieces come together by examining an example road map drawn by consolidating insights from past consulting experience. We'll look back at all the work done so far in laying the foundations for road map development. Our discussion of the actual 6-month road map will include sections on the following:

- Creation of the core CMDB System team, including the definition of core team responsibilities
- Creation of a detailed requirements document
- Technology adoption, including the creation of technology-relevant policies
- Value statement (after initial proof of concept)
- Goals
- Milestones
- Costs
- Projected production status at the end of 6 months

The discussion of the 12-month and 2-year road maps will include

- goals
- milestones
- costs
- production status

In order to help you visualize how all these pieces fit together, we will reintroduce relevant segments (e.g., CMDB team definition) as they apply to the case example of a three-tiered road map.

ONE CASE EXAMPLE: ACME FINANCIAL SERVICES CORPORATION'S THREE-TIERED ROAD MAP

One of the best ways to clarify what should go into a three-tiered road map is to examine real cases, drawn from prior consulting engagements. While the following section is in part a theoretical narrative drawn from multiple consulting efforts, dialogs, and interviews, it draws most heavily from a single consulting engagement done for a large financial services software company, which we will call "Acme Financial Services." The following analysis and recommendations are taken at least in part from that report.

In reading this road map for Acme Corporation, you should realize that it reflects a unique moment in time—in particular step seven of the Eight-Step Ladder to CMDB Success. For consistency's sake, we'll place this "moment" roughly 5 months into the first 6 months of the initiative, when Acme is trying to

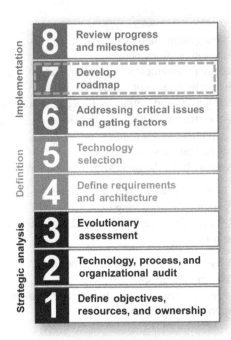

FIGURE 14.2

Where is Acme Financial Services now—as it develops its three-tiered road map? As shown above, it is at step seven of the Eight-Step Ladder to CMDB System Success. Developing the road map requires looking back at steps one through six and bringing the work already done, or in progress, into a single integrated plan for present and future objectives, requirements, and goals. In other words, it draws on work that should already have been done and brings the pieces together into single cohesive framework.

pull what's been done so far into a single coherent road map. At this point at Acme, some tasks, such as the proof of concept for technology selection, have been completed. Some decisions, such as final commitments for staffing the CMDB team, are still in play, while others await further progress to even begin—specifically the goals and milestones in the 12-month and 2-year road maps. These time dependencies will vary from company to company, but we chose to create a narrative around one individual deployment to show how these tasks can come together cohesively (Figure 14.2).

INITIAL SUMMARY AND ANALYSIS

Any introduction to a phased, or tiered, road map should include a summary look back at the processes involved in getting there and the lessons learned. In order to assess the situation at Acme Corporation, interviews were conducted with relevant stakeholders across the organization. The results of these 27 interviews were used to establish goals and the overall approach to the road map. The perspectives below reflect the results of those interviews—which came out of the audit (step two of the Eight-Step Ladder).

ACME CORPORATION'S CMDB SYSTEM GOALS

- Improve operational efficiency by aligning IT operations with the business units.
- Better identify current configuration states (software, hardware, and dependencies).
- Improve analysis and efficiencies for change decisions (impact, scheduling, etc.).
- Advance IT maturity from a reactive mode to a more proactive mode.
- Investigate an additional citizen CMDB for managing the application layer of the enterprise—with strong support for more real-time insights into application-to-infrastructure interdependencies and impacts on service performance.

APPROACH

Acme Financial Services followed the Eight-Step Ladder to CMDB Success:

- The team reviewed current status of IT management at Acme—what's working and what's not.
  - To do this, Acme required 27 interviews with staff members. These interviews were meant to gather information and educate.
  - The interviews focused on tools, process, and organization.
  - The goal was to gather facts and to assess perceptions, as perceptions can be roadblocks to project success.
- From this work, the CMDB team formulated an initial set of requirements and objectives.
- Then, the team determined prerequisites and gating factors.

Strategic Insights

The data points gathered in the staff interviews helped to inform Acme's strategy for going forward.

- Acme is growing quickly, 20% per year, with a current staff of 7000.
- IT at Acme has a very capable technical staff—with excellent execution on tactical requirements.
- Acme IT enjoys good employee satisfaction with a focus on work/life balance.
- Availability and performance for application services are all acceptable within margins, but outages, especially from change, are an escalating problem.
- The risk is that Acme cannot do "business as usual." Increasing complexity and size require the following:
  - A more scalable IT organization capable of shifting skill sets and focus. This means streamlining in some places while adding resources in others, such as development and user experience management. Scalability here also requires that Acme's IT move from a predominantly domain-defined organization to a more cross domain organization. Acme should plan to create teams focused on areas such as service delivery and configuration and change as an overlay to domain-specific roles such as network, systems, or end point management. This cross-domain focus will also be critical to Acme as it attempts to leverage both internal and external cloud resources to help facilitate growth.
  - Technology investments should include analytics and automation to enable much-needed efficiencies in supporting more dynamic awareness while minimizing manual requirements for routine, repeatable processes.

Issues surrounding vision and perception

Across the broader IT population, Acme currently lacks a concrete understanding of vision and strategy for its proposed CMDB System:

- Most staff interviewees stated that there is no consistent CMDB vision.
- Therefore, the core team must define the "big picture" in order for Acme to move forward.
- For the CMDB System to succeed, it needs to be viewed as a "macro project" relevant to (and bringing value to) the broader IT organization instead of a "niche project" or "pet project" in the hands of a few evangelists.
- Adding to this confusion, at least three core CMDB efforts have surfaced—service desk, enterprise application development, and operations. These will need to be reprioritized and integrated into a single CMDB System initiative.

Articulating a value proposition across three distinct sets of priorities

There are three overarching perspectives to consider in articulating a value proposition within Acme's organizational landscape:

1. IT executives at Acme are heavily motivated by cost avoidance (e.g., avoiding future headcount increases by improving the efficiency of information exchange via the CMDB System).
2. The lines of business are motivated by risk avoidance (e.g., avoiding outages by better Change Management data) in aligning with the CMDB effort.
3. IT staff are looking to advance IT maturity and work/life balance (e.g., fewer off-hour calls for support) as the main motivator for the implementation of a CMDB System.

OTHER ISSUES

The following five areas were also identified as issues within Acme Financial Services: *diverse expectations, communications, siloed vs. centralized IT issues, cost center vs. partner issues,* and *staffing*.

While these are far from universal, they are typical issues experienced by many organizations. Other common issues may relate to process or stem from a lack of executive leadership. As we will soon see, *staffing* and *costs* are in fact the top issues at Acme.

Diverse expectations

As seen in Figure 14.3, expectations were extremely diverse at Acme as they ranged from asset and configuration management to user experience management and virtualization. Prioritizing phase one goals therefore required explicit efforts at socialization and communication, both to evaluate stakeholder readiness and to help manage those expectations that could not be addressed within 12, or even 24, months.

Communications

Only 24% of interviewees felt that there was a communications problem at Acme, while 67% stated that communications were improving. This was a very good sign since good communication was critical for the CMDB System at Acme, which impacted virtually all technology silos. The most common complaint about communications was *inconsistency*—providing either too little or too much information.

Siloed vs. centralized

Eighty-three percent of interviewees thought that Acme was siloed. Yet, few felt that communication between silos was a problem. Nevertheless, the CMDB System required a team with clear cross silo authority for implementation of the CMDB System.

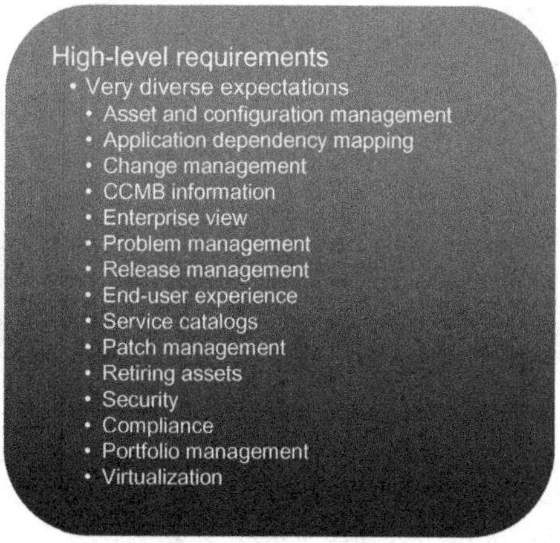

High-level requirements
- Very diverse expectations
  - Asset and configuration management
  - Application dependency mapping
  - Change management
  - CCMB information
  - Enterprise view
  - Problem management
  - Release management
  - End-user experience
  - Service catalogs
  - Patch management
  - Retiring assets
  - Security
  - Compliance
  - Portfolio management
  - Virtualization

FIGURE 14.3

Acme's CMDB initiative evolved out of a tremendous range of priorities, as indicated above. To address this problem, Acme had to develop a detailed requirement document to refine and prioritize CMDB System objectives and then work to communicate and socialize results across the broader IT corporation.

Cost center vs. business partner

In general, a "cost center" IT organization focuses on minimizing costs and cutting staff. Eighty-six percent of those interviewed thought that Acme IT was a cost center. The exception (and this represented a challenge to core IT) was found in the business units, where localized IT teams were viewed as business partners. The CMDB System initiative is therefore seeking to elevate the broader IT organization at Acme to a business-partner level. This should help the CMDB to function more effectively, while also providing a yardstick for showing real value to IT executives.

Staffing

Ninety-one percent felt that staffing was a problem and that the IT organization had no bandwidth for new projects. This was a red flag for the CMDB initiative at Acme. Personnel turnover could easily have become an issue if this trend continued, especially because Acme routinely overburdened its experts.

While the CMDB System would eventually help overall staffing issues by increasing the efficiency of Acme IT, there was a short-term price to pay. For the CMDB initiative to work, it will be imperative that the CMDB and its sponsors don't give in to staffing pressure at Acme and attempt a CMDB project with only part-time staff. This remains an open issue even as the CMDB team at Acme begins assembling its three-tiered road map.

GATING FACTORS

The gating factors (as shown in Figure 14.4) provide a baseline for prioritizing actions, policies, and communications for the CMDB System initiative at Acme.

TARGET AREAS FOR PHASE ONE

Contrast the goals described below in this section with the list of expectations in Figure 14.3. These much more focused objectives constitute the core priorities underlying Acme's phase one rollout and provided a foundation for the 2-year road map, which will expand beyond these core goals.

```
1.  Cost and staffing (7 interview votes)
2.  Demonstrating the value (5)
3.  Common strategic vision (4)
4.  Management support (3)
5.  Detailed requirements (2)
6.  Communications (2)
7.  Follow-thru (2)
8.  Integration (1)
9.  Tactical action (1)
10. Process (0)
```

FIGURE 14.4

This figure shows a ranked set of gating factors of concern for Acme Corporation taken from 27 interviews across management and staff. Having such a list prepared in advance through audits and assessments provides a much-needed backdrop for developing a staged road map.

Change Management and the CMDB System

At Acme, planned and unplanned changes drive as many as 80% of incidents related to the delivery of critical application services. This is higher than the industry average, which is between 50% and 60%. While freezing change might result in a decrease in the number of incidents, it isn't a long-term option at Acme, especially given growing pressures from cloud, agile, and the move to create a more consumer-friendly IT organization.

Eighty-five percent of the interviewees at Acme feel that the change process is poorly managed. In particular, the following concerns were expressed regarding the change control management board:

- The Change Management Board is highly reliant on tribal knowledge and therefore vulnerable to the opinions of "available experts."
- A Change Management tool is needed to provide consistent data to support document change histories and provide reliable and consistent insights into the impacts of change.
- Acme currently has more change notification than real change control, so individuals are aware of changes but lack clarity of context, impact, or a means to prevent inappropriate changes.
- In particular, there is a lack of broad architectural insights into change impacts that cut across domains.

Because of these currently unaddressed needs and hence a place where the CMDB System could show strong value quickly, Acme is prioritizing Change Management tools to integrate with CMDB and become a part of the broader CMDB System.

Incident and problem management

(Incidents are disruptive events. Problems are the underlying cause of the incidents.)

Acme is in the *active operational* stage of maturity and is hindered in moving to the *proactive service-driven* stage because IT's structure is primarily silo-based. That leads to narrow, silo-driven perspectives rather than broader, big-picture insights. As a corollary to this, problem management at Acme is still just emerging. For this reason, phase one priorities include support for a stronger problem management position. Expectations are that while Change Management should move significantly forward into production during the 12-month road map, the move to a more fully progressed focus on problem management will require the full 2-year road map.

AN OVERVIEW GRAPHIC OF ACME FINANCIAL SERVICES CORPORATION'S THREE-TIERED ROAD MAP

Little will help you inform your stakeholders how your CMDB System initiative will move forward more than a chart summary such as in Figure 14.5. Such a summary is an excellent way to initially get the attention of your stakeholders, including executives, and set the stage for more specific detailed discussions. It will also be a strong statement that you've taken the reins and thought through the process in a meaningful and constructive way.

The following graphic shows the short-term deliverables for Acme's 6-month and 12-month road maps with a sketch of priorities for 2 years out. In the first 6 months, the primary goals are centered on completing several vendor proof-of-concept exercises, building the CMDB team, and putting together a comprehensive detailed requirements document (as described in Chapter 10).

The second 6-month period is focused on implementing the core CMDB and service desk implementation selected from a vendor we'll call "vendor A," an Application Discovery and Dependency Mapping vendor ("vendor B"), and an asset management solution from "vendor C." In other words, this second 6-month period is directed at deploying the core CMDB and populating it with inventory and ADDM data. During this period, Acme should begin to address its first target area of concern: Change Management. As you can see in Figure 14.5, the road map overview also includes a pricing summary and other relevant details, such as critical team roles and associated tasks.

Finally, the 2-year road map reflects the move from a core CMDB deployment to a more fully evolved CMDB System with support for disaster recovery (DR), service-level management (SLM), service catalogs, and an executive dashboard.

6-MONTH ROAD MAP FOR ACME CORPORATION

Acme's look back at the first 5 months of planning, assessment, and preliminary technology prioritization is reflected in the summary of CMDB System issues and milestones codified below.

CREATION OF AN EFFECTIVE CORE CMDB TEAM WITH STRONG MANAGEMENT OVERSIGHT

After 5 months of assessments, planning, and communication, Acme has just finally formalized a core CMDB team under the auspices of the VP of operations. The team is still petitioning for the full support of the CIO in order to grant it the authority it needed to effectively implement a CMDB at Acme among groups outside of operations, such as the service desk and application development. While this team of individuals has already been working together to do assessments and planning, its formalization with full executive support and fully committed ongoing resource will be an important milestone in Acme's CMDB initiative.

The CMDB team at Acme is composed of four IT professionals who filled the following roles:

- The *team leader* is an articulate and easy-to-approach evangelist for the values that the CMDB will bring to Acme. He is also a good project manager with good intragroup communication skills since initial success depended on the timely completion of key projects.

	6 Month roadmap	12 Month roadmap	3 Year roadmap			
	0 6	12 18	24	30	36	
Tasks	Core CMDB POC Citizen CMDB POC (EAD) App mapping (OEI) Discovery (OEI) Detailed require doc build CMDB team	Core CMDB Citizen CMDB (EAD) Integration with park and currents Integration with park and Acme	Upgrade park service desk to current version Change management Disaster recovery SLM Service catalogs		Exec dashboard	
Software and hardware	Currents (dependency mapping) Acme asset management (desktops)	Acme asset management (servers) Park CMDB Park configuration manager (Patch management) (Application management) (Content management)				
Staff	Team leader CMDB expert CMDB expert Info architect EAD CMDB expert EMA review	Team leader CMDB expert CMDB expert Info architect EAD CMDB expert EMA review	Team leader CMDB expert CMDB expert Info architect EMA review			
Costs	Software: $0 Hardware: $15 K IT staff: $416 K Consult staff: $14 K CMDB only: $445 K Total: $445 K	Software: $X Hardware: $X IT staff: $416 K Consult staff: $14 K CMDB only: $430 K Total: $430 K	Software: $X Hardware: $X IT staff: $1331 K Consult staff: $56 K CMDB only: $1387 K Total: $1387 K			

Assumptions: Fully loaded IT staff costs are $80 per h.

	Six month roadmap	Twelve month roadmap	Two year roadmap			
	0 6	12	15 18	21	24	
Tasks	Core CMDB POC Citizen CMDB POC (EAD) App mapping (OEI) Discovery (OEI) Detailed require doc build CMDB team	Core CMDB Citizen CMDB (EAD) Integration with vendor A and vendor B Integration with vendor A and vendor C	Upgrade help desk (vendor R) into vendor A Change management Disaster recovery SLM Service catalogs		Exec dashboard	
Software and hardware	Vendor B (dependency mapping) Vendor C (desktops)	Vendor C (servers) Vendor A CMDB Vendor A configuration manager (Patch management) (Application management) (Content management)				
Staff	Team leader CMDB expert CMDB expert Info architect EAD CMDB expert EMA review	Team leader CMDB expert CMDB expert Info architect EAD CMDB expert EMA review	Team leader CMDB expert CMDB expert Info architect EMA review			
Costs	Software: $0 Hardware: $15 K IT staff: $416 K Consult staff: $14 K CMDB only: $445 K Total: $445 K	Software: $X Hardware: $X IT staff: $416 K Consult staff: $14 K CMDB only: $430 K Total: $430 K	Software: $X Hardware: $X IT staff: $1331 K Consult staff: $56 K CMDB only: $1387 K Total: $1387 K			

Assumptions: Fully loaded Z Corporation IT staff costs are $80 per h.

FIGURE 14.5

This overview graphic for Acme Corporation's CMDB System road map is designed to support high-level communication and planning both within the CMDB team and with executives and other critical stakeholders. It will be updated as progress is made and priorities shift, with more detail coming into the 12-month road map and the 2-year road map once the 6-month road map is complete.

- Two *CMDB specialists* will be supporting the implementation and integration of the CMDB solution. Both of these are planned as part-time resources initially (about 0.5 FTE each). They are responsible for working with the various technology silos to determine the initial low-level requirements, acting as liaisons with the CMDB vendor, installing software, writing reconciliation rules, adjudicating any issues with systems of records, making recommendations for tool consolidation, testing the CMDB schemas, and rolling solutions into production. One of these individuals also has solid, hands-on familiarity with the vendor A's core CMDB.
- A *database specialist* completes the team. This person is responsible for categorizing and scrubbing the requirements, analyzing the data model and schema, identifying CI-level data elements (and duplication), generating updates to the Web site, and reporting on project progress. This position is planned as full-time initially but may become part-time (about 0.5 FTE) by or before phase one completion.
- Acme's CMDB team of four includes two *ITIL-certified* members responsible for the CMDB implementation. As process always plays a strong role in the success of the CMDB implementation, these individuals have already been sharing tasks ranging from process review, drafting CMDB process policy, and educating the staff on ITIL practices as they apply to the CMDB.

Acme Corporation CMDB team responsibilities

Detailed requirements document: While the road map is primarily the responsibility of the CMDB team leader, all team members were well versed in the overall CMDB strategy and road map. In an effort that requires significant grassroots education, it is imperative that the team present a clear and consistent message to Acme's IT staff regarding its goals. All team members have already participated in the creation, refinement, and measurement of the strategy and road map. This effort took approximately 20% of the staff's time initially.

Data management: The CMDB team at Acme is responsible for providing process guidelines for gathering and automating data collection; establishing and enforcing rules for data integrity and quality; setting best practices for gathering and establishing integration with the tools that collect the data; minimizing or eliminating drift management; reporting on the CMDB; etc. It is not possible for the CMDB team to be responsible for individual data management tasks.

Tool adoption: In terms of tool adoption, the CMDB should help significantly in eliminating redundancy in data collection. However, many stakeholders may continue to use their own tools for management and discovery—even as they become integrated into the broader CMDB System.

Budget and costs: The core CMDB team has already ensured that both initial CapEx and OpEx resources at Acme were well defined, socialized, and understood. As such, they were already approved by most key stakeholders, although still waiting for final, formal executive review. Acme has approached both its 6-month and 12-month road map objectives as "funded projects" with specific beginning and end points. However, by the time the 2-year road map is complete, the hopes are that the CMDB System will receive budgetary investments as an ongoing line item in the budget of the IT organization.

CREATION OF A DETAILED REQUIREMENTS DOCUMENT

A key priority of Acme's CMDB team is education: providing a clear definition and project plan around the CMDB initiative. This includes publishing the CMDB requirements document, strategy, and road maps. Acme has done this in part by using an internal Web site to establish the CMDB System project and track progress. A key part of this communications effort was the publication of CMDB System policies for technology adoption as described below in "Technology Adoption" section that follows.

Another critical area addressed in the detailed requirements document was *process readiness*. Acme reviewed its enterprise-wide ITIL initiative, focusing on delivering "deep" value in a few prioritized areas, such as asset management, before widening the scope of the program. Acme has also already adopted a tool capable of mapping ITIL practices to Acme's processes, roles, and work products.

Yet another critical part of the detailed requirements document is *a list of analytic tools* that would utilize CMDB data. The document includes a *gap analysis* to highlight the delta between available and desired levels of functionality. In association with this, Acme is developing a list of *initial integration points* that focus on identifying and eliminating overlapping data sets and redundant configuration items related to analytic integrations.

In parallel, the application development process at Acme is being updated to include the instrumentation of mandatory "hooks" in new code for more effective usage of existing monitoring and management tools for improved performance monitoring. This is especially critical to Acme IT's move to advance its support for problem management by leveraging its investments in vendor B Application Discovery and Dependency Mapping.

Finally, the CMDB team has already established a strict set of procedures for resolving conflicts over data ownership and integration to support stakeholder dialogs, codify best practices, and manage expectations. While these procedures will continue to evolve over time, they have already become one of the most critical ingredients in the detailed requirements document.

TECHNOLOGY ADOPTION

Acme undertook a proof of concept in order to explore the strengths of its CMDB/service desk product in relationship to already defined priorities and goals. This followed Acme's practice of testing out solutions "vertically" in a focused or limited environment, in order to later optimize them "horizontally" across the broader IT environment.

Policies for technology adoption

The CMDB team established policies for the adoption of technologies as a ramp-up to its proof of concept efforts. These policies set expectations for customers and stakeholders, while showing them what benefits they would derive from the CMDB. These policies have already been published so that they could be shared and revised throughout the initial phases of the project.

Acme currently leverages a CMDB System-specific Web page on the internal IT Web site to provide a centralized place for employees to view the policies, CMDB System announcements, and results.

1. As a general rule, Acme prioritizes using off-the-shelf IT management software over building its own solutions. This represents a significantly lower risk to the organization; provides adequate functionality; reduces the need to develop, maintain, and integrate homegrown solutions; and streamlines certification and auditing.
2. This preference for off-the-shelf solutions has already been applied to both the core CMDB. Within the broader CMDB System, it will also be applied to all new IT management tools required to integrate with the core CMDB. Some more specific examples of technology adoption policies include the following:

a. Preference will be given to those tools that provide a native or proven integration with the core CMDB. This will allow Acme to leverage its current investment in tools and infrastructure components while providing the greatest degree of flexibility in sharing the data via the CMDB.

b. Secondary consideration will be given to commercial tools that provide a function not available in a tool that integrates with the CMDB. In this case, Acme will consider the cost of integration with the CMDB as an additional cost to purchase the software.

c. Internally developed solutions will be considered only as a last resort where no commercially available solution exists. Integration with the core CMDB should be considered as part of the initial development costs of the software.

Most internally developed solutions and commercial management tools within Acme have already been eliminated using the approach outlined above. Acme's preparations for selecting CMDB-related technologies are summarized in Figure 14.6.

Evaluations

The following areas were prioritized for tool set evaluations at Acme IT during the first 6 months. As you can see, some of the objectives described below have already been achieved at 5 months out, while others are still in process:

- *Core CMDB evaluation*: Evaluate and demonstrate the capabilities of vendor A's CMDB to provide data and integration throughout Acme's infrastructure. The proof of concept was directed

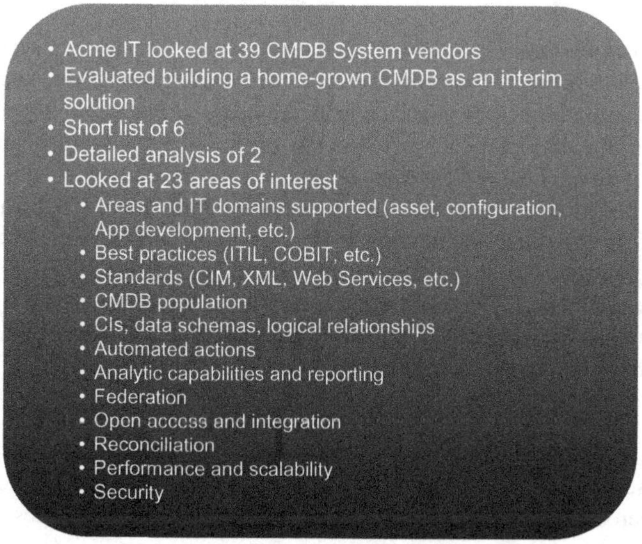

- Acme IT looked at 39 CMDB System vendors
- Evaluated building a home-grown CMDB as an interim solution
- Short list of 6
- Detailed analysis of 2
- Looked at 23 areas of interest
  - Areas and IT domains supported (asset, configuration, App development, etc.)
  - Best practices (ITIL, COBIT, etc.)
  - Standards (CIM, XML, Web Services, etc.)
  - CMDB population
  - CIs, data schemas, logical relationships
  - Automated actions
  - Analytic capabilities and reporting
  - Federation
  - Open access and integration
  - Reconciliation
  - Performance and scalability
  - Security

FIGURE 14.6

Tool set analysis required establishing priorities or "areas of interest" across multiple IT groups. These areas of interest showed a broad and well-considered approach to CMDB System planning and adoption at Acme. This, in turn, also provided an excellent foundation for technology evaluation and planning.

at specific, phase one goals. This included assessing the integration potential of the vendor A CMDB with the existing systems management investments.

- *ADDM evaluation*: Acme IT is working with vendor B's ADDM tool to establish a meaningful set of application relationships. For enterprise application development, this means that unique fingerprints will need to be developed for individual custom-developed applications. Ideally, this will be done as a part of the DevOps process—so that application dependencies can be defined prior to deployment in production. This will extend the value of the CMDB-optimized Change Management process to support life cycle application management requirements. It will provide a baseline for Acme to establish change impact-related processes and will estimate the skills and time required for any future application mapping efforts.

- *ADDM integration*: Integration of vendor A's core CMDB with vendor B's Application Discovery and Dependency Mapping solution is also a critical initial objective. Vendor B's ADDM tool is currently in the process of being deployed by operations. Successful extension of the CMDB System will require using vendor A's integration platform to create a mapping between vendor B's federated ADDM and the core CMDB. Doing this will have the added advantage of providing Acme IT with baseline experience for doing future integrations and for estimating costs, time, and skills relevant to future integration projects.

- *Asset management integration with vendor C*: Another critical integration is between the core CMDB and vendor C's asset management for servers and desktops. Similar to the application dependency mapping efforts, this integration will also provide a baseline for assessing the efforts to create mappings between the vendor C data and the core CMDB. So far, Acme has done targeted testing in a preproduction development environment that included the servers, applications, and workstations—sufficient for evaluating vendor C integrations within the first 6 months.

- *Vendor A server configuration management testing*: Testing of vendor A's server configuration management solution will also be required—as it's deployed by enterprise application development. This should include at least one use case for *ad hoc* deployment and synchronization of the development environment—potentially extending Acme IT's CMDB System to support more enhanced DevOps values.

- *CMDB team process review*: As a part of this integration work, there will be a process review by the CMDB team for each case, including ADDM, asset, and configuration. This will establish a baseline expectation and a "best practices" methodology for approaching process requirements for CMDB implementation going forward. This review should focus on what processes are followed when new servers are added to the infrastructure and how new application dependencies are defined and how automation is applied to gathering CIs throughout the infrastructure.

Training
During interviews, several individuals stated that training was not a priority at Acme. As a result, the utilization of tools across all of Acme IT was suboptimal as the following quotes show:

- We deploy only 40% of applications [commercial software tools] and utilize only 20% of their power.
- Our tools are not sufficient—not because of the tools themselves, but because of our people.

This carried over to the CMDB core team, where the view was that the "team members weren't sufficiently trained and the tools aren't being fully utilized." As a result, Acme conducted formal training in vendor A's core CMDB for all the members of the CMDB team.

PHASE-ONE TECHNOLOGY VALUE TARGETS

Acme solidified its "phase one technology value targets" during the proof of concept for vendor A's core CMDB software and vendor B ADDM capabilities:

- *OpEx efficiencies in inventory, discovery, and application dependency mapping*: These will be achieved by leveraging currently deployed technologies in order to create a more complete inventory across domains at Acme IT. These inventory data should be assessed in conjunction with the automated application dependency mapping that's currently undergoing proof of concept in operations. ROI here will evolve over time through new OpEx efficiencies. These should be very significant; however, they may be difficult to calculate.
- *Multipurpose values from harvesting CMDB System data*: Here, the CMDB team should be prepared to provide an effective demonstration of how CMDB System-related information can be made available to the Acme IT organization as a whole. This improved access to data across domains will drive value across the organization in the following ways (as projected across both the 6-month and the 12-month road maps):
  - *Change management* can use the information to make more informed decisions about the impact of proposed changes. ROI can be calculated based on fewer incidents related to change. This also supports line of business priorities for risk avoidance.
  - *Incident and problem management* can use the combined insights on change, change histories, and application-to-infrastructure interdependencies to more quickly and more effectively resolve application-related issues. OpEx ROI can be calculated in terms of faster mean time to repair (MTTR) and mean time between failure (MTBF). For business services, cost of downtime for critical transactions can significantly be added to this ROI calculation. This supports IT priorities for cost avoidance and IT efficiencies and line of business priorities for undisrupted business services.

MILESTONES

By the end of the 6 months, Acme expects to have completed all the objectives articulated in its 6-month road map. Unless otherwise indicated, these goals have already been achieved by or before 5 months out. These include the following:

1. Creation of a CMDB System team (done at 5 months pending final executive approval)
2. Creation of guidelines for ITIL processes within the CMDB team relevant to phase one objectives (i.e., as articulated in the 6-month and 12-month road map).
3. Purchase and customization of a tool for mapping ITIL concepts to existing Acme processes
4. Publication of the CMDB strategy and road map on an internal Web site
5. Creation of a CMDB intranet information page in order to engage stakeholders and customers, to provide information on status and requirements relevant to stakeholders, and to promote ongoing dialog to help fine-tune the CMDB System opportunity

6. Publication of the "CMDB strategy and road map" and the "CMDB policies"
7. Creation of a detailed requirements document
8. Installation and initial proof-of-concept testing of the vendor A's core CMDB
9. Completion of a proof-of-concept ADDM project across the Acme infrastructure
10. Creation of "integration teams" to establish procedures and guidelines for reconciliation and remediation of data *(in process)*
    a. Resolving system-of-record questions
    b. Identification of redundant data and tools
11. Training and cross training of the CMDB team *(in process)*

COSTS (See Figure 14.5)

Costs for the initial 6 months are mostly associated with building the CMDB staff. This is largely because Acme has benefited from the fact that both vendor A's core CMDB and vendor B's ADDM solution were already paid for before the CMDB initiative began.

When looking ahead to optimizing the CMDB System, the CMDB team reinforced the fact that a CMDB is an *enabling technology*. While there were some visualization and reporting capabilities inherent within the core CMDB, the real value of the implementation of the broader system would be to enable higher-level analytic tools and automation capabilities to access both the data and the associated interdependency modeling.

The CMDB team compiled a list of analytic tools necessary to fully maximize the value of the broader system in present and future phases; however, the cost of these tools was outside the scope of the CMDB System initiative at Acme *per se*. These tools ranged from Change Management analytics or performance and capacity planning analytics to business impact analysis to an executive dashboard. Some of these analytic tools are being implemented and integrated concurrently with, or shortly after, the phase one. Others, like the executive dashboard, are longer-term projects at Acme and fall into the time frame of the 2-year road map.

PRODUCTION INFRASTRUCTURE STATUS AT THE END OF THE 6-MONTH ROAD MAP

At the end of the 6 months, Acme expects to show little change in production-level technology status as most of the work so far has targeted the creation of the CMDB System team, the undertaking a proof of concept, and the need to address gating factors required to close the post-PoC gap as identified through interviews and assessments. Both the CMDB and autodiscovery remain in "gray" in the Figure 14.7 because Acme's 6-month road map leads up through, but not beyond, proof of concept and socialization.

Of particular interest for CMDB deployments is determining whether the foundational elements of the CMDB are in place. This includes ensuring both that the underlying data are in place and that the tools necessary for keeping the data current and populating the CMDB System are also in place. In the case of Acme, both the CMDB and autodiscovery are projected to show strong improvement in the 12-month road map, but they are expected to remain outside production at the end of the first 6 months.

12-MONTH ROAD MAP FOR ACME FINANCIAL SERVICES

The 12-month road map at Acme represents the initial *production* deployment of the CMDB. At the time of developing its initial three-tiered road map, Acme targeted the following objectives:

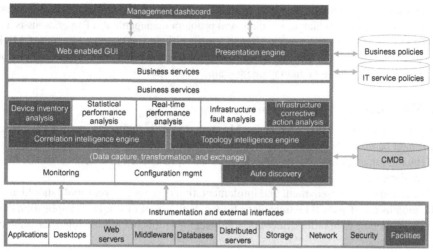

FIGURE 14.7

Projected production status at the end of the 6-month road map. White means "fully implemented." Gray means "partially implemented in production." And black means "not yet in production." The model shown above is designed to support CMDB System planning by highlighting areas of technical deficiencies and strengths. The idea is to provide an overall view of all the management technologies (either planned or in current use) and then map existing technology realities to the ideal. The gaps in black show areas in which the organization can choose to invest to gain more value.

UPDATED DETAILED REQUIREMENTS

Acme projected a further update to the detailed requirements document with yet more granular metrics. This will include a further prioritization of requirements, which in turn should lead to logical groupings of requirements by functional and organizational areas. For instance, inventory and asset management requirements for both data management and value delivery are currently "owned" by a mix of designated stakeholders working in both the service desk and operations. These stakeholders will help to refine and clarify data management and value/benefits expectations in the 12-month window.

From these groupings, itemized requirements will be addressed through the integration of existing tools or the implementation of new tools used to gather the data for the CMDB. These clusters of requirements will also serve to further clarify key stakeholder roles and processes in support of the broader CMDB System.

TARGETING THE RIGHT STAKEHOLDER TEAM

12-Month priorities are being chosen to support enthusiastic and well-prepared groups within Acme IT with well-defined, highly visible needs. In other words, the scope of the 12-month road map is being designed with careful attention placed on meeting a finite set of particular detailed requirements that map well to identified stakeholders and organizations willing, ready, and able to help optimize the CMDB System initiative at Acme.

In following these guidelines, Acme is primarily targeting IT operations, which had established clear priorities in the areas of change, incident, and problem management. IT operations is also a good choice—as opposed to an IT organization aligned to a specific business unit—since the CMDB System initiative will ultimately establish broad-based inventory, CI, and process guidelines that favor the purview of a centralized executive IT management team.

CHANGE MANAGEMENT AT THE TOP

In ranking priorities, Acme is placing Change Management at the top of its list. This prioritization has been determined based on high-level requirements gathered during assessment-related interviews. As such, implementation of Change Management analytics represents an excellent candidate for proof-of-concept work during the 12-month road map.

A final decision on the deployment and implementation of autodiscovery tools should also be complete by 12-months out. This will include plans for the deployment of vendor B application dependency mapping in conjunction with other discovery and inventory tools being scheduled for implementation on a case-by-case basis.

TIPPING POINT

The end of the 12-month road map should provide a true "tipping point" for the core CMDB and, to a lesser degree, for the broader CMDB System to deliver benefits beyond project progress. After 12 months, the value both to the production staff and to management should become clearly understood, the approach of the CMDB team became validated, and the CMDB project should begin far more aggressively to sell itself. Figure 14.8 shows project status for 12 months out—reflecting critical "tipping point" values.

GOALS

At the end of the 12-month road map, the following general goals should be accomplished:

- Management investments across IT will be at minimum domain-focused not element-focused.
- Intersilo communication should meaningfully improve.
- Integration between domains should meaningfully improve.
- Enhanced levels of automation will be deployed in support of Change Management and other phase one requirements.
- More business-relevant real-time performance and availability metrics will be used to measure SLAs in conjunction with core CMDB data and ADDM dependency insights.
- Security and DR will have meaningfully improved.
- IT will have extended its reach to facilities in support of some change, incident, and problem management requirements via CI inclusion in Acme's CMDB System.

MILESTONES

At the end of 12 months, the CMDB team should have accomplished the following milestones:

- Enterprise-wide CMDB standards will be far better understood at Acme than they were at the beginning of the initiative. This effort includes the following:
  - Communicating and publishing CMDB System standards for all stakeholders and customers relevant to both the 6-month and the 12-month road maps

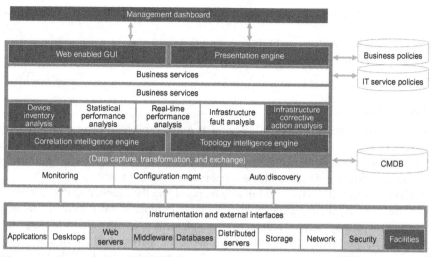

FIGURE 14.8

Projected production status at Acme Corporation 12 months out. At the end of 12 months, the core CMDB should be in full deployment, and the implementations of autodiscovery and application dependency mapping should be well under way. In addition, standards around internal application monitoring should be well established and understood, and monitoring issues in the silos should be at least partially resolved. Finally, the valuable inclusion of "facilities" for change, incident, and problem management into the detailed requirements document should be complete.

- Ensuring that configuration data gathering and updating are performed consistently as opposed to in an *ad hoc* manner
- Implementation of the core CMDB will be complete and in production.
  - Scoping this effort will be informed by the experience gained by the team during those first 6 months.
  - Prioritization of objectives and scope will be done in conjunction with the end users and technology silos.
  - No additional headcount should be needed to undertake this effort, as extensions of CMDB System activities are integrated into current stakeholder roles. However, the CMDB team is requesting the services of an enterprise architect currently in operations to support its Change Management priorities.
  - A revised budget will be provided to executive management at this point.

SOME IMPLEMENTATION SPECIFICS

Initial project implementations of the broader CMDB System and of the core CMDB will be fully under way and in production at Acme after 12 months, including the following:

- Automatic discovery and topology intelligence to detect new systems as they are inserted into the infrastructure
- Device inventory analysis

- Event correlation intelligence to allow events to be tied to the infrastructure components and applications
- Statistical performance analysis and infrastructure fault analysis
- Real-time and root cause performance analysis and corrective actions

COSTS (See Figure 14.5)

During between 6 and 12 months, the CMDB team at Acme expects to require the support of an enterprise architect currently residing in operations. In order to ensure that core business requirements are met, this position should be backfilled by a part-time contract resource, who can function as the enterprise architect's virtual assistant while he supported the CMDB team.

As the CMDB project will be focused initially on providing the foundation data for the enterprise, Acme should not incur significant expenditures on analytic tools in early in deployment. However, over time, some groups may decide to proactively implement new software to leverage the CMDB. For example, the Change Management team may choose an analytic tool for mining change-related data. As the specifics around this effort are outside the scope of the core CMDB, they should not be included in this project plan. However, the CMDB System initiative at Acme will remain responsible for *integration costs*.

This is consistent with how Acme plans to allocate costs across the broader CMDB System going forward. Stakeholders with unique interests will be encouraged to invest in capabilities that leverage the core data and service-modeling functions of the broader system—and the core team shall make every effort to support appropriate integrations and use-case extensions. However, the budget specific to the CMDB initiative does not include unique stakeholder analytic, automation, and other investments—only integration efforts. Otherwise, the CMDB System initiative will find itself funding virtually every new discovery, monitoring, analytic, and automation investment across all of Acme IT.

2-YEAR ROAD MAP AT ACME FINANCIAL SERVICES

The 2-year road map shows a completed vision for phase one use-case requirements first prioritized in Acme's detailed requirements document. The objectives below will be further revised 12 months out—updated, enriched, and presented more definitively in the 2-year road map as the CMDB initiative at Acme IT progresses. At this point, 2 years out, Acme should begin to plan for yearly evolutionary road maps based on changing business objectives and shifting technology requirements such as the move to cloud or agile and more robust support for mobile users inside and outside of IT.

ANALYTICS

The 2-year road map at Acme includes the following high-level analytic projects (Figure 14.9):

- *Change management*: As Change Management is a priority in the 12-month road map, Acme will extend the value of Change Management across domains and stakeholders through additional integrations and investments with analytic and automation tools. Investments in these solutions

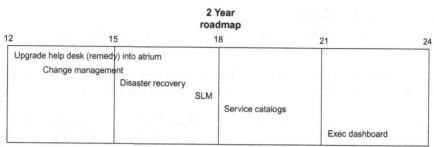

FIGURE 14.9

Acme Corporation's 2-year road map overview.

should not only help to accelerate Change Management effectiveness but also enable superior OpEx efficiencies in incident and problem management and superior asset life cycle management across domains. At the same time, these analytic investments will help to reduce MTTR and MTBF. Acme should never lose sight of the fact that Change Management is a foundational benefit central to the CMDB System, itself, and as such can extend to support many other use cases.

- *Disaster recovery*: Acme already has plans to leverage the CMDB System for DR in its data center in Nebraska. This represents a logical target area where the CMDB can provide much-needed underlying data. The application-to-infrastructure interdependencies captured via ADDM are also critical for this DR project.
- *Service-level management (SLM)*: At Acme, SLM and SLAs were initially based on easily available, or convenient, vs. *relevant* data, which were often manually gathered and hence rarely current. As such, SLM and supporting measures in availability and performance management represented areas that could strongly benefit from Acme's evolving CMDB System. By creating visibility across the infrastructure, the CMDB System will allow for SLAs to be constructed to measure appropriate KPIs (e.g., using CI-related end-user response times). Moreover, by harnessing appropriate levels of analytics and automation, the CMDB System will help to ensure that impacting metrics can also be assessed more proactively, reducing MTTR or even eliminating problems before they occur.
- *Service catalog enrichment*: Service catalogs will be redefined using the data in the CMDB. The value and power of having an integrated modeling capability between the CMDB System and service catalogs should become evident in faster time to provision new services, more accurate insights into service costs, usage, and overall requirements. An integrated modeling system between the CMDB and the service catalog will also provide a more consistent foundation with which to plan and manage Acme's IT service portfolio.
- *Executive dashboard*: Integration of an executive dashboard will provide value by extending the CMDB System stakeholder community and offering direct support for executive decision making. This will not only enable greater efficiencies in managing IT as a whole but also help to enhance the respect, position, and role of IT within the larger business (Acme) that it serves. As a by-product, executive support should also reinforce the value of budgeting for CMDB System enhancements, making OpEx and CapEx resources easier to come by.

IT MATURITY-RELATED GOALS

Within 2 years, Acme IT as a whole should be clearly moving well into the proactive, service-driven stage of maturity.

- As an extension of this, Acme will have shifted away from reactive *incident management* to gathering information for service planning with a more salient focus on *problem management.*
- Management solutions will be increasingly chosen strategically rather than reactively.
- Primary investments at this stage will be in the areas of analytics and visualization in order to capture service performance and business impact priorities more proactively.
- Workflow will become more automated and more integrated with broader IT process automation capabilities in order to capture and extend more efficient best practice processes across Acme IT.
- Acme will increasingly prioritize documenting metrics to demonstrate business value, including reduced cost of business services, while providing more relevant service levels to match the business priorities of the functional area requesting any given service.

COSTS (See Figure 14.5)

The overall cost for the 2-year implementation of the CMDB System at Acme will include CMDB and ADDM software and maintenance, a four-FTE CMDB team headcount, and one domain expert back-filled by a part-time contractor for the first 2 years of implementation.

These costs do not include higher-level analytic tools.

Finally, there are expected to be additional integration costs associated with bringing online the last 20% of systems that did not have standard interfaces. While these costs should be outweighed by the cost savings from eliminating redundant tools and correcting overlicensing issues, they will still represent a very real material investment for Acme IT.

At the end of the 2-year road map, Acme Corporation will have completed the following capabilities as expressed through Figure 14.10:

- The underlying instrumentation and external interfaces for the entire infrastructure should be complete based on CMDB System priorities and objectives.
- Monitoring, configuration management and autodiscovery should be implemented and widespread throughout the Acme IT organization. Policies and procedures should be in place to ensure that new technologies meet CMDB standards before being purchased and rolled into production.
- The core CMDB will have been fully implemented.
- Intelligence engines, high-level analytics, and the executive management dashboard will become newly empowered with CMDB System data.
- The transition from technology silos to a centralized IT management model will be largely complete.
- By now, Acme IT should be viewed as a true service organization and an essential partner to the business—a profit center with service levels matching business priorities and an innovator driving improved business performance.

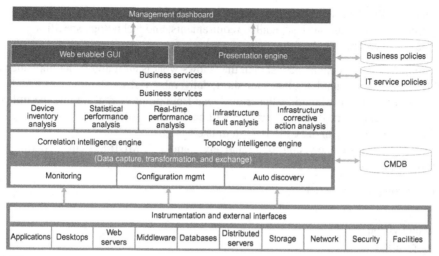

FIGURE 14.10

Production status after 2 years.

WRAPPING UP

An effective three-tiered road map provides a well-structured format for bringing yet more detailed work and planning together into a single coherent structure. As such, it should deliver a critical overview of status, objectives, costs, and obstacles with defined reference points in other documents such as a detailed requirements document or internal metrics for CMDB System planning and "external" or "use case"-driven metrics with ROI potential. The road map is the hub that connects all the spokes of the CMDB System wheel.

Road maps should enable you to look backward and forward, much as an explorer might chart the course for a critical expedition across yet undocumented waters. Road maps are also dynamic documents—helping you to gain more detailed insights as you move ahead in time and value with your CMDB System initiative.

Finally, your road map should be a critical catalyst for socializing requirements and achievements with stakeholders and executives and with members internal to the CMDB team.

SUMMARY TAKEAWAYS

This chapter provides guidelines for creating a three-tiered road map, a formal structure for helping you pull together much of the work associated with the Eight-Step Ladder to CMDB Success. It is a contextual hub for looking at more detailed insights derived from formal assessments and interviews and at detailed metrics and requirements, technology evaluations, and lessons learned during proof of concept.

Once created, the road map becomes the single most critical document for assessing the progress of the CMDB System; it also serves as a resource for communicating and socializing benefits and requirements. Finally, it becomes the best single venue for accessing and interrelating other more detailed documents—such as metrics, detailed requirements, and technology specifics.

Key takeaways here include the following:

- *6-Month road map.* This is the tactical plan that shows what is currently being implemented by the CMDB team. It sets hard deadlines for short, deliverable tasks.
- *12-Month road map.* This should be the critical leap from proof of concept into the full core CMDB deployment. Its goals and milestones will be directed at delivering value through stakeholder interaction with the CMDB System itself.
- *2-Year road map.* This is the vision for a relatively complete CMDB System supporting initial high-priority use cases.

Core road map components include

- goals
- strategy and vision
- value proposition
- issues
- gating factors
- target areas for phase one

Then the 6-month road map will include sections on

- creation of core CMDB System team, including the definition of core team responsibilities
- creation of a detailed requirements document
- technology adoption, including the creation of technology-relevant policies
- value statement (after initial proof of concept)
- milestones
- costs
- projected production status at the end of 6 months

The 12-month and 2-year road maps will both include

- goals
- milestones
- costs
- production status

In order to help visualize how all these pieces come together, this chapter provides a narrative summary of a three-tiered road map drawn from past consulting experience.

THE CMDB SYSTEM MOVES TO CLOUD AND BEYOND!

15

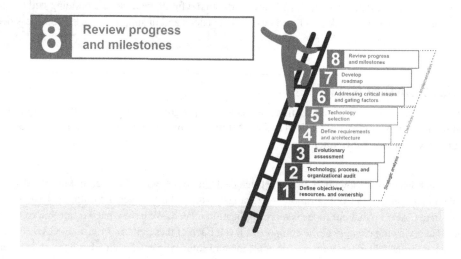

8 Review progress and milestones

Even though the first 6 months of a CMDB System initiative need to deliver value, in most cases, that value will be realized primarily in terms of project-related progress, insights into IT issues and gaps, and the creation of a clear roadmap featuring requirements and objectives, budget and resource, and technology selection. The insights you've gained and forward progress you've made during this phase should help to sell your executive sponsors on value, but the big shoe to drop is yet to come.

During the next 6 months leading up to 12-month milestone, you should approach a meaningful tipping point with benefits in IT efficiency and service quality only achievable through an actual production-level CMDB deployment—a tipping point, in other words, in which many or most of the phase 1 values of the CMDB System become fulfilled.

As such, it is a natural moment for raising stakeholder (and executive) enthusiasm. It is also a critical time for taking stock of where you've been and where you're going—adjusting your Three-Tiered Roadmap to look ahead to new requirements and opportunities while documenting present tense successes, learning from past and emergent issues, and refining present tense needs.

In order to paint a picture of what this stage might look like, we have organized the following comments from past research and consulting to provide examples from 12-month CMDB deployments in the following areas:

- Progress and benefits
- Issues and advice
- Future directions and plans

But first, we'd like to share a quote from one CMDB team leader that reflects his newfound understanding of what he'd achieved after 12 months:

> Our CMDB offers consistent visibility into how critical systems are being administered and changed across many multiple organizations, each with sensitive access rights to the context of critical financial and business information. The CMDB System enables effective change, configuration and release control without violating data access policies. I consider it to be 'Business Intelligence for Operations' akin to a data warehouse and data marts. In the future what we are building will be used for business intelligence—linking IT and business decisions and in supporting actual business decisions through a single pane of glass.

PROGRESS AND BENEFITS

The following three quotes present realistic snapshots of progress at the 12-month tipping point. The first comment is an example of what we'd call a CMDB System deployment in full motion—as changes are occurring with dramatic frequency:

> We've established workflow links to our service desk and our CMDB System, linking Incident and Problem management to Configuration and Change. With 3,000 changes a month, we have a tiered approach to CABs, so that our focus is more application related. We have what we call 'micro-CABs' targeted at reviewing changes at the component level. Each of these micro- or virtual- CABs have allocated individual CI owners who remain constant, and some who can be added or deleted depending on the nature of the change.

Next, we'll look at something many people neglect when considering metrics and requirements for a CMDB System—benefits delivered in terms of vendor and service provider management:

> The biggest benefit of our Phase-One CMDB deployment is impact analysis on changes to help to better stabilize the infrastructure. Also, we are looking forward to better service provider management. We have already seen that our service providers have become more circumspect about making changes on the fly. So better change control overall, including meaningful handshakes with our service-provider interdependencies, is our biggest benefit. We also see benefits in terms of billing—[specifically] in terms of managing our service provider costs and in supporting cost management when it comes to our lines of business. We are not paying for infrastructure services we don't need or aren't using, and so we are better able to account for what we provide to our own business customers.

The third quote looks at progress of a kind and also sets the stage for addressing "Issues and Advice" section. In this case, the deployed CMDB exposed two contentious misconceptions and promoted better Change Management, as well as more informed Change Management-related dialogue:

> We discovered that there were a lot of misperceptions once we started to drive the silos to talk to each other and work together. For instance, we went to our server team and we were told that a particular server was only dependent on two different switches. And the network team claimed that all of its switches were redundant, so that a switch going down wouldn't pull a server down. We found that both assumptions were wrong—when a switch went offline for a code update and impacted ten servers unexpectedly. In the past, these teams weren't compelled to talk and to validate changes across groups.

ISSUES AND ADVICE

The following quotes provide some advice for issues experienced at the 12-month-out stage, when it's easy to notice those things you "could have done differently" while at the same time, you may still be facing some surprises in terms of how your CMDB is being received.

The first two quotes involve very human stakeholder issues that still need to be addressed. The first reinforces one of the biggest CMDB System challenges—resistance to change:

> The challenge is still making the organization use it. Today we still have some teams that use Excel instead of our CMDB, and don't even want to use a discovery tool because they don't trust it. It's like having a jet plane for people in the Middle Ages. But at least the time and tide are with us—our CIO would like us to move into the 21st century and leverage our CMDB investment.

The next quote reflects something that's perhaps less common but is still something to take into account when promoting your CMDB System resistance to acknowledge *the benefits* of the deployment:

> I knew that we reduced incidents from badly planned changes by leveraging the newly deployed CMDB. But other people tried to take credit. When something's going badly there are no takers, but when something's going better, everybody tries to take credit.

The next two comments address that "what I might have done differently" category—each one looking back in the rearview mirror from 12 months out. As these CMDB team leaders reflect, they expose a range of issues from technical (discovery) to strategic (CI definition), from resource-related (cost) to communications (setting expectations):

> - If we were to do one thing in particular differently, it would be to pay more attention to the problem of fragmented discovery and getting our arms more around capturing our infrastructure. We have a very distributed environment—no mainframes—and a lot of tool fragmentation and false assumptions. Now we're doing a management tool audit just to find out what we've got to see if we're missing something even after our CMDB has been deployed. I know now it should have been the other way around.

> • If I had it all to do over, I would probably have started with a more stringent definition of CIs and CI attributes and focused more on the processes to control data as well as the data themselves. We already have a couple of thousand regular users—and now many are not clear on the initial use case and are expecting data that isn't yet in the CMS. I would also try not to set expectations too high, and to make sure that requirements are well understood. Any strategic project gets a life of its own, and you have to balance that and maintain scope. Everyone thinks their wish list is top priority, of course, and so having a well-defined set of core objectives is key.

One very positive bit of advice is also worth mentioning here—and in many respects, it is a subtext for the majority of the CMDB-related conversations we have once they reach the "tipping point" for value:

> My advice to others is to DO IT! Don't be scared. But don't listen to consultants who tell you they can do everything for you, either.

FUTURE DIRECTIONS AND PLANS

Once you're actually there, the 12-month roadmap should be reinvigorated by taking a fresh look at future objectives. This means fleshing out details of requirements that have been high-level up until now. It may also mean taking on new opportunities that reflect changing requirements and goals within your own IT organization.

Many CMDB System deployments take next steps beyond the 12-month mark in somewhat more modest, yet no less productive, ways. The example below highlights a not uncommon (and often successful) priority as captured in an interview done for our research:

> As a next step, we're expecting to expand the scope of the CMDB to include PCs, PDAs and mobile devices to enhance our information about people. Right now we're not very robust on the people side of things—but we want to identify impacts to service in context with specific business units and candidates.

The next comment, also taken from research interviews, looks at progress past the 12-month point but reflects a pattern fairly typical to earlier stages of many CMDB System deployments:

> Over the last two years, we've expanded our CMDB System—putting in, incident, request, problem, change, configuration, and asset management. We've also integrated some application management requirements, and now we're starting a big metrics push so we can more automatically capture the hard-number and hard-dollar values from the work we've done.

Federation is usually the most natural way to expand and enrich a CMDB System. So it's no surprise that at the 12-month mark, federation becomes an even higher priority than it normally is at 6 months out. The following three quotes provide three distinct perspectives on federation for next-stage CMDB System deployments:

- As we grow we will move more and more toward a federated system, and are already developing mappings in our open-source performance management system to feed data into the CMDB. From there, we'll move to include some of our other monitoring systems.
- I think that we have begun to discover the values of federation through trial and error. Most of the capabilities are there in the technology, but our vendor never really told us the WHY—and so we're kind of getting there on our own.
- Federation is an absolute imperative!

Not all progress involves moving forward with new functions and use cases. There may still be some cleaning up to do after 12 months, as indicated by the comment below:

Aside from growing the CMDB System, another focus will still have to be data clean-up and data integrity. We want to come up with metrics to support improved data integrity from our 'Data Stewards.' We're planning to do this in the coming weeks.

Finally, this last quote provides a sober reminder of why the CMDB System was so critical in the first place. The implied goal of the CMDB initiative in this case is nothing less than the very survival of IT itself:

Complexity is doubling every three or four years along with the size of the infrastructure. Business demands are also escalating as our business is also growing rapidly. And yet IT staffing remains level. That's a huge pain point. There's a realization that over time we won't be able to scale if this trend continues. We're already facing mandatory nights and weekends. Something's going to break. We can see the writing on the wall. The only way out is to continue to build out our CMDB System with more analytics and automation and follow this up with more cross-domain ways of working and increased IT efficiencies. Our initiative, which we once thought was a 'good thing,' is now looking more and more 'essential.'

MOVING FROM PHASE 1 TO PHASE 2: AN INTERVIEW WITH AN IT ORGANIZATION SUPPORTING A US-BASED INVESTMENT RESEARCH FIRM

This interview highlights both the opportunities and the challenges of going beyond phase 1.[1] On the one hand, the speaker describes a solid beginning for his initiative with real benefits enjoyed by people who "feel the pain" of managing and optimizing change responsibly. On the other hand, he is faced with competing priorities for investing in phase 2 and, given this, makes some telling suggestions for how to overcome the obstacles of delay. Also of note here is the clear linkage between his cloud and his CMDB System initiative.

Could You Describe Your Role and IT Environment?

I'm an IT director responsible for infrastructure, including storage networking and systems, as well as data centers overall, security and desktop management. Our goal is to help our employees to be productive. This also includes support for the applications running over that infrastructure, some of which are customer-facing. I have a peer in the NOC more focused specifically on incident and problem management. There are about 7000 in IT worldwide, but the majority of these are in software development, so our combined groups total about 250.

What Were the Drivers for Moving Toward a CMDB Deployment?

We realized that a CMDB would be a core value in supporting our ability to track inventories and configuration. This also included investment in an Application Discovery and Dependency Mapping (ADDM) solution provided by the same vendor. The ADDM solution is feeding our CMDB, which collectively represents our dynamic source of truth for day-to-day operational work.

Prior to our CMDB, we were awash in multiple sources—wiki, spreadsheets, SharePoint, and other data sources. Now we are more functionally aligned through this single source of truth for all our technology elements.

Was Cloud a Part of Your Initiative?

Yes, as a matter of fact. One of the reasons we went forward with the CMDB was investment in cloud lifecycle management and cloud automation. The CMDB was at the core of that. We had a service blueprint of what we wanted in our cloud automation capability, and that got added to our CMDB virtually for free. It allowed us to leapfrog the process. Right now we are building what we call a 'next-generation infrastructure' and we have a start with 400 VMs.

How Many People Do You Have Administering the CMDB?

Right now we have one individual dedicated to keeping out CMDB System current and operational.

What is the Status After Your Initial Phase 1 Deployment?

Everyone in tech operations is looking for us to build on this base and add metadata to tie CMDB elements to business and technical services. But our progress has been slowed based on pressure to address other priorities. For instance, right now our CMDB inputs include ADDM, but other inputs are manual—such as Microsoft's System Center Configuration Manager (SCCM). Another one of our next-step targets is to map CI owners to CIs as well as evolve better linkages between our current service catalog and our CMDB.

One of our parallel efforts is to improve our processes for incident and Change Management, and for event management in our sister IT organization. We started our ITIL journey about two years ago and are just now staffing it properly. This will help in achieving better accuracy for the CMDB in the future. We're also beginning to invest more in automation.

How Do Your Stakeholders View Your Current CMDB System?

It depends on whom you ask. I think people who feel the pain everyday are very anxious to go forward. The people not as close to the pain don't see why the CMDB should be a priority. The 'pain' I'm referring to here hits anyone who needs clean data for incident or problem management on a day-to-day basis or who is involved with managing changes around the infrastructure.

How Do You See the Rekindling Effort for Moving to a Phase 2 Deployment?

The best path will be to look at the business reasons for going forward and presenting those to the CIO in terms of efficiency, productivity, and pain points. That will help to make it a priority for other stakeholders.

[1]Interview with a large financial institution based in the United States using BMC's Atrium CMDB.

WHAT'S HAPPENING WITH THE CMDB SYSTEM TODAY AND IN THE FUTURE: INSIGHTS GLEANED FROM FOUR KEY RESEARCH PROJECTS

The good news for those of you planning a CMDB System initiative is that there is real progress and growth in your technology options both today and going forward. These advances are reflected in how CMDB-related deployments are achieving benefits in context with many of the more prominent industry trends.

In the sections below, we'll examine four key areas of growth taken from data from recent research projects,[2] as well as interviews done in the course of writing this book. These include

- the need to support more cross domain Service-Aware Asset Management initiatives,
- the move to cloud,
- the requirements to link advanced analytics to service modeling and data in the broader Configuration Management System,
- the push to support agile software development with better DevOps capabilities.

THE CMDB SYSTEM AS A FOUNDATION FOR SERVICE-AWARE ASSET MANAGEMENT

As discussed in Chapter 5, IT is going through a transformation that's both cultural and technological—a shift toward *showing value* and *managing costs*. Moreover, as described in Chapter 7, asset management in its various forms is one of the most prominent CMDB use cases—and probably still the single most popular one.

However, you should realize that asset management is itself going through a transformation. *Service-Aware Asset Management*, which unites IT Asset Management (ITAM) with IT Service Management (ITSM), is emerging as a new force for managing IT assets throughout their life cycles as components of critical IT services. Recent research[2] underscores IT's clear wish to provide a more cohesive cross domain view into IT assets and where they reside. Nearly 40% of respondents are seeking to create an organizational role for looking at IT investments across all domains, and that number shoots up to nearly 60% once telecommunications accounting is excluded.

Even more striking in this research is the need to bring service management, or ITSM, together with ITAM. Integrated ITSM and ITAM holds the promise of managing both CapEx and OpEx costs with support for the full IT asset life cycle—whatever the domain. Moreover, integrated ITSM and ITAM can empower IT to link assets to true services; in other words, it allows IT to link "costs" to "value" so that IT can be managed far more effectively as a business. Those who either currently manage assets and services together or have clear plans to do so also represent a more progressive population overall. For instance, those currently combining asset and service management are more likely to

- have a CMDB/CMS deployed or have plans to deploy;
- plan to deploy or have already deployed Application Discovery and Dependency Mapping (ADDM);
- have automated discovery and inventory;
- have integrated cloud into their next-generation asset capabilities;
- link best practices, such as those in the IT Infrastructure Library (ITIL), to their asset management strategy;

---

[2]Three key research projects featured here, in sequence to the sections where they're applied, are as follows:

a. *"Next-Generation Asset Management and Financial Analytics: Optimizing IT Value in a World of Change,"* EMA, May, 2014.

b. *"Ecosystem Cloud: Managing and Optimizing IT Services Across the Full Cloud Mosaic,"* EMA, June, 2013.

c. *"EMA Radar for Advanced Performance Analytics,"* EMA, Q4, 2012.

- achieve superior data accuracy;
- have linkages across multiple data sources well established;
- support service modeling for linking asset attributes;
- optimize software license usage overall;
- track usage for desktop applications and reassign or cancel unused licenses;
- have a service catalog in place and support cost and usage insights;
- prioritize and integrate application portfolio rationalization;
- get a raise in their IT budget because of their superior business alignment.

And this is only a partial list.

Now, let's zero in more specifically on the role of the CMDB System in all this. We found out that 62% of our respondents are linking their IT assets to service modeling in some form and 57% of the respondents have a CMDB either deployed or in plans for deployment. Figure 15.1 shows how the CMDB is being used to bring assets into Configuration Management Systems, either as a part of the core CMDB or through a set of federated resources linked to a CMDB.

The progressive virtues of a CMDB System for Service-Aware Asset Management also became clear when we analyzed the differences between the IT organizations with a CMDB in play and those without CMDB.

Those with a CMDB were

- significantly more likely to have a single coordinating organization presiding over asset and financial management;
- twice as likely to have plans to bring service and asset management together;
- more than twice as likely to have a link to ITIL in their asset/ITSM strategies;
- twice as likely to have automated asset and inventory in place and update at least multiple times a day;
- significantly more likely to link multiple data sources meaningfully;
- nearly two times more likely to track usage effectively for desktops and perform reharvesting of unused licenses;
- three times more likely to have a service catalog in place;
- four times more likely to have an App Store for managing SW requests;
- nearly four times more likely to have ADDM deployed or in plan;
- three-and-a-half times more likely to have application portfolio planning integrated with asset/financial plans;
- two times more likely to have IT Process Automation or runbook automation deployed;
- nearly two times more likely to have automated configuration management deployed;
- nearly three times more likely to support green IT;
- more than twice as likely to support enterprise services outside of IT services—such as those for HR or facilities;
- nearly two times more likely to include a move to cloud as an integrated part of their Service-Aware Asset Management direction.

Whenever we do these analyses, we recognize the natural chicken-and-the-egg question. Is this group more progressive because they have a CMDB or do they have a CMDB because they are more progressive? The truth is that we don't have hard data to close out the issue either way, but both common sense and a significant number of dialogues with CMDB deployments would suggest that it's a

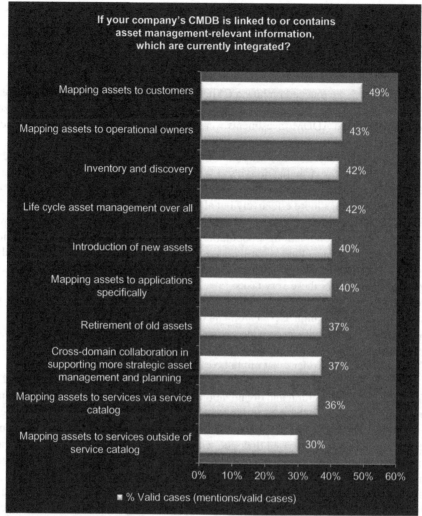

If your company's CMDB is linked to or contains asset management-relevant information, which are currently integrated?

Mapping assets to customers	49%
Mapping assets to operational owners	43%
Inventory and discovery	42%
Life cycle asset management over all	42%
Introduction of new assets	40%
Mapping assets to applications specifically	40%
Retirement of old assets	37%
Cross-domain collaboration in supporting more strategic asset management and planning	37%
Mapping assets to services via service catalog	36%
Mapping assets to services outside of service catalog	30%

■ % Valid cases (mentions/valid cases)

Sample size = 84, valid cases = 84

FIGURE 15.1

Current research shows a strong value in linking IT assets into a CMDB System for a more service-aware approach to asset management. Managing assets in context with customers and owners, managing IT assets throughout their lifecycles, and support for more automated and reconciled inventory and discovery are three requirements that stand out as leading requirements. More advanced requirements, such as mapping assets to applications and service catalogs, are not surprisingly further down on the list, but still show relatively strongly as priorities.

both/and situation: The CMDB enables the IT organization to advance, and the more mature or progressive the IT organization, the more likely it is to succeed with its CMDB System.

THE MOVE TO THE CLOUD

In both Chapters 2 and 5, we touched on how a CMDB System can empower IT organizations to manage business services more effectively across hybrid cloud environments. Figure 2.4 dramatized the fact that those with CMDBs and ADDM investments were nearly twice as likely to be "very successful" in their cloud deployments as those who weren't!

Certainly, if you're 12 months out with your CMDB System and haven't yet considered requirements for cloud or at least for virtualization, it's at least time to consider these as a next-phase option. Recent research[3] not only shows how much a CMDB, as a "system of relevance," can empower you to optimize your cloud offerings more effectively but also sheds some light on how and why.

First of all, let's revisit what we like to call the "cloud mosaic." Figures 15.2–15.5 show just how mixed business services are even among a population already selected for their commitment to cloud. As you can see from these data, cloud is hardly a single or even a singular destination. It truly is a mosaic of options that need to be planned, managed, and optimized—ideally with cloud service providers willing to partner with you for these very tasks.

Some related research data[4] show that many IT organizations struggle with cloud service providers, sometimes with failure rates as high as 57%, for a mixture of reasons—most significantly security, cost, compliance, complexity, difficulty in moving applications, and overall lack of support. So managing business services across the cloud mosaic as indicated here will require looking well beyond your immediate IT organization to consider what might be called the full "Extended Enterprise."

Before going looking further at how a CMDB System can take you "to cloud and beyond," it's worth noting some of the dominant cultural and organizational trends that cloud adoptions are driving. As you may remember from Chapter 5, the data in Figure 15.6 highlight a number of trends that clearly run parallel to those associated with CMDB System adoption. These include a move to support more cross domain, service-aware values, increased dialogue with business clients for better business alignment, and the rising importance of best practices for managing services—in particular in those from the ITIL. As you can see, we asked the question so that votes could go either way—ITIL was either gaining or losing in importance—and "accelerated ITIL adoption" came out solidly on top. This became all the more emphatic when those who were "very successful" in delivering business services over cloud were four times more likely to view ITIL as "extremely important" and five times more likely to see ITIL as "significantly gaining in importance." Also worthy of note is the move for operations to take back control of shadow or fragmented cloud adoptions.

A closer look at CMDB System-relevant data from this research is telling. As mentioned in Chapter 5, 83% of the respondents had some involvement in service modeling. Of those respondents involved in service modeling, 30% had deployed a CMDB, 39% had deployed a federated CMS, and 44% had deployed ADDM for change. The highest percentages were those leveraging either ADDM for performance (50%) or a service modeling dashboard for business impact (54%). These data points

---

[3] Ibid.

[4] "*Casualties of Cloud Wars: Customers are Paying the Price,*" EMA research commissioned by Iland and VMware, May, 2014.

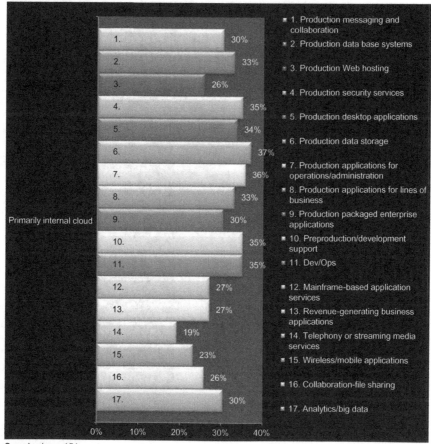

1. Production messaging and collaboration
2. Production data base systems
3. Production Web hosting
4. Production security services
5. Production desktop applications
6. Production data storage
7. Production applications for operations/administration
8. Production applications for lines of business
9. Production packaged enterprise applications
10. Preproduction/development support
11. Dev/Ops
12. Mainframe-based application services
13. Revenue-generating business applications
14. Telephony or streaming media services
15. Wireless/mobile applications
16. Collaboration-file sharing
17. Analytics/big data

Primarily internal cloud

1. 30%
2. 33%
3. 26%
4. 35%
5. 34%
6. 37%
7. 36%
8. 33%
9. 30%
10. 35%
11. 35%
12. 27%
13. 27%
14. 19%
15. 23%
16. 26%
17. 30%

Sample size = 151

FIGURE 15.2

Mosaic of services: primarily internal cloud. This mosaic of plans for placing business services in the cloud reflects the perspectives of respondents already committed to cloud at some level. Nonetheless, it shows a clear pattern of mix and match versus a singular destination for business application services. This mix-and-match pattern is all the more emphatic once you take into account that these same respondents believe that even their cloud-delivered business services are significantly dependent on noncloud infrastructures.

tend to reinforce our belief that modeling interdependencies, and in particular modeling service inter-dependencies, are becoming the real spine of the Configuration Management System as a venue for accessing, in service-aware context, multiple federated data stores.

When we asked respondents if they were leveraging these in support of cloud or virtualized in-frastructure, 85% said that they either were already leveraging (74%) or had plans to leverage (11%). Figures 15.7–15.9 provide a closer look at how the CMDB System is being applied and managed overall by cloud adopters.

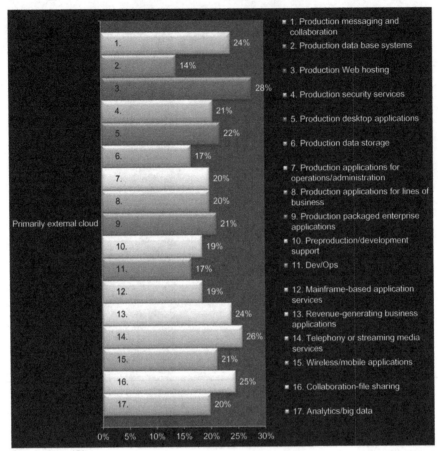

Primarily external cloud

Sample size = 151

FIGURE 15.3

Mosaic of services: primarily external cloud. This mosaic of plans for placing business services in the cloud reflects the perspectives of respondents already committed to cloud at some level. Nonetheless, it shows a clear pattern of mix and match versus a singular destination for business application services. This mix-and-match pattern is all the more emphatic once you take into account that these same respondents believe that even their cloud-delivered business services are significantly dependent on noncloud infrastructures.

These figures target

- the need for automation in updating the broader CMDB System,
- the ability to track CI states with more frequency than every 24 h (which is especially true for more dynamic, virtualized environments),
- service modeling integrations that prioritized service desk, virtualized infrastructure, security analytics, and virtualized application performance.

When our cloud-user respondents were asked about CI states being tracked, the most common answers were, not surprisingly, "desired" or "approved state," "discovered state," and "historical state."

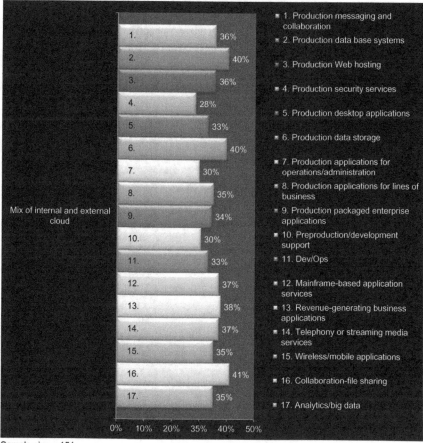

Sample size = 151

FIGURE 15.4

Mosaic of services: mix of internal and external cloud. This mosaic of plans for placing business services in the cloud reflects the perspectives of respondents already committed to cloud at some level. Nonetheless, it shows a clear pattern of mix and match versus a singular destination for business application services. This mix-and-match pattern is all the more emphatic once you take into account that these same respondents believe that even their cloud-delivered business services are significantly dependent on noncloud infrastructures.

However, a significant number—nearly half—were also tracking preproduction states in support of DevOps. This may help to explain some of the more anecdotal, interview-driven activity around DevOps later in this chapter. Interestingly enough, "future state" for longer-term planned changes rose to the top as a priority in the coming 12 months. This is a telling statement on how a CMDB System can be used to support if/then analytics for capacity planning and optimization so critical in the move to cloud.

Figure 15.10 highlights priorities for reporting and visualization not only across the CMS but also across broader service management investments for those cloud users with commitments to service modeling. The top four—reports on service usage for accounting and planning, reports for executive

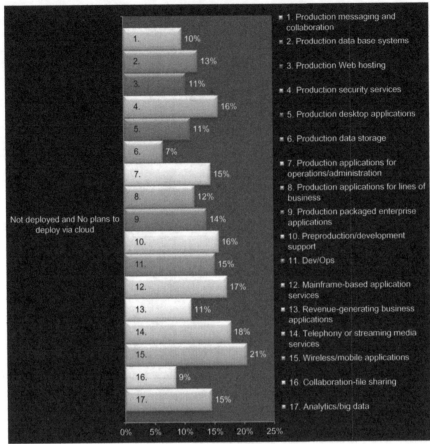

Not deployed and No plans to deploy via cloud

1. 10%
2. 13%
3. 11%
4. 16%
5. 11%
6. 7%
7. 15%
8. 12%
9. 14%
10. 16%
11. 15%
12. 17%
13. 11%
14. 18%
15. 21%
16. 9%
17. 15%

■ 1. Production messaging and collaboration
■ 2. Production data base systems
■ 3. Production Web hosting
■ 4. Production security services
■ 5. Production desktop applications
■ 6. Production data storage
■ 7. Production applications for operations/administration
■ 8. Production applications for lines of business
■ 9. Production packaged enterprise applications
■ 10. Preproduction/development support
■ 11. Dev/Ops
■ 12. Mainframe-based application services
■ 13. Revenue-generating business applications
■ 14. Telephony or streaming media services
■ 15. Wireless/mobile applications
■ 16. Collaboration-file sharing
■ 17. Analytics/big data

Sample size = 151

FIGURE 15.5

Mosaic of services: no plans for cloud deployment. This mosaic of plans for placing business services in the cloud reflects the perspectives of respondents already committed to cloud at some level. Nonetheless, it shows a clear pattern of mix and match versus a singular destination for business application services. This mix-and-match pattern is all the more emphatic once you take into account that these same respondents believe that even their cloud-delivered business services are significantly dependent on noncloud infrastructures.

support, reports for governance in managing stakeholders, and reports on security or compliance violations—help to provide a portrait of service management in the age of cloud. Understanding how, when, and by whom services are being used is central to helping IT emerge from being a back-office function to becoming a front-office value provider capable of competing with and optimizing the "shopping mall of cloud services." *Executive* and *stakeholder governance* are clearly central to the CMDB System just as they are to cloud, while still meaningful percentages targeted CMDB *maintenance* (34%) and *Change Advisory Board* reviews (33%).

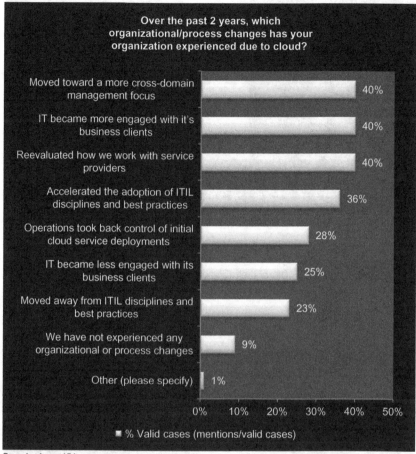

Over the past 2 years, which organizational/process changes has your organization experienced due to cloud?

Category	%
Moved toward a more cross-domain management focus	40%
IT became more engaged with it's business clients	40%
Reevaluated how we work with service providers	40%
Accelerated the adoption of ITIL disciplines and best practices	36%
Operations took back control of initial cloud service deployments	28%
IT became less engaged with its business clients	25%
Moved away from ITIL disciplines and best practices	23%
We have not experienced any organizational or process changes	9%
Other (please specify)	1%

■ % Valid cases (mentions/valid cases)

Sample size = 151

FIGURE 15.6

Organizational, process, and cultural trends around cloud adoptions favor CMDB System adoption—in terms of cross domain, business alignment, and accelerated ITIL adoption.

HOW ADDM CAN IMPROVE THE "JOURNEY TO THE CLOUD"

The eight points cited in the following list came from a product manager with one of the leading CMDB Systems vendors who works closely with many customers to understand their requirements, roadmaps, and challenges—including the move to cloud.[5] When asked about the value of ADDM in supporting the transition to public, private, and hybrid cloud environments, he had documented a number of proven values. The eight examples listed below are highlights from his list:

[5]Interview with a BMC customer-facing support manager regarding the usage of ADDM technology and cloud.

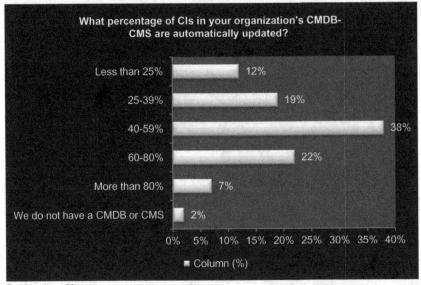

FIGURE 15.7

Automation is key to making a CMDB System cloud-ready. As you can see above, among our cloud-ready respondents, 67% update more than 40% of their CIs automatically.

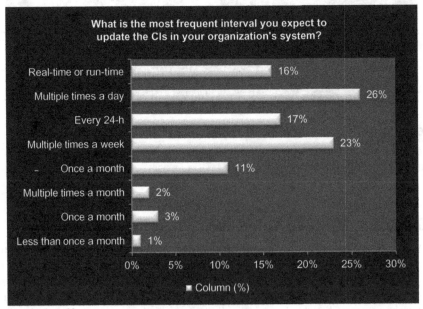

FIGURE 15.8

Given the dynamic nature of cloud and virtualized environments, it's not surprising that nearly half (42%) of cloud-ready CMDB Systems tend to update at least some of their CIs more frequently than every 24 h and 16% claim real-time or runtime frequencies.

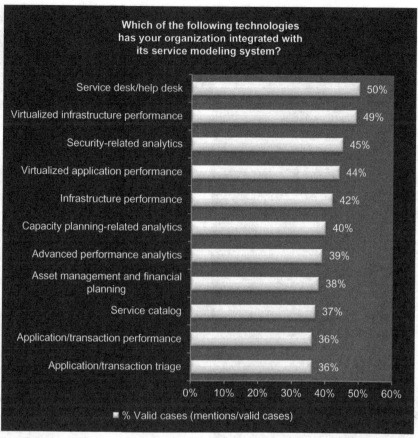

Which of the following technologies has your organization integrated with its service modeling system?

Service desk/help desk — 50%
Virtualized infrastructure performance — 49%
Security-related analytics — 45%
Virtualized application performance — 44%
Infrastructure performance — 42%
Capacity planning-related analytics — 40%
Advanced performance analytics — 39%
Asset management and financial planning — 38%
Service catalog — 37%
Application/transaction performance — 36%
Application/transaction triage — 36%

■ % Valid cases (mentions/valid cases)

FIGURE 15.9

Service desk, virtualized infrastructure performance, security-related analytics, and virtualized application performance are the leading cloud-ready service modeling integrations. The average number of integrations per respondent is high at 5.4, which underscores the dimensional breadth required for optimizing service modeling in cloud environments.

1. *Understanding the data center.*

This is probably the top use case for ADDM as, if you think about it, the move to cloud requires *more*, not less, visibility across the full data center and the broader IT environment. It may also require insight into interdependencies across public cloud service providers. Either way, IT needs to know what's running, and if something changes, what it is. This also allows for consistent population of the CMDB. If you're at a help desk and you open up a trouble ticket, you want to be able to associate the CI with the impact and see what other infrastructure or application components are impacted as well. Having this data enables faster mean time to repair and facilitates more effective communication to the stakeholders associated with the resource.

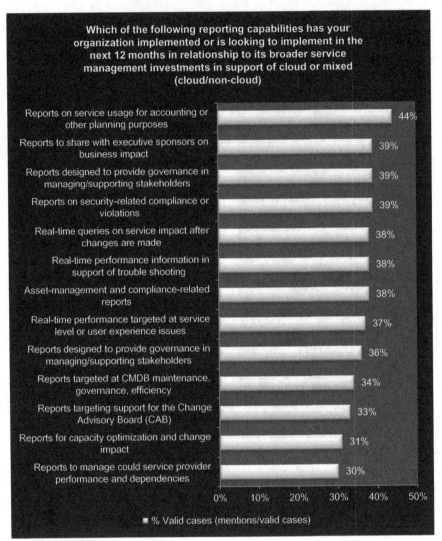

Which of the following reporting capabilities has your organization implemented or is looking to implement in the next 12 months in relationship to its broader service management investments in support of cloud or mixed (cloud/non-cloud)

Reports on service usage for accounting or other planning purposes	44%
Reports to share with executive sponsors on business impact	39%
Reports designed to provide governance in managing/supporting stakeholders	39%
Reports on security-related compliance or violations	39%
Real-time queries on service impact after changes are made	38%
Real-time performance information in support of trouble shooting	38%
Asset-management and compliance-related reports	38%
Real-time performance targeted at service level or user experience issues	37%
Reports designed to provide governance in managing/supporting stakeholders	36%
Reports targeted at CMDB maintenance, governance, efficiency	34%
Reports targeting support for the Change Advisory Board (CAB)	33%
Reports for capacity optimization and change impact	31%
Reports to manage could service provider performance and dependencies	30%

■ % Valid cases (mentions/valid cases)

Sample size = 101

FIGURE 15.10

Reporting and visualization priorities for cloud-ready respondents who leveraged service modeling help to paint a picture of service management priorities in the age of cloud. Insights into usage for accounting, portfolio planning, and other priorities lay a foundation for helping IT progress to a more consumer-aware, front-office value provider versus a back-office cost center. Executive governance and stakeholder governance are key for cloud, just as they are for the CMDB System. And CMDB maintenance and Change Advisory Board reviews also show a meaningful uptake.

2. *Provisioning.*

During the provisioning process, many IT organizations trigger a targeted discovery of the servers involved via ADDM and then update the CMDB. This can become a routinely automated process for services and applications that regularly get updated or deployed multiple times, or it could also support a developer requesting, for instance, a WebSphere development environment.

3. *Service impact.*

When you're planning to make a change in a cloud or hybrid cloud environment, ADDM can generate an impact model that provides critical insights into what pieces of a given service will be impacted by the change. This model is used by other tools for performance insights and more effective root cause identification when there's a service disruption.

4. *Continual insight.*

Related to service impact is ongoing visibility into very dynamic internal and external cloud resources. For instance, workloads can move from one host to another to optimize the performance of a VMware DRS cluster. If the impact model is not dynamically updated, it can prohibit IT from accurately assessing root cause and correctly notifying the affected users. A sudden triggering of vMotion can disrupt service performance, and ADDM can catch that either in routine updates or in near real-time.

5. *Compliance risk assessment.*

Security is one of the top concerns for Cloud adoption. Application discovery can help manage those risks. For instance, ADDM can catch outliers when there's a patch update or when there's a security issue such as the Heartbleed Open SSL bug—which can become even more important in dynamic cloud environments.

6. *No server left behind.*

There are multiple dimensions to this use case, but the general idea is to leverage ADDM visibility for consistency across the cloud and hybrid cloud environments so that you can identify servers that are not registered in your configuration management tools. Moreover, public clouds have given rise to Shadow IT. It is not uncommon for IT departments to learn that their development teams are using public cloud servers without any IT oversight. Without appropriate OS hardening and management, a server could very easily be at risk of vulnerabilities. Many of the public clouds support community built templates. In Amazon Web Service's US-East region, there are over 30,000 community built Amazon Machine Images. As you might expect, many of these images are missing patches that leave the server susceptible to hackers.

7. *Application/workload migration.*

> While there is no single magic wand for moving workloads and their associated application services into cloud environments, ADDM can add a lot of value by providing a reliable model of the interdependencies that need to be re-established. This is especially true when, as is often the case, this depends on migrating multiple servers, databases, and application components consistently and cohesively.

8. *Software license management.*

> Both private and public cloud can make software license management a challenge. ADDM has been a valuable resource in both environments, and I've seen a lot of benefits achieved in managing and optimizing software licenses—especially in private cloud—by showing where software sits in context with application service interdependencies. Or conversely, you can see if a server, a workload, and its OS license are not being utilized by an application service and so reduce unneeded license costs. So the value is both avoiding costly license compliance violations, and also for identifying and reclaiming licenses that are no longer in use.

THE CMDB/CMS, ADDM, SERVICE MODELING AND ADVANCED OPERATIONS ANALYTICS

As we have pointed out, if the CMDB System is an enabler, it can enable advanced analytic investments where insight into interdependencies can either directly or indirectly support improved contextual awareness. By "directly support," we mean direct integration with analytic and advanced monitoring solutions. By "indirectly support," we mean that the CMDB System with its broad insights into change, ownership, and service-to-infrastructure interdependencies can help solidify actions—whether for remediation, capacity optimization, or activating changes—as a parallel and complementary resource to analytic investments.

Research shows that analytics adoption for IT operations and IT more broadly is still very new, but it already indicates a strong affinity for CMDB Systems (especially when you include ADDM), even when the analytic tools involved don't require service modeling in and of themselves. Of 22 analytics vendors interviewed, 15 offered ties to a CMDB System, coming either from within the vendor's own portfolio or from a third-party CMDB investment.[1] Moreover, most analytics for IT operations can provide inherent insight into interdependencies critical to an evolving CMDB System, as shown in Figure 15.11.

ADVANCED OPERATIONS ANALYTICS: A CLOSER LOOK

Given the above, it makes sense to examine in more depth just what we mean by Advanced Operations Analytics (AOA). AOA has evolved from classic service performance management, but with a twist—rather than siloed approaches to monitoring and analysis, AOA demands more eclectic data collection, significantly higher levels of analytic scalability and strong insights into cross domain and/or business outcomes.

In part, because AOA is a relatively new area, it's premature to attempt to create a definitive market landscape. However, all AOA solutions combine big data in volume with eclectic data collection and

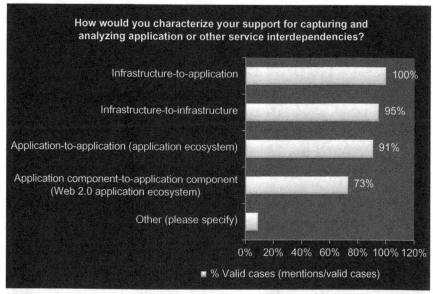

FIGURE 15.11

Advanced Operations Analytics capabilities can shed light on service- or application-related interdependencies critical to a CMDB System as it matures. All 22 analytics vendors surveyed were able to capture insights in application-to-infrastructure interdependencies, and all but one were able to help clarify infrastructure-to-infrastructure issues.

focus on data related to IT services, sometimes including business and financial outcomes. All AOA solutions also have meaningful investments in advanced analytic heuristics. When we asked about relevant heuristics, the vendors surveyed showed a wide range of options and values (see Figure 15.12).

AOA's most prominent use cases map well to the CMDB System use cases described in Chapter 7, albeit with a unique flavor all their own. Here is a look at how the use cases align:

- *Technical performance analytics*: These are focused on optimizing the resiliency of critical application and other business services with a strong focus on triage, diagnostics, roles supported, self-learning capabilities, and associated automation. This aligns well with the third CMDB System use case—performance management.
- *Business impact management*: This includes user experience, customer experience and customer management, business process impacts, business activity management, and data such as revenue per transaction, abandonment rates, competitive impact, and IT operational efficiency. Once again, this aligns more with performance management, but with a distinctive focus on business alignment and optimization.
- *Change impact and capacity optimization/planning*: These share requirements in terms of understanding interdependencies across the application/service infrastructure as volumes increase, changes are made, configuration issues arise, and actions—including relevant automations—are required. This corresponds to the Change Management use case for CMDB Systems and is the AOA area most closely aligned to core CMDB investments.

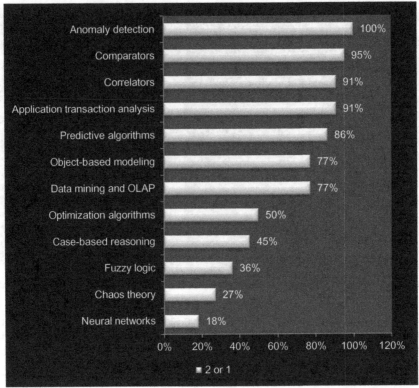

Sample size = 22

FIGURE 15.12

AOA solutions typically leverage more than one type of analytic heuristic, but anomaly detection is not surprisingly the dominant one. Comparators provide dynamic insights into ongoing performance metrics or KPIs, such as CPU utilization or transaction latencies, whereas correlation often looks at events or other data related at a single moment in time. Not broken out separately here, if/then analytics typically leverage combinations of heuristics (such as data mining and correlation) to predict the actual impacts of changes in advance, which can become a key advantage in optimizing a CMDB System for change impact and capacity management.

- *Financial optimization for IT as a business*: There are also some emerging AOA capabilities related to Asset Management and Financial Optimization, some of which already are closely aligned with CMDB System technologies. These often combine an ability to absorb a significant amount of eclectic data with a knowledge base and strong correlation capabilities. While many AOA solutions currently have, or will soon have, software-as-a-service options from cloud, this priority is most progressed in areas relating to the Asset Management and Financial Optimization use case for CMDB Systems.
- *Security* and *DevOps*: These are two strong areas for AOA investments. In fact, recent data show that "security" across a broad set of respondents (including a healthy number from the security operations center) was the number one ranked AOA use case in terms of current deployments

and planned investments. As discussed in Chapter 7, CMDB Systems can provide strong value for security initiatives, even if they don't typically originate there. A discussion of DevOps will follow shortly—but it, too, is a strongly emergent area for CMDB-related value.

As many AOA deployments are targeted at delivering cross domain values, they may also require process and cultural adjustments where stakeholders are used to working in silos. Because of this, the groundwork done for assessing and planning CMDB deployments can help to isolate roadblocks relevant to AOA adoption and ideally even lay the foundation for an integrated CMDB/analytics strategy.

This, combined with the parallel values of providing cross domain insights through service modeling, is no doubt largely responsible for the following data points.[6] When examining a list of twelve service management technologies, it became apparent that those IT organizations who were "extremely successful" in their AOA deployments were also further along in core service management investments overall. However, there were some dramatic "stars" in the service management arena. IT organizations with service-level management and User Experience Management investments were twice as likely to be "extremely successful" with AOA. But IT organizations with CMDB/CMS and/or ADDM for Change Management were *three times* more likely as those without these CMDB System cornerstones to be "extremely successful" with their advanced analytics deployments!

DEVOPS AND THE CMDB SYSTEM

In the course of writing this book, we conducted a number of interviews targeted at CMDB System deployments for currency and added insight. (A list of these interviews is provided in "Bibliography.") In the course of doing these interviews, it became apparent that DevOps, in one form or another, was a more prominent use case than any of us had expected.

We have already shared some comments from DevOps CMDB System deployments in Chapter 7, as well as in the interview excerpt provided in Chapter 10. The interview excerpt in "How CMS Modeling Can Support DevOps" section of Chapter 13 is in many respects the most definitive. It explains how the CMDB System is already extended to support requests from development for servers, databases, and other parts of the application ecosystem and also how this allows operations and development to come together with superior attention to monitoring and configuration changes moving from development, to test, to production.

The following Q&A offers a unique twist on this discussion as the CMDB in this case was actually purchased by development and then moved into operations for full DevOps support.[7] This interview underscores the growing potential of CMDB System to break down silos in operations and to bridge the still-lingering chasm between operations and development. Also of note in this interview is the "tipping point" discussion. As discussed at the beginning of the chapter, the *tipping point* is when the true value of the CMDB investment begins to show itself to a broader array of stakeholders and executives so that the CMDB System begins to sell itself.

---

[6]"*The Many Faces of Advanced Operations Analytics*," EMA, September, 2014.
[7]Interview with a midtier financial services company based in the United States using the ITinvolve Collaborative CMDB.

INTERVIEW WITH A MIDTIER FINANCIAL PLANNING COMPANY

At the time of the interview, this company, headquartered in the United States, was at the phase 1 "Tipping Point" of their CMDB deployment.

Could you fill us in a little about your IT organization and the broader business it serves?

"Our business provides 'tax audit defense' in prep for IRS and state tax agencies—with more than 5 million customers to date across the U.S. as well as globally.

"Our total IT organization is fairly consolidated, however. It has two flavors. The first group is what you might call a traditional IT operations team—focused on managing network and system equipment. We also have a development team we call the 'software engineering group,' which is where my own roots are. This group writes applications and provides support for application users in conjunction with the more operations-centric IT team.

"I'm the Director of Technology and oversee both departments.

"In terms of infrastructure our servers are spread across three locations, although they're concentrated in one location on the West Coast. We have both virtual and physical servers, and right now most are virtual servers. We're primarily a Windows shop so our virtual servers are Hyper-V. Where we have connectivity, we also manage end devices supporting our offices across the U.S., as well as some globally."

What types of applications are you developing in software engineering?

"We develop both customer-facing and Line-of-Business internal applications to support our business. Most of these are Web-based. We also have a customer-facing website with multi-national outreach so that we can support financial planning decisions in every country where we have a presence. Right now we are primarily U.S., but global outreach is a growth opportunity for us.

"In addition, we support a secure customer portal to transfer messaging and documents. It provides workflow to support planning and audit processes, which helps us to orchestrate our customer services.

"Finally, we also support third-party applications, mostly ERP for HR or other back office requirements—but these generally require less of our attention."

How did you come to select your CMDB?

"Before investing in the CMDB we were very fragmented in how we saved information. Some of it was in Visio, for instance. Some were in OneNote or in Excel. We also had a lot of Word documents—so it was difficult-to-impossible to get insight into impacts when we were about to make a change. We had no advanced configuration tools to go back in time and look at what we'd done.

"At that time, development was ahead of operations in terms of maturity. Our operations organization was fairly siloed and hadn't yet invested in best practices. We often had no clear idea what would happen if, for instance, we unplugged a server. Most of our change records there resided inside someone's head. It was pretty much tribal knowledge owned by isolated individuals. If somebody was sick at the wrong time, it could be very disruptive. When we needed anything beyond that, it was fairly primitive. For instance, we'd apply a spreadsheet to show which IP addresses had configuration changes.

"But we did have some best practices that had evolved in development for source control. So when we saw what a CMDB could do, we felt we had a chance to transform our way of working when it came to managing change."

Can you describe your change/review process?

We don't have a formal change review board, but we do have a structure where we have to get buy-in on any change that's going to affect the larger business. When a change is submitted, it has to be approved by one of two managers within Operations or SW Engineering—and then it goes to the Director or a Vice President level. This is done in a bi-weekly meeting in which we review all proposed changes and requests to our services and their impact on our HW and SW infrastructure.

"Our approval process arose not from the operations side of the house but from development. SW Engineering had more mature processes in place than the IT/operations team. So our best practices/process roots are Scrum and CMMI, although ITIL has come up from time to time. We essentially developed our own in-house best practices from these sources, borrowing heavily from Scrum in particular. In my experience, nobody runs textbook Scrum. It's all about taking the pieces that you need and making them work for you."

How is the deployment progressing?

"About two months ago, I would say we hit a tipping point. Getting there was a critical step because that's when stakeholders across both organizations really began to see the value in using the system and planning changes through it. Right from the start we had been asking our stakeholders to put information into the system before activating a change. But now they're clearly seeing value in complying.

"One of the things that helped us was that we adopted Change Management processes soon after deployment. Any changes to the servers and other devices had to go into our CMDB. Taking this tack helped us a great deal. One of the strengths of the solution we chose is that it clarifies how making a change will impact the broader environment—so you can plan based on impact or go back in time to look for diagnostics.

"But taking advantage of this required a change in policy. What rules should we set for our people to make sure that the data we need gets into our CMDB? Needless to say, because it was a new tool, there was a kind of pushback. Not about the idea of using the system so much as prioritizing how to use it. In other words, at first people were making changes the way they always did and figured that they'd enter the data sometime later. People were thinking, 'Work is more important than documentation, so I'll get the work done first.' But too often the second half of that equation never happened. So we implemented a firm policy that no change happened without it going into the CMDB.

"Part of this was getting our operations organization to understand that they weren't just managing devices. That what they did often impacted critical business services. That we, as an organization, are providing services versus just managing systems. It was something of a transformation to get IT to think about managing a change as connected to a business service called 'Sales to Customers,' because operations didn't think in those terms."

How did you make that transition? Was it just implementing policy?

"We got to a point six months ago where we decided we needed some consulting help to get over this hurdle. With any solution that's strategic to be of use, you have to get to a tipping point where the information that makes it valuable is there. We were at the cusp, and our CMDB provider's consulting took it past that critical tipping point—so that the broader organization really began to see value. It was only a two-week engagement, but it did what we needed it to. They helped us to understand where we were missing things, and after that, how to more effectively populate the system and make the connections we needed."

How are you administrating your CMDB?

"Much of the work is done across stakeholders. But we do have an individual tasked with looking at helping to chart the application/infrastructure interdependencies. He comes out of our SW Engineering development team, but his roots were in operations, so he understands both groups, and he understands where the apps are and how they run. I wouldn't say that he actually spends any more of his day on this than the average stakeholder. My best guess would be about three or four hours a week. To be clear, we don't have new applications coming out all the time. Most of what we're doing in development is reworking existing applications."

What were some of the benefits?

"Beyond making non-disruptive changes and significantly improving service availability, adopting this solution also facilitated a new kind of dialog between SW Engineering and operations. Our CMDB has become a critical liaison in helping the two groups work more effectively together. Now each group has a better understanding of what the other is doing and what the interdependencies are."

What advice would you give someone embarking on a CMDB or CMS initiative?

"The one thing I wish I'd known when I came into this role was what the tipping point for value would be and then how to manage toward that. Once you can establish a fair idea of when your stakeholders will become incented to participate based on achieved value, the initiative catches fire."

SUMMARY TAKEAWAYS

This chapter provides insight into two related areas: how to take stock of your progress and plan ahead after 12 months (or phase 1 completion) and key areas for CMDB System advancement given current industry trends that you might want to include in your future plans. The trends examined here are Service-Aware Asset Management, the move to cloud, analytics for IT, and DevOps.

In the area of "taking stock," we looked at assessing *progress and benefits* and cite examples of success ranging from achieving true cross domain visibility in support of service management, to managing frequent changes (3000 a month) from application development, to more effective handling of service providers for billing and capacity optimization, to eliminating debates about how and where critical CIs were interconnected.

For *issues and advice*, we provided examples ranging from resistance to using the new system, to refusing to give credit for real progress made, to things "we would have done differently." Examples of "doing things differently" included putting more emphasis on cohesive discovery, a more stringent definition of CIs, and firm expectation setting.

In a third area of taking stock, *future directions and plans*, we provided examples of next-step directions that include life cycle endpoint (including mobile) management, better metrics to show value, the move to federation, and improved data management and data integrity.

The first critical industry trend addressed in this chapter is *Service-Aware Asset Management* in which ITSM combines with strategic cross domain ITAM for superior service relevance and IT efficiencies. We also provided examples from research that show why and how a CMDB System can facilitate this transformation, including improved levels of automation, superior data quality, broader cross domain outreach, and improved support for portfolio planning, Green IT, and service catalogs.

This chapter includes a rich set of research data that not only reaffirms the importance of CMDB Systems in **the move to cloud** but also highlights how cloud-ready organizations are deploying and managing their CMDBs in terms of automated updates, supported CI states, visualization, and reports. In conjunction with this, we also discussed how initiatives directed at managing and optimizing business services over the hybrid cloud mosaic map well to CMDB System initiatives in terms of requirements for a more cross domain approach to service management and accelerated support for ITIL best practices.

This chapter introduces **AOA** as a third critical area of industry innovation and provides insights into how advanced analytic tools today are beginning to leverage service modeling, ADDM, and CMDB Systems more aggressively. Recent research indicates a strong correlation between AOA success and ADDM and CMDB System adoption.

DevOps is reintroduced as a fourth industry trend suited for CMDB System expansion, with reference back to interviews underscoring how development was supported through CMDB modeling so that moving from development into production could become a smoother, more consistent, and more realistically monitored process. A unique Q&A explores an entire CMDB deployment driven from development with a focus on Scrum best practices. This Q&A also calls attention to the "tipping-point" nature of phase 1 completion, when tangible benefits are achieved and the CMDB System begins to sell itself.

APPENDICES

APPENDICES

GLOSSARY OF TERMS
AND CONCEPTS

Agile software development   Agile software development includes multiple software development methods designed to optimize collaboration across cross-functional teams in support of more responsiveness to business demands and other changing requirements. It promotes adaptive planning, evolutionary development, and continuous improvement.

Analytics   If the CMDB System is, above all, about insight, that insight needs to be fed and optimized through good analytic tools. Analytic tools may range in capabilities from advanced reporting to truly advanced heuristics, including self-learning algorithms, transaction analytics, and big data in various forms. Big data for IT, which EMA calls "Advanced Operations Analytics" (or "AOA"), are becoming a high-growth area applicable to virtually all CMDB System use cases.

Application Discovery and Dependency Mapping (ADDM)   The core value for all ADDM solutions is to discover, in as automated a fashion as possible, application-to-infrastructure and infrastructure-to-infrastructure interdependencies critical for both the CMDB System and effective service management overall. ADDM solutions may be agentless, agent-based, or a combination of both. EMA classifies the ADDM market into multi-use case ADDM and performance-optimized ADDM.

Asset Management and Financial Optimization use case   Current research underscores the fact that IT organizations are looking for more cohesive approaches to managing assets throughout their life cycles. This includes understanding how all assets (CapEx and OpEx) relate to the critical business of IT in provisioning and delivering services from a costs/value perspective. Both asset life cycle management and effective Service-Aware Asset Management depend on a strong CMDB System foundation. Subsets of this overarching use case include *asset inventory and analysis*, *asset life cycle management*, *compliance audits*, and *financial optimization*.

Automation   Automation is critical both in exploiting and in maintaining a CMDB System. A partial list of automation options to consider includes PC configuration and patch management, system configuration and VM provisioning, network configuration, service desk workflow, development-centric automation, automated application provisioning, security-related identity and access management, and runbook or IT process automation.

"Big Vision, Baby Steps"   This is our consultants' mantra for proceeding with any CMDB System deployment, which requires a staged focus of evolving use cases, as opposed to an attempt to harvest the full value of the CMDB System all at once.

Business Service Management (BSM)   At its core, BSM is about optimizing IT services in support of business requirements—in terms of both maximizing value and minimizing costs. In ITIL v3, BSM is strongly focused on business alignment, in which meaningful dialogue and effective technologies are both key. In EMA's definition, BSM requires a cohesive approach to integrating performance with Change Management, operations with service desk, asset management with financial management, and business alignment with the day-to-day OpEx effectiveness of IT.

CapEx and OpEx   Throughout the book, these refer to "capital expenses" and "operational expenses," respectively.

Change Advisory Board (CAB)   A Change Advisory Board or CAB is an ITIL concept. The CAB has the authority to approve and prioritize critical or potentially business-impacting changes. It should be made up of appropriate stakeholders representing both IT and its business customers. Third parties such as partner and suppliers may also be applicable in some cases.

Change Impact Management and Change Automation use case   Change Management is at the very heart of the CMDB System value set. Change Management includes impact analysis of changes to configuration items (CIs) and their associated services, as well as change automation for activating changes more effectively. Use cases related to this overarching banner are *governance and compliance, data center consolidation (mergers and acquisitions), the move to cloud, disaster recovery, facilities management,* and *Green IT.*

Change Management   As an ITIL-defined process, Change Management is directed at managing changes across the IT HW/SW infrastructure from a life cycle perspective—with minimal to no service disruptions.

Closing the "gap"   The term "gap" as used in this book (Chapter 13 in particular) refers to the tuning required to move from proof of concept to actual phase 1 CMDB System deployment. It is in this stage that objectives, modeling parameters, integration priorities, lingering communication requirements, and other potential issues need to become refined, solidified, and fully actionable.

Cloud computing   This is a diverse set of resources classically enabled on demand to empower IT to become more nimble and responsive to business requirements. These resources include software as a service (SaaS), infrastructure as a service (IaaS), and platform as a service (PaaS). Cloud resources may be either internal to IT or provided through cloud service providers (CSPs).

Common Information Model (CIM)   CIM is the basis for most Distributed Management Task Force (DMTF) standards, including the CMDB Federation (CMDBf) standard. CIM is a conceptual schema that defines how managed CIs can be represented as a common set of objects and how relationships between them can be consistently represented. CIM is extensible to support individual product requirements. CIM is based on the Unified Modeling Language (UML) adopted as a standard by the Object Management Group (OMG).

Configuration item (CI)   Configuration items or CIs and their interdependencies are central to understanding CMDB System value. As ITIL represents them, CIs include software, devices, and components thereof that require management to support the delivery of IT services. But CIs also extend to include IT services themselves, as well as people, locations, documentation. With the advent of cloud, CIs might also extend to represent cloud service provider dependencies, for instance—thus creating a mosaic around which the logical and physical interdependencies critical to optimizing IT services can be more easily visualized and understood.

Configuration Management Database (CMDB)   The CMDB is a central data store of critical IT environmental information with links to such information stored in other systems to document the location, configuration, and interdependency of key IT assets, both physical assets and applications. The CMDB can support the change process by identifying interdependencies, improve regression testing by capturing insights surrounding these interdependencies, and help diagnose problems impacted by changes to the IT environment. (See also "core CMDB.")

CMDB Federation Working Group (CMDBf)   In Q4 2007, the CMDB Federation (CMDBf) Working Group submitted CMDB Federation (*CMDBf*) to the DMTF. The CMDB Federation is a group of six companies (BMC, CA, Fujitsu, HP, IBM, and Microsoft) working jointly to develop standard architecture and specifications for CMDBs. The CMDBf standard describes interfaces for Configuration Management Databases and management data repositories (MDRs) to share data through federation.

CMDB System   This is an enabling set of software-delivered capabilities to discover, reconcile, manage, and optimize critical IT service interdependencies in the face of change. CMDB Systems are multidimensional in benefits that over time can support the full IT organization while providing a foundation for more effective alignment between IT and the business or organization it serves. CMDB Systems generally require attention to process, culture, and communication and technology to achieve their full value. The CMDB System as described in this book bridges three ITIL-defined terms: "Configuration Management Database," "Configuration Management System," and "Service Knowledge Management System," where CMDB System investments can truly come to life through analytics and automation.

Configuration Management System (CMS)   "CMS" is an ITIL/industry term that closely approximates the yet broader concept of "CMDB System" used throughout this book. As a federated system in which more detailed data (e.g., asset, configuration, performance, etc.) can be stored locally and updated via service modeling, the CMS is beginning to rise into prominence in the industry as a more dynamic answer to having to place all data in a single, mammoth repository.

Consumer-driven IT   There are multiple dimensions to consumer-driven IT, all of which reflect the need for a more business-aligned, service-centric approach to running IT in support of both internal and external service consumers. Cloud, mobile, and agile software developments all contribute to making IT more aware of and responsive to its diverse internal and external customer base.

Core CMDB   This is a Configuration Management Database that's part of a broader federated system and serves as the primary data source for critical Change Management-related interdependencies. (See also CMDB.)

Core CMDB team   While there is not a pure, set formula for establishing a core CMDB team, there are consistent skill set requirements relevant to almost every CMDB System initiative. Generally recommended is a *team manager* with leadership and communication skills. *CMDB specialists* are responsible for working with the various technology silos to determine the initial low-level requirements, acting as liaisons to the CMDB vendor, installing software, writing reconciliation rules, adjudicating any issues with systems of records, making recommendations for tool consolidation, testing the CMDB schemas, and rolling solutions into production. An *information architect/database specialist* is responsible for categorizing and scrubbing the requirements, analyzing the data model and schema, identifying CI-level data elements (and duplication), generating updates to the Web site, and reporting on project progress.

Cost center versus business partner   Critical to the success of the CMDB System is a commitment to support the transition as IT moves from being a cost center to becoming a business partner—a transition for which the CMDB System should also become a valuable enabler and catalyst. The many dimensions of this transition, as discussed in this book, include a more strategic role for IT, a superior awareness of business needs and hence an improved ability to prioritize initiatives and service requirements, and a more cross-domain, service-aware way of working with enhanced processes and dialogue.

Data Optimization Analytics   This new market/technology provides a proven analytic framework for assimilating and reconciling "trusted sources" including gaps in coverage (such as in monitoring and security) and for ranking contextual efficiencies for a given inventory or discovery tool (asking, for instance, "Which inventory tool brings in the best coverage for Windows desktops?").

Definitive Media Library (DML)   A critical component to the Configuration Management System is the "Definitive Media Library" (DML), which was called "Definitive Software Library" in ITIL v2 but was expanded in v3 to represent more diverse media (video, voice, etc.) in order to capture a more complete array of IT-delivered services. The DML can become a common resource for empowering and clarifying the development-to-operations dialogs and processes that are rightly becoming such a priority today in many IT organizations.

Detailed requirement   A good detailed requirement clearly links CMDB-related data with a defined process that spans technology silos or is otherwise only manually available. A detailed requirement should be understood by everyone from the CIO to mainframe programmers and demonstrate clear value to the business. It should be tied to CIs in the CMDB schema, focused on current business issues and information needed, and inclusive of data provided by multiple technology silos. Ideally, it can be assigned to one or more measurable success metrics and an annual savings target.

DevOps use case   DevOps has received significant attention in a growing number of CMDB System deployments. The reasons for this are probably self-evident given the current buzz around "agile" and the pressures on IT organizations to deliver new application services and application enhancements with dramatically increasing frequency. While many of these clearly do not warrant proactive CMDB or CAB attention, their cumulative impact needs to be understood and assessed. As shown in this book, a CMDB System can become a powerful catalyst for promoting the more efficient introduction of new services into production, as well as enabling development and operations to communicate and work more effectively together.

Eight-Step Ladder to CMDB System Success   The Eight-Step Ladder provides clear guidelines for approaching CMDB System deployments in a methodical way. Its efficacy has been borne out in multiple consulting engagements—and stresses dialogue, process awareness, and organizational awareness as well as technology planning and adoption. The eight steps are as follows:

1. Define objectives, resources, and ownership
2. Technology, process, and organizational audit
3. Evolutionary assessment
4. Define requirements and architecture and finalize team
5. Technology selection
6. Closing the gap with critical issues and gating factors
7. Develop roadmap
8. Review progress and milestones

EMA Semantic Model The EMA Semantic Model is designed to highlight the transition from siloed tools and technology to broader, cross-domain integrations. It addresses IT management architectures from the following perspectives: instrumentation and data collection; data store, data sharing, and integration; analytics; automated actions; and visualization, data access, and business alignment. The CMDB System serves as an enabler for bringing siloed toolset designs into a more unified, cohesive, and service-aware perspective.

Extended Enterprise Both IT and IT-driven business models are evolving to optimize service delivery across a patchwork of partners and in some cases suppliers—for both geographic outreach and service/product outreach. Web-based applications and cloud computing are dramatically accelerating this trend, which now requires IT to become more aware of interdependencies not only internal to its own organization but also across a widening array of external relationships. These factors all contribute to the emergence of the Extended Enterprise as the new frontier in which IT organizations must seek to optimize value.

External CMDB System metrics External metrics typically involve more than just the CMDB investment. They are indications of the real value to operations and ultimately to the business, as CMDB Systems enable better access to information, better analysis, and better collaboration across IT—just as a superhighway enables a car to travel at faster speeds than it can on a pot-holed country road. Some external CMDB System metrics can be developed into clear ROI benefits. External metrics' values can be best understood in terms of metrics associated with CMDB System use cases—such as Change Impact Management and Change Automation, Asset Management and Financial Optimization, Service Impact Management and Capacity Optimization, and security/governance/compliance.

Federation Federating the CMDB System can mean many different things. Strictly speaking, federation means that data can be accessed and core CMDB System modeling can be updated without having to duplicate or move data. However, many deployments treat federation as having multiple resident "trusted sources" that are aligned with a core CMDB and update the system based on policy, largely through data duplication.

If/then change impact analysis Change impact analysis is critical not only for managing change but also for minimizing service disruptions. This analysis not only shows where and how a service might be disrupted but also adds insight into the impacts of change on critical IT-delivered business services.

Internal CMDB System metrics These are metrics directed at ensuring effective milestones in the evolution of the CMDB System itself. These metrics generally can be divided into three areas: *scope (breadth* of coverage), *accuracy (integrity* of information), and *efficiency* metrics documenting improvements in the maintenance and evolution of the CMDB System.

IT Asset Management (ITAM) Asset management is the process responsible for tracking and reporting on the value and ownership of IT financial assets throughout their life cycles. While an asset management database can easily become a part of a CMDB System, it is not in itself a CMDB. Practitioners must be careful not to find, label, and document every IT asset within the CMDB, which typically focuses on those assets that can be managed and optimized for change, service impact, and business value.

ITIL Formally known as the "IT Infrastructure Library," ITIL is the leading global source of best practices for service management. ITIL's quiet rise through the 1990s led to a substantial and growing awareness in the early years of this millennium, as IT organizations increasingly sought to take charge of their services in a more cohesive, more business-aligned, more measured, and more cross-domain manner than in the past. ITIL is a part of Axelos, a joint venture between Capita and the UK Project Office. Axelos brings ITIL best practices for service management together with a number of other best practices, such as PRINCE2 for project management and MoP (Management of Portfolios) for prioritizing investments across organizations, programs, and projects.

IT Maturity Levels   Maximizing the value of the CMDB System depends on a realistic approach to maturity levels, combining insights into technology adoption, organizational requirements, and process readiness. The four phases of IT Maturity discussed in this book are reactive infrastructure management, Active Operations Management, proactive service-driven management, and dynamic business-driven management. These have associated "personalities" starting with "reactive heroes" for reactive infrastructure management and evolving to "operationally empowered tribes," to "internal service provider," to "proactive business partner." Many CMDB deployments begin in the Active Operations Management period and become a bridge to proactive service-driven management.

IT Service Management (ITSM)   ITSM is generally viewed as an approach to managing and optimizing IT services focused on best practices and processes such as ITIL.

Metadata   Metadata are data about data and as such can provide a context for creating relationship-driven models, extending model-related associations and attributes, and linking in federated data sources.

Modeling studio   Support for developing and modifying service models includes factors such as unique access rights management, unique GUIs, unique reports, automated discovery for CI classes and types, automated model population when new CIs appear, support for approved versus discovered CIs, drag-and-drop model image creation, model libraries, and policies to support consistent model groupings.

Reconciliation   In context with CMDB updates and discovery, reconciliation (either automated or manual) can provide element-level checking of configuration items (CIs) to ensure that each CI is valid. This includes matching the source, avoiding duplication of data, and reflecting an accurate current value for each CI.

Return on investment (ROI)   The simplest formula for ROI is ROI = cost savings and added values/costs incurred. However, in most CMDB System adoptions, neither "cost savings" and "added values" (e.g., faster time to provision new or existing services) nor "costs incurred" is a trivial discussion. Limiting costs incurred to those costs specifically for deployment, software, training, and operational overhead of the CMDB System deployment itself is strongly recommended.

Scope creep   Pressure to satisfy stakeholders—along with executive pressure—can lead to scope creep. This will invariably produce dissatisfaction as reality fails to live up to expectations and derail the planned evolution of the CMDB System, itself.

Security and Compliance use case   CMDB System initiatives can deliver strong value in terms of improved Security and Compliance-related governance. However, given the generally different cultural and political environments separating the security operations center (SOC) from the broader community focusing on service management, this use case usually provides added benefits to other drivers, such as managing changes or life cycle governance for assets.

Service Asset and Configuration Management (SACM)   ITIL's Service Asset and Configuration Management (SACM) provides a comprehensive look at how service-related assets are controlled, managed, and optimized by understanding what they are, where they are, and capturing their interdependencies. As such, SACM is at the heart of a Configuration Management System.

Service-Aware Asset Management (SAAM)   Service-Aware Asset Management unites IT Asset Management (ITAM) with IT Service Management (ITSM). SAAM is emerging as a new force for managing IT assets throughout their life cycles as components of critical IT services.

Service catalog   Service catalogs ideally provide a solid matrix of options for IT service consumers to choose and select services with built-in levels of automation tied to the modeling in the CMDB System—although in many environments, the service catalog and the CMDB are still not integrated. Information such as costs, service-level guarantees, and approvals should be visible to consumers while IT links might include configuration requirements, service owners, and security, license, and usage data, among other data points. Increasingly, IT organizations are blending on-premise with public cloud-provided services in a single integrated service catalog for their consumers.

Service Impact, Performance Management, and Capacity Optimization use case Operational professionals, with concerns such as mean time to repair (MTTR) and mean time between failure (MTBF), can benefit greatly from a "reconciled view of truth" including the impacts of change on performance—insights that ultimately depend on a dynamic CMDB System foundation. Some of the subordinate use cases here include the following: *reconciled view of truth across many multiple sources, reflexive insights into change and configuration for diagnostics, validation that a newly provisioned service is performing effectively, incident and problem management automation and governance, finding the owner of the problem, linking capacity and performance for diagnostics, optimizing capacity for more effective service delivery,* and *business process and service-specific benefits.*

Service Knowledge Management System (SKMS) ITIL's vision of the SKMS unifies the broad insights of a CMS as defined above, with broader capabilities for analyzing and visualizing service management-related data. As such, it reflects many of the attributes of what we call a "CMDB System" in this book, which becomes the true leveraging point for obtaining full value from a core CMDB investment—through integrations with analytics, automation, and other capabilities.

Stakeholder or CI owner Critical to the success of a CMDB System is optimizing stakeholder involvement. Stakeholders are typically responsible for managing the integrity of an individual CI or a set of CIs. To optimize deployment, stakeholders need to see value for themselves in actively participating in the rollout— usually achieved at the "tipping point" when the CMDB begins to deliver value after six months. Managing stakeholder expectations is also a critical part of success—so that realities remain in-line with what stakeholders demand or expect without breakage or "scope creep."

Standard (preauthorized) changes This is ITIL's term for changes requiring no formal reviews, for which, therefore, automation can play an especially large role. Nonetheless, it's critical that these changes are also captured and documented to understand potential impacts on service quality, security vulnerabilities, and potential asset or other related issues.

"Standing in the middle of the storm" This concept refers to recognizing and optimizing the interdependencies across process, technology, and organizational realities—a critical mind-set for CMDB System success.

Synchronization Synchronization here refers to identifying changes to the CMDB as they occur to ensure the same "version of the truth" across integrated systems.

System of record/"trusted source" The system of record (or "trusted source") refers to the best data source for a given CI or CI attribute—and in a federated system, it can be a source accessed through modeling, Web Services, and/or other means without actually moving data.

System of relevance Rather than claiming that the CMDB is a "single source of truth," the term "system of relevance" reinforces the idea that the CMDB System requires "what's relevant" to enable a given use case—such as Change Management, asset management, or service impact management—in the current, dynamic world of IT.

Three-Tiered Roadmap This is a critical capability for documenting past progress and for planning effectively moving forward. It includes a 6-month tactical implementation plan, a 1-year roadmap, and a 2-year roadmap. Requirements for the initial 6-month plan include the creation of the core CMDB team, such as the definition of core team responsibilities; creation of a detailed requirements document; technology adoption, such as the creation of technology-relevant policies; value statement (after initial proof of concept); milestones; costs; and projected production status at the end of 6 months.

The "two CMDBs" This term refers to the dual nature of some more progressive CMDB System deployments that include a near real-time, performance-centric modeled view of IT services with classic CMDB capabilities more typically targeted at change and asset management. The unifying thread across the "two CMDBs" is usually a consistent service modeling system, often affiliated with Application Discovery and Dependency Mapping investments.

Web Services Web Services are becoming the industry's best answer for federation, especially where data need to be accessed without actual duplication. A *Web service* utilizes Extensible Markup Language (XML)-based communication as developed by the World Wide Web Consortium (W3C). XML favors simplicity, generality, and usability and allows for Web service connections to be identified and linked on demand.

SAMPLE REQUEST FOR PRODUCT INFORMATION

B

INTRODUCTION

The following questions are taken from prior research used to evaluate CMDB System-relevant offerings. They are optimized to support use-case requirements as discussed in this book. This form is intended as a useful departure point for assessing and comparing multiple vendor offerings. As a general rule, when multiple-choice options apply, the vendor should "select all." This questionnaire can be used either as a form or as a guide for vendor interviews. The sections targeted at discussion are similarly designed for interviews based on topical concerns addressed in the preceding questions.

DISTINGUISHING PRODUCT FEATURES

Please enter a brief description of the top five (5) to seven (7) distinguishing product suite features overall. Please limit feature descriptions to 25 words or less.

Feature 1
Feature 2
Feature 3
Feature 4
Feature 5
Feature 6
Feature 7

DEPLOYMENT COST EFFICIENCY
DEPLOYMENT AND ADMINISTRATION
Ease of administration
Time-related and FTE

What is the shortest time frame in which your CMDB/CMS solution has paid for software and services (ROI)?

Less than 2 weeks
2 weeks up to 1 month
1 month up to 3 months
3 months up to 6 months

6 months up to 9 months
9 months up to 1 year
1 year up to 1.5 years
1.5 years up to 2 years
2 or more years
Don't know

In the above scenario, what was the size of the deployment in terms of CIs?

500 or less
501-1000
1001-5000
5001-10,000
10,001-20,000
20,001-40,000
40,001-60,000
More than 60,000
N/A

Did your CI count include desktops?

Yes
No
N/A

If yes, what was the percentage of desktops?

50% or less
Greater than 50%

Do you offer proof of concept support for customers prior to deployment?

Yes
No

Through what methods can data be brought into the CMDB/CMS other than through automated discovery to enable initial CMDB population?

Scripting
Templates
Drag and drop
Bulk data load (ETL)
Excel import
Others (please specify)

What is the **most prevalent way** that data are captured to support initial CMDB population other than automated discovery?

Scripting
Templates

Drag and drop
Bulk data load (ETL)
Excel import
Others (please specify)

What is the average required full-time employee (FTE) allotment on a percentage basis for ongoing administration of your full CMDB solution suite in an enterprise environment with 10,000 or more CIs (can include PCs)?

Less than 50% of an FTE
50% up to 100%
100% up to 150%
150% up to 200%
200% up to 250%
250% up to 300%
300% up to 400%
400% up to 500%
500% up to 1000%
1000% or more

Administration automation

Please indicate any areas where **automation** plays a major role in the deployment, administration, or Change Management of *your* CMDB solution suite as a whole?

Self-configuration
Automatic adjustments to changing environmental conditions
Auto population
Others (please specify)

Which of the following **CMDB deployment, administrative, and Change Management roles and tasks** do you support across your CMDB and/or overall service modeling portfolio, including integrated sources (yours or third party) without unique services?

CI and service modeling
Unique integration requirements
CMDB maintenance—reports on CI accuracy
CMDB maintenance—reports on CI scope
CMDB maintenance—reports on CI updates (approved versus discovered)
CMDB maintenance—individualized stakeholder reports
Change Management histories—systems (successful versus unsuccessful changes)
Change Management histories—desktops
Change Management histories—networks
Change Management histories—applications
Change Management histories—others
CAB review support
Others (please specify)

For discussion: Automation to accelerate deployment. How do you use automation to accelerate the speed and ease of deployment for your CMDB? Be specific about *use cases* that apply, as well as size and complexity of different environments.

Modeling support

Do you offer the equivalent of a modeling studio or other types of workspace support for helping your customers develop and/or modify models?

Yes
No

If yes, what type of support do you offer your customers for developing and modifying service models?

Unique GUIs
Unique reports
Unique access rights
Model libraries
Drag-and-drop model linkages
Discovery for CI classes and/or types
Automated model population/deletion when new CIs appear/age out
Policies to support consistent model groupings
Approved versus discovered CI reports
Others (please specify)

What types of service modeling support do you offer outside of the CMDB itself that's fully reconciled with the CMDB?

Reconciled modeling between the service catalog and/or service portfolio and the CMDB
Service modeling in service management dashboards for application and infrastructure performance and availability management
Service modeling for creating blueprints of new services
Service modeling in support of automation technologies such as IT process automation or runbook
Service modeling in support of business planning and financial analytics
Service modeling to support business process use cases
We do offer service modeling but it's not reconciled with the CMDB
We don't offer any service modeling outside of the CMDB
Others (please specify)

Do you offer the equivalent of a modeling studio or other types of workspace support for helping your customers develop and/or modify models _beyond_ the CMDB itself, for instance, in support of real-time service models that sometimes appear in service management dashboards?

Yes
No

If yes, what type of support do you offer your customers for developing and modifying service models beyond pure play CMDB support?

Unique GUIs
Unique reports
Unique access rights
Model libraries
Drag-and-drop model linkages
Discovery for CI classes and/or types
Automated model population when new CIs appear
Policies to support consistent model groupings
Approved versus discovered CI reports
Others (please specify)

For discussion: Modeling customization. How do you support model customizations across versions? How can customers preserve their customized CI and CI attribute definitions when you introduce a new CMDB release?

Discovery and update support

How do you create policies or establish patterns for CMDB population?

Scripting
Mouse click(s)
Drag and drop
Templates
Others (please specify)

Do these policies also support application dependency mapping?

Yes
No

Which of the following ways **are most used** to create policies for CMDB population through discovery?

Scripting
Mouse click(s)
Drag and drop
Templates
Others (please specify)

Through what methods can domain expertise be manually entered to establish polices or patterns for CMDB updates after initial deployment?

Scripting
Templates
Text

Drag and drop
Bulk data load (ETL)
Excel import
Others (please specify)

What is the **most prevalent way** that domain expertise is manually entered to support CMDB updates after initial deployment?

Scripting
Templates
Text
Drag and drop
Bulk data load (ETL)
Excel import
Others (please specify)

For discussion: Administration for discovery and updates. How can you accelerate the speed and ease of discovery and updates through automation?

Customer support and services
Customer support
Which levels of customer support do you offer?

Online support
Business hour phone support
24×7 phone support
On-site support
Others (please specify)

Upon notification of a business-critical service problem, what is the guaranteed response time for the vendor's highest level of support?

Immediate access at time of call
1-15 min
16-30 min
30 min to 1 h
1-6 h
6-12 h
12-24 h
More than 24 min

Do you support a user group for customers?

Vendor-supported online forum
Sporadic meetings in one or more sites
Regular meetings in one or more sites
Regular vendor conferences

Professional services

What professional services do you provide to assist the customer during the **strategic planning process** (including baselining, maturity assessments, phase definitions, and metrics) that are most offered/used?

We provide our own professional services.
We partner with third parties for services.
Minimal services offered.

What professional services do you provide to assist the customer with **best practices as per ITIL including process planning and definitions?** Select the service that is most offered/used.

We provide our own professional services.
We partner with third parties for services.
Minimal services offered.
Others (please specify).

What professional services do you provide to assist the customer during the **implementation/ deployment process?** Select the service that is most offered/used.

We provide our own professional services.
We partner with third parties for services.
Minimal services offered.

For each of the following, what professional services do you provide for each of the following categories? Select the service that is most offered/used.

Modeling support, including customization and extensions.

We provide our own professional services.
We partner with third parties for services.
Minimal services offered.
Others (please specify).

Application dependency mapping and discovery.

We provide our own professional services.
We partner with third parties for services.
Minimal services offered.
Others (please specify).

Service change, compliance, and control management.

We provide our own professional services.
We partner with third parties for services.
Minimal services offered.
Others (please specify).

Support for asset management capabilities including Service Asset and Configuration Management (SACM) and asset lifecycle management.

We provide our own professional services.
We partner with third parties for services.
Minimal services offered.
Others (please specify).

Service impact planning including incident, problem, and/or real-time operational support such as SLM and service or business impact.

We provide our own professional services.
We partner with third parties for services.
Minimal services offered.
Others (please specify).

For discussion: Consulting and services Please be prepared to discuss your capabilities for CMDB-related consulting and services with specific *use cases* in mind (e.g., asset management, change management, incident management, and problem management).

COST ADVANTAGE

Price

CMDBs are packaged in many different ways and not all are priced separately. Please provide the actual full package purchase price even if function goes beyond the CMDB itself—e.g., if it's typically packaged in the service desk, include the base service desk price. If the cost is CI-dependent, please calculate to the best of your ability based on 10,000 (or whatever number is relevant) CIs.

List Price (in $ US)

Are there any hardware and/or software dependencies (e.g., server hardware and OS software) for your CMDB/CMS product to run not included in the base price?

Yes
No

Are there any hardware and/or software dependencies (e.g., server hardware and OS software) for your CMDB/CMS product to run not included in the base price?

($ US)?

Is your product available as software as a service (SaaS)?

Yes
No

If available as SaaS, please describe your pricing model. Please calculate based on 5,000 CIs.

Licensing model and environments supported

What operating systems do you support as environments for running your product?

Windows
HP-UX

AIX
Solaris
Red Hat
Linux
SUSE Linux
VMware
Appliance
Virtual appliance

If your product can run on windows, please specify versions supported.
Please specify any other Unix, Linux, or virtual operating systems that are not listed above.
What databases can be used in conjunction with your product?

SQL Server
MySQL
Oracle
DB2
Sybase
Informix
Others (please specify)

How is your CMDB/CMS solution licensed?

CI-based
User-based
Usage-based
Processor-based
Enterprise-based
Others (please specify)

Do you offer support for application dependency mapping as fully integrated with your CMDB?

Yes
No

If yes, what is the rough list cost for your preferred application dependency mapping software in a typical deployment? If cost is CI-dependent, please calculate based on a CMDB environment of 20,000 CIs (or whatever is appropriate) when a CI is a managed resource, such as a server or a desktop.

$5000 or less
$5001-10,000
$10,001-25,000
$25,001-50,000
$50,001-75,000
$75,001-100,000
$100,001-150,000
$150,001-200,000
$200,000 or more

Service-related costs
Do you offer fixed price professional services for CMDB/CMS deployment?

Yes
No

Maintenance costs
What are your maintenance fees (as a percent of list price) for highest level of service?

No maintenance fees
1-5%
6-10%
11-14%
15-18%
19-22%
More than 22%

PRODUCT STRENGTH
ARCHITECTURE AND INTEGRATION
Architecture
Scalability
How many CIs can be supported by your solution when a CI is a managed resource, such as a server or a desktop?

Fewer than 1000
1000-5000
5001-10,000
10,001-20,000
20,001-50,000
50,001-100,000
100,001-500,000
500,001-1,000,000
1,000,001-10,000,000
Greater than 10,000,000

To date, what is your largest deployment in terms of CIs?

Fewer than 1000
1000-5000
5001-10,000
10,001-20,000
20,001-50,000
50,001-100,000

100,001-500,000
500,001-1,000,000
1,000,000-10,000,000
Greater than 10,000,000

How many simultaneous users can your solution support out of the box?

Fewer than 5
5-10
11-20
21-30
31-50
51-100
More than 100

Range of discovery

What is the range of domains you can **discover and model** directly through your **own integrated management software** portfolio?

Network
Systems
Virtual systems
Virtual cross domain
Mainframe
Desktop
Mobile
Web applications
Web 2.0 applications
Third-party packaged applications
Custom applications
SOA applications
Storage
Database
Asset inventory
Asset license/usage
Security/vulnerability

What is the range of domains you can discover and model through **third-party or outside sources** as an **integrated and reconciled resource at the data level**? Please do *not* include integrations that require extensive (more than one week) custom support or special services.

Network
Systems
Virtual systems
Virtual cross domain
Mainframe

Desktop
Mobile
Web applications
Web 2.0 applications
Third-party packaged applications
Custom applications
SOA applications
Storage
Database
Asset inventory
Asset license/usage
Security/vulnerability

What is the range of domains you can discover and model directly through your **own integrated** portfolio **for purposes of change, configuration, and release management**?

Network
Systems
Virtual systems
Virtual cross domain
Mainframe
Desktop
Mobile
Storage
Database
Security/vulnerability
Application provisioning
Virtual application infrastructure provisioning
Others (please specify)

What is the range of domains you can discover and model through **fully supported third-party** integrations **for purposes of change, configuration, and release management**?

Network
Systems
Virtual systems
Virtual cross domain
Mainframe
Desktop
Storage
Database
Security/vulnerability
Application provisioning
Virtual application infrastructure provisioning
Others (please specify)

For discussion: Discovery capabilities. What are your discovery capabilities in terms of breadth, range, and *use case*. including partner or other fully supported integrations with your own or third-party software.

Service interdependencies

How would you characterize your support for capturing **service interdependencies**?

Infrastructure-to-infrastructure
Infrastructure-to-application
Application-to-application (application ecosystem)
Application component-to-application component (Web 2.0 application ecosystem)
Others (please specify)

Do you offer application dependency mapping **as a fully integrated extension to your CMDB**?

Yes
No

If yes, please list the product name(s) through which you support application dependency mapping directly **through your own portfolio**.

Do you also offer application dependency mapping through **fully supported third-party integrations**?

Yes
No

If yes, please list the product name(s) through which you support application dependency mapping through **fully supported (by you) third-party integrations**.

Which of the following infrastructure and software/applications are components **directly discovered** through your CMDB/CMS or an integrated application dependency mapping solution?

Network topology
Network configuration
Systems configuration
Virtual systems
Virtual cross domain
Mainframe
Mainframe configuration
Desktop
Desktop configurations
Browsers
Web applications
Web 2.0 applications
Third-party packaged applications
Custom applications
SOA applications
n-tier application interdependencies

Storage
Storage configurations
Database
Database configurations
Asset inventory
Does not apply to our product

To what degree do you recommend leveraging your preferred application dependency mapping solution (yours or third party) to reconcile information from other MDRs such as performance monitoring trusted sources and other tools?

Heavily
Somewhat
Slightly
Not at all
Does not apply to our product

For discussion: Capturing interdependencies. How you can capture interdependencies across HW, SW, services, or other interdependencies through your CMDB and your own or integrations from other vendors. Be *use case*-specific as appropriate.

Reconciliation and normalization

Does your CMDB/CMS solution support unique workspaces or other resources specifically targeted to support the administration of data reconciliation policies across multiple "trusted" data sources?

Yes
No

Does your overall CMDB/CMS solution provide data synchronization or time stamping for time-sensitive data sources such as performance-related data?

Yes
No

Does your CMDB solution offer unique workspaces or other resources specifically targeted to support the administration of data normalization policies across multiple trusted data sources?

Yes
No

If there are any special components (applications, modules, workspaces, etc.) exposed to IT administrators in support of reconciliation, synchronization, and/or normalization, please list what they are and provide a brief (50 words or less) description of each.

For discussion: Synchronization, reconciliation, and normalization. Please be prepared to discuss synchronization, reconciliation, and normalization. Be *use case*-specific, as appropriate, for example, access to an asset management database versus access to performance-related CI attributes may require different technologies.

Integration/interoperability
Functional sources

Which of the following types of data-level integration (import/export or data access—e.g., on-demand federated data access) do you provide **from your own portfolio** without requiring unique services?

Change and configuration management visibility/histories
Service catalog integration (for service visibility)
Service desk records
Performance monitoring and diagnostic tools
Security monitoring tools
Portals or dashboards for BSM
Service-level agreements
Asset management tools/inventories
Asset management/contracts
Asset management/other
Application development tools
Others (please specify)

Which of the following types of data-level integration (import/export or data access) do you provide **from third-party sources** without requiring unique services?

Change and configuration management visibility/histories
Service catalog integration (for service visibility)
Service desk records
Performance monitoring and diagnostic tools
Security monitoring tools
Portals or dashboards for BSM
Service-level agreements
Asset management tools/inventories
Asset management/contracts
Asset management/other
Application development tools
Others (please specify)

MDRS and data access

How many management software data repositories (MDRs) such as monitoring or asset management **internal to your portfolio** can you **import data from**? Please do *not* include those requiring unique, "special effort" integration services.

None
1-5
6-10
11-20
21-25
More than 25

Please list some key examples of the management sources (MDRs) from your own portfolio that you can import data from.

How many management software data repositories **(MDRs) internal to your portfolio** can you **export data to?** Please do *not* include those requiring unique, "special effort" integration services.

None
1-5
6-10
11-20
21-25
More than 25

Please list some key examples of the management sources (MDRs) from your own portfolio that you can export data to.

How many management software data repositories **(MDRs) from third-party sources *external* to your portfolio** can you **import data from**? Please do *not* include those requiring unique, "special effort" integration services.

None
1-5
6-10
11-20
21-25
More than 25

Please list some key examples of the management sources (MDRs) *external* to your own portfolio that you can import data from.

How many management software data repositories **(MDRs) from third-party sources *external* to your portfolio** can you **export data to?** Please do *not* include those requiring unique, "special effort" integration services.

None
1-5
6-10
11-20
21-25
More than 25

Please list some key examples of the management sources (MDRs) *external* to your own portfolio that you can export data to.

How many management software sources **(MDRs or other) internal to your portfolio** can you *access* **as reconciled, federated trusted sources without moving or replicating data?** Please do *not* include those requiring unique, "special effort" integration services.

None
1-5
6-10
11-20

21-25
More than 25

Please list some key examples of the management sources (MDRs or other) from your own portfolio that you can *access* as reconciled, trusted sources without moving or replicating data.

How many management software sources **(MDRs or other)** *external* **to your portfolio** can you **access as reconciled, trusted sources without moving or replicating data?** Please do *not* include those requiring unique, "special effort" integration services.

None
1-5
6-10
11-20
21-25
More than 25

Please list some key examples of the management sources (MDRs or others) *external* to your own portfolio that you can *access* as reconciled, trusted sources without moving or replicating data.

Standards and other conventions

Which of the following standards and other conventions does your solution support for: modeling, importing, exporting, and/or accessing information, from other data sources?

XML
CIM
ODBC
CMDBf
OVF
ITIL
eTOM
SID
SMI
BPEL
BPMN
HTML
SNMP
TCP
SOAP
WSDL
CSS
OpenSSL
Global Namespace
Proprietary API
Adapters
Tool kit
Others (please specify)

For discussion: Integration and data access. What are your capabilities for integration and data access as relevant to the above questions with the analyst?

FUNCTIONALITY

Features
Service modeling capabilities

Which of the following CI relationships can your solution model **out of the box** in terms of services and service interdependencies?

> Parent/child
> Adjacency (connected to)
> Inheritance
> Depends on
> Deployed on/installed on
> Member of
> Owner of
> Executes on
> Monitored by
> Communications through (e.g., network link)
> Consumer (consumes services from)
> Provider (provides services to)
> Secures (provides security for)
> Others (please specify)

How many CI relationship types can your solution support out of the box?

> Fewer than 20
> 20-50
> 51-75
> 76-100
> 101-150
> More than 150

How many CI classes can your solution support?

> Fewer than 20
> 20-50
> 51-75
> 76-100
> 101-150
> More than 150

How many CI subclasses can your solution support?

> Fewer than 20
> 20-50
> 51-75

76-100
101-150
151-200
201-300
301-500
More than 500

Which of the following CI attributes (or class characteristics) can your solution define/support out of the box?

Cluster
Contract
Organization
SLA
Location
Document
Facilities
Hardware
Owner
Project
Department
Others (please list or characterize in 50 words or less)

How many CI attributes across all classes can your solution support **out of the box**?

Fewer than 100
100-200
201-300
301-500
501-1,000
More than 1000

What CI states can your solution support **directly**?

Desired/approved
Actual
Future/planned
Historical/past
Others (please specify)

For discussion: Service modeling capabilities and metadata. What are your capabilities for modeling not including ease of administration already addressed?

Change impact and analytics

Analytics can add value for optimizing CMDB/CMS deployments in terms of maintenance, capacity planning, service vulnerability assessments, if/then change analysis, asset reconciliation, and other functions associated with governance, planning, and infrastructure-to-service optimization.

What are your CMDB solution set's capabilities for assimilating change impact information? Please include only fully supported integrations that do not require unique services.

Real-time **network configuration** service impact analysis
Historical **network configuration** service impact analysis
Real-time **system configuration** service impact analysis
Historical **system configuration** service impact analysis
Real-time **desktop configuration** service impact analysis
Historical **desktop configuration** service impact analysis
Real-time **storage configuration** service impact analysis
Historical **storage configuration** service impact analysis
Real-time **security-related** service impact analysis
Historical **security-related** service impact analysis
Real-time **virtualized infrastructure** service impact analysis
Trending and optimization across **virtualized infrastructure** for service optimization
Others (please specify)

What type of analytics/advanced intelligence do you support "under the cover" or through direct integrations **as a part of your CMDB/CMS product suite** to enable superior CMDB analysis, maintenance, reporting and planning, etc.?

If/then change impact analysis
Correlation
Anomaly/anomalous behaviors
Predictive trending
Data mining and OLAP
Self-learning heuristics (please specify)
We don't offer analytics as a part of our CMDB/CMS product set
Others (please specify)

What type of analytics/advanced intelligence do you support "under the cover" or through direct integrations **through fully supported integrations from your own product portfolio** to enable superior CMDB analysis, maintenance, reporting and planning, etc.?

If/then change impact analysis
Correlation
Anomaly/anomalous behaviors
Predictive trending
Data mining and OLAP
Self-learning heuristics (please specify)
We don't offer analytics through integrations across our own product portfolio
Others (please specify)

Please list some key examples of product names relevant to the above.

What types of analytics in support of CMDB/CMS governance do you employ directly as a part of your CMDB/CMS offering through integration with other products **with third-party sources** that do not require unique services?

If/then change impact
Correlation
Anomaly/anomalous behaviors
Predictive trending
Data mining and OLAP
Self-learning heuristics (please specify)
We don't offer analytics for CMS/CMDB through third-party integrations
Others (please specify)

Please list some key examples of product names if analytics are indicated.

For discussion: CMDB/CMS-related analytics. How would you describe your fully supported/integrated CMDB/CMS-related analytics? Areas of focus are CMDB/CMS maintenance, change management, asset management, problem management, incident management, and SLM/BSM.

Automation

Do you provide any automation capabilities directly packaged with your CMDB?

Yes
No

If yes, what types of automation capabilities do you support **directly through your CMDB/CMS suite**?

Change and configuration management tools
ITPA or runbook automation tools
ITIL process automation
Other process automation
Service desk workflows
Service desk trouble ticketing
Workload automation tools
Service catalog integration (for service provisioning)
Automated diagnostics
Automated security compliance audits
Automated asset compliance audits
Others (please specify)

What types of automation capabilities do you support **directly through your integrations across your own management portfolio?**

Change and configuration management tools
ITPA or runbook automation tools
ITIL process automation
Other process automation
Service desk workflows
Service desk trouble ticketing
Workload automation tools
Service catalog integration (for service provisioning)

Automated diagnostics
Automated security compliance audits
Automated asset compliance audits
Others (please specify)

Please list some key examples of the product or functional names of automation capabilities provided through your own portfolio.

What types of automation capabilities do you support **through fully supported third-party integrations?** Select all that apply.

Change and configuration management tools
ITPA or runbook automation tools
ITIL process automation
Other process automation
Service desk workflows
Service desk trouble ticketing
Workload automation tools
Service catalog integration (for service provisioning)
Automated diagnostics
Automated security compliance audits
Automated asset compliance audits
Others (please specify)

Please list some key examples of the product or functional names of automation capabilities provided through fully supported third-party integrations.

Which of the following ITSM processes does your product suite enable directly through fully supported integrations with **your own portfolio**?

Availability management
Incident management
Problem management
Continuity management
Service management
IT financial management
IT asset management
Capacity management
Security management
Change management
Configuration management
Release management
Service desk

Which of the following ITSM processes does your product suite enable directly through fully supported integrations with **third-party solutions**?

Availability management
Incident management

Problem management
Continuity management
Service management
IT financial management
IT asset management
Capacity management
Security management
Change management
Configuration management
Release management
Service desk

For discussion: CMDB/CMS-driven automation. How does your CMDB/CMS can support *use case*-specific automation either directly or through fully supported integrations?

Ease of use
Visualization/reporting
Which of the following do you offer as fully supported integrated extensions to your CMDB/CMS-related product suite? Select all that apply.

Executive dashboard
Portal
Scorecards
Templates
Widgets/gadgets
Mash-ups
Browser-based support
Others (please specify)

Roles supported
Which of the following **domain-related** roles/stakeholders do you support as fully supported extensions to your CMDB/CMS suite, including integrated sources (yours or third party) without unique (no more than one consultant for one week) services?

Network
Systems
Systems virtualization
Other virtualization
Database
Desktop
Mobile
Security
Help desk/service desk
Applications management/support
Applications development

Desktop management
Storage
Other domains (please specify)

Which of the following **cross domain** roles do you support as fully integrated extensions to your CMDB/CMS portfolio, including integrated sources (yours or third party) without unique services?

Engineering
Infrastructure management
Architecture
Service portfolio planning
Service delivery
Other cross domain service management
Configuration management
Change management
Release management
Asset management
Financial planning
Vendor management
User experience management
Online operations
Executive IT

Which of the following **non-IT-related** roles do you support across as fully supported extensions to your CMDB/CMS portfolio, including integrated sources (yours or third party) without unique services?

Enterprise financial planning
Executive non-IT
Asset management
Online operations
Partner management
User experience management
Other non-IT-related roles (please specify)

For discussion: Visualization and reporting. How would you describe your capabilities to support visualization and reporting?

SOME ADDITIONAL QUESTIONS

Can data be brought into your CMDB via Web Services?

Yes
No

Do you offer out of-the-box support for baselining and auditing data stored in your CMDB?

Yes
No

Do you offer version management for data stored inside your CMDB?

Yes
No

Do you provide capabilities to track data provenance, so that stakeholders and CMDB administrators can quickly and easily understand what the source was for a certain CI, CI attribute, or other CI update?

Yes
No

SELF-ASSESSMENT: WHAT IF YOU'RE *NOT* READY?

In Chapter 4, we asked the question: *How do you know if you're ready?*

We pointed out that sometimes, you just need to recognize and accept the fact that you aren't yet ready for an actual CMDB System deployment. Some of the more common reasons for this may reflect broader organizational or business conditions, such as in enterprises with global sprawl, multiple autonomous data centers, and individualized teams with different toolsets, cultures, process readiness, etc. Mergers and acquisitions can be another cause for concern. As we said in Chapter 4, "Trying to impose a CMDB as a unifying force across these organizations without taking initial steps to plan for coherence in other areas is bound to fail. The software may be up and running. It may even include data from all localities. But the chances of anything meaningful being done with it are slim to none if there aren't consistent processes, objectives, and stakeholder expectations."

CHAPTER 9'S "ONE-CHAPTER READINESS ASSESSMENT"

To be honest, there are lots of other examples when an IT organization is simply not ready for an actual CMDB System deployment. With its structured look at the four stages of IT maturity, Chapter 9 is the best resource in this book to help you determine your readiness. As a rule, if you are squarely in the *reactive infrastructure management* stage, you're probably *not* ready for deployment. Most successful CMDB System initiatives emerge out of the *active operational* stage in support of the transition to *proactive service-oriented management*. In some of the more advanced situations, we've seen CMDB-related investments can spur a transition into *dynamic business-driven management*, especially when the IT organization recognizes that insight into IT business service interdependencies is a critical enabler for effective automation, advanced analytics, and superior business value and relevance.

In any case, Chapter 9 is designed to serve as a one-chapter readiness assessment—a way of getting a meaningful snapshot of where you are in order to move forward. By mapping your organization, its processes, and its technology to the maturity levels and dimensions outlined, you'll have a quick picture of just where you stand. This is something you may be able to do yourself, with no interviews—or you may wish to inquire in several areas across your organization to flesh out your own insights. But these needn't be formal interviews. This process may be something you can achieve after an hour's reflection or after a few days of informal correspondence and dialog with your peers and management.

COMPLEMENTARY SELF-ASSESSMENT TEST

In support of the assessment process, here are 13 questions you will want to answer in framing this decision:

1. How would you place your IT organization? (20 points)
   a. Both our IT executives and our business executives view us as a business partner. (20 points)
   b. We are well along the road to becoming a business partner but still have ways to go. (15 points)
   c. We are still largely a cost center but are becoming more of a business partner/value provider. (10 points)
   d. We are still predominantly a cost center. (5 points)
   e. We are exclusively a cost center. (0 points)
2. How do communications occur across your IT organization? (20 points)
   a. Well across silos (20 points)
   b. Poorly across silos but well within silos (10 points)
   c. Poorly within silos (0 points)
3. To what degree are processes documented and shared? (20 points)
   a. Well across silos (20 points)
   b. Hit or miss across silos but well within silos (10 points)
   c. Hit or miss within silos (5 points)
   d. Not at all (0 points)
4. To what degree does your organization follow ITIL or other best practices? (10 points)
   a. To a large degree—ITIL (or some other best practice for establishing processes) is a major direction for us, and we continue to make investments in training. (10 points)
   b. To some degree—we have had made some efforts at training across our organization, but these are still partial and tentative. (5 points)
   c. Somewhat, but efforts are made mostly by isolated individuals. (3 points)
   d. Not at all. (0 points)
5. How are changes currently managed? (20 points)
   a. We have consistent policies in place for managing change and approach Change Management as a cross domain, service-aware requirement. (20 points)
   b. We have some policies for managing change, although currently Change Management is done primarily as a siloed set of decision-making. (10 points)
   c. We do not have policies for change, and most changes are undocumented and are being made at an individual level. (0 points)
6. To what degree are operations and the service desk functioning as integrated partners? (10 points)
   a. We have thoroughly integrated processes and dialog between operations and the service desk. (10 points)
   b. We have some dialog and common processes between operations and the service desk. (7 points)
   c. We have minimal dialog and common processes between operations and the service desk—which remain fundamentally two separate worlds. (0 points)

7. To what degree do security and operations work together? (10 points)
   a. Security and operations are in dialog and already have common processes. (10 points)
   b. Security and operations are beginning to share processes and dialog more proactively. (7 points)
   c. Security and operations are two separate worlds. (0 points)
8. Are there investments in cross domain, service-aware IT management teams? (yes or no) (10 points)
   a. Yes (10 points)
   b. No (0 points)
9. Is executive leadership promoting a more cross domain, service-aware approach to management? (10 points)
   a. Yes (10 points)
   b. No (0 points)
10. To what degree is data currently shared? (20 points)
    a. Well across all of IT. (20 points)
    b. Somewhat across all of IT but primarily within silos. (15 points)
    c. Only somewhat within silos, and only minimally across IT for executive reporting. (7 points)
    d. Not at all—data are generally not shared among our professionals. (0 points)
11. Which domains are covered for inventory, topology, and/or application dependency insights? Is this? (20 points)
    a. All domains across all silos, including application dependency mapping. (20 points)
    b. All domains across all silos, but without application dependency mapping. (15 points)
    c. Some domains across some silos but mostly just within silos. (10 points)
    d. All silos have some level of inventory and discovery. (7 points)
    e. Only some silos have inventory and discovery. (5 points)
    f. Inventory and discovery are fragmented, siloed, and incomplete. (0 points)
12. To what degree are advanced analytics (big data for IT) in place? (10 points)
    a. We've already deployed some cross domain analytics capability for our IT organization. (10 points)
    b. We're moving toward a cross domain way of sharing data through analytics. (7 points)
    c. Somewhat, but more on a domain basis when it's there. (5 points)
    d. Not at all—all our tools are siloed and we're not sure what advanced analytics for IT really is. (0 points)
13. To what degree is automation a core investment in your organization? (10 points)
    a. We have already begun to deliver cross domain automation at meaningful levels across our IT organization. (10 points)
    b. We have committed plans to unify our automation investments across domains. (7 points)
    c. We have strong pockets of automation in configuration management, diagnostics, and workflow but haven't brought these pockets together under a common umbrella. (5 points)
    d. Minimally—we have some workflow automation and some tool-specific automation diagnostics. (3 points)
    e. Not at all—we're still mostly manual. (0 points)

If you scored fewer than 80 points, you're probably not yet ready for a CMDB System deployment.

DON'T THINK YOU'RE READY, BUT WANT TO SET THE STAGE?

Even if you don't think you're ready—for any of the reasons already described—making some progress up the Eight-Step Ladder may still be a good preliminary investment. We recommend going forward with this process as a "feasibility assessment" as opposed to using "CMDB deployment" as the overarching banner. The assessment should bring value in and of itself by supporting improved IT efficiencies and helping you and other stakeholders to do your jobs more effectively. Once completed and socialized, the assessment may indeed set the stage for a modest first-phase CMDB deployment.

We recommend the following steps (in the spirit of the Eight-Step Ladder to CMDB System Success):

1. Once you've read this book, go back to Chapter 7 for CMDB System use cases and try to determine what eventually might be right for you in phase 1.

2. Now it's probably time to have your first conversation with at least a midlevel executive—you have an idea of what might be done and how you might approach it as a readiness assessment. Chapter 6 should provide some useful ammunition in terms of the value that a readiness assessment can show to IT executives—as it promotes superior dialog and awareness of just where you and your organization need to go.

3. With this in mind, go back to Chapter 9 and revisit *why* you are where you are on the IT maturity curve. This is your own private resource for mapping your IT organization to your CMDB ambitions. Try to get a handle on processes—to what degree are they documented and shared? To what degree do they still live in silos or, worse, solely with individuals? Map out your existing capabilities for understanding inventory and interdependencies and, if appropriate, any CMDB investment that may well be already a part of your service desk, for instance. Leverage Chapter 3 for more insight into process and Chapter 12 and Appendix B for more insight into technology requirements. Finally, consider organization and cultural issues—as well as which stakeholders are most willing and ready to go forward with your CMDB hopes. Do they map to the initial use case you singled out? If not, you may want to reconsider first-phase priorities. Chapter 8 provides an excellent framework to help you to seek out and define issues across process, culture, organization, and technology before going forward.

4. Now it's time to go back to the executive and share some of your insights. You will also want to evaluate resource readiness. What kind of team will you need when the time is right? (See Chapter 11.) Are the skill sets already in-house, or will you likely need more consulting investments?

5. If there is some executive support for going forward, you're ready to take the next step and begin a more articulated project plan (see Chapter 10). Make sure that you have a mix of internal and external metrics. Try to anticipate some of the benefits you expect to receive in the phase 1 deployment and document these as explicitly as possible. This plan will serve as the foundation when you're ready to move forward with technology selection and deployment.

6. Next, consider your own readiness. Assess your time commitment and personal goals. The CMDB initiative won't work if you become a martyr to it. Beyond your organization, are you, yourself, ready—assuming the team resources you need are in place? If something's changed to either accentuate or degrade your own enthusiasm, what is it? You don't need to document this to anyone but yourself, unless it makes sense to share some of the issues with your management. But of all the "gating factors," your own personal commitment is, believe it or not, near the top of the charts.

7. Lastly, revisit Chapter 5 and consider the impacts of current trends—the move to cloud, agile software development, and other business-driven changes, such as mergers and acquisition—that may change and possibly accelerate the need for a CMDB System. This is the final step in your readiness assessment: providing a big-picture eye toward the future so that you can anticipate changes in direction proactively and promote the initiative in that light.

8. Using insights from the previous steps, be prepared to create an action plan for going forward when the time is right. The first steps may still not be a CMDB investment, but rather an investment in filling in gaps in inventory and discovery, providing process training for better process awareness to move beyond siloed ways of working, and supporting higher levels of workflow and other automation once the processes are defined. By addressing these and other gaps, all of a sudden you may see that your IT organization has moved past *reactive infrastructure management* into *active operational management*—and you're ready to move forward with your CMDB investment after all.

PRODUCT MAP

D

The brief "Product Map" provided here is a useful guide for planning your technology selection. By exploring the options below, you will have a chance to assess examples of different design points, cost points, and appropriateness as per use case.

This Product Map features four key categories:

- Core CMDB capabilities integrated with service desk or IT Service Management solutions
- Unique CMDB or CMDB-related offerings
- General-purpose Application Discovery and Dependency Mapping solutions
- Application Discovery and Dependency Mapping optimized for performance and/or other more real-time values

However, this Product Map is not intended to be a complete list of available vendor offerings for any number of reasons. Chief among them is that new products come and go with sometimes lightning speed, and markets themselves morph as new requirements and new technologies come on the scene. Another reason is that what one vendor calls a "CMDB" and what another calls a "CMDB" may be strikingly different. One isn't necessarily more correct than the other, but each may reflect skews to different use cases, stakeholders, and scale and complexity requirements. Finally, a list of hundreds of vendor offerings is probably less useful as a reference point than the far more modest list of 31 offerings below. (A more complete list of CMDB and ADDM offerings will be available on the www.emausa.com website.)

You should also be aware that few CMDB solutions are currently packaged as stand-alone options. For instance, a CMDB that's not yet even in use may already be embedded in your service desk. However, you may decide for any number of reasons that your current investment isn't the one to take you the whole distance going forward. Moreover, there are a growing number of "variations on a theme"—as some CMDBs are packaged primarily as Business Service Management (BSM) solutions optimized for service impact and performance, others target workflow and automation, and some CMDB solutions are extensions of Application Discovery and Dependency Mapping tools.

The list of offerings below should be a helpful beginning reference for framing your thinking around these and other options.

CORE CMDB CAPABILITIES INTEGRATED WITH SERVICE DESK OR IT SERVICE MANAGEMENT SOLUTIONS

The partial list below presents offerings integrated with IT Service Management or service desk capabilities. These are examples of what have been, and to a large degree remain, the heart of the CMDB market:

- Axios assyst CMDB
- BMC Atrium CMDB

- CA Technologies, Service Desk Manager CMDB
- Cherwell Software CMDB
- FrontRange CMDB
- HP Universal CMDB (UCMDB)
- IBM SmartCloud Control Desk (SCCD)
- iET Solutions, iET CMDB
- LANDESK Service Desk Suite
- ManageEngine IT360 CMDB
- Scalable Software (asset optimized CMDB)
- ServiceNow CMDB
- SysAid CMDB

UNIQUE CMDB OR CMDB-RELATED OFFERINGS

These solutions vary—some are more associated with BSM performance management, while others have yet more unique footprints. For instance, Blazent's offering is often used as a complement to core CMDB investments in reconciling many multiple data sources, while ITinvolve offers some industry-leading social IT capabilities in conjunction with some ITSM capabilities. eMite, FireScope, and Interlink are all associated with strong BSM platforms. The ASG metaCMDB is a versatile offering equally affiliated with both BSM and ITSM functionalities. Evolven provides an integrated platform for Change Management analytics and automation.

- ASG metaCMDB
- Blazent CMDB Accuracy and Intelligence
- eMite CMDB
- Evolven Change and Configuration Analytics
- FireScope Orchestrate
- Interlink Software Service Configuration Manager
- ITinvolve Collaborative CMDB

GENERAL-PURPOSE APPLICATION DISCOVERY AND DEPENDENCY MAPPING SOLUTIONS

Multiuse case ADDM first became an area of extreme innovation almost 10 years ago with the initial tidal wave of interest in CMDB deployments and the need to capture service-related interdependencies more effectively. That initial crop of companies was largely acquired and became foundational technologies for leading platform solutions with native CMDB integrations. As a group, these ADDM pioneers were focused on capturing configuration-related changes as well as application-to-infrastructure residency, with updates most frequently on a 24-h basis. More recently, some of these solutions, along with newer entrants into the multiuse case class, are evolving to support more real-time requirements, including performance management:

- ASG-DDM/Trackbird
- BMC Atrium Discovery and Dependency Mapping (ADDM)
- HP Universal Discovery
- IBM Tivoli Application Dependency Discovery Manager (TADDM)
- ManageEngine Application Discovery
- ServiceNow Application Dependency Mapping

APPLICATION DISCOVERY AND DEPENDENCY MAPPING OPTIMIZED FOR PERFORMANCE AND/OR OTHER REAL-TIME VALUES

Performance-optimized ADDM meaningfully emerged about 5 years ago, when the industry began to see a new crop of ADDM solutions more focused on performance interdependencies, transactional awareness, and more real-time dynamic currency. Many of these also supported CMDB integrations; all were highly automated and, to some degree, were complementary to ADDM-related investments from the first wave. Vendors in this category are raising the bar on in-depth transactional awareness; dynamic, operational insights into application-to-application and application-to-infrastructure interdependencies; and higher levels of automation in terms of discovery and currency:

- AccelOps
- AppDynamics
- AppEnsure
- Riverbed SteelCentral AppMapper
- ServiceNow ServiceWatch (from Neebula)
- VNT IlluminIT

Bibliography

1. C. Araujo, The Quantum Age of IT, IT Governance Publishing, 2012.
2. *Enterprise Management Associates Consulting*. This research heavily leverages eight extensive CMDB System consulting reports done between 2007 and 2014. Because these were custom engagements, the clients will remain anonymous. While several of the consulting customers had global outreach, all consults most were conducted within the United States. These include four financial services organizations, one large retail organization, one large government organization in the United States, one large government organization in Canada and one global biotechnology company based in the United States.
3. *Enterprise Management Associates Research*. The following is a chronological list of Enterprise Management Associates-driven research projects leveraged and sometimes cited in this book.
   a. The Many Faces of Advanced Operations Analytics, September 2014.
   b. Next-Generation Asset Management and IT Financial Analytics: Optimizing IT Value in a World of Change, May 2014.
   c. ITIL and CMDB Implementations: Case Studies and Lessons Learned, (presentation) April 2014.
   d. ITIL Resources Adoption Priorities and Values: A Global View, Custom Research for Axelos, February 2014.
   e. EMA Radar™ for Application Discovery and Dependency Mapping, November 2013.
   f. The Changing Role of the Service Desk in the Age of Cloud and Agile, EMA and le CXP, April 2013.
   g. Ecosystem Cloud: Managing and Optimizing IT Services Across the Full Cloud Mosaic, June 2013.
   h. User Experience Management and Business Impact—A Cornerstone for IT Transformation, August 2012.
   i. EMA Radar™ for CMDB/CMS Use Cases: From Database to Federation, January 2012.
   j. EMA Radar™ for CMDB/CMS Use Cases—Innovation Through Diversity, June 2011.
   k. Service-Centric Asset Management in the Age of Cloud Computing, February 2011.
   l. Responsible Cloud, EMA, 2010.
   m. Making Your CMDB System Deployment Count: Who's Winning the Battle to Show Value and Why?, April, 2009.
   n. CMDB Deployments in 2008: The Search for Value, August 2008.
   o. Defining Value for CMDB Systems—Some Internal and External Metrics to Help you Get Started, March 2008.
   p. Actionable CMDB Systems: How to Succeed at Your CMDB Project, June 2009.
   q. Winning Strategies in CMDB Adoption: What's Working in the Real World, What Isn't, and Why, June 2007.
   r. CMDB Adoption in the Real World: Just How Real Is It?, June 2006.
4. IT Infrastructure Library:
   a. ITIL® Continual Service Improvement, The Stationery Office (TSO), UK, 2011.
   b. ITIL® Service Design, The Stationery Office (TSO), UK, 2011.
   c. ITIL® Service Operation, The Stationery Office (TSO), UK, 2011.

d. ITIL® Service Strategy, The Stationery Office (TSO), UK, 2011.

e. ITIL® Service Transition, The Stationery Office (TSO), UK, 2011.

5. itSMF International, Metrics for IT Service Management, Van Haren Publishing, 2006.

6. G. Kim, K. Behr, G. Stafford, The Pheonix Project: A Novel About IT, DevOps, and Helping Your Business Win, IT Revolution Press, 2013.

7. G. O'Donnell, C. Casanova, The CMDB Imperative: How to Realize the Dream and Avoid the Nightmares, Prentice Hall, 2009.

8. R. Sturm, W. Morris, M. Jander, Foundations of Service Level Management, Sams, 2000.

QUESTION AND ANSWER INTERVIEWS

There are eleven Q&As used throughout this book. Some are resident in just one chapter and others are used in sections in multiple chapters. The following list provides a summary based on the date of the interview.

- May 2012: Colloquium with a large manufacturer and a mid-tier insurance company both using the ServiceNow CMDB. (Chapter 4 in its entirety—used in short segments in several other chapters)
- September 2013: Interview with a large technology services organization based in the United States regarding their deployment of IBM's Tivoli Application Dependency Discovery Manager (TADDM). (Chapter 12)
- February 2014: Interview with a European-based global financial services company using Interlink Software's BSM software including the Service Configuration Manager. (Chapter 9)
- February 2014: Interview with a large global transportation company based in the United States using HP's Universal CMDB and Universal Discovery. (Chapters 9 and 13)
- February 2014: Interview with a large financial services company based in the United States using Blazent CMDB Accuracy and Intelligence. (Chapters 9 and 13)
- March 2014: Interview with a large European-based global transportation company using Interlink Software's BSM software including the Service Configuration Manager. (Chapters 8 and 10)
- March 2014: Interview with a large financial services company based in the United States using Blazent CMDB Accuracy and Intelligence. (Chapters 10 and 13)
- March 2014: Interview with a mid-tier healthcare services company based in the United States using CA Technologies' Service Operations Insight. (Chapter 6)
- April 2014: Interview with a mid-tier financial services company based in the United States using the ITinvolve Collaborative CMDB. (Chapter 15)
- September 2015: Interview with a BMC customer-facing support manager regarding the usage of ADDM technology and cloud. (Chapter 15)
- September 2015: Interview with a large financial institution based in the United States using BMC's Atrium CMDB. (Chapter 15)

Index

Note: Page numbers followed by *f* indicate figures, *b* indicate boxes and *t* indicate tables.

A

Active operational management, 65
  IT organization maturity stage, 172, 173*f*
ADDM. *See* Application discovery and dependency
    mapping (ADDM)
Advanced Operations Analytics (AOA), 318–321
  capabilities, 319*f*
  directly/indirectly support, 318
Agile software development and DevOps, 86–88
  case study, 321–323
Analytics, 45, 164, 236, 268–269
Application discovery and dependency mapping
    (ADDM), 43, 44*f*, 46, 247–250, 304,
    313–318
  all-in-one ADDM *vs.* ADDM plus integrations, 250
  application dependency, 228
  capabilities, 233*f*
  for change management, 21, 21*f*
  deployment perspectives on, 250–251, 251*b*
  integrated sources for, 234*f*
Asset management, 19–20, 121, 127–131
  aspects of, 20
  automation for, 157–158
  benefits, 131
  data and dependency insights, 156
  ITIL process, 129–130
  process issues, 157
  service-aware, 305–308
  technology considerations, 131
Audit-derived metrics, 158
Automation, 44–45, 164, 242
  for asset management, 157–158
  change (*see* Change automation)
  cloud-ready, 314*f*
Availability management, 135

B

Big vision, baby steps, 45–46
Blogs, 154
BRM. *See* Business relationship management (BRM)
BSM. *See* Business Service Management (BSM)
Business alignment, 164, 169–170
Business management, impacts, 319
Business relationship management (BRM), 88
Business service management (BSM), 88–90,
    89*f*, 96*f*, 220

C

Capacity management, 124
  definition, 37
  ITIL process, 37
Capacity Management Information System (CMIS), 37
Capacity optimization, 131–136
  AOA, 319
  audits, 159
  benefits, 136
  ITIL process, 133–135
  technology considerations, 135–136
CapEx, 127, 128*f*
Change advisory board (CAB), 49*f*, 215–216, 216*f*
  definition, 36
  process, 155
Change automation, 121, 122–123
  audits, 154–156
  benefits, 126
  ITIL process, 123, 125*f*
  technology considerations, 125–126
Change configuration and release (CCR) manager, 212
Change impact analysis, 19
Change impact management, 121–126
  AOA, 319
  benefits, 126
  ITIL process, 123–125, 125*f*
  perceptions, 154–155
  technology considerations, 125–126
  technology issues, 156
Change management, 19–20
  Acme Financial Services Corporation, 282, 292, 294–295
  ADDM solutions for, 21, 21*f*
  CMDBs, 21, 21*f*
  ITIL process, 36
Checklist, CMDB System, 5
Closing the "gap"
  accountability, 271–272
  administration, 266
  analytics, 268–269
  application team, 266
  attributes, 265
  bottom-up approach, 262
  CIs, 261–268, 264*f*
  CMDB/CMS deployments, 273
  CMDB configuration, 263*f*
  CMS modeling, 266–268
  communication, 258–259

Closing the "gap" *(Continued)*
  definition, 257
  extending data models, 265
  federation, 267*b*, 269–270
  follow-through, 270–271
  integration, 267*b*, 268–269
  interview, 265, 268
  maintenance, 270–271
  managing process requirements, 260–261
  metrics, 271–272
  middle-layer outward, 262
  modeling, 261–268, 267*b*
  normalization, 268–269
  objectives, 271–272
  priority, 264
  proof of concept (PoC), 257, 258–261
  scope creep, 259–260
  single source of truth, 263
  system of relevance, 263
  top-down approach, 262
  workflow, 270–271
Cloud
  and extended enterprise, 84
  mosaic, 308, 309*f*, 310*f*, 311*f*
  optimizing service delivery, 97
  trends, 93–94, 94*f*
Cloud adoption, 21*f*, 22–23
  diversity of, 85*f*
  impacts of public and private, 105
Cloud service providers (CSPs), 86
CMDB federation, 46*f*, 267–268
CMDB federation working group (CMDBf), 231,
    267–268
CMDB System
  consulting engagements, 146, 150, 153
  definition, 4, 5
  ecosystem, 46, 46*f*
  skill sets based on past research, 143*f*
CMDB System deployments
  eight-step methodology for, 53, 54–55, 57–58, 57*f*
    addressing critical issues and gating factors, 70–72,
      70*f*, 71*f*
    define objectives and consider resources, 58–61,
      58*f*, 60*f*
    define requirements, architecture, and metrics, 66–68,
      66*f*, 67*f*
    develop roadmap, 72–73, 73*f*
    evolutionary/maturity-level assessment, 64–66, 64*f*
    review progress and milestones, 74, 74*f*
    technology, process, and organizational audit, 61–63,
      61*f*, 62*f*
    technology selection, 68–70, 68*f*, 69*f*
  process of, 54

CMDB System foundations
  history, 29
  ITIL and, 27–29, 28*f*
CMDB System possibilities, changing dimensions in
  agile, 86–88
  mobile, 88
CMS. *See* Configuration management systems (CMS)
CMS modeling, 266–268
Common Information Model (CIM), 267
Communications, 151–153
  Acme Financial Services Corporation, 280
  effective, 153
  executive, 152–153, 154
Compliance
  audits, 127
  use cases, 137
Configuration items (CIs), 31–32, 188, 200–201, 209,
    264–265, 264*f*
  categories, 40
  modeling and defining, 261–268
Configuration management database (CMDB)
  data and configuration, 38–41
  definition, 5, 31–32
  deployment to ITIL workflows, 40*f*
  ITIL, 31–32
  process-centric, 47*f*
  success rates, 14, 15, 15*f*
  technologies, 43
Configuration management, definition, 36
Configuration management systems (CMS), 4, 14
  definition, 32
  ITIL, 32–33
Consumer-driven IT, 13
Continual service improvement, 124
Core CMDB, 5, 42–46, 244
Core CMDB team, 208, 210, 211*f*, 215, 216–217, 283–285
Cost center *vs.* business partner, 281
Costs, Acme Financial Services Corporation, 281, 290,
    294, 296
Cross-domain ITAM initiative, 110*f*
Cross domain IT organization, 90–93, 91*f*
Cross domain service management, 166
CSPs. *See* Cloud service providers (CSPs)
Customer-facing IT service, 29

D

Dashboards, 45
Data
  breadth, 148–149
  and dependency insights, 156
  issues, 147–149
  ownership, 149
  quality, 147–149

Data optimization analytics, 251–252
Definitive media library (DML), 33
Definitive software library, 33
Detailed requirement, 195–203, 285–286, 291
DevOps. *See* Agile software development and DevOps
Disaster recovery, 119, 122
    Acme Financial Services Corporation, 295
Discovery tools, 43–44
Distributed Management Task Force (DMTF), 267
DML. *See* Definitive media library (DML)
Domain-centric organization *vs.* service-centric, 106*f*
Drivers, CMDB System, 16, 16*f*, 18
Dynamic business-driven management, 65–66, 65*f*
    IT organization maturity stage, 175, 176*f*

E

Eight-Step Ladder to CMDB System Success,
    53–78
Enterprise Management Associates (EMA), xxi
Evolutionary/maturity-level assessment, 161–178
Executive communication, 99–114, 152–154
Executive leadership, 100
Executive support, 18
Executive team
    cloud adoption, 105–106
    communication, 104
    distractions, 103
    eight-step ladder and, 108–113, 108*f*, 110*f*, 111*f*
    executive imperative, 100–103, 101*f*, 102*f*, 106*f*
    executive perspectives, 105–106
    failures and successes, 107
    resources, 104
    stakeholder buy-in, 102–103
Extended enterprise, 308
    cloud and, 84
    CMDB Systems for, 22*f*, 23
    data sharing and, 86
External CIs, 40
External CMDB System metrics
    asset management, 189–190
    capacity optimization, 190–191
    change impact management and change
        automation, 189
    financial optimization, 189–190
    vs. return on investment (ROI), 184–192
    security/governance/compliance, 191
    service impact management, 190–191
    summary circle of values, 191–192, 192*f*

F

Facilities management, 122
Federation, 267*b*, 302

Financial optimization, 121, 127, 156–158
    benefits, 131
    for IT as business, 320
    ITIL process, 129–130
    technology considerations, 131
Formal change reviews, 125, 322

G

Gap, 257. *See also* Closing the "gap"
Gating factors, Acme Financial Services Corporation,
    281, 282*f*
Governance, 122
Green IT, 122

H

Hamster scenario, 151
Healthcare services, case study, 113*b*

I

IaaS. *See* Infrastructure as a service (IaaS)
Identify informal *vs.* formal process, 63
If/then change impact analysis, 240
Incident management, 135
Information architect/database specialist, 212
Information Technology Infrastructure Library (ITIL),
    27–32
    adoption, ranking values, 32*f*
    asset management/financial optimization, 129–130
    change impact management/change automation,
        123–125, 125*f*
    CI attribute, 41
    cloud and virtualization trends, 93–94, 94*f*
    CMDB, 31–32
    and CMDB System foundations, 27–29, 28*f*
    human face to service management, 29, 30*f*
    life cycle approach, 29, 30*f*
        continual service improvement, 31
        service design, 30
        service operation, 31
        service strategy, 30
        service transition, 30
    process, 38, 39*f*, 164–166, 165*f*
        capacity management, 37
        change management, 36
        deployment management, 37, 38*f*
        release management, 37, 38*f*
        SACM, 36–37
    resistance to, 9
    service impact management/capacity optimization,
        133–135
    SKMS, 33–34, 34*f*
    workflows, CMDB deployment to, 40*f*

Infrastructure as a service (IaaS), 21
Instrumentation and data collection, 162–164
Integrated service knowledge management system, 163*f*
Interface CIs, 40
Internal CIs, 40
Internal CMDB System metrics, 186–189
  for accuracy and integrity, 188
  for efficiency, 189, 190*f*
  questions for, 188
  vs. return on investment (ROI), 184–192
Interviews
  process, 142
  with team leaders, 154
IT asset management (ITAM), 130, 130*f*, 305
ITIL. *See* Information Technology Infrastructure
    Library (ITIL)
IT OpEx efficiencies optimization, 18–19
IT organization
  asset management initiative, 108–113
  and business alignment, 88–90
  as business partner model, 88
  evolution, 166–170
    internal service provider, 168
    operationally empowered tribes, 167–168
    proactive business partner, 168
    reactive heroes, 167
IT organization maturity
  criteria influencing, 168–170
  dynamics for technology adoption, 162
  and evolutionary assessments, 164
  stages, 170*f*
    active operational management, 172, 173*f*
    dynamic business-driven management, 175, 176*f*
    proactive service-oriented management, 174–175,
      174*f*, 177*b*
    reactive infrastructure management, 170–172, 171*f*
    salient trends, 175–177
IT service continuity management, 124, 135

L

Life cycle management, 127

M

Management data repositories (MDRs), 228–229
Management of Portfolio (MoP), 29
Mean time between failure (MTBF), 20
Mean time to find someone (MTTFS), 119
Mean time to repair (MTTR), 17, 20, 118, 119
Mergers and acquisitions, 122
Metrics, 183–205
  architectural requirements, 199*f*, 201–203, 202*f*
  CMDB System, 184, 185–186, 185*f*, 187*f*

    CI details, 200–201
    interview, 203*b*
    requirement, 196–201, 197*f*, 198*f*, 199*f*
    value proposition, 200
  external CMDB System
    asset management, 189–190
    capacity optimization, 190–191
    change impact management and change
      automation, 189
    financial optimization, 189–190
    security/governance/compliance, 191
    service impact management, 190–191
    summary circle of values, 191–192, 192*f*
  general categories for, 184–185
  internal CMDB System, 186–189
    for accuracy and integrity, 188
    for efficiency, 189, 190*f*
    questions for, 188
  project plan, 183
  return on investment (ROI)
    vs. internal and external metrics, 184–192
    total cost of ownership (TCO), 193–195
    words of wisdom, 194–195
  translating metrics, 195–203, 196*f*
Milestones, Acme Financial Services Corporation, 289–290,
    292–293
Move to cloud, 20–23, 21*f*, 22*f*, 122
  cloud mosaic, 308, 309*f*, 310*f*, 311*f*
  deployments, 308–311
  extended enterprise, 308
  ITIL, 308
  respondents in service modeling, 308–309, 310–312
MTTFS. *See* Mean time to find someone (MTTFS)
MTTR. *See* Mean time to repair (MTTR)

O

One-year roadmap, 72–73
Optimization
  IT financial, 19–20
  IT OpEx efficiencies, 18–19
  service delivery, 97
Organizational dynamics, maturity stages, 165
Organizational model, 165*f*

P

PaaS. *See* Platform as a service (PaaS)
Performance management, 131–132
Performance-optimized ADDM, 248
Phase-One CMDB deployment, 300
Platform as a service (PaaS), 21
Predictive trending, 240–241
Problem management, 135

Process-centric CMDB, 47*f*
Proof of concept (PoC), 257, 258–261

Q

The Quantum Age of IT (Araujo), 81, 82
Quick time to value, CMDB System, 18

R

Release and deployment management, 124
Release management, ITIL process, 37, 38*f*
Return on investment (ROI)
  EMA research and consulting, 17–18
  vs. internal and external metrics, 184–192
  total cost of ownership (TCO), 193–195
  words of wisdom, 194–195
Road map, 275–297, 276*f*. *See also* 6-month road map;
    12-month road map; 2-year road map
  Acme Financial Services Corporation, 277–278
    approach, 279–280
    gating factors, 281, 282*f*
    goals, 279
    graphic overview, 283, 284*f*
    issues, 280–281
    target areas for phase one, 281–282
  components, 298
  ingredients, 276–277
  wrapping up, 297
ROI. *See* Return on investment (ROI)

S

SaaS. *See* Software as a service (SaaS)
SACM. *See* Service asset and configuration management
    (SACM)
Scope creep, 259–260
Security
  AOA, 320–321
  use cases, 137
Service asset and configuration management (SACM), 123
  ITIL process, 36–37
Service-aware asset management (SAAM), 305–308
Service catalogs, 252, 295
Service-centric asset management, 127
  ITIL process, 129
Service-centric IT asset management initiative,
    108–113
Service impact management, 131–136
  ADDM, 317
  benefits, 136
  ITIL process, 133–135
  SLA, 159
  technology considerations, 135–136
  use case audit, 159

Service impact management CMDB system deployments, 48*f*
Service knowledge management system (SKMS), 33–34, 34*f*
Service level agreement (SLA), 134, 159
Service-level management (SLM), 134
  Acme Financial Services Corporation, 295
Service life cycle CIs, 40
Service modeling, 50–51, 50*f*, 261–266
Siloed IT issues, Acme Financial Services Corporation, 280
6-month road map, 72, 275–276, 277, 283–290,
    291*f*, 298
  Acme Financial Services Corporation, 298
    costs, 290
    milestones, 289–290
    phase-one technology value targets, 289
    production infrastructure status, 290
    requirements document creation, 285–286
    responsibilities of team, 285
    team creation, 283–285
    technology adoption, 286–289
  description, 275–276
SKMS. *See* Service knowledge management system (SKMS)
SLA. *See* Service level agreement (SLA)
SLM. *See* Service-level management (SLM)
Software as a service (SaaS), 21, 221
Staffing, 150–151, 210–214
  Acme Financial Services Corporation, 281
Staffing issues, 209
Stakeholders, 208–210
Stakeholder team, Acme Financial Services Corporation,
    291–292
Standard (preauthorized) changes, 36
Standing in the middle of the storm, 54–55, 55*f*, 162*f*
Strong ITIL (Information Technology Infrastructure Library)
    roots, 5
System of relevance, 5, 13, 122

T

Team building
  change advisory board (CAB), 215–216, 216*f*
  consumers, 207–208
  creation for Acme Corporation, 283–285, 291–292
  finalizing the core team, 210–216, 211*f*
  optimizing ITIL processes, 213
  recommended core team matrix
    CMDB specialists, 212
    CMDB strategy, 213
    data responsibilities, 213
    information architect/database specialist, 212
    ITIL, 213
    team manager, 212
  reporting in, 214–215, 215*f*
  staffing challenges, 214

Team building *(Continued)*
  stakeholders, 208–210
  wrapping up, 216–217
Team manager, 212
Technical performance analytics, 319
Technology adoption, Acme Financial Services Corporation,
    286–289
Technology parent, CMDB Systems, 6
Technology selection
  ADDM, deployment perspectives on, 250–251, 251*b*
  analytic and automation specifics, 238–242, 240*f*, 241*f*
  application discovery, 247–251
  architecture and integration, 228–235
    discovery, 235
    integrations and data sourcing, 232
    scope and phased growth, 232
  automation capabilities, 243*f*
  CI metrics, 229, 229*f*, 230*f*, 237*f*, 238*f*
  CI state support, 244
  CMDB investment, 251
  core CMDB packaging, 220–222
  core interdependencies, 229–230, 232*f*
  data import, 230–231, 235*f*
  data optimization analytics, 251–252
  dependency mapping, 247–251
  deployment and administration, 224–228, 224*f*, 225*f*, 226*f*, 227*f*
  domain reach, 229, 231*f*, 249*f*
  federated universe, 230–231
  functional concerns
    analytics, 236
    automation, 236
    modeling and metadata, 236
    visualization, 236
  functional power and outreach, 248
  gamification, 252
  investment, 251
  modeling, 244
  one client engagement, 245–247, 245*t*
  outreach, 229–230
  project management, 252
  reporting, 242–243, 245
  scope, 229–230
  service catalog, 252
  social IT, 252
  software as a service (SaaS), 221
  trade-offs
    all-in-one ADDM *vs.* ADDM plus integrations, 250
    performance-optimized *vs.* multiuse case, 248–250
  trending, 245
  use case, 238–242, 239*f*, 243–244
  visualization, 242–243, 244*f*, 245
Three-tiered roadmap, 72–73, 204, 275–298. *See also* Acme
    Financial Services Corporation; 6-month road map;
    12-month road map; 2-year road map

Transaction-centric analytics, 45
Translating metrics, 195–203, 196*f*
12-month road map, 276, 277, 290–294, 302
  Acme Financial Services Corporation, 290, 298
    change management, 292
    costs, 294
    detailed requirements document, 291
    goals, 292
    implementation, 293–294
    milestones, 292–293
    targeting right stakeholder team, 291–292
  description, 276
The "two CMDBs," 34*f*, 42–51, 212, 285
2-year road map, 73, 276, 277, 294–296
  Acme Financial Services Corporation, 294, 298
    analytics, 294–295
    costs, 296
    goals, 296
  description, 276

U

UEM. *See* User experience management (UEM)
Use cases, 118*f*
  asset management and financial optimization, 121, 127–131
    benefits, 131
    ITIL process, 129–130
    technology considerations, 131
  audits, 154–159
  change impact management/automation, 121–126
    benefits, 126
    ITIL process, 123, 125*f*
    technology considerations, 125–126
  DevOps, 138
  security/compliance, 137
  service impact management/capacity optimization,
    131–136
    benefits, 136
    ITIL process, 133–135
    technology considerations, 135–136
  sprawl, 144, 145*f*
  technology selection, 238–242, 239*f*, 243–244
User experience management (UEM), 49

V

Vendor failure, CMDB System, 10
Virtualization, 20–23, 84
  trends, 93–94, 94*f*
vMotion, 21–22

W

Web services, 231, 268
Wiki, 154

Printed in the United States
By Bookmasters